WHEAT AND WOMAN

An established writer before she came to Canada, Georgina Binnie-Clark (1872–1947) bought land near Fort Qu'Appelle, Saskatchewan, in 1905. She had no experience with agriculture, and her family members thought she was mad, but she persevered. Profoundly influenced by the ideologies of the British Empire, she was motivated by the belief that she was helping the 'mother country' to rear the 'daughter nation' of Canada through her own farming efforts and through her promotion of farming as an occupation for British women. She believed that marriage need not be the sole destination for women, that there were alternatives such as agriculture which could permit women to support themselves and have a rewarding profession.

Originally published in 1914, *Wheat and Woman* is an autobiographical account of Georgina Binnie-Clark's first three years of farming the prairies – her mistakes and misfortunes but also the kindness of neighbours, her love for the prairies, and her remarkable determination. As well, it documents the inequities of the land laws of western Canada, which permitted only a handful of women to obtain the homestead grant available to males. While Binnie-Clark's brother could acquire a homestead for free, she had to purchase her land. For this reason, there were few women farmers in western Canada, and *Wheat and Woman* is a rare document, being the only book-length, published account of a woman farmer in the region.

This new reprint includes an introduction by Susan Jackel, written for a 1979 edition of the text, as well as a new scholarly introduction by historian Sarah A. Carter, who received a Killam Fellowship for the study of Great Plains women of Canada and the United States. *Wheat and Woman* is a fascinating, lively, and often humorous account of a gifted and determined woman's experience in prairie farming, and it is a unique document in Canadian social history.

SARAH A. CARTER is Henry Marshall Tory Chair in the Department of History and Classics and the Faculty of Native Studies at the University of Alberta.

GEORGINA BINNIE-CLARK

Wheat and Woman

WITH A NEW INTRODUCTION
BY SARAH A. CARTER

UNIVERSITY OF TORONTO PRESS
Toronto Buffalo London

First published in Toronto by Bell and Cockburn, 1914
© University of Toronto Press Incorporated 1979
Reprinted with a new Introduction 2007
© Introduction Sarah A. Carter 2007

Toronto Buffalo London
Printed in Canada

ISBN-10: 0-8020-3813-1
ISBN-13: 978-0-8020-3813-5

Printed on acid-free paper

Library and Archives Canada Cataloguing in Publication

Binnie-Clark, Georgina, 1871–1955.
Wheat and woman / Georgina Binnie-Clark ; with a new introduction
by Sarah Carter.

Includes bibliographical references.
ISBN-13: 978-0-8020-3813-5
ISBN-10: 0-8020-3813-1

1. Binnie-Clark, Georgina, 1871–1955.   2. Women farmers –
Saskatchewan – Fort Qu'Appelle – Biography.   3. Frontier and
pioneer life – Saskatchewan – Fort Qu'Appelle.   I. Carter, Sarah,
1954–   II. Title.

S417.B545A3 2006   630.92   C2006-904556-9

University of Toronto Press acknowledges the financial assistance to
its publishing program of the Canada Council for the Arts and the
Ontario Arts Council.

University of Toronto Press acknowledges the financial support for its
publishing activities of the Government of Canada through the Book
Publishing Industry Development Program (BPIDP).

SARAH A. CARTER

Introduction

It was very fitting that five horses should be grazing contentedly on Georgina Binnie-Clark's farm near Fort Qu'Appelle, Saskatchewan, when I visited on a sunny harvest day in September 2005, one hundred years after she purchased this land.[1] Just as she described the horses of long ago, 'even these seemed invested with the Canadian spirit of inquiry and turned their heads to take stock of the passer-by.'[2] As readers of *Wheat and Woman* will learn, Binnie-Clark was devoted to her horses and other members of her 'four-footed family.'[3] Although the house at the farm she called 'Binning' was destroyed by fire long ago, much remains the same as in 1905, particularly the view that she cherished 'away across four miles of peaceful prairie towards the line of land on the far side of the Qu'Appelle valley, which from that distance looks like a friendly sea, blue as the Mediterranean.'[4] Binnie-Clark loved the prairie, particularly the 'exquisite environment' of the Qu'Appelle valley.[5]

Georgina Binnie-Clark was a thirty-three-year-old journalist with no farming experience and, according to her own account, r.o particular intentions of becoming a farmer when she bought her 'improved' farm of 320 acres, despite the advice of family members who told her it was the 'maddest thing which you have ever done.'[6] *Wheat and Woman* is her delightfully self-deprecating, often humorous account of her first three years of farming – her ignorance of agriculture and the many customs of the country;

her mistakes, misfortunes, financial woes, and adventures, which
included being lost on the prairies in a summer deluge and being
tossed head first into a snowbank when her beloved horse Nancy
came to an unexpected and abrupt stop and then bolted, leaving
Binnie-Clark on her own. It includes an account of the long and
viciously cold winter of 1906–7, perhaps the worst in prairie history.[7] But *Wheat and Woman* is also the story of the courtesy and
kindness of her neighbours, of her love for the prairies and for
her animals, of her fascination with wheat (a 'tall mass of living
loveliness'), and of her own remarkable persistence and determination.[8] It is a sort of early twentieth-century, western Canadian
version of Susanna Moodie's 1852 *Roughing It in the Bush*, but it is
aimed in particular at women contemplating farming on their
own.[9] Despite the humour, it is a sobering tale of 'years of arduous toil and seasons of bitter disappointment,' but ultimately the
message is that women can succeed if they have capital, forti-
tude, tenacity, and good humour.[10] Capital was particularly vital
for women, as *Wheat and Woman* is also a sharp critique of
Canadian land laws that denied single (and married) women the
right to the homestead grant of 160 acres that was available to
men, regardless of marital status. *Wheat and Woman* challenged
accepted norms of white, middle-class femininity; Binnie-Clark
never mentioned marriage as the final destination for her or her
sister, and she did not take kindly to domestic duties such as having to prepare meals for her hired men. 'From the beginning,' she
wrote, 'I was perfectly happy working on the land, only I wished
it was some one else's turn to get those tiresome three meals a
day.'[11]

As it is one hundred years since Binnie-Clark purchased her
farm and twenty-five years since the second edition of *Wheat and
Woman*, with an introduction by Susan Jackel, it is time to intro-
duce this book and its author to a new generation and to reconsider both in the light of new approaches to the past and new
research on women in Canada, in the British Empire, and on the
Great Plains of North America. The introduction to the 2006
reprint builds on, and should be read in conjunction with,
Jackel's 1979 introduction. It is unfortunate that Binnie-Clark has

attracted little attention since Jackel's introduction.[12] Jackel wrote optimistically that there were signs of a renewed interest in Binnie-Clark, but this did not materialize, even though the field of women's history has blossomed in the last quarter-century. In this field it became suspect by about the mid-1980s to focus on notable women 'worthies,' who were invariably Anglo, white, and privileged. Biographical approaches were also frowned upon, as they echoed the old 'great men' approach to history and meant that the lives of the vast majority of ordinary women would go unexamined.[13] This criticism and dismissal was unfortunate and narrow, particularly in the case of western Canada, where the field of women's history has only ever attracted modest attention and the work of rescuing women from obscurity, both the exceptional and the ordinary, is still just beginning.[14] Women such as Binnie-Clark deserve attention, and not because we need female additions to heroic tales of rugged individuals in the narrative of western Canada. Her life raises significant questions and sheds light on many dimensions of the early twentieth-century Canadian West, particularly the privileges, limitations, and complexities of race and gender categories. She can also assist in opening conversations between historians of western women in the United States and Canada, and with international scholars who are adopting transnational approaches to gender, race, and empire. As a journalist, travel writer, farmer, and enthusiastic promoter of the British Empire and the opportunities for women in the British settler colonies, Binnie-Clark belongs in these conversations and in these studies. The purpose of my introduction is to draw attention to her and to situate her in the context of some of the new research that has emerged since the second edition.

As Susan Jackel found, there are many puzzles and gaps in the Binnie-Clark story. She was clearly well educated, and she must have been accustomed to servants, as she could not cook when she arrived in Canada, and although she was an experienced rider, she was not able to harness her own horse. (Initially she had to call on her neighbours whenever this was required!)[15] But just how 'elite' was she? Her parents were from modest backgrounds. Her father, Arthur Walter Binnie Clark, the son of a labourer, was a valet when in 1866 he married Georgina's mother, Maria Letheby, the daughter of a gamekeeper.[16] Georgina, born in 1872 in Sherborne, Dorset, was their third child. The 1901 census lists Georgina's father as the proprietor of the Digby Arms Hotel in Sherborne. Her financial situation was always precarious, according to her books and from evidence found in family papers. She had to write and publish to sustain herself and her farm and in order to purchase the labour she required. But she also had to learn to milk, make bread, clean out the stables, pickle seed, stook, and to do numerous other chores, since she could not afford to have these done for her. Binnie-Clark described herself as 'desperately short of money' in the winter of 1906–7, and in later correspondence, she wrote that she was 'always more or less hard up.'[17] It does not appear that her financial situation ever dramatically improved. (In 1936, for example, she wrote from England to a Fort Qu'Appelle acquaintance asking for the $12.00 she had loaned her five years earlier.)[18] As a British, educated woman, she had power and privilege, but these were unstable categories, made all the more unstable by the uncertainties of farming on the northern Great Plains. She did not enjoy the power and privilege bestowed upon men, since she did not qualify for a homestead because of her gender. She was genteel but not well-to-do, and she had to support herself throughout her life. Binnie-Clark also donated to causes that diminished any income she made from her writing. Profits from *Wheat and Woman*, for example, were donated to the Blue Cross.[19] She would not have been recognized as superior or elite in the Saskatchewan community she adopted; she was keenly aware of her status as an eccentric, 'green' Englishwoman. She cast herself, however, as well above the people of the East End of London, whom she encountered (for the first time) in an emigrant shed in Quebec in their 'grotesque attire' and 'squalid degradation.'[20]

It is important to emphasize, as Jackel pointed out, that it is not clear whether the information provided in Binnie-Clark's books about herself, her family, and her farming is entirely reliable. She changed the names of her family members, her neighbours, and her hired men. 'Lal,' for example, was her brother Louis, whose homestead records indicate that he was married and that his wife lived with him on his homestead from March 1906.[21] Yet Louis's wife does not appear in *Wheat and Woman*; rather, it is important to the narrative that Lal be presented as a lazy bachelor who wants to desert the homestead while she insists that he stay and 'prove up.'[22] Binnie-Clark's sister, called 'Hilaria,' was probably Ethel, but if so, it is likely not the case that she hated the rural prairies and farming in the way Binnie-Clark describes, since Ethel became a much more permanent resident of the farm than her sister. But for her narrative, it is important to develop Hilaria's distaste for farm life on the prairies, to form a contrast to Georgina's growing fascination, and through Hilaria's efforts to find a job as a nurse and domestic servant, readers learn about the limited options for single women in Canada.

There remain significant gaps in important aspects of Binnie-Clark's life, such as where she was educated and where and how she established a reputation as a journalist before her arrival in Canada in 1905. As Susan Jackel discovered, it is also not clear precisely when and for how many years she was resident on her Saskatchewan farm.[23] What is now clear is that Binnie-Clark never entirely switched her allegiance or her abode to her Saskatchewan farm. She had a flat in London's Chelsea district, on Cheyne Walk on the Embankment, with a view of the Thames from at least the First World War to her death in 1947, although there were times when it was rented out.[24] Chelsea, in particular Cheyne Walk, is a district that has long been associated with writers, artists, and activists, and she was part of a literary and artistic circle that included a very good friend and neighbour, Dame Ethel Walker, a leading British painter of her day.[25] Walker also lived at the south end of Cheyne Walk, right on the Thames. Her home was described by one her acquaintances as 'opposite the house-boats ... at the slummy end. The studio was a first-floor room and the light from the Thames was reflected inside, flickering with the tides, the wind and the sky. It was almost like being in one of the house-boats on the river.'[26] Another close neighbour on Cheyne Walk was prominent feminist Sylvia Pankhurst. Binnie-Clark's accommodation was modest; she described hers as the 'vagabond end' of Cheyne Walk.[27]

During the First World War, Binnie-Clark was one of seven agriculturalists appointed by the Ministry of Labour to organize the work of women on the land, and she was assigned the Yorkshire and Lincolnshire districts.[28] She wrote a book for children during the war called *Tippy*, about a little puppy's adventures and set mainly on Cheyne Walk, with any profits to 'buy comfort for the wounded soldiers and horses fighting in the Great War for Liberty.'[29] Binnie-Clark also had a business on Woodstock Street, a small street off Oxford Street, London's main shopping district, from the First World War into the 1930s called The Fashion Journals Guild, where she sold patterns for dresses and hats. As a young boy of nine or ten in the 1930s, her great-nephew Dennis Jenks recalls visiting Avril (as family and friends called Georgina) at this small, cluttered office; which she managed with the assistance of one employee.[30] Just how she juggled this business and her farm in Saskatchewan is one of many puzzles about Georgina Binnie-Clark.

Binnie-Clark's first allegiance was to the British Empire. This loyalty was expressed through her writing, farming, training of young English women agriculturalists, lectures, and finally the organization of the Union Jack Farm Settlement. She counted herself among those who were 'fighting out the battle of our Empire with the pick and spade on unbroken soil.'[31] She was charmed by Quebec City, as it was 'stamped with associations which bear the glorious seal of dauntless, deathless, effectual moments in our imperial history, when we English knew how to fight for causes.'[32] Binnie-Clark was devoted to the 'Mother Country' and was helping to rear the 'daughter nation' of Canada, 'our most important colony.'[33] In recent years scholars have challenged earlier, male-dominated approaches to imperial history by focusing on women and empire from a variety of perspectives and in diverse locales.[34] Binnie-Clark and many other British women were profoundly influenced by imperialist ideologies and practices, and they supported, promoted, and helped to shape the British Empire, at home and in the colonies. Binnie-Clark was convinced that the empire was a force for great good in the world, and she was particularly interested in publicizing and promoting the contribution English women could make to the settler dominions.

She shared the view that the British Empire would uplift the 'darker' races, but this was not her main concern or issue.[35] She devoted little time and attention to issues of Aboriginal dispossession in her writing and appeared to know little about Native people, even though her farm was located on Treaty 4 land and it was surrounded by the reserves of the Cree, Assiniboine, and Saulteaux. In *Wheat and Woman* she praised the work being done at the industrial school for Aboriginal children at Lebret in the Qu'Appelle valley, though admitting a tinge of regret that they had been robbed of their freedom to travel the valley and prairies she had grown to love. A photograph included in *Wheat and Woman* of four industrial school children with two elders was one of the propaganda images that the Department of Indian Affairs used to demonstrate the contrasts between the old and new generations. Binnie-Clark's other major passage on Aboriginal people, which appears in *A Summer on the Canadian Prairie* (1910), conveys a typical settler mentality that much was being done to 'graft civilization on the aborigines of our colonies with generosity and excellent intention.' but that they refused to live in the good houses or till the good farms they were given because they had been robbed 'of their liberty and the joy of the hunter.'[36]

Aboriginal people had little place in the book *Wheat and Woman* and no place in the new agricultural economy, defined mainly as a white, male enterprise. Binnie-Clark's only Aboriginal acquaintances, according to her books, were the Métis (whom she called 'half breeds') she encountered in her district and who fenced for her. Her writing, however, was not characterized by the kind of pejorative descriptions of Aboriginal people that were to be found in the work of her contemporaries, and she may have been trying to challenge misconceptions and assumptions. When her suspicion that two 'half breeds' had stolen her bag of oats proved untrue, and they actually helped her to find the oats and hoist it onto her buggy, she 'vowed to scorn suspicion and colour prejudice for evermore.'[37] Binnie-Clark was also critical of what she described as 'the creed of every Englishman to dislike or at best tolerate foreigners.' She described the Hungarians who settled near her brother, for example, as generous and industrious; they commanded her 'unqualified admiration.' Her brother, however, 'imagines he detests them.'[38] Binnie-Clark's admiration did not extend to 'Chinamen,' as she called them, providing her version of the familiar 'no ticky no washy' story.[39]

As historian Lisa Chilton has argued, female imperialists such as Binnie-Clark were devoted to the idea that 'educated women would use their inherent personal advantages to carve out strong roles and identities for themselves in the mutable environment of the colonial frontier, to civilise and extend the boundaries of the British world.'[40] She was a contributor to the *Imperial Colonist*, the official organ of the British Women's Emigration Association and South African Colonization Society, designed to promote female emigration to the colonies.[41] While domestic service was the career path most enthusiastically promoted, it was seldom presented as an end in itself. Marriage was a likely destination for many, but alternative occupations for single women, including farming, were regularly presented. Smart, plucky, successful female farmers were described as owners of grain, poultry, and dairy farms throughout the colonies. The author of a 1910 article entitled 'A Lady's Farm in Tasmania,' for example, had been engaged in agricultural pursuits for years and found them 'pleasant and remunerative.' She 'could not bear the idea of becoming a companion or a clerk, but the independent life of a farmer appealed to me.' She intended to open an agricultural college on her farm in order to train women 'in any branch of agriculture they wish to take up.'[42] Binnie-Clark's articles encouraged single women to consider farming in western Canada as a rewarding and fulfilling profession.

At a 1909 conference in Portsmouth of the National Union of Women Workers of Great Britain and Ireland, Binnie-Clark gave a talk during the day devoted to 'Women in Britain and Beyond the Seas.' She began her talk, on 'Conditions of Life for Women in Canada,' by saying that 'the immigration of English women is a matter of vital importance to the Canadian race.'[43] She described her own farming experiences and the arguments she put before the minister of the interior to extend the grant of homestead land to women. Englishwomen, she said, were eager for the free land grant because it was in their nature to 'love outdoor pursuits,' and because of 'a grave and ever increasing necessity for English-women to support themselves in youth, and to make provision for old age.'[44]

Around 1910, Binnie-Clark took her devotion to this cause to another level when she began to train English female pupils at her farm to work on the land, advertising in the *Times* of London for recruits and taking in students from the prestigious Roedean School near Brighton. Mrs Thomas Lavington, employed by the Canadian Pacific Railway to assess opportunities for British women in western Canada, spent a month at Binnie-Clark's farm in 1910. In her reminiscences Lavington described four young English women 'full of hope and earnest endeavour' who were being charged a 'substantial premium' for lessons in prairie farm-ing. The pupils were 'much assisted by willing males who seemed to appear from every quarter to offer their services.' Three of the pupils were married within the year, she reported. Lavington learned to bake, milk, and make butter during her stay on Binnie-Clark's farm, but was she not enthusiastic about the accommodation, writing that the house was 'heated by a maze of pipes running from the kitchen stove. When the stove went off the heat went off, and the first night I spent there I thought I should never live till morning, so terrible was the cold.'[45]

One pupil was Kathleen Laughrin, who came out with six oth-ers in 1910, having seen an advertisement in the *Times*.[46] Kath-leen's main memory of the short-lived experience was that the kettle at Binning was a block of ice in the morning and the bed could not be made be-cause the bedding stuck to the frozen wall. Laughrin subsequently married James Harrison, a neighbour of Binnie-Clark's. Georgina Binnie-Clark was well informed and up to date about similar training initiatives throughout the empire, describing in *Wheat and Woman*, for example, the new Fairbridge Farm School in Western Australia for the resettlement of underprivileged British working-class children, who received practical vocational training.[47]

But there were doubters and dissenters on the suitability and ability of women farmers both in Canada and in other settler colonies of the British Empire, where women's ownership of and work on the land disrupted cherished versions of white femininity and was perceived to be a subversion of the heterosexual order, particularly if the women were single and childless.[48] Women were among the sceptics. A Miss Beevor, a discussant at the 1909 Portsmouth conference, cautioned that Binnie-Clark had purchased an 'improved' farm, that she had not done the 'pioneer work,' and that only exceptional women could succeed. She concluded by saying, 'I am afraid that one swallow does not make a summer and one Miss Binnie-Clark won't exactly carry this scheme ... [but] if I were younger I would be off tomorrow.'[49] Eileen L. Burns, president of the Calgary Women's Hostel, was another critic of Binnie-Clark's promotion of women farmers in western Canada, writing in 1910 that it was an unsuitable and impossible occupation for women, and that 'unsuspecting, romantic and inexperienced women ... [should] not be led to waste time and capital on a scheme which cannot fail to entail bitter disappointment and disillusion.' Moreover, they would be looked on 'askance by their Canadian neighbours as women of eccentric and suspicious character.'[50] In her report on British women and farming in western Canada, Mrs Lavington advised that 'no woman on her own could possibly brave the elements and the super human activities required for this type of farming.' After a year of investigation she agreed with the 'rather grim ladies representing various organizations' whom she met in Montreal at the beginning of her sojourn, who informed her that the only British women required were 'Home Helps.'[51]

Yet Binnie-Clark was correct; many women were interested in obtaining and farming land in western Canada, and there were other examples of successful solo women farmers. Women's interest in farming was evident from the 1870s, when for a brief period of time, the wording of the Dominion Lands legislation permitted single women to homestead. This legislation was deliberately changed in 1876 to exclude single women.[52] Surveyor General J.S. Dennis made the recommendation in October 1875, following a visit to Manitoba and the North-West Territories, that the legislation be changed 'To render females, not being heads of families, ineligible to enter for homesteads.'[53] Before that date there had been a significant number of women applicants.[54] The first woman to 'prove up' was Susanna Jane Kennedy, who applied for a homestead in Manitoba in 1873 and received patent to her land five years later. In 1873, 41 women filed for homesteads, and 10 (24 per cent) of these women successfully proved up. In 1874, 111 women filed, and 30 (27 per cent) proved up. Males were somewhat more successful in proving up, but not dramatically so. In 1874, for example, 1,279 males filed for homesteads, and of these 416 proved up (33 per cent). But after 1874 the number of women applicants plummeted – there were a mere 6 in 1875 and 4 in 1876. From then on, women qualified only if they were heads of families with dependent children.

Yet there were a significant number of solo women farmers in western Canada, although their numbers were small compared to male farm owners. The January 1925 edition of the *Imperial Colonist* proclaimed that 'there are now 15,840 women farmers in Canada, many in the prairie provinces. Of these 15,094 are owners and managers of farms, 255 gardeners or florists, 204 market gardeners and 104 ranchers and stock raisers.'[55] Historian Kathryn McPherson has found that in southwestern Manitoba, not too far from Binnie-Clark's farm, at least 283 women possessed title to 418 quarter sections. Most had purchased their land, but 92 had homesteaded as widows with dependent children.[56] She discovered that they were overwhelmingly of British ancestry; access to land was determined by ethnicity, nationality, and racial category. In Binnie-Clark's municipality, several women were among the first patentees, or owners of the land, including Mary McAskill and Hannah Rolley.[57] Some landowners, such as Madeline Klyne, Susette S. Denis, and Anne Inkster, may have acquired their land through Métis scrip. Women went to extraordinary lengths to acquire land. In May 1910 a young, single

Saskatoon schoolteacher, Mildred Williams, waited for twelve days and nights at the top of the stairs outside of the land office in Saskatoon in order to be able to file on a half section of valuable land near Kindersley.[58] She was permitted to file on a homestead as a single woman by purchasing South African scrip. Volunteers who had served the British crown in the Boer War were entitled to make entry on two adjoining quarter sections of dominion land as homesteads, and if they did not wish to take advantage of this offer, they could sell their scrip to anyone, regardless of gender or marital status, entitling the buyer to homestead land. In this way Mildred Williams, and many other single women, obtained homestead land. Williams successfully filed and proved up, earning her patent in 1914.[59] She was not alone; there were many women who acquired land in western Canada by purchasing South African scrip.[60]

In the American West, thousands of single women homesteaded because, in contrast to Canada, the land legislation permitted them to do so. It may have been a somewhat exaggerated statement, but one woman in Dakota territory remarked that 'the woman who has not some kind of claim proved up is either a newcomer or a curiosity.'[61] Single women had filed on homesteads as early as the 1860s, and their numbers increased significantly after the turn of the century.[62] They proved up at a rate that was comparable to that of men.[63] In Valley County, Montana, which shares the border with Saskatchewan, nearly 900 women filed on homesteads, out of a total of nearly 6,000 entrants.[64] The homestead rush in that county was most intense during the years 1910–15. Women filed for a variety of reasons: to establish themselves permanently as farmers, to enlarge their family's property, or to acquire investment property and earn a profit from the sale of their claims.[65] Profits (if any) could be used to establish them in business or to pursue education. Many supported their homesteads by raising income in non-agricultural occupations. A great number of teachers were also homesteaders. Women homesteaders were diverse, despite the fact that homesteading was cast as the salvation of white America in the early twentieth century. A recent study found Anglo Protestant, Mormon, and Mexican

American women homesteaders in Arizona.[66] A significant number of women homesteaders in the American West were from Canada.[67] The phenomenon was not reported in the *Imperial Colonist*; nor did Binnie-Clark comment upon it in *Wheat and Woman*, likely because it might have attracted British women away from the colonies, and there is evidence that such was the case.[68]

In Canada Binnie-Clark's *Wheat and Woman* was a unique account of a single woman farmer, but in the United States a 'female homesteading genre swept popular literature with stories that spoke metaphorically to the challenges of New Womanhood.'[69] The theme of courageous and intrepid single women proving themselves capable and self-reliant in unorthodox ways was extremely popular; magazines such as *Atlantic Monthly*, *Collier's*, *Overland Monthly*, and *Outlook* published over thirty articles by women about homesteading between 1913 and 1928.[70] As historian Dee Garceau writes, 'The woman homesteader of popular literature tested herself against traditional assumptions about her gender and discovered new strengths. Literary homesteaders presented their experience as a vehicle for developing emotional self-reliance, economic autonomy and political clout ... In these ways, homesteading writers spoke thematically to the challenges of female role change, as New Women increasingly defined themselves in individualistic, egalitarian terms.'[71] The rewards were many, including improved health, economic independence, property ownership, and inner strength. The literary homesteaders 'pushed their own limits and emerged with a broader sense of their own capabilities,' Garceau writes.[72] Proving up was used as a metaphor for demonstrating female competence beyond domestic duties. But these laudatory articles implicated women in the white triumph over the American West. Homesteading was promoted for men and women by national leaders such as Theodore Roosevelt because they were concerned about farms being 'occupied by a lower type of people.'[73] *Wheat and Woman* should in part be understood as a Canadian contribution to the literary genre of the single woman homesteader, but it emerged from a dramatically different context, although just a few miles north of the forty-ninth parallel. Unlike many of the literary homesteaders, Binnie-Clark does not celebrate an egalitarian West, but rather, she provides a critique of the inequities of the Canadian West. Farming was not an easy solution to poverty in her book, in contrast to the account of her contemporary in the United States, Elinore Pruitt Stewart, in her very popular *Letters of a Woman Homesteader*, published the same year as *Wheat and Woman* (but serialized earlier in *Atlantic Monthly*).[74] Binnie-Clark did not escape domestic drudgery and poverty in an idealized West; she had to confront them squarely.

As Susan Jackel has described, a homesteads-for-women movement gained momentum in western Canada in the years leading to the First World War, which culminated in a petition submitted to Parliament in 1913. Binnie-Clark was an important advocate of the cause, and she was used to illustrate the success of single women farmers. Her own arguments for the cause were articulated in a letter of November 1908 to the Department of the Interior, asking the minister to 'give personal consideration to the idea of "Free Homesteads for Women."'[75] She argued that there was 'no insurmountable obstacle to a woman in the working of a farm ... if they do not get through as much work as a man in a day, they will get through considerably more in a season.' Women would not 'roam around' during the off season and would seize on sidelines of stock raising and dairy produce; 'the woman's homestead will be Home, the centre of life and interest.' Binnie-Clark emphasized their 'civilizing' role, since schools and churches would result. She described the class of woman she had in mind as 'working gentlewomen of education.' She proposed that the Canadian government offer a limited number of home-steads to Englishwomen, and she was confident the 'experiment would succeed beyond imagination.' Binnie-Clark understood that the law was the only barrier, and she concluded by writing, 'The laws of a Liberal Government are always awaiting expansion & the ear of the true law-giver is always alert for the whisper of Reason.' The brief answer to her letter stated simply that her arguments had been noted, 'but unfortunately the law does not allow this and the Department does not make a law and has no power to alter it in this particular.'[76]

A wide variety of arguments were drawn on by other supporters of homesteads for women, but increasingly the one made most forcibly was that homestead rights should not be given to 'foreign' men when British women were denied that right. They keenly felt it to be an injustice that 'our own Canadian men – our fathers and our brothers – deliberately set aside us as undeserving of a share in our country,' while permitting 'ignorant, uncouth, lawless foreigners to occupy lands that we desire, and that we have laboured for, yet cannot have.'[77] This point of view is presented in *Wheat and Woman*, as Binnie-Clark notes that the land laws enriched the 'stranger.'[78] Isabel Graham, women's editor of the *Grain Growers' Guide*, was the most prominent and dedicated activist for the cause. She wrote in a 1913 letter to the president of the National Council of Women that Canadians must 'Keep back the foreigner. Give us good, sound British stock – women already British, already civilized.'[79] Graham claimed sole responsibility for the clause in the petition asking that homestead rights be extended to 'all women of British birth who have resided in Canada for one year.'[80] Thousands of women and men agreed as they signed the petition, which was not circulated in areas settled by the 'foreigner' or 'new' Canadians who had arrived after the turn of the century from eastern and central Europe, many from impoverished backgrounds.

There were many who disagreed, however, arguing that if there were to be changes to the homestead laws, they should benefit all, not just British women. These individuals expressed concern that such narrowness might diminish their quest for equity and justice. 'The women of British birth should not be so selfish and short-sighted as to try to put through a law of this kind with the words "of British birth" therein,' wrote one reader of the *Grain Growers' Guide*, 'for if they succeed it will be a blot on the degree of their intelligence, and a factor of their lack of Christianity as practiced by them, which our historians will be sorry to relate.'[81] 'What have women of British birth done that entitles them to the land more than the thousands of other nationalities?' asked another.[82] American and former American women were disappointed that they too were to be excluded from homestead-

ing rights in Canada, if the petition succeeded in persuading leg-
islators.[83] As Susan Jackel noted, the homesteads-for-women
campaign was unsuccessful: the petition was shelved and forgotten. Unfortunately, *Wheat and Woman* was published just at the
outset of the First World War, and it had little impact at a time
when the issue of women's homestead rights did not loom
large.[84]

Binnie-Clark's last major initiative at her farm in Fort
Qu'Appelle, also in the cause of the British Empire, was the
establishment of the Union Jack Farm Settlement (UJFS) in 1930
for British immigrants. She was living on her farm and working
on this project from at least 1929 to 1935. As with the publication
date of *Wheat and Woman*, this initiative could not have begun at a
worse time because this was the start of the ten-year Depression,
which hit rural Saskatchewan more severely than all other
regions of Canada. The purpose of the UJFS was to assist British
immigrant families to adapt to the conditions of the West by
teaching them farming and helping them to find work. Binnie-
Clark believed that 'such families are the most eligible type for
the "army of occupation" we need for the guardianship of the
King's Dominions Overseas.'[85] 'In the Union Jack Farm Settlement,' she wrote, 'we try to accomplish for human beings what
the Experimental Farms, established throughout Canada by the
Canadian government, have accomplished for the care and
development of all that is most valuable in the life of seeds and
plants and birds and stock.'

The idea for the UJFS took shape in 1929 when Binnie-Clark
published a letter in the *Times* of London, in answer to a proposal
by five members of Parliament that the British government
should acquire a 'large estate' in Canada for the purpose of settling unemployed Britons, particularly disinherited miners, who
would work on roads and railways and lay out townships. The
scheme would benefit Britain as well as Canada, the MPs argued,
as it was the chance for a fresh wave of British emigration, 'not a
driblet, but a wave, which might well mark a new stage in the
history of Canadian life.'[86] Binnie-Clark responded as a 'hard-
worn farmer of many years' experience in raising stock and grain

on an average farm on the Canadian prairie.'[87] She felt there was little hope of happiness or prosperity for the settlers in the plan as outlined by the five MPs. Settlers needed their own land, lumber for building, cattle, pigs, implements, and other essentials. 'Instead of an "estate,"' she wrote, 'why not establish home-farms here and there among the settlers and use them as centres of reception and distribution for men and good stock?' Binnie-Clark by this time had clearly given up on any special plea for women homesteaders or farmers. She concluded her letter to the *Times* by writing; 'Any project or policy which threatens the supremacy of the homestead-grant of free land as the ruling factor in the settlement of men on the land in Canada is to be mistrusted and rejected.'

From this seed grew the idea of the UJFS, which was to be one of her proposed 'home farms.' Another half section of land near Binning, called 'Settler's Rest,' was purchased for the UJFS with the assistance of an elderly, wealthy benefactor, Rachel Mary Punshon, who visited Binnie-Clark on her farm in the late 1920s, just when she was 'elated' that the *Times* had chosen to publish the letter.[88] Binnie-Clark then sought assistance through the Empire Settlement Act of 1922, which was intended to advance British emigration to the colonies through land settlement schemes, assisted passages, training courses, and other methods.[89] Binnie-Clark persuaded Florence Amery, wife of Leo Amery, the leading political spokesman of the empire settlement movement after 1918, to make the appeal for funding for her plan. The Overseas Settlement Department, which administered the act, informed Mrs Amery in 1931, however, that 'we have not been able to secure authority to contribute to any land settlement scheme, even with well established organizations, for a considerable time. It would therefore be quite impossible to assist a private individual however efficient.'[90] There was little enthusiasm for empire settlement schemes in Canada through much of the 1920s, and they were a lost cause as the Depression deepened.[91] Confidence in the British Empire itself was eroding. Binnie-Clark's devotion to the empire was out of step with the thinking and writing of many of her contemporaries in western Canada, such as journalist

Violet McNaughton, who had qualms about British imperialism and was an internationalist and a pacifist.[92] Binnie-Clark's plan was also frustrated because no more land was available for free homestead grants in Saskatchewan; there were new 'purchase provisions,' but these were open only to those resident within the province for five years.[93] Binnie-Clark also sought royal sponsorship for the project, which she hoped to attract by setting aside, as a mark of allegiance, an acre in each farm to be known as the 'King's Acre,' a promise she kept on her own land, as Susan Jackel described.[94] *A Birthday Book for the Farm Settlement on the Canadian Prairie*, compiled by Binnie-Clark, was another fund-raising effort. She chose 365 messages from the Bible, one for each day of the year, and beside each day was a space for the owner of the book to pledge an amount to the UJFS.[95]

The project received no significant financial backing, and it limped along, remaining in operation until 1937. The Canadian government cut off immigration to Canada at the end of the summer of 1930, but Binnie-Clark appears to have found an ample number of applicants already in Saskatchewan, who were likely willing to take advantage of any opportunity for housing and employment in the midst of the Depression.[96] In 1932 she wrote that she was going to Regina to interview thirty married couples with children.[97] Each year Binnie-Clark wrote to the *Times* of London to ask for support for the settlement, particularly 'warm woollies.' In January 1933 she wrote that the UJFS supported three men, three women, and six children. In the spring each man would receive his 'bit of saved pay to cheer him on his search for a job.'[98]

By 1936, however, Binnie-Clark was living in London. Her 11 February 1936 appeal to the *Times* for 'woollies' was sent from 125 Cheyne Walk, and it is not clear whether she ever returned to her farm after that date. The same year she joined London's Lyceum Club for women artists and writers.[99] She continued her appeals to the *Times* on behalf of the UJFS until 1937. Three years later she published a letter in the *Times* describing her success with 'Sixty Days Barley in Canada,' also written from her Cheyne Walk address.[100] Chelsea, in particular Cheyne Walk, was badly damaged by bombing during the Second World War, as it was on the Thames and between two power stations. It would be hard to imagine a place more worlds away from the tranquility of Binnie-Clark's Fort Qu'Appelle farm than her flat on Cheyne Walk, where she died in 1947.

Wheat and Woman is an important text in the history of western Canada. It remains the only published book-length account of a single woman farmer, a dynamic individual who challenged the conventions of her day, flouting definitions of appropriate possession and use of the land. She exemplified the potential choices that British women could make, but unlike the literary homesteaders of the United States, she did not romanticize the West as a place where single women could be freed from domesticity, drudgery, and poverty. *Wheat and Woman* revealed the extreme inequity of the homestead laws and the uneven distribution of power between men and women. Yet Binnie-Clark and others in the homesteads-for-women movement advocated the homestead rights of British and not all women. The book, and Georgina Binnie-Clark's career, remind us of how western Canada is a landscape profoundly shaped by ideas of gender, race, and empire.

NOTES

1 Many thanks to Lynn Anderson, Derek Harrison, and Doug and Marge Dawson, Fort Qu'Appelle, Saskatchewan.

2 Georgina Binnie-Clark, *A Summer on the Canadian Prairie* (London: Edward Arnold, 1910), 133.

3 Georgina Binnie-Clark, *Wheat and Woman* (1914; rpt., Toronto: University of Toronto Press, 1979), introd. Susan Jackel, 188–9.

4 Ibid., 121.

5 Binnie-Clark, *Summer*, 134.

6 Ibid., 303.

7 Simon Evans, *The Bar U: Canadian Ranching History* (Calgary: University of Calgary Press, 2004), 134–41.

8 Binnie-Clark, *Wheat and Woman*, 236.

9 Susanna Moodie, *Roughing It in the Bush, or Forest Life in Canada* (1852; repr., Toronto: McClelland and Stewart, 1962).

10 Binnie-Clark, *Wheat and Woman*, 119.

11 Ibid., 151.

12 An exception is the work of Lisa Chilton. See her article 'A New Class of Women for the Colonies: *The Imperial Colonist* and the Construction of Empire,' in Carl Bridge and Kent Fedorowich, eds., 'The British World: Diaspora, Culture and Identity,' special issue of the *Journal of Imperial and Commonwealth History* 31, no. 2 (May 2003): 36–55. Pernille Jakobsen includes Georgina Binnie-Clark's *A Summer on the Canadian Prairie* in her analysis of the travel writing of fourteen British women who visited Western Canada. See Pernille Jakobsen, 'Touring Strange Lands: Women Travel Writers in western Canada, 1876–1914' (MA thesis, Department of History, University of Calgary, 1996). For an example of recent attention to Binnie-Clark with reliance on Susan Jackel's introduction, see Anne Innis Dagg, *The Feminine Gaze: A Canadian Compendium of Non-Fiction Women Authors and Their Books, 1836–1945* (Waterloo: Wilfrid Laurier University Press, 2001), 39,

13 Dee Garceau-Hagen discusses the suspicion of biography in the field of women's history, but argues that these portraits can 'reveal interweavings of race, gender, and class as plural sources of identity, and as unstable categories of power and privilege,' in her introduction to Dee Garceau-Hagen, ed., *Portraits of Women in the American West* (New York: Routledge, 2005), 1.

14 There is evidence of a renewal of interest in biographical approaches to western Canadian women. See, for example, Lesley A. Erickson, '"Bury Our Sorrows in the Sacred Heart": Gender and the Metis Response to Colonialism – The Case of Sara and Louis Riel, 1848–83'; and Patricia A. Roome, '"From One Whose Home Is among the Indians": Henrietta Muir Edwards and Aboriginal Peoples,' in Sarah Carter, Lesley A. Erickson, Patricia A. Roome, and Char Smith, eds., *Unsettled Pasts: Reconceiving the West through Women's History* (Calgary: University of Calgary Press, 2005). See also Catherine A. Cavanaugh, 'Irene Marryat Parlby: An "Imperial Daughter" in the Canadian West, 1896–1934,' and Ann Leger-Anderson, 'Marriage, Family, and the Cooperative Ideal,' in Catherine A. Cavanaugh and

Randi R.Warne, eds., *Telling Tales: Essays in Western Women's History* (Vancouver: University of British Columbia Press, 2000).

15 Binnie-Clark, *Wheat and Woman*, 53.

16 Thanks to Binnie-Clark's great-nephews Richard and Dennis Jenks for sharing 'The Family History of Clark' and other papers. Thanks also for their comments on the final draft of this introduction. Georgina's father was sometimes listed in the census returns as 'Binnie-Clark' and sometimes just as 'Clark.' For example, in the 1901 census he appears as Arthur W.B. Clark. Seven children were born to Arthur and Maria: Maria Elizabeth (b. 1868), Walter Douglas (b. 1869), Georgina (b. 1872), Louis (b. 1873), Arthur Cameron (b. 1874), Mabel (b. 1874), and Ethel (b. 1880). Georgina's brother Louis signed his name Louis B. Clark. See Saskatchewan Archives Board (SAB), Homestead Records, file no. 1328338, Louis B. Clark (SW ¼ Section 6, Township 26, Range 14, West of the 2nd Meridian).

17 Binnie-Clark, *Wheat and Woman*, 190; Richard and Dennis Jenks papers, typed untitled document by Georgina Binnie-Clark, beginning on p. 2, n.d. (c. 1932), 2.

18 Derek Harrison papers, Fort Qu'Appelle, Sask., Georgina Binnie-Clark to Dorothy Harrison, 21 February 1936. Thanks to Derek Harrison for sharing these papers and for his comments on the final draft of this introduction.

19 Harrison papers, Advertising flyer for *Wheat and Woman*, n.d.: 'The profit of this edition (1st) goes to the Blue Cross. Will you do all you can to help make known the book, as we hope to get £100.'

20 Binnie-Clark, *Summer*, 30.

21 SAB, Homestead Records, file. no. 1328338, Louis B. Clark.

22 To 'prove up' a homestead meant to fulfil all the obligations required under the Dominion Lands Act in order to acquire patent to the land. For a $10.00 registration fee a homesteader could file on a quarter section of unoccupied land. Patent would be issued after three years if residential duties were performed (resident on the homestead for three months each year) and if a specified number of acres were broken.

23 In an undated seven-page typed manuscript in the Jenks papers, Binnie-Clark wrote that she was at her farm in 1926 and 1928, and at that time 'I was just pulling out from the embarrassment that awaited me

on my return to Canada after my absence during the war and following years.' She also noted that 'Binning House had been destroyed by
fire during the war and never replaced.' (2).

24 Binnie-Clark may have had two different homes on Cheyne Walk. On
6 November 1932 she wrote to Dorothy Cooper-Abs, 'Our old house
in Cheyne Walk was demolished.' She had been renting the flat out
for £100 a year, and this was an important source of income for her
(Harrison papers). By February 1936 she was living at 125 Cheyne
Walk, and she stayed there until her death in 1947 (*Times* [London],
11 February 1936, 10).

25 Thanks to Dennis Jenks for sharing his memories of Avril, London,
5 October 2005, and for taking me to the Cheyne Walk location of her
flat, now demolished.

26 Nicolette Devas, *Two Flamboyant Fathers* (London: Readers Union-
Collins, 1968), 213; Thea Holme, *Chelsea* (London: Hamish Hamilton,
1972).

27 Georgina Binnie-Clark, *Tippy: The Autobiography of a Pekingese Puppy*
(London: The Fashion Journals Guild, n.d., c. 1916), in Jenks papers.

28 Jenks papers, handwritten document, 'The Union Jack Farm Settlement,' 113.

29 Binnie-Clark, *Tippy*, front cover.

30 Dennis Jenks to Sarah Carter, email correspondence, 14 December,
2005.

31 Binnie-Clark, *Wheat and Woman*, 60.

32 Binnie-Clark, *Summer*, 27.

33 Ibid., 230, and *Wheat and Woman*, 60.

34 For an introduction to this field, see Phillipa Levine, ed., *Gender and
Empire* (Oxford: Oxford University Press, 2004). See also Julia Bush,
Edwardian Ladies and Imperial Power (London: Leicester University
Press, 2000). For recent approaches to single women and empire, see
Jan Gothard, *Blue China: Single Female Migration to Colonial Australia*
(Melbourne: Melbourne University Press, 2001); Rita S. Kranidis, *The
Victorian Spinster and Colonial Emigration: Contested Subjects* (London:
St. Martin's Press, 1999); Katie Pickles, 'Pink Cheeked and Surplus:
Single British Women's Inter-War Migration to New Zealand,' in
Shifting Centres: Women and Migration in New Zealand History (Dune-
din: University of Otago Press, 2002); and Cecile Swaisland, *Servants*

and Gentlewomen to the Golden Land: The Emigration of Single Women from Britain to Southern Africa, 1820–1939 (Pietermaritzburg: University of Natal Press, 1993). On western Canadian women and empire, see Nadine Small, 'The "Lady Imperialists" and the Great War: The Imperial Order Daughters of the Empire in Saskatchewan, 1914–1918,' in David De Brou and Eileen Moffatt, eds., *'Other' Voices: Historical Essays on Saskatchewan Women*, (Regina: Canadian Plains Research Centre, 1995), 76–93.

35 Binnie-Clark, *Summer*, 245.

36 The Aboriginal people of the reserves surrounding Binnie-Clark's farm had made concerted efforts to farm from the time of Treaty 4 in 1874, and their endeavours were meeting with a measure of success by the early 1880s. Government policies intervened to atrophy this development, however, especially a 'peasant' farming policy, introduced in the late 1880s, which demanded that reserve farmers limit their acreage and grow root, not grain, crops, and prohibited them from using labour-saving machinery. A concerted government- and settler-supported effort to reduce the size of the reserves gained momentum after the turn of the twentieth century, just at the time Binnie-Clark's farm was established, and this severely limited the amount of arable land on most Treaty 4 reserves. See Sarah Carter, *Lost Harvests: Prairie Indian Reserve Farmers and Government Policy* (Montreal: McGill-Queen's University Press, 1990).

37 Binnie-Clark, *Summer*, 218.

38 Ibid., 124.

39 Ibid., 240.

40 Chilton, 'A New Class of Women,' 53.

41 Thanks to researcher Patricia Gordon for her work on the *Imperial Colonist* and other sources for this introduction. Binnie-Clark's three-part series 'Are Educated Women Wanted in Canada?' appeared in the *Imperial Colonist* 8, no. 98 (February 1910): 22–4; 8, no. 99 (March 1910): 39–42; 8, no. 100 (April 1910): 52–7. See also Susan Jackel, ed., *A Flannel Shirt and Liberty: British Emigrant Gentlewomen in the Canadian West, 1880–1914* (Vancouver: University of British Columbia Press, 1982).

42 *Imperial Colonist* 8, no. 100 (April 1910): 57–8.

43 G. Binnie-Clark, ' The Conditions of Life for Women in Canada,' in

Women Workers (papers read at the conference held in Portsmouth, 18–22 October 1909, arranged by the National Union of Women Workers of Great Britain and Ireland), 110.

44 Ibid., 119–20.

45 Libary and Archives Canada (LAC), Mrs Thomas Lavington, 'Reminiscences of Life on the Prairies, 1910–1914,' 3.

46 Thanks to Derek Harrison, Fort Qu'Appelle, for this information about his mother, Kathleen Laughrin Harrison. Another of Binnie-Clark's protégés, Dorothy Cooper-Abs, also married a Harrison, Captain Stanley Harrison. See Grant MacEwan, *The Rhyming Horseman of the Qu'Appelle: Captain Stanley Harrison* (Saskatoon: Western Producer Prairie Books, 1978).

47 Binnie-Clark, *Wheat and Woman*, 310.

48 Kate Hunter, 'The Big Picture Problem: Race and Gender in the Histories of Single Farming Women in Victoria, 1880–1930,' in Patricia Grimshaw and Diane Kirkby, eds., *Dealing with Difference: Essays in Gender, Culture and History* (Melbourne: History Department, University of Melbourne, 1997), 59–66.

49 *Women Workers*, 122.

50 *Imperial Colonist* 8 (August 1910): 127–8.

51 LAC, Lavington, 'Reminiscences,' 5.

52 LAC, Records of the Department of the Interior (RG 15), D-II-1, vol. 228, file 798 (1872), *Memorandum on the Subject of the Public Lands of Manitoba* (approved by the governor general in council on the 15 April 1871), 4, provided: 'Any person who is the head of a family, or has attained the age of twenty-one years, shall ... be entitled to be entered for one quarter section.' Under this wording, single women were eligible to apply, and they were so until the wording was deliberately changed in 1876 to 'Any person, male or female, who is the sole head of a family, or any male who has attained the age of eighteen years, shall be entitled to be entered for one quarter section.' See ibid., vol. 235, file 4730, 'Provisions Respecting Dominion Public Lands, Homestead Rights and Forest Tree Culture,' 12.

53 Canada, *Sessional Papers*, 1876, no. 9, part III, no. 7, 'Annual Report of the Department of the Interior for the Year Ended June 30, 1875,' Surveyor General J.S. Dennis to Minister of the Interior David Laird, 31 October 1875, 6.

54 LAC, RG 15, Homestead Land Registers from 1872 (reel T-2). Thanks
to Leslie Hall for her research and analysis of the homestead land
registers.

55 *Imperial Colonist* 23, no. 1 (January 1925): 1.

56 Kathryn McPherson, 'Was the "Frontier" Good for Women? Historical Approaches to Women and Agricultural Settlement in the Prairie
West, 1870–1925,' *Atlantis* 25, no. 1 (Fall 200): 80–1.

57 Map of names, dates, and locations of the original 'Dominion Land
Grants,' 1871–1930, Rural Municipality of North Qu'Appelle, no. 187;
available at the Municipality of North Qu'Appelle office, Fort
Qu'Appelle. Thanks to Beverly Van der Breggen, administrator, Rural
Municipality 187.

58 *Daily Phoenix* (Saskatoon), 16 May 1910; *Kindersley Clarion*, 27 May
1910.

59 SAB, Homestead Records, file 1915194, Mildred Catherine Williams,
N.O. Coté to M.C. Williams, 3 February 1914.

60 My research on women and South African scrip continues, and I do
not have a precise number as yet. So far I have found twenty-nine
single women (and many more married or widowed women) who
homesteaded in Saskatchewan through purchasing South African
scrip. One enterprising single woman, Sarah Birtles, was in her early
sixties when she homesteaded and proved up on two homesteads,
both half-sections of land, one near Colonsay, Saskatchewan, and the
other near Provost, Alberta. See SAB, Homestead Records, file
108200A, Sarah Birtles.

61 Quoted in H. Elaine Lindgren, 'Ethnic Women Homesteading on the
Plains of North Dakota,' *Great Plains Quarterly* 9 (Summer 1989): 158.

62 James Muhn, 'Women and the Homestead Act: Land Department
Administration of a Legal Imbroglio, 1863–1934,' *Western Legal History* 7, no. 2 (Summer/ Fall 1994): 283–307.

63 H. Elaine Lindgren, *Land in Her Own Name: Women as Homesteaders in
North Dakota*, foreword by Elizabeth Jameson (1991; repr., Norman
and London: University of Oklahoma Press, 1996), 224.

64 List of homesteaders in *Footprints in the Valley: A History of Valley
County, Montana* (Glasgow: Glasgow Courier and Printing, 1991),
637–51. Thanks to researcher Amy McKinney for her work on the
women homesteaders of Valley County. There were 894 women who

filed for homesteads (of these 22 were 'Indian Allotments'). There were 103 'unknown' who provided initials only, and it was not clear in the case of 123 whether they were men or women. The total number of entrants was 5,948. The original research covered 104 plats of townships and ranges in Valley County; 47 plats are missing.

65 Dee Garceau, 'Single Women Homesteaders and the Meanings of Independence: Places on the Map, Places in the Mind,' *Frontiers* 15, no. 3 (Spring 1995): 1–26.

66 Katherine Benton-Cohen, 'Common Purposes, Worlds Apart: Mexican-American, Mormon, and Midwestern Women Homesteaders in Cochise County, Arizona,' *Western Historical Quarterly* 36 (Winter 2005): 429–52.

67 See the appendix to Lindgren, *Land in Her Own Name*. For two examples, see Sarah Carter, 'Transnational Perspectives on the History of Great Plains Women: Gender, Race, Nations and the Forty-ninth Parallel,' *American Review of Canadian Studies* 33, no. 4 (Winter, 2003): 590.

68 See, for example, Sandra Varney MacMahon, 'Fine Hands for Sowing: The Homesteading Experiences of Remittance Woman Jessie de Prado MacMillan,' *New Mexico Historical Review* 74, no. 3 (July 1999): 271–94.

69 Garceau, 'Single Women Homesteaders,' 6.

70 Ibid., 12–13.

71 Ibid., 12.

72 Ibid., 16.

73 Benton-Cohen, 'Common Purposes,' 433.

74 Elinore Pruitt Stewart, *Letters of a Woman Homesteader* (1914; repr., Lincoln: University of Nebraska Press, 1961). There are many scholarly studies of Stewart, including Natalie A. Dykstra, 'The Curative Space of the American West in the Life and Letters of Elinore Pruitt Stewart,' in Garceau-Hagen, ed., *Portraits of Women in the American West*, 209–30; Susan K. George, *The Adventures of the Woman Homesteader: The Life and Letters of Elinore Pruitt Stewart* (Lincoln: University of Nebraska Press, 1992); and Sherry L. Smith, 'Single Women Homesteaders: The Perplexing Case of Elinore Pruitt Stewart,' *Western Historical Quarterly* 22, no. 2 (May 1991): 163–83.

75 LAC, RG 15, vol. 1039, file, 1713679, Georgina Binnie-Clark to Interior Department, Ottawa, 17 November 1908.

76 Ibid., W.D. Scott to G. Binnie-Clark, 12 November 1908. (The reason for the discrepancies in the dates is unclear. Binnie-Clark's letter was written on 17 November; so the reply of 12 November must be misdated.)

77 Ibid., vol. 1062, file 202953, clipping 'Homesteads for Women: A Western Woman's View of Man's Duty to women,' by Isabelle Beaton Graham (n.d., n.p., 1910).

78 Binnie-Clark, *Wheat and Woman*, 307.

79 Quoted in Carol Lee Bacchi, *Liberation Deferred? The Ideas of the English-Canadian Suffragists, 1877–1918* (Toronto: University of Toronto Press, 1983), 52–3.

80 LAC, RG 15, vol. 1105, file 2876596, Petition signed by the Winnipeg Board of Trade, 12 June 1911.

81 *Grain Growers' Guide* 3, no. 52 (26 July 1911): 17.

82 Ibid., vol. 4, no. 23 (3 January 1912): 23.

83 Ibid., 3, no. 47 (21 June 1911): 21.

84 *Wheat and Woman* received a very favourable review in the *Times Literary Supplement*, 30 April 1914 (p. 207), although the reviewer thought there was too much emphasis on how women were handicapped by the homestead laws. Rather, the 'main interest of the book for the general reader lies in its graphic and clear account of the difficulties Miss Binnie-Clark encountered in buying her experience and winning her way to practical success through sheer pluck, persistence and, it is important to add, the indispensable equipment of a tough constitution capable of enduring an astonishing amount of hardship and fatigue.'

85 *A Birthday Book for the Farm Settlement on the Canadian Prairie*, foreword G. Binnie-Clark (London: The Fashion Journals Guild, c. 1935), 5 (copy in British Library, 3089, a 33).

86 *Times*, 6 March 1929, 12, Letters to the Editor: 'New Methods with Unemployment: A Colony in Canada,' signed John Buchan, Geoffrey Ellis, L.R. Lumley, Angus McDonnell, and Oliver Stanley.

87 Ibid., 15 March 1929, 12.

88 Rachel Mary Punshon (née Cooper-Abs) lived at the Punshon estate, Ingleby House, Northallerton, Yorkshire. She had established the High Barnes estate in Sunderland, northern England. Punshon died in 1932, and there followed two years of acrimonious legal wrangling

over the ownership of 'Settler's Rest.' This was decided in 1934 when Binnie-Clark purchased the property, the money being deducted from the legacy Punshon had bequeathed to the Union Jack Farm Settlement.

89 Stephen Constantine, 'Introduction: Empire Migration and Imperial Harmony,' in Stephen Constantine, ed., *Emigrants and Empire: British Settlement in the Dominions Between the Wars* (Manchester and New York: Manchester University Press, 1990), 4.

90 Jenks papers, Geoffrey Whitehead to Mrs L.S. Amery, 6 July 1931.

91 John A. Schultz, '"Leaven for the Lump": Canada and Empire Settlement,' in Constantine, *Emigrants and Empire*, 121–49.

92 Georgina M. Taylor, '"A Maid of Kent": and British Imperialism,' revisions in progress to Georgina M. Taylor, '"Ground for Common Action": Violet McNaughton's Agrarian Feminism and the Origins of the Farm Women's Movement in Canada' (PhD diss., Carleton University, 1997). See also Georgina M. Taylor, '"If We Are Really British We Must Be Fair": Violet McNaughton's Attitudes toward the British Empire and the First Nations and the Metis on the Canadian Prairies' (unpublished paper presented to the British World Conference II, University of Calgary, July 2003).

93 Jenks papers, John Barnett to G. Binnie-Clark, 8 January 1931.

94 Ibid., handwritten document 'The Home Farm Settlement,' 1933.

95 *A Birthday Book*. Of the 365 messages from the Bible, 362 were from the Psalms of David because 'The presence of the Shepherd-King seems to brood over and belong to the vast silent spaces of the Prairie, and in the radiant stillness of the Canadian night the silver voice seems very clear as it calls across the boundless tract of snow-veiled solitude to lift one's heart to the test of the moment, and to render familiar and serene all that is awesome in the shadows' (5).

96 Schultz, '"Leaven for the Lump,"' 168.

97 Harrison papers, Binnie-Clark to Dorothy Cooper-Abs, 8 April 1932.

98 *Times*, 25 January 1933, 6.

99 Harrison papers, Binnie-Clark to Dorothy Harrison, 31 March 1936.

100 *Times*, 3 June, 1940, 10.

SUSAN JACKEL

Introduction

1

When the land around Fort Qu'Appelle was opened for homesteading in the early 1880s, the rich level plains above the river
valley soon filled up with settlers. The pages of the Land Titles
Registry in Regina bear witness to the influx. In 1883, for example,
one John McLay filed on the northwest quarter of a section in
township twenty, range thirteen west of the second meridian.
Before the decade was out, Sam Brodie, Guy May, George Robb,
and the Sam Carroll family had all taken up land along the
Touchwood Trail, which joined the old fur-trading post of Fort
Qu'Appelle to the new railway town of South Qu'Appelle, eighteen miles away. The district prospered, especially during the
years of good harvests and rising land values after the turn of the
century. Even a decade of drought and depression in the 1930s
could not seriously disrupt what had by then become a stable,
well-consolidated farming community. Today, as the residents
of Fort Qu'Appelle round out a century of settlement, a small but
scrupulously maintained museum testifies to their sense of the
district's continuity. The town's telephone book offers its own
corroboration: in it are listed Gord McLay, Everett Robb, Jessie
Carroll; and these, along with others in the town, talk with evident enjoyment about Georgina Binnie-Clark. 'She caused a sensation around here,' recalls one, '– a woman farmer, you know.

She did everything the hard way, but she had courage.' On the testimony of her former friends and neighbours, it is clear that despite the more than thirty years that have elapsed since her death, Georgina Binnie-Clark lives on as local legend: a woman farmer, and a published writer into the bargain.

Wheat and Woman was first issued in November 1914, in London by William Heinemann and in Toronto by Bell and Cockburn. The timing of its appearance could hardly have been worse. Two years of downturn in western Canada's economy had rubbed the roseate hue from 'the last best west,' and now England and Canada were both caught up in war. Accounts of western settlement, long a staple of Anglo-American publishing, became virtually unmarketable. Reviewers paid the book scant notice, and the first printing remained the last.

Circumstances have conspired to make it scarcely better known today. Dealers in out-of-print books have few copies to offer, and the price is correspondingly high. Meanwhile, the vagaries of library systems contribute their mite to the book's invisibility. The title, so explicit and apt, nonetheless puts cataloguers in a quandary: where should something called *Wheat and Woman* be shelved? With the books on wheat? on women? on western Canada? Wheat usually triumphs; this record of wheat farming in Saskatchewan from 1905 to 1908 is to be found in the Agricultural Sciences section of most provincial and university libraries in Canada. Maverick to the end, the University of Alberta library gets round the difficulty in a manner one hopes is unique: there, *Wheat and Woman* keeps solemn company with the books on British rural life.

Recently, however, there have been signs of renewed interest in Georgina Binnie-Clark by Canadian readers and scholars. Norah Story led the way when in *The Oxford Companion to Canadian History and Literature* (1967) she described Binnie-Clark's two books of life on the prairies as 'self-revealing accounts by an upper-class Englishwoman who came to the west to visit her brother, found that he and a friend were failing because they despised labour, conquered her own *hauteur* sufficiently to learn from pioneers of humbler backgrounds, bought a farm, and managed it successfully.' Veronica Strong-Boag also mentioned her in the 'Biographies and Autobiographies' section of 'Cousin Cinderella,' a bibliographical essay on sources for Canadian women's history published in 1973; in Strong-Boag's view, Binnie-Clark's writings have been 'unappreciated.'[1] Since then, two popularizers in the field have placed Binnie-Clark's name before a wider reading public: Eve Zaremba in *Privilege of Sex: A Century of Canadian Women* (Toronto 1974) and Candace Savage in *Foremothers* (Saskatoon 1975).

Strong-Boag's decision to classify *Wheat and Woman* as autobiography is understandable, for the book is nothing if not 'self-revealing,' in Story's apt phrase. In the diary that formed the basis for her book, Binnie-Clark confided: 'One thing I have learned – to criticize myself without flinching. "Know thyself." One can't do that everywhere!' (272). One could do it on the Canadian prairies, however, especially if one were well educated, much travelled, and of an enquiring and reflective bent. As the musings of a well-stocked mind, *Wheat and Woman* makes excellent reading on these grounds alone. Yet its interest for the scholar and general reader alike extends well beyond the merely personal; here is a writer who looks outward as well as inward, and does so with impressive cogency and insight. A journalist before she came to Canada, Binnie-Clark was vitally interested in the country's development on all fronts – political, economic, social, religious, and cultural – during the heady years of growth which preceded the First World War. She was also vitally interested in her Canadian neighbours, and observed with fascination the intricacies of social intercourse in the prairie farm community in which she settled. In consequence, *Wheat and Woman* has much to offer the student of social history in Canada, both in matters of detail and in forming the broader picture of attitudes and values as western settlement proceeded.

Perhaps its strongest claim to re-examination, however, lies in the light it sheds on sexual politics in this country during the century's early years. From her experiment in prairie wheat farming, Georgina Binnie-Clark came to know only too well the peculiar disabilities that Canadian law and custom placed on the woman who chose agriculture as a means of self-support. Chief among these was the homestead law, which excluded all but a handful of women from the right to claim a free farm from the Dominion's so-called 'public lands.' How one woman farmer learned to define and deal with her anomalous position in pre-war prairie society forms the plot, so to speak, of this long and detailed narrative.

Essentially, then, what the reader encounters in *Wheat and Woman* is a record of personal experience, shaped by intelligence and informed by humour. Assuredly it is about wheat, and about woman too; but it is also about the lessons of life on the land in Canada, as met and digested by an observant, articulate, and witty individual. Perhaps with this re-issue of her most important book, Binnie-Clark will begin to receive the appreciation she deserves.

2

If *Wheat and Woman* has lingered in obscurity these sixty years and more, so too has its author, Georgina Binnie-Clark. Penetrating the mystery of her identity has turned out to be no easy task, for the standard biographical dictionaries are silent as to her very existence. One turns then for clues to her published writing – principally, *A Summer on the Canadian Prairie*, issued by the London firm of Edward Arnold in 1910, and the volume reprinted here. From both books one learns much of the mind and character of this personable and talented writer, but the larger outlines of her life story remain shadowy. When was she born? When did she die? How long did she live in Canada? Why did she not write more books? These and other questions confront the reader of these volumes, and the answers do not come readily.

A Summer on the Canadian Prairie, although told from a first-person point of view, is not strictly autobiographical in intent. Rather, it belongs to a somewhat different genre, the Edwardian book of travel to the Dominions. By 1910 this was a well-established branch of British prose writing, with its own rapidly

hardening conventions and numbering close to a hundred titles.
In general, these books were all directed towards a common aim:
to educate the British reader, whether tourist, intending emigrant, or merely fireside traveller, as to conditions of life and
travel in the colonies. There was a limit, however, to how much
of this kind of thing the reading public could absorb, and Binnie-
Clark was well aware that cliché had set in. '"The book market is
fed up with Canada,"' she was told (7), but the warning proved
more a challenge than a deterrent. With rare enterprise she
turned to the devices of the fiction writer – plot, dialogue, dramatic incident, and well-rounded characterization – to tempt the
jaded palate of the British reader. By these means Binnie-Clark
obviously hoped to camouflage the fact that she, too, was dis-
pensing useful information for tourists and would-be settlers, à
la Baedeker and the innumerable emigrant guides of the period.
Her hope was not misplaced, for even after seventy years *A Summer on the Canadian Prairie* makes delightful reading, despite the
heavy interlarding of factual material about Canada as a field for
emigration.

Facts about Georgina herself, on the other hand, are harder to
extract with assurance. If considerations of dramatic heightening
and comic tone can be seen to govern the narrative, there are no
firm grounds for assuming that the speaking voice is entirely
immune to their operations. The form and purpose of *A Summer
on the Canadian Prairie* make it impossible to know with certainty
whether the 'I' of this book is primarily self-revealing or self-
creating: whether we are dealing here with the confessional
tones of the autobiographer, or the plausible but largely fictive
revelations of an artfully-projected narrative persona. Yet even
when all due allowance has been made for the hazards posed by
her procedure, one can piece together enough fragments of the
Binnie-Clark story to lay the groundwork for research elsewhere.

Three major figures in that story are introduced in *A Summer
on the Canadian Prairie*: Georgina herself, her younger sister
Hilaria, and their brother Lal. All three of the Binnie-Clark
siblings are unmarried, and they come from a family in England

sufficiently well off for Lal to be counted among that perennial source of high comedy among early comers to the prairies, the English remittance man. Their story begins in the summer of 1905. Lal has come west the previous year to Lipton, Saskatchewan, ostensibly to homestead; Georgina and Hilaria have followed him merely on a visit of inspection, to find out what their ne'er-do-well brother has accomplished. Little enough, they discover on arrival at the homestead: a tiny patch of broken land, a nondescript shack of poplar poles, and a brother fully determined to effect his escape from the back-breaking work expected of the prairie settler.

Lal soon has an ally in Hilaria, who after less than a month of roughing it on the prairies is in total agreement with her brother's maledictions on the land and its people. '"Stay here another week I will not,"' she announces, '"it is a waste of life"' (193). And off she goes to Winnipeg to try her hand at nursing. But Georgina is roused to resolution by the knowledge that of all the settlers around them, Lal and his partner Hicks are the only ones who cannot make wheat farming pay. She determines to redeem the reputation of her family, and her country, by making good where Lal has failed. 'As we drove through patches of amber wheat I vowed I would not acquiesce in failure,' she records. 'I would make one straight strong effort to get on the line of prosperity which others seemed to find in Canada, and often in spite of utter poverty, and frequent mischance at the start' (292). Her resolve leads her to purchase a half section of land from a well-established farmer some four miles out of Fort Qu'Appelle. Although she does not name him here, this farmer was in fact old Alan McLay, father of John, and the man Georgina upbraids in the opening lines of *Wheat and Woman*.

Wheat and Woman covers three years in the life of its author, from the harvest of 1905 to the harvest of 1908, and the presentation is sufficiently candid to earn without reservation the term autobiography. Nevertheless, many unanswered questions remain, especially in relation to the years before and after this period. There are a few clues to be gleaned: Binnie-Clark alludes, for example, to the previous summer spent in Paris (185), and to musical studies in Europe (66). She also confirms at several points in this second book a claim made in the earlier one, that before coming to Canada in the spring of 1905 she was an established writer for magazines. There are scattered references as well to the period from 1908 to 1913. 'I was not in Canada in 1909,' she writes (233). Rather, as one can discover from other sources, she was in England, where she read a paper on 'Conditions of Life for Women in Canada' to the annual meeting of the National Union of Women Workers held in Portsmouth in October of that year.[2] It is probably safe to surmise, too, that at least part of 1909 was spent in seeing *A Summer on the Canadian Prairie* through the press.

From the late fall of 1909 to the outbreak of war, Binnie-Clark seems to have worked her farm in Canada, spending occasional winter holidays in England and publishing articles on western settlement in the British and American periodical press.[3] In 1913 she fulfilled another speaking engagement in Britain, addressing the meeting on 8 April of the Royal Colonial Institute in London, chaired by Sir Charles P. Lucas. Here she read a paper entitled 'Land and the Woman in Canada,' which generated vigorous debate from those present.[4] But just at this interesting juncture the trail goes cold. After the publication of *Wheat and Woman* in 1914, the name of Georgina Binnie-Clark disappears from the documentary record, and the would-be biographer reaches an impasse.

The sole remaining clue to her fate – and it is a tenuous one at best – is an entry in the British Museum catalogue that attributes an anonymous publication of 1934 to Binnie-Clark's hand. This entry reads: '*A Birthday Book for the Union Jack Farm Settlement on the Canadian Prairie*. Compiled from the Psalms of David by a British emigrant. London: Fashion Journals Guild, [1934].' There is no explanation given for the catalogue's dating of this item, nor for its seemingly gratuitous identification of the nameless 'British emigrant' as Georgina Binnie-Clark. Nonetheless, both pieces of information are correct: for the author of *Wheat and Woman* was indeed still alive in 1934, still very much the British emigrant, and still actively involved in what she now called the

Union Jack Farm Settlement on the outskirts of Fort Qu'Appelle. There she lived with her sister Ethel (in all probability the 'Hilaria' of the two published books) from after the war until sometime in the late 1930s; and from old-timers in the neighbourhood, as well as from members of the family in England, some of the missing pieces in the Binnie-Clark story can be filled in.

The known facts are these: Georgina was born 25 April 1871 in Dorset, England, daughter of Arthur Walter Binnie Clark and Maria Clark. Her father's occupation is given on the birth certificate as 'innkeeper.' There were at least six children in the family, four of whom spent varying portions of their lives in Saskatchewan. Residents of Fort Qu'Appelle remember Ethel best, because it was she who lived there longest, from sometime in the early 1920s until her death in 1955 at the age of sixty-nine. 'Lal' occupies no place in local memory; in all probability he spent only four years in Canada, from 1904 to 1908; his real name was Louis or Lou.[5] But the people of Fort Qu'Appelle and environs do remember Arthur Cameron Binnie-Clark (born 18 August 1875), who farmed in the district from before the war until his death in 1921.[6] Georgina, who returned to Canada from England when Arthur died, was known by a variety of names: to her family and very close friends she was 'Avril,' in honour of her birth month, while to her neighbours she was Miss Binnie-Clark, or more usually 'Binnie' – but only out of her hearing, never to her face. Ethel seems to have used the shorter of the family surnames: people who had known her concurred in speaking of her as Miss Ethel or Miss Clark. The two sisters shared the management of N-½-18-13-20-W2, adding NE-¼-20-13-20-W2 around 1925; by 1930 they had 275 acres in production.[7]

Then there are the anecdotes. Tommy Paton, for example, who with his wife worked for 'Binnie' from 1930 to 1932, recalls an incident involving a clogged seeder, which he proposed to clean by the simple expedient of running it through some idle land referred to between the Clark sisters as 'The King's Acre.' What Mr Paton did not know at the time was that this small vacant field had been earmarked for a very special purpose, the raising of seed wheat for the Union Jack Farm Settlement for British Emigrants, soon to be established (or so Binnie-Clark earnestly hoped) under the sponsorship of no less a personage than His Majesty King George V.[8] Knowing, however, that her philanthropic ventures, of which there were many over the years, tended to make her a comic figure in the eyes of her Canadian neighbours, Binnie-Clark did not explain herself very fully to her hired man; she simply forbade him to use the King's Acre and told him to clean the seeder by hand. Not unreasonably, he objected, whereupon she said she would do it herself. But when Mr Paton continued to remonstrate, pointing out the unnecessary expenditure of time and effort which this entailed, she cut off discussion by saying tartly: 'Paton, if I'd wanted to be dictated to by a man, I'd have married one and let him keep me.'

This incident was just one of several that Binnie-Clark's former neighbours adduced as evidence of her impractical attitude towards farming. On the other side of the ledger are their numerous testimonials to her kindness and generosity. All made a point of remarking on her fondness for children, and her active interest in school matters. During the depression she arranged for shipments of long-wearing clothes to be sent out from England, and Mr Paton recalls going around the district with her to distribute these clothes and sometimes food as well. But the prevailing picture of 'Binnie' that remains with those who knew her is one of benign eccentricity: of britches and leggings and a large floppy hat, worn seven days a week on the farm and off; of a high-wheeled buggy from England that she continued to drive even after Ethel bought a car; of cats that slept on the flour bag in the kitchen, and horses kept on as family pets long after they had outlived their usefulness on the farm. This, of course, was the Binnie-Clark of 1930 and later, when she was into her sixties.

How much time Georgina spent in Canada after the mid-1930s is not clear, for accounts differ. Her return to England as a resident may have taken place as early as 1936; certainly she spent all of the Second World War there.[9] In the meantime, Ethel continued to run the farm in Saskatchewan. Ethel's later years were marred by a rather serious accident: she was kicked in the face by a horse and permanently disfigured. Having been by all accounts a remarkably handsome woman before this happened, she suffered more than physical effects, becoming something of a recluse and even refusing on occasion to see her long-time friends from the district. She kept up a steady correspondence with Georgina, though, and letters that passed between them during the periods of their separation show that the Union Jack Farm Settlement remained a subject of consuming interest to them both.[10]

Early in 1947 Ethel was called home by the family in England with news that her sister was ill. Georgina died of myocardial failure on 22 April, just three days short of her seventy-sixth birthday. After the funeral Ethel returned to Canada, bringing with her Georgina's ashes, which she scattered over the fields her sister had bought more than forty years before. For the next few years she lived alone on the farm; then, her own health becoming uncertain, she moved in with Stanley and Dorothy Harrison, her neighbours to the south. On 13 December 1955 Ethel died after a short illness; she is buried beside her brother Arthur in the cemetery on the hillside above Fort Qu'Appelle.

3

For Georgina Binnie-Clark the change from British gentlewoman to Canadian grain grower was far from automatic; in fact, there were those among her neighbours who doubted, with much justice, whether the transition ever fully took place. 'She was no farmer,' said Everett Robb, who grew up not far from the Clark sisters' farm. 'She was just an English lady who liked to live in the country.' It was a shrewd comment, although voiced in accents which hinted strongly at distrust of so odd a preference. Neither the tone nor the substance of his verdict would have surprised Georgina. As one raised to a life of relative leisure in England, she had many difficult adjustments to make to her new life in Saskatchewan: how difficult, few of her Canadian-born neighbours could know. Over the years, the special challenges facing the middle-class British emigrant to Canada became one of her central preoccupations. Her books document the grounds for her concern. *A Summer on the Canadian Prairie* dramatizes the shock of Binnie-Clark's personal discovery that as a member of the privileged classes of England she was an alien in a British colony; while *Wheat and Woman* highlights her realization that as a woman she was, in some measure at least, an alien wherever she lived.

A Summer on the Canadian Prairie explores in some depth the problems of 'green English' among the pioneers of prairie settlement, problems having largely to do with social and cultural adaptation. Her first insight into the complexities of this issue occurs when she visits an emigrant shed in Quebec City, where 'many classes of English people were represented in the crowd':

I had never been one with an East End of London crowd before that night. In England the East End is always on the other side. Under the roof of the emigrant shed in Canada each and all of us represented England. In the main the women took care of the men, but the men seemed kinder to the little ill-trained, frightened children than the mothers; all of it, the general lack of consideration among families, the absence of mutual respect, the grotesque attire, the noisy helplessness, the murdered language of the mother-country, the squalid degradation, was a bit of oneself. The vaunted strength and chivalry of England, to which every British member of that crowd had birthright, would have been conspicuous in any solitary member of it – never was symbol so far removed from tradition. Is it a wonder that Canada fights with all her fine, fresh strength against class distinction, since she looks upon the unhappy condition of the majority of our emigrants as its direct result? Or turning to the members of our upper classes, who, many of them, leave our country for our country's good, can she be expected to find justification? Is that all you have to show for the other? she asks. Is that your sample of the class that England fosters at the cost of the physical, moral, and mental degradation of your under-grown, ill-speaking, half-starved battalions? (30)

Further enlightenment comes from a friendly Canadian who undertakes to explain why the English custom of tipping public employees is looked down on in Canada. '"I guess it's in great measure owing to that tipping business that so many Englishmen find it pretty hard to behave as man to man,"' the Canadian says. '"Guess you could keep a few of them without their pay altogether, if you tipped them pretty frequent to forget it."' Binnie-Clark comments: 'This frank summing up, and a note in the tone in which it was uttered, was as a douche of cold water down one's back. With whatever significance of accent one may permit oneself to make use of the distinguishing adjective "English," it had never even occurred to me that people of a kindred nation could utter it without burning incense at the altar of the people of the mother-country' (54).

But the lesson is driven home in Georgina's experiences among the settlers near Lipton, where of all the several nations represented, the English are least popular. '"You know the English ain't much considered out here,"' a neighbour informs her. '"The Scotch is highly respected, and the Irish is well liked. But there is too much affectation and nonsense and laziness about the Englishmen"' (158). And with the example of her brother Lal and his equally indolent partner Hicks in plain view, Georgina is in no position to argue. '"You should hear what the other settlers think about them,"' Hilaria cries in shame and despair. '"They are called remittance-men, and as far as I can make out remittance-men are just at the very bottom of things in Canadian estimation"' (177).

The problem, the sisters conclude, is largely the result of background, that is, of income, education, tastes, expectations, and habits of social deference: that whole complex bundle of factors that are included in concepts of class identity. Georgina sums up their dilemma in a family conclave: '"You know as well as I do that those of us who come out here expecting to find respect and sympathy waiting for us because we are English find ourselves against a brick wall. There is material kindness waiting for us, provided by the Government; but Canadian opinion divides the English into two groups, the ignorant English who can work, or the English wasters, who, having been dowered with every advantage which wealth can procure in a highly civilised country, won't work – although both divisions look to Canada for a living. We are dumped together as the helpless English, affected or ignorant, helpless or hopeless, snobs or slaves, and every one of us has to make his or her individual way through that barrier of prejudice"'' (231).

The barrier of prejudice against her nationality and class, then, was one unforseen condition awaiting Georgina Binnie-Clark in Canada; yet even during that first summer on the prairie she began to have inklings that more than nationality and class stood in her way. Having observed the patient and productive labour of the wife of a former London Bobby, she remarks pointedly to him: '"No wonder English*women* have so high a reputation in Canada, if there are many like her"'' (226). And she concludes: '"In England I used to think that men worked whilst women gossiped. On a prairie settlement the women work, and it isn't the women who gossip. I owe one debt to my life on the prairie, and that is a fair appreciation of my own sex"'' (278).

A prominent theme, of course, in the past century of feminist writing has been the relation of work to status, the books of Charlotte Perkins Gilman (*Women and Economics*, 1899) and Olive Schreiner (*Woman and Labour*, 1911) having their direct descendants in the more scholarly findings of writers like Jessie Bernard and Alice Rossi in America, Ann Oakley in England, and, closer to home, that industrious group which has launched and maintained the Canadian Women's Educational Press. There is nothing in *Wheat and Woman* to suggest, except by inference, that Binnie-Clark ever read any of the extensive debate over feminist objectives during the century's first decade; yet she had no great difficulty in pin-pointing the essential issues, particularly as they applied to her personal situation. On the Canadian prairies, as turn-of-the-century commentators never tired of remarking, work was the condition of survival, hard work the condition of success, and both these conditions bore on every newcomer regardless of nationality, class, or sex. The result was a levelling process which wrought undoubted hardship on those born and reared to a life of leisure, men and women alike. Nevertheless, there is cause to think that women as a group were more vulnerable than men to loss of social prestige, by reason of their inability to escape from prevailing attitudes to domestic labour. A man might take up land in Canada and still be a gentleman in his own eyes, even though he had callouses on his hands and mud on his boots; but a woman who scrubbed her own floors and did the laundry herself could retain few pretensions to gentility. The case was succinctly put by British journalist and travel writer Marion Dudley Cran, when in *A Woman in Canada*, a very popular book of 1910, she advised emigrating middle-class Englishwomen to cast aside their prejudices against domestic service as a means of self-support, because 'every woman is a servant where labour is so scarce' (163).

Wheat and Woman offers a variation on this theme unique in the extensive literature of settlement. Where other British observers of Canadian social organization stressed the difficulties facing the émigrée farm wife, who must learn to get along without her accustomed household servants, Binnie-Clark was able to speak from experience on what the chronic scarcity of labour in Canada meant to the woman farmer. There was a distinction here on which she was quick to insist. 'The life of a woman-farmer is very different from the life of a farmer's wife on the prairie,' she asserts in *Wheat and Woman*. 'Some may prefer one, some the other; but the one is an entirely different proposition from the other' (215). Having found out, the hard way, exactly what the life of a woman farmer entailed, she assembled the lessons of her first three years on the prairies for the guidance of other women hoping to earn their livelihood by agriculture – principally, we may assume (although Binnie-Clark herself never uses the term), the 'superfluous' or 'redundant' women who so troubled the consciences of late Victorian and Edwardian social commentators.

The debate over Britain's redundant population was nearly a century old when *Wheat and Woman* was published, although even in the late 1700s the concept if not the exact term was well known, especially in Scotland. In the mid-nineteenth century, however, public attention in Britain began to focus on one particular trend in the census figures, the numerical disproportion between the sexes. If there were extra people occupying those crowded isles, there were many more extra women than men. Yet it was the men who more often sailed away on the emigrant ships to Australia, New Zealand, South Africa, America, and Canada, and so the imbalance worsened as the century progressed. By the census of 1901, the excess of women over men in England and Wales alone had passed the one million mark, in a total population of thirty-two million.

Although 'superfluous women' – that is, women who statistically stood no chance of finding a marriage partner in Great Britain – were to be found among all levels of society, it was the predicament of the 'distressed gentlewoman' that dominated the public debate; for unlike her working-class sisters the gentlewoman was by definition barred from engaging in all but a severely limited range of paid employments. According to the expectations of her class, factory labour was out; domestic service was out; work as a shop assistant, except in a few *chic* establishments, was out. The approved genteel occupations – teaching, governessing, needlework, nursing – were badly overcrowded and underpaid, and although new forms of employment were beginning to gain social acceptance (typing and telephone operating were two of the most popular), still there were not nearly enough jobs to go around. Meanwhile, the benevolent male Briton who had for so long assumed financial responsibility for his sisters and his cousins and his aunts began to grow restive and to resent his customary obligation to maintain his unmarried female relatives.

Believing that 'marriage was accepted by many women as the sole resource against labour in a world governed by laws made by men for men, where there is but the scantest justice and scant wages for the labour of women,' Georgina Binnie-Clark proposed a novel solution to the plight of the redundant woman: farming in Canada. The governing purpose of *Wheat and Woman* was to convince the English reader that 'what men had done for themselves in agricultural pursuits on the prairie, women could also do for themselves. Woman can earn for herself independence and in time wealth. The minimum sum of independence I

defined then, as now, in the sum of £5000, and I consider that a
woman should be able to command that amount at least after
twenty years' work on the land, providing she has a fair start'
(304-5).

'Providing she has a fair start': there lay the rub. Precisely
what Binnie-Clark meant by this phrase may not be immediately
apparent to the present-day reader, removed by three generations from the conditions that gave rise to her concern. From
other passages in the book, however, it is easy enough to see
where her argument was leading – straight to reform of the
homestead laws of Canada. Having recorded a profit of seven
hundred dollars on her farming operations in 1908, for example,
she then comments:

It was not good, but ... it was enough to prove to me that farming on the
prairie properly done is farming easily done, and that, worked out on a
well-thought-out plan, it is a practical and should be a highly profitable
means of independence and wealth for women as it has always proved
for men. But on every side my neighbours had obtained their land as a
gift from the Government, or at least one hundred and sixty acres of it,
and a further hundred and sixty had been added on the condition of
pre-emption, which is by payment of three dollars an acre in addition
to the performance of the homestead duties; in this way a farm in every
way equal to the one which had cost me five thousand dollars was to be
obtained by any man for nine hundred and seventy dollars. So that
even allowing that a woman farmer is at a slight disadvantage in working out a farm proposition, she has the killing weight of extra payment
thrust on her at the very outset. She may be the best farmer in Canada,
she may buy land, work it, take prizes for seed and stock, but she is
denied the right to claim from the Government the hundred and sixty
acres of land held out as a bait to every man.

I talked to every man about it, and almost to a man they said: 'Too
bad!' (299-300)

4

The early-twentieth-century movement to obtain homestead
rights for women on the same basis as men is not one of the

better-known episodes in Canadian history. One of many re-
forms to originate in the pre-war prairie west, the object of this
movement was to alter certain provisions in the Dominion
Lands Act of 1872. This was the act which governed alienation
of public lands 'for the purposes of the Dominion' in the huge
western territories acquired from Britain in 1870. Although the
act was amended several times during the settlement period, the
paragraphs defining eligibility for homestead application remained essentially unchanged. These paragraphs became the
target of the homesteads-for-women movement carried on by
western journalists and farmers, most intensively between 1909
and 1913, and then sporadically thereafter right up to 1930,
when the three prairie provinces inherited control of public
lands. Throughout the entire period, Georgina Binnie-Clark
was one of the movement's most devoted supporters, and in
Wheat and Woman she provided its most extended and articulate
rationale.

Section 9 of the Dominion Lands Act provided that 'every person who is the sole head of a family' could apply to take up one
hundred and sixty acres of homestead land in the surveyed portions of the west, subject to the usual conditions of entry fee,
residence, and improvements. Furthermore, any male eighteen
years of age or over was similarly entitled to apply. In the capa-
city of 'sole head of a family,' therefore, there were from the
1870s onwards three categories of women qualified to enter for
homestead lands: widows, divorcées, and, in scrupulously
documented cases, separated or deserted wives – providing, that
is, that they had children under eighteen dependent on them for
support. Judging from publications of the period, enough women
in these categories made use of their right to draw some public
notice, both here and overseas. *Home Life of Women in Western
Canada*, *Words from Women in Western Canada*, and *Women's
Work in Western Canada*, pamphlets issued by the Canadian
Pacific Railway in 1906 and 1907 and circulated widely in Great
Britain, all feature accounts by successful widow farmers on the
prairies.

It is clear, however, that the ins and outs of these regulations
were not well understood by the reading public at large. Mrs

Cran, for one, could not fathom why there should be so many unattached men in the west, and so few of what she called 'bachelor women.' 'I am constrained to wonder if there is any reason why women should not come out and work the land as well as men,' she wrote in *A Woman in Canada*. 'No one questions its fertility and abundant profits, nor the fact that hundreds of healthy Englishwomen are encumbering the old country and leading profitless lives. The labour of "homesteading" would be very great for women, I can understand their shirking it; and the lure of 160 acres of free land is not so golden, when faced in detail, now that Canada is fast settling up, as it is impossible to homestead within easy reach of the railway ... To "make good" on a free farm a woman would need either much courage and capital, or considerable male labour, besides agricultural skill' (153-4). But in her talk of 'a free farm' and '160 acres of free land' Mrs Cran proved how completely she had misapprehended the homestead laws. For the fact was there were no free farms being offered to bachelor women in Canada; if they were not widows, divorcées, or deserted wives, who must in any case be responsible for dependent children in order to qualify, women could only buy their way into farming as a livelihood.

Formal protest against this discriminatory regulation gathered slowly at first, consisting largely in the early years of local and unco-ordinated agitations among prairie farm organizations. Then in 1908 the *Grain Growers' Guide* came on the scene, providing the homesteads-for-women movement with a forum. Over the next five years the *Guide*, ably supported by the *Manitoba Free Press* and other Winnipeg newspapers, brought the question of homestead rights into national prominence.

The women's editor of the *Guide* from 1909 to 1911 was Isabel Beaton Graham, who with her husband Francis Graham had emigrated west from Ontario in 1885. She was a founding member of the Winnipeg Women's Press Club, and honorary secretary of the Winnipeg Women's Canadian Club for many years. Isabel Graham (or 'Isobel,' as she called herself in the pages of the *Guide*) was to become the movement's most visible and influential leader, and she clearly deserves full credit for the vigour and persistence with which the campaign was conducted. But it is also clear that the immediate occasion of her first major pronouncement on the need for homestead reform – virtually the whole of her 'Around the Fireside' page in the *Guide* of 17 November 1909 – was a long talk with Georgina Binnie-Clark.

The two women had discussed the issue before. In the late fall of 1908 Binnie-Clark, in her own words, 'set out for Ottawa to claim the right of women to their share in the homestead land of Canada' (306). En route she stopped off in Winnipeg, where she learned from talking with Mrs Graham and Cora Hind that 'Canadian women had already taken up the matter of Homesteads for Women with a deep sense of the injustice of a law which, whilst seeking to secure the prosperity of the country in enriching the stranger, ignores the claim of the sex which bore the brunt of the battle in those early and difficult days when every inch of our great wheat-garden of the North-West had to be won with courage and held with endurance' (307).[11] A year later, returning westward to her farm from England, Binnie-Clark resumed the topic with Mrs Graham, who by this time was in a position to air their common grievance in the women's pages of the *Guide*. The result was a three-column article entitled 'Woman's Sphere in Life and Labour. Homesteads for Women. A Western Woman's View of Man's Duty to Women.'

Mrs Graham began her article by raising several arguments that were to recur with variations throughout the campaign. 'How many men ever thought that the present homestead law is unfair, even to men themselves?' she wrote. 'Here are two farmers, pioneer homesteaders, the family of one consisting of sons, the other of daughters – a common case in the west. In a few years the man with the sons spreads out, homesteads right and left, gobbling up a wide area of land; the man with the daughters cannot extend his homestead rights. The accident of sex in the family enriches one and impoverishes the other. The law steps in and provides a birthright dowry for the man having sons, and none for the man with the daughters.' As the mother of four daughters and one son, Mrs Graham had a personal interest in seeing this particular injustice removed, as she can-

didly admitted many times. But she had other arguments to
press as well: among them, the form of the homesteading laws
south of the border, which permitted women to homestead
without restriction; and, more compelling in the long run, the
bar which the discriminatory clause in the Canadian law placed
in the way of women who sought economic equality with men.
Wrote Mrs Graham on this head:

Oh, yes! We are sure to have that jollified masculine specimen of our
kind who would promptly wipe the question of unequal dowry off the
slate by marrying the girls of Poverty Ranch to the men of the Free
Homestead. Unfortunately, the expedience of marrying portionless
girls to men of means is good for neither. It gives the man an advantage
over the woman that is hurtful to both; to him because it tends to arrogance, to her because it tends to undue humility, and the 'mighty dollar' in such a case is not a blessing. There are times when every such
man, however liberal minded, feels that he has been a 'capital fellow' in
having 'made good' to a penniless fiancee. Overcome by the intensity of
self admiration, he takes her into his confidence, that she may lose no
atom of cause for adoration. The result is often pitiful. At the back of
every woman's mind lies resentment that, through no fault of hers, she
should be so humiliated.

Her article continued for several paragraphs more to explore
the theoretical grounds for the extension of the homesteading
privilege to women; but in the concluding section, 'Isobel' turned
to actual cases: to be precise, one actual case, where someone had
exploded the myth that a single woman could not farm successfully. Under the subhead 'Miss Clark's Success' we read:

A very modern farmer-ess who startles the ear aesthetic wherever her
exploits are told, one Miss Georgina Binnie-Clark, an English woman
of moderate means, considerable culture, unusual enterprise, and rare
pluck, on behalf of herself and numbers of her single country-women
similarly situated, came in the summer of '06 [1905] to experiment in
farming in the Canadian west ... Finding a discouraged farmer in the
Qu'Appelle Valley, she bought outright his whole plant, including
farm, machinery, crop, two cows and three horses, and started in to

work, breaking twenty-five acres with a sulky plow the first season. She lived entirely alone through the long bitter winter of '06-'07, getting her own wood, caring wholly for her own stock, two miles from any neighbour, and had a dog and revolver for her body-guard.

Miss Binnie-Clark still prosecutes farming in the west and continues to make a brilliant success of it. She does not do the heavy work herself. She hires a man and his wife, and she makes it pay just as so many bachelors do. Possessed of some means, it was not her intention to continue at the heavy work; she simply experimented to know exactly what it was and to prove that woman in an emergency could farm were she so minded.

This article evidently struck a responsive chord among readers of the *Guide*, for the early months of 1910 brought a rash of enquiries about women and homesteads to the Department of the Interior. Frank Oliver, minister of that department in Sir Wilfrid Laurier's Liberal government, was not disposed to be sympathetic; and, since the minister exercised discretionary power in all cases of homestead applicants not clearly covered by the regulations, Oliver's personal feelings had some bearing on the question. The minister's first response, in a series of rulings dated 24 January 1910, was to *narrow* the existing categories of eligible women, by tightening up several loopholes in the law. Henceforth, Oliver wrote in a memo to J.W. Greenway, no entry for homestead land was to be granted to

a widow who is the legal guardian of a minor child, nor to a widow who has an adopted minor child dependent on her for support except in cases where the adoption was made a sufficiently long time prior to the application for entry to satisfy the Department that such adoption was not made for the mere purpose of making her eligible for homestead entry as the sole head of a family.

Nor is entry to be granted to a widow who has a daughter over twenty-one years of age except it can be satisfactorily established that such daughter through physical infirmity is dependent for support upon the widowed mother, in which case it may be submitted to the Minister for consideration.[12]

What kind of 'consideration,' Oliver made quite clear when the case of Mrs Oxilia Grant, widow, was referred to him for a ruling later that year. In asking the department's permission to homestead, Mrs Grant supplied a medical certificate stating that her daughter, though an adult, was an invalid and totally dependent on her mother for support. Across the bottom of the memorandum detailing this case, 'F.O.' scrawled the summary ruling: 'Not eligible. Daughter is not a minor.'[13]

In the meantime, another influential journalist in Winnipeg had taken up the cause: Lilian Laurie, women's editor of the *Manitoba Free Press*. In private life Lilian Laurie was Lilian Beynon Thomas, sister of Marion Francis Beynon, women's editor of the *Grain Growers' Guide* from 1912 to 1917. In an article in the *Free Press* of 9 May 1910 headed 'No Homesteads for Women,' 'L.L.' wrote:

Were you ever at a meeting, where the men, being in power, were discussing the adviseability of giving women something they were asking for? If you have and the men referred to the women as the 'fair sex,' you will know that they did not grant their request. When men intend to face the rights of women, and consider their requests from the standpoint of justice, they refer to them by the old but dignified term of 'women,' and it is quite good enough.

Last week, in the House of Commons in Ottawa, women and homesteads were mentioned. Dr. Roche, [Conservative member] of Marquette, mentioned them, and favored giving women homesteads, and used two really strong arguments, at least so I read, for I was not there. One argument was that women are needed in the west, and if women could get land they would come west and supply that need.

The other was that public opinion strongly favors this, and he quoted letters and press clippings to prove it.

Mr. Oliver acknowledged that the matter had been brought to his notice, but he did not think it would be in the best interest of the west to give women homesteads for the object in giving homesteads is to make the land productive, and this would not be the case if held by women. He also stated that a widow with children old enough to work the land could homestead and he considered that quite as much as is for the good of the country.[14]

'Since reading this I have been asking myself, whether it is Mr. Oliver or I who cannot read,' 'L.L.' continued, going on to quote the relevant sections of the homestead regulations and exposing the minister's blatant misrepresentations and inconsistencies. She concluded her article: 'The letters and press notices Mr. Oliver brushes aside quite easily. He evidently thinks that in this matter his opinion is the important thing, and not the wishes of those interested. The "fair sex" have no votes.'

The debate over homestead reform continued for several weeks more in the Winnipeg papers, notably the *Free Press* and *Town Topics*. When in her column of 24 May 'L.L.' called for women to 'stand shoulder to shoulder' on this as on 'all matters of progressive legislation for women,' letters to the editor poured in.[15] The *Free Press* of 18 June even carried a petition from the Edmonton area, addressed to Frank Oliver and asking that 'we, the undersigned, unmarried women of Canada ... be allowed to take up homestead lands in any of the provinces.' Needless to say, this petition met with the same fate as the letters and press clippings which Dr Roche of Marquette had produced in Parliament two months before.

'The "fair sex" have no votes': all roads led to the suffrage issue. Still Mrs Graham hoped to circumvent this political roadblock by applying pressure on the federal government through those who *did* have votes. After a resolution in favour of homestead reform had been passed at the Brandon convention of the Manitoba Women's Christian Temperance Union in the spring of 1911, 'Isobel' returned to the fray. In the *Guide* of 24 May 1911 she published a copy of her own petition, addressed to 'His Excellency, the Governor General of Canada, in Council,' and asking, after eleven 'whereases': 'that as soon as possible a bill may be introduced by your government and enacted by the Parliament of Canada, providing that all women of British birth who have resided in Canada for six months, and if residing with their father or mother or a near relative, are of the age of eighteen years, or if otherwise, are of the age of twenty-one years, shall be granted the privilege of homesteading.' Following the text of the petition was a note on strategy: 'The plan of campaign is to distribute these printed petitions very widely and, no doubt, some interested party in each district will volunteer to superintend the work of getting the signatures. Only men are requested to sign. It will be taken for granted that all women desire the homestead privilege for their sisters even though they do not intend to take advantage of it themselves. Let those who are willing to take charge of a petition write to The Guide and one will be forwarded with full instructions. A post office is a good place to use one.'[16]

The fortunes of Mrs Graham's petition cannot be traced in detail here, except to note that when it was finally presented to the responsible minister in Ottawa in the spring of 1913 it had gained the signatures of over 11,000 electors, which is to say men, from the three prairie provinces, as well as the declared support of the Winnipeg Board of Trade, the three provincial Grain Growers' Associations, the National Council of Women, Women's Press Clubs in cities coast to coast, the national board of the WCTU, and a host of other influential organizations and functionaries. By then, the minister of the interior for Sir Robert Borden's Conservative administration was none other than Dr Roche of Marquette, and the petition's supporters no doubt considered this a favourable omen. If so, they were to be disappointed. Roche's reply to Mrs Graham on receipt of the petition was properly non-commital: 'Permit me to express my appreciation of the matter referred to in the petition and to assure you that any matter pertaining to the welfare of the Canadian people will always receive my close and favorable consideration. Yours faithfully, W.J. Roche.'[17] Whether Dr Roche had changed his mind since coming into responsibility for the homestead laws or whether he was simply a minority voice within his own party is difficult to determine on the existing evidence. One thing is certain: no government bill on the issue was introduced, and the regulations barring single women from homesteading remained unchanged.

'Dear Isobel,' began one of the many letters to the *Guide* at the height of Mrs Graham's crusade: 'What is your latest movement in regard to Homesteads? Is there any fresh hope from this government?' The date was 1 November 1911, less than two months after the election that saw reciprocity defeated and the Conservatives returned to power after fifteen years in the wilderness. The remainder of this letter reads:

You will perhaps remember my telling when I last saw you in Winnipeg last May, that I still had some of my 1910 crop on hand. I did very well on it, having sold it all at $1.00 a bushel for No. 1 Nor. This year I am frozen rather badly over an 80 acre summerfallow, but the stubble crop will grade No. 3 or 4 Nor. I thought I was going to bring off a great haul this year, and could have interviewed a whole cabinet on our Homesteads with confidence – but the Gods won't have these hasty arrivals.

Last year I had quality, this year I have quantity, and next year perhaps both. Though a woman farmer, I did not find Jack Frost less courteous to me than to my men neighbours. Providence does not seem to object to homesteads for women.

I thresh this week and am then going through to the coast to report on some women farmers to the English press.

I go to England in November for the winter and should like so much to have a chat with you when I reach the city.

Kind greetings to you and yours.

GEORGINA BINNIE-CLARK

To which 'Isobel' responded, in a 'Note' appended to the end of the letter: 'Miss Binnie-Clark is a woman of pluck and determination. She came to Canada to farm, to experiment not only for her own benefit but also for the benefit of single women of her own social level left behind in England. Unable to persuade the Dominion government to grant her a free homestead she courageously bought a half-section of land in the beautiful Qu'Appelle Valley and started in to pioneer, with the great financial handicap of being compelled to buy her land while her men neighbours got theirs free. Nevertheless she is 'making good' and would make a great immigration agent to the old land among women like herself, women of culture and some means, when the Canadian government grants free homesteads to women.'

But that 'when' never materialized. Official reasons for the federal government's failure to amend the homestead regulations shifted ground over the years. In answer to a resolution favouring homesteads for women passed by the United Farmers of Alberta in 1919, for example, Mr Harris of the Department of the Interior wrote, in a memorandum dated 25 March 1919: 'For years past the policy of the Department has been pretty well defined with regard to extending the homestead privilege to women. There would appear to be no reason why this policy should be changed, in view of the fact that homestead land is getting scarce, and all Dominion Lands within fifteen miles of a railroad are reserved for Soldier Settlement purposes. The Soldier Settlement Act extends the same privilege to the widows of soldiers who have fallen in action as granted to members of the Expeditionary Forces.'[18] Which was quite true: but it did not thereby guarantee equal opportunity for women in post-war Canada in the matter of obtaining free public lands.

Nor did subsequent rulings by the department through the 1920s, despite several further attempts by a variety of farm groups and individuals to prod the government into action. One of the final rulings on the subject, from April 1929, reads: 'Apparently nothing has occurred during recent years to warrant the Department in changing the practice ... Land of good quality can be purchased in the West at a moderate price, and land so obtained is more advantageously situated, as a rule, with regard to churches, markets etc. than land available for homesteading. A woman who is fully qualified as a farmer need not be debarred from that occupation because she cannot get a homestead. The capital required for homesteading is not very much less than what would buy a farm.'[19] In 1929, this observation on 'the capital required for homesteading' probably carried more force than would have been the case twenty years earlier, when the homesteads-for-women movement first took shape. Yet as an argument it was no less specious than all its predecessors, for if such were really the case, then the only tenable alternative to opening the homestead privilege to women was to withdraw it altogether.

Such, in effect, was the conclusion of the governments of two of the three prairie provinces when in 1930 they assumed control of their own public lands, and with it the thorny problem of homestead eligibility. In Manitoba and Saskatchewan this problem was met by abrogating the homestead right entirely. Thereafter, the few remaining public lands were to be sold, not given away, although the price was often nominal. In Alberta, on the other hand, where land suitable for agricultural settlement was still available in some quantity, the provincial government had the option of either continuing federal government policy or drawing up its own homestead regulations. It chose the latter course; and with the successful conclusion of the Persons Case barely two years in the background, it is perhaps not surprising that the Alberta Public Lands Act, Section 15, sub-section 1, should read: 'Every person who has resided in the Province for a period of not less than three years, and has attained the age of seventeen years, and who is a British subject or declares intention to become a British subject ... shall be entitled to obtain entry for a homestead.' In the province which counted among its residents Magistrate Emily Murphy, ex-MLA Nellie McClung, ex-MLA Louise McKinney, the Honourable Irene Parlby, and Henrietta Muir Edwards, author of works on the legal status of women for both the Alberta and Dominion governments, the meaning of the word 'person' needed no elucidation.

These developments were all far in the future when Georgina Binnie-Clark embarked on her one-woman mission to Ottawa in the fall of 1908. In the absence of Frank Oliver, with whom she had been promised an interview, she talked to deputy minister W.W. Cory of the Interior Department. 'Just as I had anticipated, firstly, lastly, and all the time came the argument, "She can't,"' Binnie-Clark wrote of that interview (308). As an 'argument' it was scarcely calculated to impress someone who had just completed her third year of prairie wheat farming. Believing, however, that 'the only way of going on' lay in 'refusing to give up,'

Binnie-Clark returned the following autumn to her farm near
Fort Qu'Appelle. There she embarked on a remarkable teaching
project, in which prospective women farmers from England came
to her to gain experience in prairie agriculture – and, as she remarked in her book, to gain self-confidence as well. 'Over and
over again,' she wrote, 'I recognized the splendid qualities I had
always believed to be in women, and I don't think a woman ever
worked on my wheat-land without discovering a finer energy
and a stronger and more independent Self than she dreamed she
possessed' (308).

The farm itself prospered, but its role as a teaching station was
short-lived. With the outbreak of war, Georgina returned to England for the duration, there to accept an appointment from the
British minister of labour to organize Church of England women
into cadres for work on the land, in order to free male farm
labourers for war service.[20] By the time she returned to Canada
after the war, educated women were at work throughout the
labour force and no longer needed to look to farming for self-
support. Besides, there was a development which Binnie-Clark
herself never alluded to in her writings, but which residents of
Fort Qu'Appelle recall with invariable amusement. 'They all
married, you see,' one of Georgina's former neighbours explained. 'Those girls came out here to learn to farm, but they
used to find husbands pretty quick. They never stayed with her
long.' Given their choice of the two propositions Binnie-Clark
distinguished in *Wheat and Woman*, woman farmer or farm wife,
her pupils soon declared their preference; and Deputy Minister
Cory no doubt smiled knowingly, and waited confidently for the
birth announcements.

5

By the time she came to compose the manuscript of *Wheat and
Woman*, probably in the winter of 1913-14, Binnie-Clark knew
that her subject was work and woman as well: work, and the
place it occupied in Canadian, as distinct from English, attitudes
to individual and group status. Sometimes she aimed at general-

ity, as when she described her hard-working neighbours on the prairies as 'typical old timers ... uniting in a solemn hatred of class-distinction as the best word they knew to express their innate sense of the dignity and force of self-respect' (64); while her portrait of the grand-daughters of Samuel Brodie (65-6) was her personal tribute to the accomplishments of those 'typical Canadian girls.' Yet her most valuable insights into the links between national and sexual politics were the direct result of her own far-from-typical experience as a woman farmer on the prairies.

The accusation with which *Wheat and Woman* opens – '"You gave me your word that if I bought the farm your son should take off the crop"' – marks the first of many occasions on which Binnie-Clark had to face up to the unpleasant fact that she was, at least in the early stages of her venture, totally dependent on others to do the actual work of her farm. The labour problem continued to plague her, until experience revealed the obvious solution: 'The best system of all for the woman-farmer,' she advised, 'is to train herself to do all her own chores and hire her field labourer at special seasons by the day' (227). She could give this advice with confidence; for in three short years, she who had never mastered a practical art in her life had learned how to break, plough, harrow, and stook a field, harness a horse, milk a cow, feed and water stock, clean and pickle seed grain, cut wood for fuel, and keep painstaking accounts of the whole operation; all this in addition to the more usual 'woman's work' of butter and bread making, paper hanging, laundering, and the day-to-day cooking and washing up. Aiding her in all this, of course, were her brothers, her neighbours, and her long succession of hired men; but even here experience gave her wisdom: 'It is the greatest mistake' she wrote, 'to imagine that because you are paying a man a low salary you can't lose much by him in Canada where labour is so expensive and so scarce ... In Britain we grow up with the idea that kitchens and bedrooms are born clean and remain in that state without labour; none can make clear the labour and energy which women distribute, looking after the personal need of men who never give a thought to the work they are creating, but will spend hours meditating on the work they can evade' (227).

The one clear exception to these strictures was Roddy McMahon, the Canadian day-labourer whose portraiture in *Wheat and Woman* is one of the book's highlights;[21] but even Roddy's manly tolerance was strained to the breaking point when his employer undertook 'to learn the meaning of stoning the land': 'Roddy McMahon got off the plough and took me to a big fellow in the neighbourhood of the plough, and showed me how to test its depth and raise it if possible by inserting the crowbar as a lever, and when it was too tightly set to move in this manner to free it from the imprisoning earth with the pick; and all without a word, barring the usual phrase of encouragement at the end, "I guess you'll get them out all right – but it ain't no work for a woman"' (146).

Roddy's feelings were shared by many of Binnie-Clark's Canadian neighbours, who seldom bothered to hide their disapproval of 'a woman doing everything ... she shouldn't' around the farm (198). But it was finally her brother Arthur who forced Georgina into open rebellion against the masculine patronage and presumption in which she had so far acquiesced. In one of the central passages in the book she wrote:

Always at the back of my mind had been the belief that [men] had a genuine title to the splendid term which has come to be a byword, 'lord of creation.' To make life possible one drank at the fountain of the thought of men, not women; but through the shoulder-to-shoulder rub of everyday working-life in Canada it grew clear that although more giants had issued from the male division, within the crowd men have hoisted their pretension to superior power not on the rock of superior work, but on the sands of superior wages – the misappropriation and unfair division of money. Had my brother been a little more sympathetic about the fact that I had to wash towels which were called upon to perform the united service of sponge, loofah, and occasionally of soap and water for the man on the land, I might have been a little more sympathetic about his having to use the towels I washed. As it was, he sat on the edge of the veranda with a face like a boot and washed out his

own towels in Hudson's soap, used strictly according to the directions
on the wrapper; and I heartily wished that it had been the fate of a great
many more men to wash towels all their lives (164-5).

Having thus engaged so intimately in 'the shoulder-to-
shoulder rub of everyday working-life in Canada,' with the results that she described above, Binnie-Clark might well have
chosen to throw in her lot with that vocal branch of British
feminism which saw in every man an instinctive will to oppress.
It is impossible to avoid the conclusion, however, that her personal objective was not victory but justice; having arrived at a
fair appreciation of her own sex, she sought valiantly to avoid
unfairness to the other. 'The fact is I wasn't in the mood to be
generous to men just then,' she wrote in explanation of her unkind feelings towards Arthur (164); her 'newly acquired knowledge that ... men take so much kindness and consideration from
women for granted' (184) was a revelation and a shock, and at
least one of her hired men felt the brunt of her resentment. But
these episodes were few and minor in comparison to the many
occasions in her book when Binnie-Clark paid sincere and gracious tribute to the chivalry and kindness of her neighbours, the
majority of whom were men. The list of those so acknowledged is
a long one; it includes Alan, John, and Danny McLay (which she
spells 'McLeay'), Roddy McMahon, Sam Brodie, Dick McGusty,
Guy Mazey (in historical fact Guy May), Si Booth, and Donald H.
Macdonald, banker of Fort Qu'Appelle, to mention only a few.
The net effect of these tributes is to restore Georgina Binnie-
Clark to that honourable company of feminist writers who, out
of respect to the claims of justice, refuse to erect new barriers of
prejudice to replace the ones they so ardently seek to demolish.
As for her virtual withdrawal from authorship after the publication of *Wheat and Woman*, one can only surmise that she
found satisfaction enough in her new career as a woman farmer.
In making a paying proposition of her wheat farm, she knew that
she had effectively rebutted the gibe of her brother Lal, recorded in
the closing pages of *A Summer on the Canadian Prairie*: '"A woman
work a Canadian farm! Why, you would be the laughing-stock

of the country, if you could do it, which you can't."' His words
were to be echoed by Deputy Minister Cory in Ottawa: 'Firstly,
lastly, and all the time came the argument, "She can't."' But of
course, she could: providing she had a fair start, and providing,
too, that she possessed the considerable resources of mind and
character that Georgina Binnie-Clark everywhere displayed in
the history of her experiment. If the experiment itself proved
little more than the audacity of her undertaking, shouldered so
blithely and so innocently in that harvest-season of 1905, its record in the pages of *Wheat and Woman* is monument enough to a
gifted and memorable person.

NOTES

I would like to express my appreciation to Professor L.H. Thomas of the
University of Alberta, who first turned my attention to the rich travel literature of the Edwardian period in Canada, and who has been unfailingly
kind and helpful on many occasions since. I also owe thanks to the Jenks
family of England, and to the residents of Fort Qu'Appelle, in
particular Mrs Jessie Carroll.

1 In Marylee Stephenson, ed., *Women in Canada* (Toronto 1973), 267
2 *Annual Report* of the British Women's Emigration Association, 1909,
pp. 110-20; courtesy of D.H. Simpson, Librarian, Royal Commonwealth
Society, London
3 Only fragmentary evidence of Binnie-Clark's career as a journalist has
been recovered so far, although research is proceeding. Sir Charles Lucas,
for example, told the audience at the Royal Colonial Institute that she had
contributed 'many interesting articles' to the *Canadian Gazette*, a weekly
newspaper published in England for the information of British investors.
By her own account, Binnie-Clark spent January-March 1908 in New
York writing for magazines (see pp. 272, 275). In *A History of Emigration
from the United Kingdom to North America, 1763-1912* (London 1913), 265,
Stanley C. Johnson refers to an article by Binnie-Clark in *The Quiver*.
4 *United Empire*, 1913, pp. 497-508
5 This and other information on the Binnie-Clarks in England was supplied
by Dennis and Richard Jenks, great-nephews of Georgina. According to
Dennis Jenks, his great-aunt 'may have had a very small private income
but she was always hard up and hopelessly unbusiness-like.' He adds:
'You will appreciate that Avril was very serious indeed and intellectual in
her whole approach. She was also a bit of a terror and everybody was

    frightened of her and my brothers and I as children used every now and again to be sent on a week's "course" with Avril to sharpen up our manners!' Letter 6 February 1979

6 Birth and death dates for Ethel and Arthur Cameron Binnie-Clark were provided by Charlie Horsman of Fort Qu'Appelle from gravestones in the Fort Qu'Appelle cemetery; Mr Horsman also put me in touch with the family in England.

7 Records of the Fort Qu'Appelle grain inspection station and elevator, searched and transcribed by Charlie Horsman.

8 Fragment of a draft letter to King George V, found among Binnie-Clark's papers after her death by Richard Jenks; copy in my possession, courtesy of Mr Jenks.

9 Residents of Fort Qu'Appelle recall visits by Georgina to her sister throughout the later 1930s, and again just after the Second World War; Dennis Jenks on the other hand thinks that his great-aunt lived in London from the mid-1930s and never returned to Canada.

10 Copies of letters from 'Avril' to her sister, dating chiefly from 1940 to 1942, are in my possession; copies of Georgina's birth and death certificates were supplied by Dennis Jenks.

11 In the 1914 edition of *Wheat and Woman* Binnie-Clark writes of Cora *Hine* and Mrs *Lilian* Graham (306-7). The first has been corrected in this edition, as have a small number of other minor errors in the original text. The second, left uncorrected here, probably reflects some confusion in her mind between Isabel Graham, women's editor of the *Guide*, and her counterpart at the *Manitoba Free Press*, Lilian Laurie.

12 Public Archives of Canada (PAC), Dominion Lands Branch, RG 15, vol. 1955, Ruling 417

13 *Ibid.*, Ruling 484

14 L.L.'s account of the exchange between Roche and Oliver is accurate: see *Can. H. of C. Debates*, 30 April 1910, pp. 8488-90.

15 *Manitoba Free Press*, 17, 18, 24, 27 May, 1, 18, 28 June 1910

16 The original of this petition forms a thick file in the papers of the Department of the Interior: PAC, RG 15, vol. 1105, file no 2876596.

17 *Nor-West Farmer*, 5 March 1913; through the courtesy of Elizabeth Blight, Assistant Archivist, Province of Manitoba

18 PAC, RG 15, vol. 1105, file no 2876596

19 *Ibid.*, vol. 1987, Ruling 7261

20 Letter to King George V in Binnie-Clark's papers

21 Residents of Fort Qu'Appelle were unable to identify Roddy McMahon; they did, however, recall a Roddy Macdougall who fits the description. It is more than possible that Binnie-Clark changed this surname in order to avoid embarrassing someone she considered more a friend than an employee. All other changes in actual names which have so far come to light have been remarked on in the text of this introduction, and in note 11.

Georgina Binnie-Clark at the family home in Sherborne, Dorset.
Courtesy of Mr Dennis Jenks

The industrial training schools at Le Bret

A Roedean girl stooking at Binning, 1913

The Anglican church and rectory at Fort Qu'Appelle

The water chore: a Roedean girl at work on the land
at Binning, Fort Qu'Appelle

A pioneer priest of the prairie –
the Very Rev. J.P. Sargent,
Dean of Qu'Appelle

Mr Archibald Macdonald, last of
the 'chief factors' of the Hudson
Bay's Company

The pioneer statesman of the Prairie
provinces, Hon. F.W.G. Haultain

Threshing at Binning, 1906

Shopping at Fort Qu'Appelle

My neighbour, John McLeay

Victoria Day (now Empire Day) at Fort Qu'Appelle, 1912

The round-up: two of the Mazey girls set out to round the cattle home

The present phase of development in Father Hugenard's work for the
mother country

WHEAT AND WOMAN

Contents

4 Contents

PART I: HARVEST HOME

'To burn with one clear flame, to stand erect
In natural honour, not to bend the knee
In profitless prostrations whose effect
Is by itself condemned, what alchemy
Can teach me this? What herb Medea brewed
Will bring the unexultant peace of essence not subdued.'

'This, too, I had to learn – I thank Thee Lord –
To lie crushed down in darkness and the pit –
To lose all heart and hope – and yet to work.'

1

Of agricultural equipment, horses, and hired men

'You gave me your word that if I bought the farm your son should take off the crop,' I said. 'We have been waiting nearly a week for the binder-reaper. Now that it has at last arrived and everything is ready, your son isn't here. Of what use, do you suppose, is eighty acres of wheat, or eighty thousand acres, if we can't get it off?'

'He'll not be taking less than four and a half dollars a day for himself and team, I guess,' shouted my predecessor on the note of explanation.

'I don't care what he charges,' I shouted back. 'He simply has to come. Even I can see the wheat shelling all over the place; and you are not looking after my interest as you promised you would if I bought the farm.'

'I guess he'll be along some time to-day. Dick McGusty will have let him know the binder's set up. You'd best get busy and see about stookers. 'Tis a heavy crop, and will keep two men busy all the time, I guess. An' your brother, he should be getting on to the summer fallow. 'Tis the best crop I ever see on the auld place,' he concluded with a sigh of regret.

Dick McGusty had taken the binder twice around the crop land on the preceding afternoon, which brought to a close his responsibility as engineer-agent to the Massey-Harris Implement Company at Fort Qu'Appelle, and he had departed with a promise to hurry up other help. A double row of neat stooks threw a belt around the eighty-acre field of golden wheat, which was here and there shedding its wealth reproachfully upon the bosom of Mother Earth. The brand-new binder-reaper, for which I had agreed to pay thirty-one pounds ten shillings cash, seemed to groan as it leaned at ease listening to the incessant music of its fellows which floated through the clear atmosphere from near and far. In the adjoining field it had hummed from early morning. One could see the pale belt of stubble growing wider and wider around the shrinking zone of amber which the winged and active implement was rapidly laying low.

The old man's thought followed my envious and possibly angry eyes.

'There's Rolan'. He ain't got much more than forty acres. I guess he'll have it down by to-morrow noon. Every man should stand by his neighbour at harvest-time. He's another Englishman, so I guess he'll come in with his binder and help you out all right. Two binders would soon get it down. My! but it's the finest field of wheat this side of the valley – the best I ever see on th' auld place since I came to the country. I shouldn't have sold it if it hadn't been for my missus; though you never know if the frost will knock you out till it's safe down.'

'There's a wagon and team coming along by the side trail,' announced my brother, who had been cheerfully waiting the turn of events in the heart of one of the big stooks which, even in that first year, he built neat, sound, and strong to face the fury of the prairie winds.

'That's Johnnie all right,' said the old man, 'and I guess them others is the men Dick McGusty has hired on to stook. Now you get along and tell Rolan' Dennison to come on in here with his binder as soon as he's got his own wheat down, and I guess we'll get it all down inside next week.' He went off to meet the little party with a reassuring air about the shoulders – a Canadian never gives away the negative side of a situation, but hope and confidence may sit astride and stalk abroad.

'He may continue his guessin',' said my brother scornfully. 'I should like to catch myself asking favours of a stranger – and an Englishman too! He has been over here four years. Drives a fine team. But I expect he has just got them on time like everybody else.'

I recognized the driver of the wagon as my predecessor's son from a picture in the parlour, and the man at his side as being the butcher's assistant at Fort Qu'Appelle. The third gentleman – a veritable son of Anak – towered over them both in height, in breadth, in depth.

Dick McGusty had sent the butcher's assistant on approval. The terms were to be a dollar and a half a day and his board. The 'son of Anak' was an old hand; he had left him to make his own terms.

I thought six shillings and threepence a day with board too much for the outdoor labour of an amateur, and said so.

'You had better be careful,' warned my brother Lal, drawing me aside. 'Farmers pay the most helpless greenhorns any money at harvest-time. Any fool can stook, and I didn't feel too well when I got up this morning. Twice round that field tired me more than you think, and Dr. Hall particularly cautioned me to be most careful to avoid anything approaching over-exertion for a month at least.'

I agreed rather rebelliously to follow his advice, but promptly closed with the offer of the 'son of Anak' to give him twenty dollars for twelve days' work, since he looked so altogether promising and splendid. He informed me that he had worked on Lord Brassey's farm at Indian Head boy and man, intimating that his services had not only been valuable but highly valued.

'Brassey was a downright fine feller,' he said with a tinge of patronage. ''Twas he that gave Indian Head the start, and he gave every man on the place a new suit of clothes once a year.'

I said that he must have been extraordinarily clever to induce Canadians to accept them; at which remark the 'son of Anak' winked deliberately at his fellows. Every one acquiesced in the suggestion that we should dine promptly, and get a long half-day in the harvest-field; but I noticed that neither of the stookers lent a hand to the unharnessing of the team.

Before we bade each other good-day Dick McGusty had dropped a word of wisdom in my ear which served me well. 'If you want to keep your men, feed 'em. Feed them good, plenty of meat and potatoes three times a day. Cakes and jellies ain't no stand-by to a man who has to put in his ten hours a day on the land. Porridge for breakfast they'll look for, but, porridge or no porridge, plenty of meat and potatoes three times a day.'

In those days sirloins and ribs of beef represented meat to our British understanding, and for a time after that solemn warning housekeeping was distinctly on the expensive side. But as a matter of fact the average Canadian is quite an easy person to feed. During the summer he will tackle pork, salt or fresh, three times a day without a murmur. But as I was but five miles from the butcher, fresh beef was always available, and in those days cheap, though nearly always tough. After a while I got into the way of making scones almost as well as my Canadian neighbours, and with pork and beef, bread, butter, scones, treacle, milk puddings, and stewed evaporated fruit, the advice of Dick McGusty was fulfilled.

The new binder worked exceptionally well. The weather was deliciously hot. My sister Hilaria and I spent many lazy delightful hours resting against one or another of the daily increasing stooks, and we noticed that the same manner of taking one's ease was very popular with both our stookers. At four o'clock we took out tea and cakes to them, much to the amusement of our English neighbour and the scorn of my brother, who had withdrawn entirely from the harvest-field and was gathering hay from an adjoining slough with Charles Edward, the diminutive Indian pony, and Kitty, the cart-horse mare; Jim, the leader of the big team which we had purchased from Messrs. Johnson and Creamer of South Qu'Appelle during the early days of the summer for my brother's homestead, having taken third place on the binder.

'What a supreme greenhorn old McLeay must think you!' remarked my brother in a reflective friendly tone one morning as we halted by the slough that Charles Edward might take good breath before proceeding with the load.

'Why *me* in particular?' I inquired.

'To buy a farm with its crops at the highest price on record, and then to present him with the hay crop. A nice fix you'll be in next spring, and I haven't the smallest intention of remaining in this country, so I shan't be here to help you out. There are only five acres of oats, and it is all very well for him to say that he has left us plenty of hay; but half the goodness of prairie grass passes out when it arrives at the seeding phase, and all the rest is knocked out with the first frost, which may come at any day now. If you want to save any winter's feed at all you had better get a second team at once; and Dick McGusty says that you can have that mower and rake standing by the granary for fifty dollars. They belong to the last chap that bought the place, but he didn't pay for anything; and as he hardly used them, they are in good order and will save you several dollars.'

'I got a draft for three hundred and fifty pounds yesterday,' I answered. 'I thought I would just pay the old man the two hundred pounds initial payment due on the land; then Johnson and Creamer should be paid the three hundred and sixty-five dollars due on the team, and their harness, thirty-seven dollars. Mr. McGusty asked me to settle your note for the buggy and pony harness, ninety dollars, the wagon, eighty-six, and for the binder I have arranged to pay one hundred and fifty dollars cash. I ought to save enough ready money for wages and that kind of thing; but of course if you think a second team an absolute necessity one must get them.'

'Mr. Creegan says there's a man at Fort Qu'Appelle named Shore who has a team for sale. Why not go down and see them to-day?' he suggested. 'Then to-morrow you might go out to South Qu'Appelle, cash the draft, and find out if the bank won't let you draw anything you need on the strength of the crop. The last chap let them all in pretty badly I fear, and naturally bankers and people won't trust women in business. Besides, in any case they are certain to debit you with the lesson he taught them; and I can tell you that Canada is not a pleasant country in which to be saddled with a responsibility unless you have plenty of cash to see it through. Won't you wish yourself out of it before long!'

'But, Lal,' I expostulated, 'the old man says that there are two thousand five hundred bushels of wheat at least, and two thousand five hundred bushels of wheat at a dollar a bushel is two thousand five hundred dollars, and two thousand five hundred dollars is five hundred and twenty-five pounds. If I get five hundred pounds over now I can draw from my income a further five hundred pounds in instalments if necessary, and then the wheat being worth five hundred pounds and possibly more –'

'Well, the wheat is A1, I grant you,' he allowed, 'and perhaps you may come out all right.' In those days one of us couldn't have been more optimistic than another over the illusion of the elastic property of money. 'Well, I shall have to throw up my job for the day,' he added, 'as you will need Charles Edward to take you down to the Fort.'

'I can easily walk it,' I said. 'Please go on getting in the hay. I suppose I was a fool not to have settled it at halves like the potatoes. But you see he said there was plenty left for us, and it seemed rather hard luck to take it from him as he had gathered it all himself.'

'Hard luck! Isn't it the talk of the neighbourhood that you have been silly enough to give fifteen dollars an acre for the old place?'

'*With the crops*,' I corrected. 'You may be as pessimistic as you please. I believe in the place absolutely and entirely. Since an eighty-acre field can produce five hundred pounds' worth of wheat on a three hundred and twenty acre farm, it stands to reason that if one breaks up the lot it will produce one thousand five hundred pounds, therefore it must be extraordinarily cheap at a thousand guineas, comfortably arranged on a system of two hundred and ten pounds down, two hundred and ten pounds after harvest, and the balance in annual instalments at six per cent.'

'You bought the land with the crops, and you ought to have stuck to the hay,' he insisted. 'In Britain hay represents nine-tenths of its own value, and the labour attached to its harvest the last fraction. Over here it's precisely the reverse. You could easily get a hundred tons of hay for the gathering in the neighbourhood of my homestead. But first find your labourer.'

I set out for Fort Qu'Appelle by the side trail immediately after our twelve o'clock dinner. The adjoining section of land, consisting of the orthodox six hundred and forty acres, was at that time the property of the Canadian Pacific Railway Company. I had always hoped it would become my own. In 1906 one could have bought it at five dollars an acre, in 1907 it was offered to me at seven dollars, in 1908 the price had risen to ten dollars, and at last in 1910, when I wanted the south-west quarter for a special purpose, the entire section had been purchased by its present owner at about eleven dollars an acre. So that it more than doubled its value in four years, and owed this increase solely to the rising tide of Canadian land values, and without a solitary effort in the matter of contribution from the toil of man. In the day of its virginity a well-worn trail beckoned one through this lovely bit of pasture country and on through the thickly wooded property of my neighbour, John McLeay, to pause at the door of his hospitable shack. Curling respectfully around his potato-bed, it still skirts the bonny wheat-field – which, sheltered between two giant bluffs, is always the first in our neighbourhood to pay homage to the harvest sun – to wind its way on through the lovely lingering lawless mile of the school section towards that exquisite oasis of the prairie where nature called on form and colour, wind and tide, and all the children of the morning to breathe beauty, which hovers about the hills and valley of Fort Qu'Appelle. On the brow of the southern hill is God's acre, and the very chant of its sleepers is one with the song of the spirit of the morning. 'Very pleasant was love and life in the happy valley,' they seem to say. 'Very sweet is rest in the sun-warmed bosom of its guardian hill.'

In those fascinating days, between the space of four miles, one walked from the place where 'uncertainty is hope' to the mood where hope becomes certainty. The fine exhilaration of the prairie air lures one on all the time – always up the hill, never down; and even if it is sometimes to halt at the place where the gods laugh, it is at least within the enchantment of an atmosphere where one may laugh – through one's tears – with the gods.

I ran down the narrow zigzag path full tilt and met Mr. Creegan at the gate of his house.

'My brother thinks you know a man who wants to sell a team,' I said. 'Can you really recommend them to us? Most people who have seen our present team seem to think them a little ancient. But they work splendidly. Only I should like mares.'

'Couldn't Mr. McLeay have let you have a team on good terms?' he suggested.

'He wouldn't sell his mares,' I explained, 'and as I thought he might have let me have at least one of them, I wouldn't take his son's geldings at three hundred and fifty dollars. Especially as they aren't young either, although they are fine beasts, nearly as big as our own.'

'I can show you the team Jake Shore has for sale,' he said; 'they are running over here on the flats. Good beasts and young. He bought them of old Yorke the carrier for his son's homestead, but the poor fellow died. He says he will let you have them for three hundred and ten dollars, harness thrown in. But you had better look at them first, and then go and talk to him about the deal.'

'I can't possibly pay him three hundred dollars spot cash, and they are not nearly as big as our own team,' I said. But they were good horses of the middle-weight division. Jess, the mare, was gentle, black, and quite young – she revived one's hope of baby horses. Dick was a bright bay with the friendliest eyes, and a promise of pace which even the hair on his fetlocks failed to conceal. I determined to buy them if I could come to terms.

'Do you think if I offered him sixty dollars down and the balance a month or so later he would agree to sell?' I asked Mr. Creegan.

'I feel sure he would,' he answered; 'but go and see him. You will find him in or near his shack.'

I knocked at the door of a little shanty opposite the Post Office, and a man with sad eyes and a big grey beard, who looked as though he particularly belonged to the hills of Fort Qu'Appelle, opened it. I told him of my errand and proposal of payment, and that of course I was willing to pay interest on the amount deferred.

'If you will pay the balance in October and November, you can take the horses and harness,' he said, 'and I shall not be asking any interest for that short time.'

So we arranged that Jess and Dick should join my forces, and that my brother should fetch them on the following day. At the top of the hill I looked back upon them in the valley. A happy, useful, friendly pair, browsing contentedly on the sun-cured herbage. Four and five years was the age which had been given me, but it transpired that it was rising four and five. At least they will be good for many years, I told myself; and long before I reached John McLeay's shack I am afraid I had dotted the new landscape with the foals of the new mare.

2

The custom of deferred payment – a prairie storm

On the following morning I started for Fort Qu'Appelle very early in order to avoid driving in the intense heat of midday. But Charles Edward was in his most grudging mood, and we arrived in sight of the Lake of the Woods Elevator just in time to see every one going to twelve o'clock dinner. Charles Edward settled himself to a bunch of sweet-smelling hay in one of the narrow stalls of the spacious livery barn, after nodding his head with angry but vain intelligence towards the bag containing the oats which I gave to the ostler to be given him later. At the hotel one was offered the usual midday fare of soup, a choice of roast and boiled meats with vegetables, sweets, and a cup of tea or coffee in a cool, clean dining-room for the modest sum of twenty-five cents. Afterwards I wrote letters in the 'Woman's Parlour' by way of killing the time which I knew must intervene before I could hope to find the bank manager, the butcher, or the harness-maker in the place of my several needs. 'Do your business before dinner, or get home when you may' is another unwritten law of life on the prairie.

My drafts had been made payable through the Union Bank of Canada. In the manager I was fortunate enough to find an English gentleman, who in the process of event became my adviser, my censor, and my tyrant without offence. On that first and on all subsequent occasions of our meeting he was courtesy itself. I submitted my copy of the draft, but it appeared that its duplicate had not yet arrived at the bank. However, on being informed that the harvest was well under the binder, and the wheat of the finest quality, he gave me permission to make the full payment of one thousand dollars to my predecessor, and also to draw on the bank for any further sums that might suit my convenience at the rate of seven per cent.

With a considerably lighter heart I bent my neck willingly and most gratefully towards the gilded chain of that obligation; it was not removed for many years, and the scar of temporary loan sears the pages of the history of my experiment. On that day, however, I was content to sign a bill of three hundred dollars at seven per cent. for one month, so that I should not be at the inconvenience of being without ready money. Within four days the duplicate draft had arrived, but at the end of the month its value had been distributed among the many claims of a new undertaking.

Messrs. Johnson and Creamer I found equally obliging. Dr. Creamer was out of town, and I had a hazy idea that if I didn't meet the bill for the team which fell due on September 1 I must at least personally explain the delay, lest the horses should be seized, and the initial payment of one hundred dollars forfeited. I made my way to the harvest field of Mr. Johnson, where no fewer than three binders were careering round a two-hundred-acre field of simply gorgeous wheat.

Mr. Johnson was driving the third binder himself, and willingly consented to my request that the payment might be deferred until November 1. I thought them the very pleasantest people to do business with, and nothing at all of the fact that ten per cent. became the charge for interest after the maturity of the original bill. Nor is the debtor in Canada one whit less the obliged party because of the heavy rate of interest. Had I not been able to settle the whole amount for six or even twelve months I think my two creditors would have waited with patience, but certainly not with pleasure. In Canada money can command almost anything but labour; and I haven't the smallest doubt that had I taken three hundred dollar bills to Messrs. Johnson and Creamer on the day of purchase, Jim and Kitty would have changed hands at that 'spot cash' price, instead of the original three hundred and sixty dollars plus interest on deferred payment at eight and ten per cent.

I returned home with joints of beef, harness repairs, various pots and pans, and a crate of delicious black plums from British Columbia, paying about seven shillings and sixpence for twenty pounds. As I drew near the boundary line of our neighbour's half-section I saw that he had crossed it, and that two binders were at work in the eighty-acre field. It was the first of many kind attentions he showed us during those early days of farming. I drove towards his binder to thank him, and to ask him to join our party at supper, but he refused the invitation on the plea of his evening 'chores,' and promised to come again if we hadn't finished before his own oats were down. 'I would come tomorrow,' he said, 'because, there is no mistake about it, your wheat is ahead of you, especially on the high ground. But I'm in the same place with my oats, which are shelling almost as freely. However, I expect we shall both be through by Saturday.' And we should have been only there came a violent storm.

My predecessor departed in the morning with his first instalment of a thousand dollars, which I felt quite sure he received with much surprise and some regret. 'I don't want to worry you,' he said at parting, 'but I shall be glad when you can let me have the money for the stock and the cord-wood. 'Tisn't much, but I've bought a house and two lots down at the Fort, and a thousand dollars won't go far.'

It was a matter of about a hundred and fifty dollars, and it included two milch cows and two bull calves at ninety dollars, a sow at ten dollars, and nine pigs at two and a half dollars each. Besides these, there was quite a good stock of fuel of the dimensions known as cord-wood, a kitchen table, a heater and its attendant drum. I undertook to pay the amount within a few days.

'And you should have bought my son's team,' he added; 'they would have done you well, knowing the place and the work. That second team of yours is too light for the others.'

'You should have sold me a mare,' I answered; 'if you couldn't part with even one brood mare, I don't see why I should buy your son's elderly geldings.' But events proved that it would have been a wiser deal.

'Will you buy my bull at thirty-five dollars?' he asked.

'Not if you gave him,' I answered. 'And please take him away as soon as you can. You could make a fortune putting him over fences in an English show-ring. He would beat an Irish hunter.'

'You are doing wrong not to take him,' he said. 'I'll be coming up for my things in a day or so, and maybe you'll change your mind.'

'Never!' said Hilaria from the rear. 'At least, if the bull remains, I depart. Lal and the son of Anak took fully an hour to drive him back into the pasture from the wheat field this morning. And whilst they were in the heat of argument over the height of an effectual barricade he slipped down on his knees, and most carefully conveyed his huge body beneath the bottom strand of wire, and stalked back into the wheat. It's distinctly weak of you to have allowed him to remain even for a day! ... Lal met Mrs. Creegan as he was bringing back the horses,' she added, 'and she wants you to go to the Fort this morning and drive with her to Lipton this afternoon. Some of her people have a furniture store there, and she thinks you may care to look round. We shall certainly have to buy some chairs when these people remove their household gods; but I shouldn't buy much more at present in case a chance should come to get out of it altogether.'

It is fully ten miles from Fort Qu'Appelle to Lipton, and we didn't leave until after two o'clock. Mrs. Creegan was the gentlest of whips, and on each of the many occasions she halted to give fat swift Pussy a rest I refrained with difficulty from telling her that she and Charles Edward had been made for each other. The furniture was shrill, and therefore not indispensable, but we bought a convenient camp bedstead for four and a half dollars. We left at dusk, but by the time we reached the Touchwood trail it was ominously dark, only for a lurid glow in the distance which I knew meant a bad storm.

The Creegans begged me to remain at the Fort overnight, but I thought it possible to get home. Charles Edward, fresh from his long rest, climbed Troy Hill gaily by the last gleam of light. As we emerged into the open the first growl of the oncoming storm echoed among the hills, but I hoped to reach home before it broke and blazed as it only can on the prairie. Spring rains and snowdrift have caused fainter repetitions of the main trail on its either side. After wandering off on to these many times in the black darkness, and literally feeling my way back with my fingers, I got into a place which was completely baffling. By the mocking flash of lightning I could see the country for twenty miles round, but I could not define my exact whereabouts on the trail, and I hadn't learned to trust entirely to the instinct of a horse.

Over the space of a mile I wandered up and down leading Charles Edward, and shouting in the hope that I was near the farm, and that Lal or Hilaria might hear me; but during our summer on his homestead we had grown serenely indifferent to delay, and had made it a rule to refuse to worry. Suddenly my shout seemed answered on a weird strange dominating note of profound melancholy. First one, then many other voices echoed to its calling, until it grew into a soul-chilling chorus – hungry and despairing as the 'Adsum' of tired souls in the leash of the corpse of sin. For the first time in Canada I heard the music of the prairie-wolf. I got back into the buggy and waited in silence. Gradually the storm grew and burst into magnificent fury. Peals of thunder rose and fell, like mountains in procession marching to the battle-cry of the gods by light of the unearthly splendour in motion which flashed from every corner of the heavens. The infernal orchestra of the wolves from all ends of the prairie joined in the imperial crescendo. Nothing was strange – all seemed at one with the crash of storm and the cry of the unseen hosts of the unfamiliar hours of darkness, and one had a strange desire to step out of everything and dart to one's place on the wing of the storm, as, fierce and dry-eyed, it swept on its way across those plains of peace.

But with its passing the rain fell as though it would wash away the sway and the trail of tempest with the relief of familiar discomfort. It drowned my hat, my pretty frock, my petticoats, my shoes. Finally it washed me out of the buggy to seek protection and a touch of warmth on the more sheltered of the dripping sides of Charles Edward. In time the deluge ceased, but black darkness remained until the silent shadows of dawn stole back to duty, revealing the fact that we were within half a mile of home, and like a drowned rat I made my way back to the stable and the cottage.

3

A vagabond garden

I knew nothing whatever of the law of crops beyond the fact that
one must never ride over anything that springs at springtime.
On the night of the storm I concluded that in its rage and fury it
must have laid low the golden harvest, but I was much too wet
and uncomfortable to care. However, in the morning the grain
was standing erect, all fresh and sparkling from its bath; only the
land itself was far too sodden to permit the binder to travel, and
the harvest field was abandoned for the day.

The son of my predecessor borrowed the buggy, and drove off
to Fort Qu'Appelle accompanied by the late A.D.C. of the butcher;
but the 'son of Anak,' whom we had already rechristened 'the
Great Boaster,' remained, and discussed the dilapidations of the
farm with every token of sympathetic interest, and a hint of permanent intention in his undertakings.

'My! But that's a miserable old barn of a stable they've let you
in for,' he exclaimed at dinner; 'we must get some lumber and
roof-paper and me and Lal will get busy and fix up the roof so as
to keep out the rain. I guess we'll have to put in a good window
too – horses don't like living in the dark. So soon as we've got in
the crop I shall get on to the job.'

'Why not to-day?' I inquired. 'You must get so very tired of
doing nothing. Don't any Canadians do anything on wet days?'

'Guess not many does much. Stable-cleaning, water-hauling,
milking, and wood-bucking is chores – boy's work. In this coun-

try the boss who can't keep a chore-boy he just does the chores himself. When a fellow gets paid by the day, I guess on the days you can't get on the land he principally lies round.'

'But if he turns up three times a day for his meals, Billy, he is expected to lend a hand with the chores, at least that was my experience,' struck in Lal. 'And as I got water last night, and again this morning, you just go along and do your bit now. And to-night you will milk the easy cow, and I shall milk the hard one. I'll show you which is which.'

'Why, certainly, I'll fetch the water,' he answered affably. 'But I guess you needn't go out of your way to show me which is which in the matter of cows, seeing as that old bird of Alan's is known for ten miles round. My, but he's tickled to death to have got quit of her! Not much praise up to him either, as I was telling him, rounding her off on English greenhorns. Guess you couldn't be expected to know no better.'

'Wait until you come to England,' advised Lal, with the mask of calmness stretched taut over the wrath which the term '*English* greenhorn' always kindles in his British heart. 'We'll talk about "greenhorns" then.'

'I guess I shan't never get that far, Lal,' was the rejoinder. 'I ain't what you may call a great traveller. Likely I might get so far as Regina, but that's about the limit.'

'Well, get along and get the water, and then come and give me a hand cleaning out the stable, and earn your supper.'

On that afternoon I walked around the farm. It was a mile east and west by half a mile north and south, but as it was then unfenced I found it difficult to be sure of the boundary line at the east end. I walked through the forty-acre pasture, which consists of a stretch of rough but attractive virgin prairie. Five sloughs break up this field, affording good water for beasts, and a coarse but seemingly popular herbage when the water dries out towards the end of July. On the hill at the north boundary the only bluff of the pasture keeps guard, and it is the favourite hide-and-seek playground of cattle and horses. A group of tall poplars graces the foreground, and a thicket of withies in the rear has been picturesquely graded by horns and hoofs to the pool of

water which marks its silent heart. On that first day of our association I vowed that no tree should be permitted to fall from the
stately group of poplars, which stand for beauty from the first
breath of springtime to the last fierce breath of the destroying
angel of the Fall, and through all the loneliness of the white-clad
winter months their form, even without the glory of colour, is
beauty still. Within a year I had fenced the land, and discovered
that only one-half of the bluff was on the right side of the
fence – but that half included the poplars.

Just beyond the pasture was an even stretch of prairie measuring fully twenty-five acres, and unbroken by slough or bluff. It
seemed to clearly cry out for wheat, and I dedicated it to the site
of my first new field. Beyond, again, on the other side of an en-
circling chain of hay-sloughs, I was able to get in another field of
twelve acres which runs north and south across the east line
until it dips to the edge of a most fertile and perfectly round
slough, from which the yield of hay, in England would pay the
rent of a small farm. On that day from the far side I caught a
gleam of glorious colour isolated in the contrast of the surrounding prairie. Viewed from a distance it seemed like an enchanted
garden, and I went eagerly though carefully towards it across the
intervening slough.

'And your brother should be getting on to the summer fallow;
it's forty acres and late in the year!'

My predecessor had uttered this advice on a warning note at
every meal. When I stood on the border of that living mass of
loveliness I knew that I had arrived at the place of 'forty acres,'
because running down the centre was a narrow strip of recently
turned black soil. And all the rest was fairyland.

Within the dower of Canadian soil is the supreme gift of
colour – 'the soul's bridegroom' – although the twin-gift of perfume is not there. Turn but three feet of virgin soil and within a
year bloom in every hue of violet and gold greets your labour.
How these flowers come and whence none knows, but it is supposed that an understanding exists between bird, wind, and
seed, since the seed always seems to arrive at the best place possible for its growth. On that afternoon tall groups of sunflowers

and banks of golden rod lifted rain-washed faces to the warmth of the harvest sun. Masses of mauve daisy reminded one that sweet and somewhat sad September was in London too. Gorgeous violet thistles, looking like kings of Scotland in love with exile, mingled with roses whose colour deepens and glows with the tint that the sun brings back from the land beyond the horizon. In full bloom and full head they reigned amidst vagrant beds of barley, of vagabond wild oats; they curled round the stems of the sunflowers, and clung to the beds of burr which marked the place where the blue forget-me-not had been; and even in the few solitary acres which my predecessor had turned in July the rose of the prairie triumphed over the power of the plough. From end to end of this exquisite garden the measure was half a mile. I never walk or work on 'forty acres' without remembering it as I saw it then; and although the price of that lovely vision proved to be several seasons of anxiety, toil, and an extraordinary share of that burden of financial worry which must attend every business proposition not soundly enclosed within a fence of adequate capital, it lives in one's memory as a sunbeam, and it was a phase of Canada that one knew even better than the Canadians – those flowers were peculiarly *mine*. Within the month I was a guest at a party given by a neighbour in order that I might meet other neighbours. Some one asked me what I found the chief attraction of the prairie. I said 'the flowers.' 'The flowers?' inquired my hostess, who lived in a tiny house at the corner of a section of land which was literally six hundred and forty acres of grain. 'The flowers?' echoed every voice at the table but one. 'I guess I saw you carrying an armful the other morning when I was out with my gun,' observed its owner. 'It's the weeds she means,' he explained in a tone that authorized gentle dealing, and those who succeeded in arresting their titter merely said, 'Well, there!'

From the far end of the expensive pleasure-ground I dropped into another round luxuriant slough which marks the centre of a sheltering slope, and yields from eight to ten tons of hay, and shelter from every wind that blows across the North-West. To the right another stretch of virgin soil climbed a forbidding hill which later on I compelled to the service of wheat. From that point to the western boundary the eighty-acre field stretched north and south, and I reached the plain-featured cottage well content with its surrounding land.

It was past supper-time and the meal was in progress. My brother had persuaded our neighbour to join us. We talked of the storm, which had caught him also on the trail. Then we talked of the crops, and I inquired of him the full meaning of the term summer fallow.

'Summer-fallow land,' he explained, 'should mean that particular third section of one's crop-land which should be permitted to lie fallow every year. Canadians will give you many good reasons for this system of farming; the ruling reason is that Canadian soil is not only the finest in the world for wheat, but also for weed. This third year out system gives the farmer an opportunity of keeping down the weed through careful surface cultivation with disc and harrow. And if you want a particularly impressive specimen of what the Canadian prairie can produce in the form of weed on a large scale, you have only to walk to the forty-acre field on the south-east corner of this farm.'

'I have been there this afternoon,' I said. 'It is even lovelier than the wheat-field.'

'You will be having an awful mess there next year if you are not very careful,' he said seriously.

'What do you mean?' I asked.

'We don't deprive ourselves of the use of a third, or even a fourth, of our crop-land every year in order to grow wild-flower gardens,' he answered. 'I broke that forty acres myself. When I first came to this country I hired on with Alan McLeay for a year. It is a beautiful field, and it is a shame that it is in its present condition in so short a time; but, as you may have heard, the farm was sold to an Englishman two years ago. He knew very little of farming, and in any case he had no money to farm with. The old man went to his other place up north, and the farm got into a pretty dirty condition; and although he took possession again in time to claim the harvest, the weed had got badly ahead.

Last year they managed to get the greater part of this big field twice ploughed and well worked, and so knocked out a good many of the wild oats. But they are there still, and badly in places. I should recommend you not to sow a stubble crop next year, but leave it fallow and work it well. Then in 1907 you could expect to get as fine a crop as this year, and quite free from wild oats.'

'But that would only leave the forty acres for crop-land,' I objected.

'Do you really intend to sow wheat in forty acres?' he inquired.

'I understood that the crop grown on fallow land represented the principal contribution to the grain harvest,' I said, 'and as far as I can judge the grain can be the only substantial source of one's income for a time.'

'Ah! grain grown from the fallow land which has been even fairly well worked,' he explained. 'This field is the best in the neighbourhood and I expect its prospect went to Alan's head. At any rate he put in very little work on forty acres this year. There is about fifteen acres in the centre which he ploughed in late June. Didn't you notice that it wasn't nearly so thickly covered with growth as the land on either side? If your brother ploughed that fifteen acres now, and again in the spring, after the seed which must be scattered on the present surface has had time to shoot, it will be a fairly good bed for barley next year, because barley can be sown as late as June. But wheat is out of the question; and believe me it is perfectly hopeless to think of using the remaining twenty-five acres as a seed-bed next year. You should put the mower to all that growth at once, burn the refuse, then disc and harrow. Next year plough lightly in May, then plough deep early in July, cultivate until the freeze-up, and in 1907 you should obtain a good result.'

'That means that I ought not to put in a crop at all next year.'

'Not quite. There is the fifteen acres your brother is now at work on, which should yield excellent pig-feed, and the ten- and four-acre arms of this big field are perfectly clean. You could quite well sow wheat on this stubble. But it would be wiser to spring plough and sow oats so as to make a good reserve of feed, and go nap on wheat in 1907.'

'Are all Canadian farms like this, or have I made a particularly unfortunate investment?' I asked.

'I shouldn't say that exactly,' he answered, 'the investment is all right if you have sufficient capital to work and wait for its return. It is a common saying in this country that if you don't get the better of the other man in a deal, he will get the better of you. In the main this farm owes its present plight to the first English buyer, and the vendor no doubt thinks that it is quite all right that the second English buyer should take a share in the settlement of the score. You have bought the best farm in the neighbourhood as far as the wheat-land goes – very little slough and bluff, a hundred and twenty acres of crop-land, to which you can easily add another hundred and fifty and still hold on to that useful pasture. But you mustn't forget that you have a far more expensive proposition before you in dealing with the cleaning of that forty acres than with new breaking. If you can hold over next year's crop you will be upsides on the deal; but if this is the best farm within the slough and bluff neighbourhood, which lies between the wheat plains of Wideawake and Springbrook, it is wiser to face the fact that it is also about the dirtiest. There is one neighbour who can beat you in French weed, and another in wild oats – but you have *both*!'

Our neighbour was something of a pessimist, and a more inspiring companion in good times than in bad. But he was unusually clever, and never walked blindfold through experience. On that occasion certainly his advice was sound and strong. Also I might have been guided by the sight of his own agricultural work, which, although limited in extent through lack of capital, was excellent as far as it went. But my position was too weak from every point to dare that fallow year. The further capital I depended on was but income drawn from another source of business enterprise, and, sound and remunerative as it was at that time, I knew it would probably decrease during my prolonged absence from England. My father plainly disapproved of the Canadian deal, in spite of the fact that he had advanced the initial capital. He hadn't sufficient agricultural knowledge to swallow my glowing report of wheat with a grain of salt, and I knew that to ask for more money to work and wait with, as my neighbour advised, would mean a complete loss of confidence. Family eye-witnesses in the form of my brother and sister frankly shouted, 'Evil be thou our good and take us out of Canada!' I had already spent a good deal of money over the equipment. I knew that in the long run I need not fail, and had that initial capital been my own I should not have hesitated a moment to follow my neighbour's advice. As things were I didn't hesitate to decide that it was impossible, and that since I could not have the full loaf I must make the best of the half. Lastly, but not least, I had always believed in the gods, and I hadn't found out that they won't perform agricultural miracles *for* you, but only *through* you. So even on that night I slept as soundly as one always sleeps in enchanted air, until the sun was shining on the wheat-field in face of my bedroom window.

4

Of harvest, wages, the cost of implements and plant

'Is everything ready?' I inquired of Lal, who had brought me a cream-decked cup of tea, an attention with which he never failed to meet the early morning no matter how firmly we had decided to differ the night before.

'The horses are ready and your stookers have just turned out of bed. I have been up the last two hours – fed everything, groomed the horses. We ought to finish to-day, as our neighbour expects to finish his oats before dinner and is coming along to help us through. But the Jehu of the binder has not turned up yet.'

'Not turned up!' I cried. 'Lal, what shall we do? And every hour matters! Do you think he can be ill?'

'The aftermath of conviviality, I shouldn't wonder,' he answered cheerfully. 'He isn't half a bad sort. Jolly good chap all round. Everybody likes him.'

Billy the Boaster didn't fail to turn his neighbour's possible backsliding to his own account at breakfast. 'It's a free country,' he affirmed, 'and I say if a feller has a mind to get full let him get good and full as often as he likes. But at seeding and harvest times I guess I'm off the liquor. Threshing ain't of the same account.'

'You cut it a bit fine sometimes, Billy,' said my brother. 'You were the heaviest old rip I have ever lent a hand in putting to bed in a stable since I have been in this country.'

'I ain't been so full as that night, Lal, since Sam Soundman came back from fightin' the Boers with his pockets sticking out with dollar bills and his legs tied round with bits of rag, and there was free drinks to all. Have you seen me touch liquor since I hired on?' he demanded with such force that I thought it wisdom to turn conversation my way.

'I shall go across and ask our neighbour if it is quite sure that he can come this afternoon,' I said; 'and I feel certain that our Jehu will be along within an hour.'

'If he doesn't, hadn't some one else better get on with the binder?' suggested Lal.

'I don't see how we can since he came as a kind of favour. Besides, supposing any little thing went wrong it would be a fine excuse for him to go off altogether. Better wait awhile.'

I found our neighbour already at work and expecting to finish at midday. Half-way back across the field I saw the binder at work again, and waited for it to come up. To my astonishment, the Great Boaster was in command. He stopped the horses at my signal.

'I am quite sure you mean well,' I said, 'but it really won't do for you to drive the binder, and especially with Mr. McLeay's horses. He came as a favour and at great personal inconvenience, and you must see that it is not possible to allow another man to take his place. Of course it is most annoying, but we must wait until –'

'Wait! Wait for a man at harvest-time! My, if that don't tickle a feller some! There's no favours in a free country where you're paying a man good money. You leave Jack to me. The wheat is shelling all the time. I'm on this here binder and I guess I'm stopping on it till he comes along. All the English greenhorns I've been up against yet I never heard of stopping the binder because a man –'

'Be quiet!' I shouted. 'And if you are going on, go on and don't talk so much.'

'No offence meant nor need be taken,' was the complacent comment. 'I've teached them all some. And I guess you'll larn.'

At dinner-time the missing man returned. He had the pleasantest way of being sorry about things without actually putting it into words, and I was relieved to find that he took the Great Boaster's presence on the binder as a matter of course. Our neighbour arrived in due time, and by Saturday noon the wheat was finished, and by evening the five acres of oats were laid low. The stookers, however, were miles behind; but harvest was gathered. Its labour account ran:

Binder-man with team, 6 days at $4, and one day team only	$26.75
Stooker, 12 days at $1.50	18
Stooker, 12 days	20
Total	$64.75

As the general law of the harvest-field in Canada is three stookers to two binders, and they usually finish within a few hours of each other, it will be easily understood that the two stookers who followed in the wake of the binder in the first year of my farming experiment had the harvest-time of their lives ... But wages to-day are nearly double, two dollars seventy-five or three dollars with board being average pay for stooking.

My general ignorance of agriculture proved deplorable in the matter of the selection of implements. I made a good start with the Massey-Harris up-to-date six-foot binder-reaper; but the principal implement on a farm, especially where there remains much land to be broken, is a plough; and into this booby-trap I fell headlong. Mr. McGusty was the Massey-Harris agent at Fort Qu'Appelle, and in duty bound to sell their implements when possible. I bought the Sulkey model he recommended at fifty-six dollars in good faith – later in these pages it may tell its own tale. The disc cost forty-five dollars. The mower and rake had been purchased, but not paid for, by the first buyer, and Mr. McGusty let me have them for fifty dollars. The mower still does good work; the rake was not satisfactory. The seeder, a 'Kentucky,' I bought of a neighbour, who was also its agent, for the sum of one hundred and thirty dollars; but it is wisdom to buy an implement of a direct agent, and that he should be within reach, because of the frequently urgent matter of repairs. The hay-rack was made to order at a cost of twenty-three dollars seventy, which included lumber, bolts, &c., and carpenter's charges. It was much too heavy and clumsy for its purpose, and has been succeeded by two – one was sold to me for ten dollars by the sharp son of a really clever father, and finally I had a Yankee model copied at the inclusive cost of seventeen dollars seventy-five. A hay-rack is deserving of thought, labour, and money, as it is one of the most useful of farm chattels; but most Canadians make their own, and the average collection of racks on a threshing gang is characteristic of Canada, in expressing the individuality of its particular owner untrammelled by the law of order or any sense of loyalty to form.

Bob-sleighs I was able to buy at an auction for eighteen dollars; there also I bought a second wagon at forty-six dollars, and might have bought a serviceable seeder in excellent order at twenty-five dollars had I not already ordered the 'Kentucky.' A fanning-mill should be selected with finest discretion; and here again I made the mistake of buying at the door. It was an up-to-date model of the Chatham separator, and certainly separated wild oats from wheat in a manner that seemed to me marvellous, and I didn't discover, until the agent and my cheque were both beyond recall, that it was a very slow process entailing great waste of grain. It cost twenty-six dollars, and was replaced by another in 1910 which I bought of Morgan and Vicars of South Qu'Appelle for thirty-five dollars without its bagging attachment. It did its work well, but occasionally needs the attention of the expert, which proves the theory that it is wisdom to purchase one's implements of an agent within call. A set of four sections of harrows cost twenty dollars, and some years later I bought for eleven dollars a harrow cart – an item of equipment which none should be without. It is only a slight additional weight for the horses, and saves foot-weariness and foot-wear, besides ensuring more faithful service to the land. I managed with a home-made stone-boat, and also a home-made wood-bucking board for some time, at a great cost of energy, patience, and unstoned land. It is wisdom in purchasing a ready-made farm to engage a good carpenter for a day or so to put all implements in order, and supply such chattels as are absolutely necessary for economy of time and energy.

The total cost of my original outlay in implements and chattels amounted to nearly one hundred and fifty pounds. This included the cost of buggy and harness which my brother had purchased for his homestead at about nineteen pounds, and also the second wagon, which was useful but not indispensable. There was also the cost of binder-twine, thirty-six dollars, and an account from the local iron stores for such items as brooms and buckets, grain-shovel, spades, forks, rakes, barrels, halters, and those items of stable equipment which are absolutely indispensable, and the cost of which always seems inconsiderable; but its sum demands a distinct place in the consideration of capital adequate to secure the success of agricultural experiment within reasonable time.

When all the sheaves were safely in stook, 'the Great Boaster' spent a day in repairing the stable roof. At the end of the day my brother told me that he thought he was anxious to stay on, but that he would want at least two dollars a day after that week, and that he feared I should find farming a very expensive occupation. Between the serious dilemma of the unploughed summer fallow, the ungathered hay, and, to an Englishwoman, the seeming urgent necessity of immediate repair, I might have made the deal; but I had discovered that although, after his many years' residence in the North-West, 'the Great Boaster' knew his business, he never lost an opportunity of 'resting a piece.' That day two men had chanced to call in search of employment, and offered their service at one dollar fifty; but I felt that a change was inadvisable, and decided to offer 'the Great Boaster' a renewal of the bargain – twenty dollars for twelve days – but I intended to map out service day by day.

I told Hilaria of my intention as we were saying good-night to Charles Edward, and just at that moment his voice fell on our ears.

'Be sure have the women up in good time to get our breakfast, Lal. To-morrow we ought to get in at least five loads of hay.'

'Women indeed!' said Hilaria. 'Oh, haven't you tied yourself up in a knot!'

However, 'the women' as usual served breakfast punctually, but finding the exclusively egotistical turn of the conversation a little trying at that early hour I went off to the gallery-room which Hilaria and I had fixed up at the head of the stairs.

'Billy wishes to know if you have decided that he shall work on next week at two dollars a day,' said my brother. 'And if he thinks I am going to do all the pitchin' whilst he lies on the hay and smokes, he is mistaken,' he added. 'Yesterday he sat on the stable roof like a field-marshal commanding an army whilst I did all the work. And I have done every blessed chore this morning whilst he talked on.'

'How very silly of you!' I answered. 'Of course if you wait on people – you may. And only yesterday you strongly advised me to renew his engagement at higher pay!'

'I said he was a good man, and so he is; but who do you suppose is going to work for a woman in this country without taking advantage of her ignorance? If you get rid of him, where will you be? I can't do all the work that is waitin' to be done in this place. And you simply can't get labour for love or money!'

'Can't I? Two real workmen called to ask for a job yesterday, and only asked a dollar fifty a day. "The Great Boaster" may be a good man at his work on the rare occasions when he puts his power into practice; but he is far more reliable at resting from his labour. He can take twenty dollars for twelve days' work if he chooses, but I shall dictate the work, and shall expect him to do it, and not merely bounce about what he has done for other people. You can tell him that I say so.'

However, there was no need. Through the stovepipe in Canadian houses sound carries very clearly; in this way a candid opinion has often flown straight home. On that morning the Great Boaster heard mine.

'Find fault with my work! And a woman too! Not another day! Tell her to have the dollars ready. I quit – after dinner.'

I had to pay him by cheque, and in Canada the cost of exchange not only between one bank and another, but between branches of the same company located in different cities, is twenty-five cents. In drawing the cheque I naturally allowed for this cost of exchange. He received it like an injured Viking, and left without the conventional farewell; but in explaining his sudden exit, with the opinion that we were the queerest outfit that had yet arrived in Canada from the old country, he sharply defended us against an accusation of meanness in the fact of that twenty-five cents.

We were completely fed-up with feeding hired men. Hilaria expressed the hope almost hourly and seldom devoutly that she might never again look upon roast beef and bacon to the end of her days – the meat which had been so far away as to seem a boon in the place of my brother's homestead had become as the quails of the wilderness. My brother, not altogether unpleased with the situation, decided that with a spurt he could manage to finish the ploughing; and our neighbour kindly offered to help with the carrying of the hay. I think the turning of about two-thirds of the fifteen acres was accomplished, but very little of the grass in the few sloughs which our predecessor had left became hay, and before the end of the winter we were in difficulties over feed. From the moment the harvest was down my mind attached itself to the possibility of improvement, and my neighbour warned me that it was necessary to see about new granaries, as the only one on the place would contain barely two thousand bushels, and he considered we might expect at least two thousand five hundred bushels of wheat, and about four hundred bushels of oats.

The carpenters had to come to build the granaries, and in that fact I will plant my first mistake in completely embracing the cottage with an eight-foot roofed and floored veranda, a luxury primarily designed to conceal its bald lack of attraction.

Our neighbour, who was an excellent carpenter, took the measurement of the house, and advised me to build a ten-foot mosquito-netted veranda on the entrance and south sides rather than make it eight foot all round. He explained how useful would be such an addition as a summer parlour, but I insisted that only the complete circumference of a veranda could make

the cottage possible; and that one could easily add mosquito net-
ting and dividing doors when summer came. He smiled and said
nothing – just as I now smile and say nothing when I hear newcomers discuss the plans of next summer; and I determined to
drive into town the next day to find a carpenter and make the
necessary arrangements.

On the shady side-walk in South Qu'Appelle I met an Englishwoman who seemed like an old friend, since she and her
husband had pitched their tent one midsummer night on my
brother's territory. As a matter of fact, all the hospitality had
been on their side, since they bestowed upon us a much-needed
candle and strawberry jam, whilst all that was asked of us was
boiling water and space for the tent. But the visit had been an
event in our sojourn on the prairie. He was a barrister, and I
purposely had not asked his advice about the purchase of the
farm lest he should side with my brother and sister. But I asked
her to recommend us a carpenter.

She spoke highly of one who was just then employed at the
Church House. I went in and told him my business, and he said he
would draw up the estimate immediately and give me the list of
the lumber required; but for the estimate of that cost I must inquire of the lumber merchant. Mindful of my neighbour's solemn
warning, I impressed on him the fact that I must have the estimate
for the finished work, and would have nothing to do with a *time*
arrangement; and that when the veranda was completed I wanted
two granaries built, each to hold a thousand bushels; also I needed
some odds and ends in the house, the estimate for which he could
give me when the veranda was finished. To my utter astonishment the estimate came out at thirty-five dollars.

'But are you quite sure about the sum?' I asked. 'It is considerably less than I anticipated.'

'If the measurements are correct, that estimate covers it,' he
answered.

I inquired how long it would take, and he said about two or
three days, and that if I could send out for the lumber in time for
him to start on the following Friday he would come out with his
men, start them, and discuss the estimate for the other matters.

On the Friday he arrived at about eleven o'clock with three men. To my astonishment, as so far I had considered the Canadian casual in labour, they started at once, putting in a good hour's work before dinner, and by evening the west end of the veranda was an accomplished fact, and the greater part of the flooring in the south side was laid. I poured out my admiration of this Canadian method and scale of charges to my neighbour as he sat on the newly erected flooring waiting for his milk-pail to be filled.

'The charge is all right,' he said, 'but look out that he doesn't charge you time; although if they go on at this rate that won't be far out of his reckoning either.'

The next day the master unexpectedly took his departure with one of the men, promising to return early in the following week. On Monday one of the men retired to his room with lumbago. On Tuesday down came the rain, and in came the men. It was late in the afternoon of this dull day that I suggested to one of them that I wanted two little tables, and a kitchen cupboard and some shelves. He gladly started to work on these furnishing trifles, which if purchased at a store could not have cost more than ten dollars.

Towards the end of the week the master returned, and again work went forward merrily; but it was discovered that the measurement had been three feet out, and that additional lumber must be fetched. The granaries were then started. The contractor estimated the cost of the first at fourteen dollars, the second might be a little less. I suggested twenty-six dollars for the two, and he seemed to assent; but added that the cost of the veranda would slightly exceed his estimate owing to the fault in the measurement.

'How much more?' I inquired.

'Well, the stones have taken time to remove, and one thing and another made it a more troublesome job than I expected.'

'It won't come out at more than forty-five dollars, will it?' I said with anxiety, although as a matter of fact fifty dollars had been the original estimate in my mind; but had it exceeded that sum I should have escaped the folly of the veranda.

'Oh, certainly not more than that,' he said reassuringly; and within the week the veranda, the granaries, the odds and ends were all finished, and we all bade each other a pleasant farewell.

Within the month I was at South Qu'Appelle, and, encountering him in a store, asked for my bill. It was one hundred and twenty-five dollars.

Already I had discovered that of all sorts and conditions of wealth capital is the most powerfully winged. At first sight the amount subdued me even more than it annoyed me. It would have bought three milch cows and two calves or four sows and forty little pigs – or a horse. I took counsel of my neighbour.

'I knew he would do it; they always do,' he said consolingly. 'And if you buck at it he will simply give you a time bill. Have you got his estimate in writing?'

But the scrap of pencilled paper had fluttered anywhere; although even had I been able to produce it, the measurements which my neighbour had taken were incorrect. I reminded him of this not altogether without malice.

'The writing would have been evidence, and the difference easy to estimate on the figures given for the given dimensions,' he said. 'I knew when those men stayed on day after day so jolly well pleased with themselves and their quarters that, no matter what your estimate might be, they were being paid by time.'

I paid fifty dollars on account, referred to the estimate, and demanded a corrected account. Back came an absolutely confounding misstatement of time.

I approached my friend the barrister, and determined to fight out the matter even if I had to take down every shelf and small table to stand for my case. He was of the opinion that, as I had no written evidence, I should have but a poor chance of winning the case, and in his kind and cheerful way advised me to pay and look pleasant.

I reasoned with the contractor, who wouldn't move an inch. The men had returned that time list, which I could not contradict, as, having made it clear to him that I would accept no estimate calculated on time, I hadn't thought it necessary to make any note of the hours or even days. The only possible claim I could make against it, he assured me, was a charge for their board.

'And that you know quite well I shouldn't do,' I said in the heat of the moment. And he said 'Quite so.'

In the end I paid one hundred dollars, absolutely refusing to settle the balance unless the law obliged me to do so. I don't think for one moment the contractor was guilty of intentional dishonesty. Both of us were unbusinesslike, and I have no doubt when he received the time sheet from the men it was as severe a shock to him as was my bill to me. Possibly he considered that since one of us must pay for a careless transaction it should be the more careless of the two. Bitterness rankled in my heart over that deal for many a day, but in time we forget everything in Canada. It is a matter of regret too that I have no copy of the time list, as such a record of industry could never have been beaten, or even attained, by the most conscientious bee in the hive watched over by Maeterlinck. The incident proves that it is wisdom in all new-comers to insist that estimates for labour or other services should be presented formally in black on white.

5

Threshing

'Have you made any arrangements about threshing?' inquired our neighbour. 'Because if you have not, Guy Mazey will take on your job and mine as soon as he has finished his own. It's only a small outfit, but he is a reliable chap and will thresh our crops as carefully as his own. Russell Haynes wants him to go there, but if you agree he will come straight through to us after he has threshed himself out, and then go on to Haynes and finish. I don't think you will do better. There aren't many outfits round this year.'

I closed at once with this offer, and, with one's usual way of waving away the detail of responsibility, I considered the threshing arrangement made, and that I need think nothing more of it until the engine and gang came in at the gate. But there is a certain etiquette to be observed in the ceremony of threshing in Canada. Some eight days later I got belated on my way home from South Qu'Appelle and lost my way utterly and completely in the neighbourhood of home, until Charles Edward literally fell up against Guy Mazey's fence, and, guided by the barking of many dogs and a bright light, I came step by step to the comfortable cheer of Mrs. Mazey's kitchen. In the process of conversation I found that it was quite news to him that he was to thresh out the crop. It is probable in the dazzling brightness of the kitchen my greenness, standing out from the background of the pathetic darkness in which I had lost my way, stood me in good stead, since among the entire threshing-gang only one tittered audibly at my amazed discomfiture, and he was promptly shut up. I gladly shared the evening meal, and before Charles Edward and I were set upon the right road I had asked my host if he would be kind enough to thresh for me, and he had most graciously consented.

The charge was to be four cents a bushel for oats, and five cents for wheat; and he found all the stook teams. So that if one or both my teams were in the field he was due to pay me for the use of them; and the same law held good with the neighbours. But we were all more casual about payment in those days when threshing terms were comparatively low. In due course the engine arrived at my neighbour's, and Hilaria and I went over to make acquaintance with the Mazey family, who were always in the trail of their father, always choosing some form or another of work for play, and always happy. At that time they only numbered eight of the present eleven, and each seemed to have arrived within easy distance of the other. The eldest girl was driving a stook team, the eldest boy was fireman, the third girl had stooked from dawn till dark through the gathering of the harvest, and was still busy at one thing or another in the threshing field, whilst the second girl was at home preparing meals for the gang of fifteen men, and all the younger branches took care of themselves and each other. They were a healthy, jolly, friendly group, and in time we grew to know each other well. On that occasion I remember taking their photograph on my new camera, which to this day seldom registers a success.

Hilaria and I had more than one offer of help in the entertainment of our threshing party, but the only one she would hear of was Ella Carroll, the daughter of our neighbour, – the farmer and postmaster, Sam Carroll of Strathcarrol. We liked her because she was pretty, and we stood in no awe of her because she was only sixteen. Hilaria presided over the cook-stove, and Ella Carroll made scones by the hundred and raisin pies, apple pies, lemon pies, and all sorts and conditions of cakes just as casually and quickly as the average Englishwoman sits down and sews on buttons with an air of rest. I was henchman to Hilaria, and usually dispatched to fetch the meat and merchandize in the morning, and more meat and all the other things that had been forgotten from Fort Qu'Appelle in the afternoon.

For a day and a half all went merrily. The sun was generous indeed that year, and in October it was as deliciously warm by day as is the Riviera in April, and with bright, keen, moonlit, frost-kissed nights. The two new granaries had been drawn up side by side in the centre of the eighty-acre wheat-patch. The wheat was of excellent quality, plump, and of a deep gold colour, and hard as the shell of ripe nuts. In the bliss of ignorance we were unaware that it was freely sprinkled with wild oats.

'There must be three thousand bushels of grain,' said Lal. 'We have nearly filled the first granary, and that patch of cleared land looks to be barely one-tenth of the field.'

But the fact was that those two granaries never contained a thousand bushels of grain. There is a simple table in Canadian farm statistics by which one can calculate, through the number of pounds of grain due to a bushel, the amount of grain in a granary by measuring the amount of space it takes up. The rule is to multiply length by breadth by height by eight, and cut off the final figure. Thus a granary measuring fourteen feet by fourteen by seven should contain one thousand and ninety-seven bushels of wheat. Oats and barley take up more space in relation to weight. As oats weigh but thirty-five pounds to the bushel and barley forty-five against the sixty pounds which should find place in the orthodox bushel of wheat, thus the threshing-charge for the coarser grains is nominally less, but really higher, than the charge for wheat, and the Canadian plan of feeding oats in sheaf saves the cost of threshing and renders the winter chore of stock-feeding considerably lighter as the beasts consume first the oats and then the more appetizing portions of the oat-straw, but there is always a considerable amount left over for ready-to-hand bedding. However, some farmers think that the waste which is entailed through the shelling of the oats in stack outweighs the cost of threshing, and the greater number put aside sufficient sheaves for threshing to yield at least three hundred bushels. Wheat badly frozen or cut on the green side will fall below the average standard of weight to the bushel, but on the whole the method works out well, and its rule should be securely fixed in the memory of the grain-farmer. My ignorance cost me a considerable sum in more seasons than one, although I levelled up in one year through the ignorance or carelessness of the thresher-man. A new granary had been unsoundly built, and it broke down on its first journey out. It leaned slightly on its right side on an incline, and to its care was confided the grain drawn from a newly broken sixteen-acre field. The thresher-man debited me with three hundred and fifty bushels in that granary, but afterwards when I had sold three hundred and fifty bushels there remained between eighty and a hundred bushels, which I treasured for seed. The grain was sold on the street, and the dealers at the local elevator are the last in the world to err on the wrong side. The grain, too, was very fine, and perfectly ripe; but it must have weighed out at the rate of eighty-five pounds to the bushel to have accounted for the margin.

Apropos of the newly built granaries of my first harvest a story in connexion with bulk and space will serve to show how, among other things, stories grow on the prairie. A neighbour who had been working for Guy Mazey at that first threshing, and between then and now has managed to become the possessor of three farms, was driving his own stook team at my harvest of 1911.

The weather was fiendishly cold. Many of the gang were standing by one of the two granaries waiting for something in connexion with the engine to thaw out, and the topic of conversation was, as is usual at threshing-time, the quality and quantity of the grain.

'D'you mind the first year you came to the place, and Guy Mazey threshed you out, and charged you at the rate of a thousand bushels to each of them two granaries, an' you paid it?' he inquired.

'Not he nor I,' I answered. 'I'm not likely to forget my first year for many reasons, but, as a matter of fact, the grain was not measured at all. I paid Guy Mazey a hundred dollars spot cash on account, and he took my figure of weight from the return bills of the elevator net – not even *gross*. When it was all sold we calculated what was left for seed, and in the following spring I paid him the balance.'

'Took the figures from the elevator weigh-bills! Golly! I wish all the threshing outfits would work out their sums that way. My returns ain't never once been quite up to the level of the threshing bill. Wall now, if that ain't news to me! I've always heard tell that he charged you a thousand bushels each for them two granaries – an' that you paid it. Any you fellows heard the same?' he demanded.

'Sure thing! That's right,' came the chorus.

To return to the threshing of 1905. On the second day down came a snowstorm.

'It's horribly annoying for you,' said our neighbour, 'but Guy means to shut down and pull over to Haynes. They have their wheat stacked, so it will thresh out all right in spite of the snow. But he is quite right not to risk this. We shall probably get the Indian summer after the snowstorm, which means six or eight weeks of very hot weather, so that if the grain passed into the granary in a moist condition it would probably shoot, which would be ruinous. He will pull in again directly he has finished with Haynes. But it's hard luck having the bother twice over as it were in your first experience of threshers.'

'I don't know that I am so very sorry,' said Hilaria. 'It's a respite at least. And they are all very kind and nice, and really no trouble. As for bucking wood and drawing water, why two of them bucked enough for a week in an hour. And when I think of those harvest worthies looking on with their hands in their pockets, I feel one can't be too decent to them.'

'Oh, they are pleasant enough,' I allowed, 'but it's the eternal cooking and smell of cooking. And then one's so awfully afraid that there shouldn't be enough when they come trooping in. Lal says it's a point of honour to do them *magnificently* – the farmers' wives do anything to outrival the reputation of each other. Every kind of iced cake beneath the sun – stewed fruit – canned fruit – whipped cream – junket and heaven knows what!'

'Don't take the slightest notice of Lal's fussiness,' advised Hilaria. 'He is either "pulling our leg" or doesn't know any more than we do. Yesterday just half an hour before dinner he came in with the tale that three of the men were Jews and wouldn't touch pork under any condition. I had two joints of pork in the oven, and of course there was no more room, so I had to draw on the beef-steak I had in reserve for supper – to say nothing of the extra annoyance and trouble at the last moment. And to crown it all – did *not* those three Jews eat pork? You should have seen them!'

The Indian summer followed the snowstorm, and in three days back came the threshing outfit. The little engine took things easily, and Guy Mazey had decreased the number of his gang, so that it was four days before they finished, but they were a quiet, well-behaved group of men, although drawn from many nations, and, barring the inevitable drudgery attached to the washing-up as well as the cooking of three heavy meals a day, they were no trouble.

It was on the last afternoon that I went down to the Fort to replenish our store of sausages for the final breakfast, and, taking the pace at the lazy will of Charles Edward, I only reached home just before supper.

Hilaria met me on the veranda with cheeks aflame, and wrath in her blue eyes, which always seemed the bluer in the nearness of her blue overall.

'It is quite too bad of you not to have managed to get home before,' she said resentfully. 'There have been callers – troops of them! The first contingent arrived in quite the jolliest car just after I had finished laying the table for supper, and the last just as I was hoping the others were intending to depart. Cooking beefsteak for a dozen men is hardly a merely temporary occupation. Oh, it was humiliating! This beastly country – how I loathe it! My feet are sore with walking over the stubble last Sunday, and then standing for ever and ever on that greasy kitchen floor. And I had put on the hideous pair of shoes we bought at Lipton when we were waiting for the lost baggage. That was not enough – the threshers had left the basin that twelve of them had washed their hands in on the veranda just outside the front door. – And alongside were their towels. – You know their towels!'

'It does sound a little appalling,' I allowed. 'Never mind – I hope you gave them tea.'

'Oh, I gave them tea, and they only stayed about half an hour, but it felt like eternity. They said they wouldn't have come had they known it was threshing, and that kind of thing, and I've no doubt they understood. But there was a man with them. And my blue overall, a skirt shorter than a petticoat – and those awful shoes!'

'You needn't worry about the overall,' I consoled her. 'I should never wear anything else if I were you.'

'It's all very well for you to say nice things,' she said ungratefully. 'You weren't there.'

'Who was the late arrival?' I inquired.

'Oh, Mrs. Dugald Bertie. She's charming!'

'Really! How?'

'Beautiful eyes. And at this loose end of the world *bien soignée*. She stayed quite a while after the others had gone, and was quite nice. I could almost have poured out to her about the shoes. Her gloves were most fasky – the Indians made them. She is coming again, and she wants me – that is, of course, *us* – to go down.'

'If there are to be callers and so forth, I suppose we shall have to buy chairs and that kind of thing, shan't we?' I suggested.

'Oh, I don't know. There was no hint of "Pleased to make your acquaintance" in the quite natural way in which they attached themselves to the bench and Tate's sugar boxes. I suppose the cheque-book having swallowed so many extraordinary camels lately has indigestion at the mere thought of the gnat-like proportions of tables and chairs.'

'Go for a long walk,' I recommended, 'and for once let me finish getting supper, wash up, and prepare the breakfast. Did they come early for Ella?'

'Yes; she is going to a box-social. And if you don't mind I would rather hold on to my own chores this last night. But I really am getting a little played out.'

Before noon of the next day the last bag from the last load of oats had been emptied into one end of the old granary. There seemed to be oats enough to last for ever, but our neighbour looked ominous.

'Not more than two hundred and fifty bushels,' he said. 'I'm afraid you will have to be buying in the spring. With so little hay this amount of oats won't tide you over. The old man never grew many oats, but he was the finest hay and wood gatherer in these parts. There is quite a good stack of oat-straw, which you must keep for feed, and just use the wheat-straw for bedding.'

Guy Mazey departed in the trail of his outfit. He told me he was coming back to measure the grain, but he didn't come, and it was in this way I sent him a cheque for one hundred dollars on account, and suggested that he should take the weight returns from the weigh-bills received at the elevator, and I would pay him the balance. He accepted the suggestion in his quiet even way without even a lurking smile, and I hadn't the smallest idea it was a little unusual.

It was my brother's suggestion that we should start hauling at once, and, as everybody seemed to be waiting for all the money I could get, I agreed. It was chiefly owing to this that no work was done on the land that autumn, and what hay there was remained cocked in the sloughs. Meanwhile, every morning the wagon-load of wheat went into the elevator, and afterwards we cheerfully counted dollars.

6

Wheat sales – the fall of the leaf – Le Bret

My brother and I had come to an arrangement by which he worked for me at the rate of twenty dollars a month, and over the business of hauling the grain he was far and away the best man at the game that ever fell to my lot. He got up at daylight, cooked his own breakfast, and we usually heard the wheels of the wagon as the sun rose up from the horizon. He made the fourteen miles of distance to South Qu'Appelle, which at that time was my nearest wheat town, in about three and a half hours, took from one to two hours' rest, getting home at about three thirty, in time to load up for the next day. At first we tried the big teams on one day and the middle-weight the next, but Jess, the mare, was distinctly on the light side for hauling, although Dick took it as gamely as he took everything else in his splendid life. The trails too at that early hour in the morning were soundly starched by autumn frost, which made the going easy, although on one occasion the wagon got into a rut, and Hilaria and I had to rush to the rescue in very little more than our night attire, as she had felt that my brother's shout for aid couldn't possibly signify anything less than a broken leg.

The first load went out on October 20. It graded No. 1 Northern and fetched sixty cents a bushel. Wheat is usually low in the market immediately after harvest, and if one has sufficient capital and horse-power to hold sales over until May or June, it can make anything from ten to one hundred per cent. difference in returns. For example, in 1906 the average sale of the bulk of the crop was about sixty-four cents, but I had about thirty bushels held in reserve, and in September I sold it for a dollar a bushel at the South Qu'Appelle elevator, which equals one dollar seventeen at Fort William. A farmer in my neighbourhood had twenty thousand bushels in reserve that year. I think he got out at rather over a dollar a bushel, but the price is unusual, and a sign of bad times rather than good. By December 31 I had sold over 1797 bushels, and I held about 160 in reserve for seed, although in the end I also marketed this and bought other seed. The total returns that year amounted to two hundred and fifteen pounds ten shillings and tenpence. The experience, disappointments, and mistakes of several years have taught me that the wheat crop on a Canadian farm should stand for net profit, chargeable only with its threshing bill and cost of binder-twine. Sufficient capital should be invested in stock at the outset to ensure a comfortable living and an easy mind in spite of August or early September frost, which hangs as a sword over the prairie. The sum of dairy produce from three milch cows and the annual sale of four steers and twenty pigs should be sufficient to cover the wages of a hired man, taxes, and one's household and simple personal expenditure for the year, under which plan the produce of the wheat crop would rank as an addition to one's capital.

In that first year against my harvest receipts was the sum for harvest labour, binder-twine, threshing bill, daily expenses attached to hauling; and the only addition stock offered was through the sale of seven small pigs, which cost twenty-two dollars fifty and sold for thirty-five dollars. Also in the light of the year that followed I must acknowledge my housekeeping bills to be of extraordinary amount, the sum total between August 23 and December 31 standing at five hundred and nineteen dollars thirty. Many a woman has come to me within the last two years with a proposal to start farming in Canada on less than that amount. It must be remembered that for harvest and threshing seasons, and during the visit of the carpenters, the provisions account was heavy, and nothing is cheap in Canada if one has to buy it; but it is possible to provide oneself with almost everything but groceries from the farm, and with even two good milch cows grocery bill and dairy sales should balance accounts. Indeed, I remember in looking over the ready-made farms in the Shaughnessy colonies I came across an able man and woman who assured me they were able to pay the total expenses of their living – barring, of course, the land payments – from the produce of three milch cows.

Also my housekeeping bill included some articles of furniture and a few expensive necessities such as cook-stove, fifteen dollars; wood for fuel, twenty-four dollars; second-hand box-stove with bedroom heater, eight dollars. Two bedsteads, two tables, half a dozen chairs, pots and pans, &c. Then there was a suite of bedroom furniture from Eaton's of Winnipeg, which cost eight dollars, and a bath which cost twelve dollars. The 'suite' was really a consolation through the years that followed. The dressing-table consisted of two big drawers and a bevelled mirror, eighteen inches by twenty-four; and none can fully appreciate a mirror of those dimensions so truly as the one who has shared a hand-glass for three months with two bachelor men on the prairie.

The bath I had taken out from England sprung a hopeless leak on the journey, so that directly we left the shelter of canvas for four walls and a roof we sent for one. On the day it arrived we stood like pilgrims round a shrine whilst the twelve-dollar masterpiece from Eaton's was safely delivered from its wrappings, and carefully placed upon the floor of the veranda. It was a thing of joy, and long enough even for us. At last in perfect accord we marvelled at its lustre, its convenience, its cheapness. Hilaria, with the professional air which she reserved as an effect from a voluntarily curtailed season of hospital training, affirmed that the ingenious and most convenient contrivance for letting out the water alone was worth the money, and in the delightful enthusiasm and anticipation of the moment the matter of letting in the water entirely escaped consideration. It struck my brother first.

'How in the name of the prophets and all holy wonders are we to fill it?' he demanded. 'The well is three hundred yards off, and will run dry at the very sight of it!'

I felt it my duty to support the reputation of the well – which my predecessor assured me had cost him a hundred dollars and had never been known to run dry – and I announced that the two stookers would, of course, haul the water.

'I should like to meet the Canadian who would haul water for an Englishman's bath, or an Englishwoman's either! He would be the rarest bird I have yet encountered in Canada. However, as you have bought the thing, I suppose we must see what can be done. There are four pails, two lard containers which leak, and the potato boiler. I think we might make a faint impression in three journeys.'

We ran lightly to the well with our empty pails, but my sister and I returned slowly enough beneath the burden, which in those days was new to us. My brother swung along in front, reciting 'More servants wait on man' with fine sarcasm, which I feel sure 'the beautiful psalmist of the seventeenth century' would have been the first to pardon had he found himself within kicking distance of a like circumstance. At the end of the third journey we agreed to draw lots for the bath, which had been conveyed with much difficulty into the kitchen. Afterwards it took our combined force to carry it to the veranda, which was the only place from which the water could pass through the ingeniously contrived exit without disaster. Within the month we unanimously decided to abandon it in favour of some less imposing vessel of ablution, and I agreed to sell it at its original price to a friend who embraced me at the mere suggestion of the deal. I let her have it with an easy conscience as she lived on the Lake shore. It was not my fault, but the irony of fate, that within six months her husband built a bungalow at the top of the Western Hills, to which water had to be hauled from a distance of two miles. The last time I caught sight of it was in the spring of 1910, when I went to buy seed oats of its owner. It was still a bath, but dedicated to the pickling of seed grain, and for the first time I honestly wished I hadn't parted with it.

Lal being on the trail day by day, Hilaria and I decided that it was time to return our calls. It was not quite so easy as it sounds, in spite of the fact that Jess, the mare of our light team, went really well in single harness, so that we were no longer at the mercy of the mood of Charles Edward; but the fact was that neither Hilaria nor I knew the way to hitch up. Our neighbour's shack was almost half a mile away across the big wheat-field, and whenever a desperate and unexpected occasion arose for going down to the Fort we used to shout for him; and even then neither of us thought of learning the order and detail of the harness, it looked so clumsy and heavy and complicated; and Hilaria always seemed so sure that our neighbour liked coming. As a matter of fact, it wasn't until the following spring that I mastered the simple method of strapping those three simple main fittings which contribute to the altogether of single harness.

The occasion was memorable. I had been asked to an afternoon party at which I really wanted to be present, and the hired man had gone into town. For half an hour I worked, very nearly wept, and utterly failed to make shaft strappings pan out back or front. In despair I led pony and buggy, persuaded together by an arrangement of my own, to the nearest neighbours, a Canadian family who hadn't long arrived in the neighbourhood. I knew there were quite a number of girls, and one always seemed to meet them in their buggy, so I felt sure they would be able to do it for me.

They knew very little more than I, but with some difficulty we improved on my arrangement, and all went well until I got half-way down Troy Hill, when a shaft shot up in the air. A passer-by came to the rescue, and, overcome with the frankness of his criticism, there and then I learned the simple art of hitching-up.

To return to my story. Our neighbour persuaded us that there was no hurry at all in returning calls in Canada, but that on no account should we miss seeing the hills in their glorious attire before the fall of the leaf. We promptly agreed to drive with him the next afternoon, and he came to fetch us in a buggy distinctly built for two only. However, all sense of discomfort left us as the horses raced across the prairie trail to make a bee-line for the *coulée*, which leads to the lake-shore trail.

No words can paint the beauty of the transfiguration of the fall in Canada. In the Qu'Appelle valley the trees are a maze of every tint of gold. Here and there is sometimes a touch of scarlet, and in Ontario the autumn carpet is clear vermilion, but in Saskatchewan the predominating tint of autumn is gold, and its effect against the rose and opal tint of sky and the grey-green of the landscape, and the sharp cold contrast of the water is beautiful beyond expression. At the foot of the *coulée* colour reigned on every side, the very horses seemed to feel its sway as they danced through entwining trees down the sharp incline with the gay irresponsibility of a British four-year-old dancing from cover to cover; only usually the light-heartedness of the old country horse means ignorance, whilst the light-footedness of the true Canadian stands for self-confidence born of the absolute freedom of the first three years of life.

The roads in Canada are interesting, and historical in the finest sense of the word, because indissolubly one with the history of man – of the men who tramp them, or grade them through all manner of difficulty with the dogged determination of those who refuse to look behind. Of all great examples of this making of the way in Canada, the grade of the Canadian Pacific Railway just beyond Glazier House in the heart of the Rockies seems supreme; certainly it is the most impressive, that winding, curling, persistent, indomitable man-made way, hanging by its teeth for the defence of its life to the great obstacle. In climbing or descending that splendid pass the Spirit of Power always seems to hover in the hush of the shadowed silent hole in the hills, as though God breathed eternal thanks for the patience and power of mankind in the place where just a man or so made a great way for the race.

And by the southern shore of the eastern lake of Fort Qu'Appelle there runs another conquering ribbon of a road, graded into the hip of those fertile heights which mark the awe and ache of distance between the shadowed sheet of water, stirred with the restless pain and longing of the temporal why, and that far-off shrine where the sun stands for power, and the moon for peace, and 'stars leap out through blackest night.' Winding along until it reaches an open sweep of hill-sheltered *coulée*, where the Indians and the English alike love to pitch their tents, the lake-shore way suddenly pulls itself together, tightens teeth with a snap, and climbs the vertical wall of 'Hairpin Bend' without looking backward or sideway into danger, until it reaches the sun-kissed summit where scarlet lilies first grew out of camp-fires in June time for love of those dark-eyed Indian babies, the echo of whose beauty still lingers in the flesh and the spirit about their homeland by the lovely lakes of Qu'Appelle.

Just across the lake in the height of a hill is planted the cross which marks the end of the Mission Trail, and beneath, in its shadow, is the great Industrial School for Indian boys and girls, the organization of which has been the life-work of one Father Hugenard, a French priest and one of the most useful members of the British Empire.

The village of Le Bret is built on the choicest site on the sunny or northern side of the eastern lake of Fort Qu'Appelle. Constructive genius is in evidence not only in every detail of the building and work of the industrial schools, but throughout the village. The schools are built on the lake shore at the west end of the village, and occupy very much the same site and general position as the Hôtel Bristol in Beaulieu on the Mediterranean. The garden shore curves out into the lake; one steps from a bed of brilliant poppies, across a stile, to the slim beach on which the delicate waves of the lake lap and gurgle. In summer-time the garden is a mass of bloom. Pale pink petunias, rose-coloured creeping geranium, sweet pea in profusion and a regiment of sweet william in uniform of glorious tint lend that delicious rosy glow of the morning to this charming lake-garden. Beyond is a neat and luxuriant bed of strawberries, then tomatoes, rhubarb, lettuce, carrots, onions, cucumbers, gourds of all species, monster cabbages and cauliflowers literally leap out of the fine soil directly the grip of zero is loosened, and earth awakes with redoubled energy from the enslavement of sleep to the liberty of service.

Within the schools the quiet cheerful nuns preside over the education and well-being of the girl-children, and school and craft masters train the boys; so that the girls leave school equipped with an excellent education and domestic training, and the boys are taught a useful trade or craft, besides learning by doing in the garden and farm attached to the schools, in order that they may be able to take possession of the opportunities which civilization brought to the wonderful treasure-land of their fathers. That neither education nor training can wean them altogether from the sway of the spirit of Hiawatha, who can wonder or deplore? As you walk through the bright and sunny dormitories it seems the best possible arrangement that so many dear small bodies should be tucked safely and snugly into so many snow-white beds; but when you get back to the lake-shore trail again and watch the evening sky as it makes its rose and opal offering to the lake, when you sniff the pungent odour of prairie herbs, the heart-warming smell of the camp-fires which mark the freeman's tent, when you breathe in and breathe out the air of liberty, and the sway of the fascination of life in the open tugs at the heart-strings, you know that the children of Hiawatha pay the price for those opportunities of civilization.

Not that the gentle art of pleasure is neglected in the general preparation for life. A glance through the composition books proves the culture of the imagination to be proceeding on fertile soil, and signs of the love of joy are in evidence in the playground, and in the interested and intelligent faces of the children. One glorious summer afternoon I had driven some English visitors over to the schools, and after much inspection and more inquiry; after having climbed the tower, and talked with the saddler, the bootmaker, the carpenter and the baker, we leaned over the balcony rail and rested from our labours whilst the kind nun related to us the history of one or two fair small people among the darker family, the main point of which was that Father Hugenard, who is one of the very few absolutely practical clever persons with whom 'the quality of mercy' is always at home, finds in himself a godfather and godmother on desperate occasions, and all the nuns nod Amen. Suddenly there was the impression of the opening of a great big door and a sense of wide liberty, followed by the crescendoing chorus of joy – then the patter of many bare feet treading the path of pleasure. The children were off for their daily swim in the lake, the nun explained.

And we listened to the resounding splash and watched that jolly band of bathers not without envy.

All visitors are impressed with the good manners of those boys and girls. In Britain we unveil our sense of the fitness and beauty and power of this grace in great places. How proud are we yet of the beautiful manners of King Edward VII, which persuaded the French nation to forgive 1871, and forget the long bill they had against us; and in St. Paul's Cathedral on the tomb of our great soldier, General Gordon, all who pass by read 'Manners makyth man'; but in the industrial school at Le Bret 'Manners maketh man' is carved in 'Everyman.'

But besides all these things Father Hugenard and his brother-priests of the Roman Catholic Church have most truly bestowed on the children of the darker race the consolation of religion. On Easter Day I was lunching with some friends who have a cottage among the hills which line the lake-shore trail between Le Bret and the Soo village, which is the chief centre of the remnant of the tribes in the Qu'Appelle valley. Sitting in the porch, we watched the Indians returning from their eight-mile walk to Mass. Singly or in little groups, they swung past with that soothing grace of movement which they seem to have caught from the swaying of branches, just in the same happy manner in which they have charmed into their smile the spirit of human kindness which, together with their innate dignity and simplicity, endows them with such pleasing attraction.

On that Easter morning a squaw, who walked alone, came through the gate and towards us. She had walked from the Soo village to the Mission church to make her communion, and feeling a little weary, through the length of the way and the heat of the sun, most gratefully hoped – which is the best of all possible ways to hope – for a cup of tea. She made all known to us through the sign of the Cross and a very few English words distributed generously among the fascinating sounds of her mother-tongue. It was so easy to understand that Easter Day was really a beautiful oasis in her life. The Indians are quick to catch in religion that fragrance of rosemary which all bring out 'for remembrance' from the other side of the horizon. In the brave

and patient eyes of Tosh the squaw Easter incense burned – the
sacrifice of Father Hugenard and his brother-priests was clearly
accepted.

Only the day before I had given a small child of civilization,
and another branch of the Christian Church, an Easter picture
from an English magazine.

'What is it?' demanded the child. 'Your daddy?'

'No; it is a picture of the Resurrection,' I answered lamely.

'What's that?' inquired another, whilst the picture passed
from one to the others, attracting interest, but also the unmistakable air of wonder.

'But surely you know,' I said. Suddenly a beam of intelligence
shot across the face of the eldest girl, who must have been quite
fifteen. 'I know,' said she. 'He riz.'

The Church of Rome in general and Father Hugenard in particular seem to get wonderful results in their method of dealing
with humankind. Possibly it's because they never miss the 'descent into Hades,' which is laid before them in the confessional.
'Tout comprendre c'est tout pardonner.' Not that for one moment
could one fail in admiration of the work done by the Anglican
Church in the Prairie Provinces, which is and always has been of
superlative quality as far as it goes. But in the pioneer phase of
the development of Canada, if the work was less, it was hopelessly scattered, with very little railway, few good roads, very
few men, and hardly any money to work with. Just a handful of
brave, unselfish, dauntless clergy of the wealthy and powerful
Church of England making 'bricks without straw' on the prairie.
History can never tell what they did, and did without, in those
days in order that the Church might not fail her children in their
deepest need. The diocese of Qu'Appelle was coextensive with
the old district of Assiniboia, its boundaries about five hundred
by two hundred miles; the priests of its remote and far-scattered
parishes had sometimes to make journeys of over a hundred
miles on foot for the sake of the 'two or three gathered together'
in the far corners of the Empire. Among this gallant band the
names of Rev. the Hon. A.J.R. Anson, sometime rector of Woolwich and afterwards Bishop of Qu'Appelle; Bishop Burn, for-

merly rector of St. Peter's, Jarrow; the Very Rev. J.P. Sargent, the present Dean of Qu'Appelle – who was at one time an officer in the 62nd Foot now 1st Batt. Wiltshire Regiment; Archdeacon Mackay, Archdeacon Tims, Archdeacon Dobie, Canon Stocker, Canon Beal, now Secretary to the Archbishop's Western Canada Mission – and the Rev. F. Palgrave, will never fade from the noble roll of the Church of England's pioneer priests of the prairie.

With the extension of the railway, the increase of the population and prosperity, and the extraordinary work of the archbishops, bishops and clergy and the generous support of the laity, the establishment of the Church of England along the beaten track of Western Canada became firm and far-reaching; although in the diocese of Qu'Appelle, now ruled by the Right Rev. Malcolm Macadam Harding, priests and dignitaries are still subject to the strain of incessant work, not always free from sordid and distressing worry. Nor do cathedrals and churches of Canada flatter the generosity of those dwellers in the Mother Country who have the privilege of the use of our common inheritance of Westminster, York, St. Albans, Canterbury, Salisbury, and the whole glorious group of the historic and beautiful cathedrals, abbeys, and churches of the United Kingdom, in addition to the treasures tradition has stored in Europe at the gate. There is not a church of the Anglican Church in Canada which could be named as an offering to the Church worthy of those who enjoy its gift from the past. Millions are spent freely on the great Provincial Houses of Parliament in Canada. Miles of patriotic and appreciative sentiment overflowed the British newspapers when the hope of Canada's noble contribution to the Navy was received, and, although that hope has not yet passed into act, the gift of a million to Regina to build the cathedral for which the Church of England in Saskatchewan has so ardently hoped and prayed would still be an appropriate thank-offering from those who love and value and really, if it came to the point, would quite simply and willingly give their lives to spare our sacred treasures of the past from the mad destruction of war. In England too it should be more clearly emphasized and understood that it is absolutely impossible for the Church of England in Canada to keep pace with the hundreds of thousands of immigrants who flock to the prairies from all the ends of the earth. It was to meet the special claim of this ever-growing need that the Archbishop's Western Canada Fund was started in 1910 after a conference between the Archbishops of Canterbury, York, and Rupertsland during the Pan-Anglican gathering in 1909. The Rev. Douglas Ellison and Archdeacon Boyd, leaders of proven constructive genius, were selected for the organization of the work which was to break the trail of the Church of England on the prairie alongside the trail of the newcomers to the prairie homesteads. The work is financed by the British in the Mother Country who trouble to think and to care and to help those who are fighting out the battle of our Empire with the pick and spade on unbroken soil. It is manned by a band of young British clergymen who from the first fell into step and line with their charge, enduring all those phases of life which are not easy to endure with amazing patience and cheerfulness. There are days in the life of the homesteader's first year or so when not even the inspiration of Pan in his finest mood, nor the hope of the future consolation of far more than one's fair share of dollars, can induce one to work one's way through the arduous toil of the daily round. Those sporting parsons with their splendid fund of enthusiasm for the thing that is higher somehow filled the need. The day of their coming is really *Sunday*, and patience and endurance are swift to acknowledge the fact in playing the game through all the other days. The Archbishop's Mission is doing truly great and most valuable work in the social as well as the spiritual development of the far-out prairie population in forming centres of social and religious interest, building churches, beckoning schools, and by every possible way of admirable organization binding together the Mother Country and her daughter nation with the beautiful bond of the National Church.

But on the first day of my visit to Le Bret the Archbishop's Western Canada Mission was still a voiceless thought, and the splendid example of mission work at Le Bret, which one could but admire, seemed to belong to Rome. Even in the village the

Church was in full sway. The atmosphere was and still is French. In the centre of the lake shore amid many trees and sunflowers, was the only church, and close at hand the clergy-house of the Mission. Further on there was a convent school for the higher education of girls; also there were two good stores, the post office, and a boarding-house, but no hotel; and the little village under the cross seemed to have the peace and restfulness of a quiet hive of industry.

Passing out from the school buildings, we drove towards the sunset and Fort Qu'Appelle around that winding, silent shore trail which we prophesied would become a great pleasure-ground of the North-West. At the Fort we halted to collect our mail, and directly they scented the home trail the horses flew on their way.

'Would you think it was going to rain?' inquired our neighbour, as we came within sight of the cottage.

We scanned the horizon. Across the valley the prairie might have been the deep blue sea itself on an incoming tide, but the sky was of clear pale rose, flushed here and there with the hectic glow of geranium.

'No indeed!' said Hilaria.

'We shall have rain to-morrow,' he prophesied. And on the morrow it rained, and the next day and the next; and when we drove again into the valley the glorious phase of the fall had fled, and even though the intense heat of the sun of the Indian summer forbade us to dream that winter was near, we knew that our sweet day had been drawn into the quiet chapel of memory only just in time, and that the Canadian summer had fled.

7

Friends and acquaintances
in Fort Qu'Appelle

Hilaria vowed that as she was not remaining in the country there was no need for her to pay calls or go to church.

It was not altogether surprising about church because on the only occasion we had an opportunity of being present at an Anglican service during our summer on the prairie the clergyman, who took morning service at his other parish twenty-three miles west, and afternoon service at his third parish ten miles west, had been an involuntary absentee; and in spite of the fact that the lay-reader did his best with that portion of the liturgy where lay-readers need not fear to tread, the service was a little dull. In England we had the inestimable privilege of living in the very near neighbourhood of Westminster Abbey, and in new surroundings one is inclined at first to screen the hallowed and hallowing associations of home in a winding-sheet of loyalty. But the exquisite shadows and sounds of the Abbey have a way of finding channel through the tenderest intentions, and in those early days as one sat in the simple little church of Fort Qu'Appelle, now and again the breath of the holy beauty of Westminster seemed to live in nearest nearness and full measure in the heart, and for a moment one was not homesick, but at home.

It was at the close of morning service on a Sunday in September that I made the acquaintance of the younger members of a family to whose forsaken bungalow my pony still offers the unfailing homage of a homeward turn. The head of the house, who was also the architect of the bungalow, the gardener of the garden, the father of its mistress, the grandfather of the girls and the breadwinner for all, was one Samuel Brodie, a British pioneer on survey in Canada, and the nephew of Sir Benjamin Brodie, the distinguished surgeon and founder of St. George's Hospital.

We had encountered him on more than one occasion of our visits to the Fort from the prairie. Already on the far side of his seventieth year he was a small, lithe, active person with the arresting eyes of the pioneer – eager, very blue, and quite young, they were the kind of eyes which seem to have the power of seeing what is happening across the rim of the horizon, as though certainty had flashed just one stolen glance through the window of hope. Even as strangers he had always given us pleasant greeting, and we wondered if he had learned that courtesy from the Indians.

At first we seldom caught sight of him at the bungalow, but one Sunday I had gratefully accepted the hospitality of breakfast, and he came in with a sunbeam from his morning chores. He was a member of the 'Church of St. Thomas' himself, and, as a rule, avoided discussion which might lead to argument with members of the Churches of St. Peter or St. Paul; but platitudes are impossible at breakfast, one has to be silent or talk. He was deeply interested in the trend of thought in the Mother Country, but he was also very human, and when his rather assertive reference to certain irksome conditions obliged me to say that lots of miserable old prejudices and habits had dropped off out of sheer decay, and if it was not exactly general it had at least ceased to be criminal for even the clergy to use their power to think, I am not sure that he wasn't just a little disappointed. Honest emigrants from the Mother Country know that they leave much behind that softens and sweetens life. He loved the North-West as being his very own country in the finest sense of the term, but he must have missed his intellectual peers badly, and although I feel sure he would never have acknowledged even to himself the most far-off touch of *heim weh*, he was deeply conscious of the unseverable quality of the home-tie which like the last string of the lyre in Watts' 'Hope' won't snap, because it can't. He was a keen admirer of Herbert Spencer, and on one occasion when he was driving me inch by inch into a cul-de-sac I propped up my defence on a passage of Emerson: 'Ah! Emerson,' he said, 'but you know I am afraid he permitted himself to be drawn just a little into the clouds; follow Herbert Spencer, *the one*, who has dared to think with all his mind, and striven to think with all his might.' I refused to acknowledge the limitation implied in '*the one*,' but I felt that to name others would be only to invest them in his mind with the pall of clouds. Nor was it the smallest use shouting 'clouds of glory.' His eyes had easily crossed the horizon, but he had vowed no wings should carry him where his feet might not tread. He was far and away the most interesting and fascinating intellectual personality that I encountered in Canada, and in common with some others among our most powerful thinkers he was simple, clean-hearted, human, and kind. Upon the altar of thought he had raised one of the strongest friendships ever held fast between man and man, and that with one of my neighbours, a man of keen intellect and many acres, who lived the unadorned life of a bachelor on the prairie. The greater part of each available Sabbath was passed with Sandy Stuart in the discussion of things which matter, and the very last glimpse I caught of him was in climbing the *coulée* on his short cut to the little house wherein his brave, bright, and busy mind found refreshment and inspiration in the mind of another. Nor did his influence stop short at the boundary of a kindred spirit. All the friends of Sandy Stuart – typical old timers finding love and life in the land in which they lived, and uniting in a solemn hatred of class-distinction as the best word they knew to express their innate sense of the dignity and force of self-respect – men who would work alongside Duke or Dukaboon, as man with man, using the shibboleth of Dick, Tom, and Harry, raised their hat in reverence to the claim of the master-mind.

'He'll be greatly missed,' said one of the best of them, my neighbour John McLeay, as we talked, with the regret of those who lose, of the fine and simple old man who had gone down east for a holiday, after twenty years of survey work in the North-West, and then in a brief moment of sleep had crossed the horizon. 'Eh,' said the old Highlander, 'I had a great respect for *Mister* Brodie; he was a fine scholar.'

At the time that the two Canadian-born grand-daughters of Mr. Brodie first claimed acquaintance in the most natural and kindly manner, one had just turned up her hair, and presided at the organ, the other looked about fifteen, and still attended the public school with all the other boys and girls of the village.

They walked with me to the foot of Cemetery Hill, and explained that their mother had been unable to call on us because they had no conveyance, and in the end I believe I was their guest without that tribute to the orthodox. They have always seemed to me typical Canadian girls, probably because I knew them more intimately than any others, and in the perfect appointments of their simple and delightful home I also drew my type of Canadian home which did not run the gauntlet of public opinion without occasional attack. The peculiar charm in the household appointments and delightful appearance of these North-Western girls was that everything seemed to arise without effort, never by any chance was one permitted to 'smell the lamp'; but later on I found that there lay behind it the strenuous day by day effort of a British-Canadian woman, in whom was the tradition of the Mother Country controlled by the splendid energizing impulse of the North-West.

These girls of the North-West have a peculiarly characteristic way of investing their household tasks with an air of accomplishment. I remember being their guest in a neighbouring city after they had left the happy valley. My hostess and I returned about nine o'clock to the fresh and breezy note of entertainment. The salon was asleep, and the adjoining dining-room solemn, but from the kitchen came cheer. The younger girl in her evening gown was presiding over an ironing table, and rows of snow-white, perfectly laundered linen, which included even big impossible details, such as table-cloths and sheets to mark the happy end of 'the tale of a tub.' In the background was Mademoiselle Sans-Gêne neither tired nor triumphant, martyr nor saint. The Canadian girl's artistic rendering of the daily round, of course, has its other side; unconsciously she can treat art, that so rarely reveals itself amid new conditions, as a matter of fact. In the days when I first knew this family I found the elder to be remarkably musical. Her technique was almost brilliant, her memory sure, her sense of rhythm correct, her ear true; but her touch needed tone, and her phrasing thought. I had studied music in Europe, so for a time we worked together. She worked well, sometimes almost with enthusiasm, but she could never rise above the sway of bricks and mortar, even in the most persuasive and directly consoling of all the arts. She could work for the effect of beauty, but not for just beauty. The work of Beethoven, Bach, Chopin, and Liszt was in complete possession of her fingers at the first glance of the eye, and at home in her memory almost as quickly. Her ear was so unerring that the professor seldom dared to play before the pupil. But she fell short of the artist in this same unconscious manner in which the sister performed a household task as an artist. Before the altar of Apollo himself one felt she would have cried, 'Cui bono?' A few years later she discovered from the applause of the people, but she might have learned in the whisper of a god, that she was a chosen channel of delight. 'The principles of art are eternal,' but the story seems to make the distinction between the European and the American artist.

The simple bungalow in which this delightful family lived at Fort Qu'Appelle deserves quotation. It was a square lumber and plaster building divided into three sections. The south division was a big, two-windowed lounge drawing-room; at the far end were a dining table and sideboard, and during the winter that end served as a dining-room. The floor was restained once a year and highly polished all the time, but rugs were here and there to save the situation. Quite a delightful instrument in the way of a piano, some books, many interesting photographs, and even when the temperature fell to sixty below, always ivy trailing round these windows which looked out on the lake from the one side and the hills on the other, contributed to the impression of restfulness and charm. The north division of the bungalow was subdivided into three small bedrooms, and the central aisle into two rooms, the outer was the winter kitchen and summer dining-room, and the inner the pleasant lounge hall, familiar as home itself to many English people who have passed through or sojourned in Fort Qu'Appelle. A lean-to kitchen was at the back for summer use, and a hop-curtained veranda spanned the north-east walls. The bungalow was heated entirely by a huge box-stove and drum which could swallow on demand six Yule logs nearly two feet in length; but two were usually sufficient to keep the temperature at its hospitable degree of warmth, and waking or sleeping I never felt cold in that wind and weather-proof, well-built, simple house.

Another interesting family who were friendly and kind to us were the married and unmarried children of Mr. Archibald Macdonald, a man of great distinction, not only as being the last of the chief factors of the Hudson Bay Company, but as one who played his part well in Imperial matters during the historic days of the treaties and periods of disturbance with the Indians.

It was he who stood for intelligence and integrity on the historic occasion in 1857 when the general affairs of the Hudson Bay Company passed under the review of the House of Commons, and in answer to a leading question as to what class of men the officials were sending out to Canada this prompt answer came from Mr. Ellice, M.P. for St. Andrews, Fife, 'such men as Archibald Macdonald of Invergary.' At that time he had barely reached his twentieth year. Nearly thirty years later, in 1885, during the final phase of the Riel Rebellion, the people of the Prairie Provinces were in great anxiety over the fear of the ill-will of the Indians. The Government looked to Lord Strathcona and the Hudson Bay Company for help and advice in dealing with the Tribes, and they looked to Archibald Macdonald, the boy of Invergary and the man of Fort Qu'Appelle. Relief came in his one sentence, 'We can manage the Indians.'

We were deeply interested in him long before we had passed the 'Good day' stage of acquaintance, because he seemed the patriarch of the village and was obviously the principal white man friend and adviser of the Indians, of whom there were always few or many customers in the Hudson Bay Store. He talked to them in friendliest fashion in their own tongue, was polite to the squaws and petted the charming dark-eyed children. The world and his wife called him Mr. Macdonald with great respect in his presence and 'auld Archie' with the same marked respect in his absence; but absent or present he was always 'Chief' in Fort Qu'Appelle. He was profoundly interesting; in all those years in the North-West he had gathered a wide experience of human nature; he knew men and motives well, and he had an excellent memory. One could listen to him with pleasure for hours on end. But he was also naïvely and frankly inquisitive, and very deaf. I remember on one occasion whilst he ruled over the Hudson Bay as last of the chief factors, in the process of a particularly bad time it became imperative that I bought horses, and, therefore, it was impossible that I could settle a Hudson Bay account. When I had been compelled to shout the explanation of my embarrassment on a top note and in full detail several times over, I lost all sense of guilt, and found the courage of the situation whilst doubtless every one within earshot seized on its humour. However, I obtained time for my bill and bought my horses, but although Mr. Macdonald served his adopted country, his sovereign, and the Empire with fine service, he always served the Hudson Bay Company first, and it was not the smallest tribute to his most attractive personality that much was easily forgiven in the last of the chief factors. His wife, whose lamented death occurred in December 1912, had been a Miss Ellen Inkster, and the daughter of a brother officer of the Hudson Bay Company. She was a woman of great charm, in whose quiet courtesy, dignity and gentleness seemed always peculiarly one. Isolated as were the greater number of the pioneer families of the North-West, the many official and distinguished persons who 'stopped off' to visit the historic and beautiful neighbourhood of Fort Qu'Appelle, or passed through on their way to that paradise of sportsmen known as 'the Head of the Lakes,' seldom missed the opportunity to pay their respects to Mr. and Mrs. Macdonald who, through a period extending over forty years, have shown much kindly hospitality to the English, and some of the most attractive leaves in the 'last of the chief factors'' book of memory are associated with British names of which we have good reason to be proud.

Of his several children two sons were prominent in the movement of affairs in Canada – the elder, John A. Macdonald, being Conservative member for North Qu'Appelle in the Saskatchewan Chamber of Legislature from 1908-1913; and another, Donald H. Macdonald, well known in Western Canada as being one of the biggest landowners and of particular perspicacity and knowledge in financial affairs, has also a place in the history of my farming experiment.

I think we returned the Millingtons' call last, in spite of the fact that they had been the first to seek us out, because they live two miles on the far side of Fort Qu'Appelle and on the opposite shore of the western lake, so that it was fully eight miles to drive. It was a bitterly cold afternoon on which Hilaria and I faced the wind and possible tempest, and drove rather silently along the narrow curving road of the west lake. A mile out we exclaimed in a breath at a charming cottage actually cradled in the hills. Afterwards we learned that it was Crow's Nest, and the property of an Englishman who had also served under the banner of the Hudson Bay, and having taken the trouble to understand the ways and language of the Indians is now the acknowledged medium of information and communication between the white and darker man in Fort Qu'Appelle. When in springtime the useful potato gives out and is not to be bought for love or money, it is to Mr. Rooke one goes as the unofficial agent of the Indians, who are never caught out of the necessities of life at the end or any other period of the season. From Crow's Nest we swung down the descent of the trail to sight quite a well-built house on the left; but we had been warned by the Millingtons that their house was just beyond, and literally curtained by maple-groves, north, east, and west, but on the south bounded by the narrow pebble beach of the lake shore.

The lap of the little waves of the lake upon the beach sounded in one's ears as the echo of the voice of a dear but distant friend, and the chill, melancholy breath of the English autumn seemed in the Canadian air that afternoon. The Millingtons have the most lovable garden I have ever known in the North-West, although the loveliest is the Mission school at Le Bret. But that day the frost had nipped all bloom, and even the leaves of the hops shivered in the shrunken garment of the past. A golden-haired English girl opened the door and took us to a spacious and lofty room, which opened from a pleasant and almost English-looking hall. A wood fire leapt and crackled with a mirth akin to madness in the quite open hearth. Our hostess gave us the friendliest welcome, and we were relieved to find all our threshing excuses ready-made for us. The fair-haired girl brought in tea English fashion and we spent a cheerful and delightful hour.

Listening to the voice of the lake I had a sudden longing to sojourn beside it for a while. I had intended to spend the winter in New York, learning the ways of that fascinating corner of the universe in the most enlightening of all possible methods – newspaper work – but my father was very insistent on the fact that I had no right to leave a new responsibility. However I did not find the prospect of living in the farm cottage surrounded by an ocean of snow altogether attractive, and it occurred to me as we drove towards home that perhaps I might be able to board through the winter at the convent of Le Bret. I felt sure one could write well near the lake, not having grasped the fact that it would be frozen solid. I asked Hilaria what she thought, reminding her that I should want quite a lot of money to work the farm.

'I am sure of it,' she said, 'and I told you so from the first. Now, didn't I? And everybody says you will simply freeze to death at the farm, and I believe you don't even know that you are frozen until it is too late. Go to the nuns by all means if they will have you. They are always kind, and you can easily put in a man for the winter if Lal refuses to stay. You will be able to go up now and then and see that the beasts are all right. Nearly all the wheat is sold already, so there is nothing else to worry over. Of course, the best thing possible from every point of view would be New York, but if you feel you really ought to stay in the neighbourhood, far better stay at the convent. We will go along tomorrow and see how things are. I don't mind going away now that one knows that there are really some nice people within reach. I think you have brought anything you have to get through in the way of unpleasantness on yourself, but I should hate leaving you alone at the farm. And all these people say it's preposterous and no doubt think –'

'Oh! Do stop,' I interrupted, 'if I have made a mistake at least I can pay for it. And even you must allow that I am not in the habit of dragging other people into my worries. Not that I am not absolutely content with the thing I have done. I believe in this country from end to end, but especially I believe the prairie and the wheat and –'

'The woman!' gibed Hilaria.

8

Winter quarters – Springbrook school – a political meeting

Hilaria and I drove silently out of the convent gates at Le Bret and looked about for inspiration. The nuns would have none of me. The Reverend Mother was courteous, but unyielding. The number of nuns was short, one had been sent away for her health, and none had been sent to take her place. The pupils required much care and attention; there was none to spare for boarders. She advised me to go on to the old convent, which was then being used as a boarding-house, and was under the care of people she could thoroughly recommend.

The old boarding-house is not an attractive building, but it is built facing the little church and lake and connecting in line with the cross-crowned hill. The owner was most kind, and offered to partition off for my accommodation the greater part of the old convent nursery, as it was a particularly warm room. My fellow guests would be the public school teacher, one of the masters of the Indian school, and two Frenchmen also employed there. The terms were only four dollars a week, and I think I should have accepted the offer at once, but the windows were very small and very high, so that one could not see anything without deliberately looking for it; and I obtained permission to consider her offer for a day or so before making a decision. Within three days Mr. and Mrs. Millington paid us a flying visit early in the afternoon when Hilaria and I were busy in the granary bagging grain for Lal's load. The Millington girls were pupils at the convent, and they had heard that I had sought winter quarters there in vain. Mrs. Millington kindly offered me a winter home in their roomy house. Her husband, she explained, through his office as Inspector of Fisheries to the Government, was often away during the winter, the girls were at their convent. She and her lady-help were much alone. I should be entirely welcome, and she thought I should find it quiet and very pleasant by the lake shore.

I gratefully accepted the offer and agreed to join them two days after Hilaria left for England. It would have been in that year, as in most years, quite easy to find a caretaker, but my brother after much conversation on the eternal drawback of the situation announced his decision to stay himself if he might borrow the horses in order that he might fulfil his duties on his homestead in the spring. Then he could claim his patent, sell his land, and return to England.

'Mind, I loathe life on the land as much as ever, and I am certain you will live to share my opinion,' he repeated at frequent intervals. 'But after the slavery and discomfort I put in on my homestead I may as well get anything I can out of it. And I have a conscientious objection to confer benefit directly or indirectly on the Canadian Government.'

The days flew by, exquisite days of brilliant sunshine and every night star-laden. Money came in with the return of the wheat wagon at the rate of from thirty-five to forty dollars a day, according to fluctuation of market and difference in weight of load. It was sufficiently encouraging to cause one to forget that if it was coming in it was also going out, and would continue to go out long after the granaries were empty and wheat sales were over until the new harvest. Hilaria and I drove about a good deal, and agreed to forget her approaching departure.

My brother brought back the daily news from South Qu'Appelle; the General Election was in the air, and it seemed that every one was talking politics. 'And such politics!' said my brother who, relieved from the immediate obligation of British punctilio, had learned to esteem form and ceremony as chief among the bulwarks of national superiority. 'Haultain was in town to-day,' he added, 'quite a good sort and speaks well. Not at all like a Canadian in any way whatever. He is going to speak at Lipton on the 17th. He is a barrister. There was a case on in town and he was over professionally. You should have seen the Judge! You couldn't have picked him out of a British jury – you really couldn't. "Hullo, Judge, come along and have a drink," I heard one chap say. And he went! Oh, shouldn't I like to have taken the whole gang to the London Law Courts, just to show them how the thing ought to be done.'

Mr. Haultain was at that time leader of the Conservative Party in Saskatchewan; he is now Chief Justice of Saskatchewan. The son of an officer in the British Army, he was born at Woolwich, but received his education, took his degree, and read for the Bar in Eastern Canada. Directly he had fully qualified as a barrister he went to the North-West full of the energy and sympathy of the born pioneer. After fifty years in Canada he is more typically British than any other prominent man in Canada, but he is 'best man' among friends and adversaries throughout the dominion. In Mr. Haultain the spirit of British tradition and that Canadian spirit of the morning which breathes out of the North-West is one spirit; he is one of the very sound human links between the Mother Country and the Daughter Nation.

To the development of the Prairie Provinces he gave his best; his youth, thought, energy, opportunities of wealth making; but when the electorate for whose coming this far-seeing leader of men made ready the Prairie Provinces found that he would not lend himself to the hallucination of the loaves and fishes of Reciprocity, they returned him with just six followers to the Chamber of Legislature for which he had thought and fought, and which he won for Saskatchewan. But in Canada to-day innate appreciation for the essence of personality is filtering through that resistant pavement of the national devotion to dollars which marks the prominent trait in the present phase of development in Canada. Two persons stand particularly for the term of this illusive and indefinable quality – Sir Wilfrid Laurier and Mr. Haultain. So that quite unconsciously the new country gives the 'best man' the best it has to give.

I was eager to know something of Canadian politics and to hear Mr. Haultain speak, so finding the date was at the time of full moon I said that I would drive over, in spite of the fact that it would be my last night at the farm.

'Why don't you,' encouraged Hilaria, 'I don't suppose it will be particularly entertaining, but as you like that kind of thing it will break the monotony. And the drive will be delightful.'

On November 13 Hilaria left for England. For the first and only time in Canada I felt a breath of the ghost of solitude. By way of protest, I invited all the little Mazey children to tea on one day, and on the next I walked over to Springbrook where a kind and friendly neighbour had promised to take me to call on the village schoolmaster that I might see the children at work.

There were about thirty of them in all – boys and girls together, and this, my first glimpse of co-education, seemed as delightful and desirable as George Meredith's dream of it. There are but few married labourers in Canada, nearly every man works for himself. The pupils were mainly the children of the farmers of the neighbourhood – men of substance, growing anything between two thousand and fourteen thousand bushels of wheat a year. Probably the greater number of the small band had been born in the typical shack, but many of them at the time of my visit were located in imposing villa residences wherein is to be found the altar of a bathroom. I listened to some reading, a little recitation, and then a selection of copybooks and some writing matter was placed before me.

It was in passing from one copybook to another that I caught sight of the familiar face of Sam Carroll, who had vainly endeavoured to teach me to shoot during some jolly half-holidays which we had spent together on the prairie in company with my brand-new .22 rifle and a box of shells. Forgetting the direful anecdote and event of my own schoolroom days and all that has been written in praise of silence, I asked if I might see his copybook.

'I shouldn't have selected Sammy's copybook if you hadn't asked for it,' said the master, on a note which was as a familiar arrow from the past.

I could have knelt at the feet of Sam Carroll for forgiveness for my tactless blunder, and in the embarrassment of the moment I pleaded that he was a remarkably promising shot; but his re-

proachful face seemed literally set in the giggles of his school-
mates, and it made no secret of his share in my wish that I hadn't
come. But in any case the rifle is mightier than the pen on the
Canadian prairie, and to-day Sam Carroll is not only a fine shot
but among all horsemen in the Qu'Appelle valley, as a race-
course jockey easily first.

When the boys and girls had been dismissed for the day I remained for a while and chatted with the schoolmaster. In the
North-West there are often more schools than teachers, and many
Canadian men obtain their teacher's certificate and put in an
occasional period of school teaching. Some take it up altogether as
a far less arduous means of making a living than working on the
land, some as providing them the means to pass on to other pro-
fessions such as medicine, or the law, others by way of diversion,
or comparative rest. At any rate, many callings must have been
open to this particular teacher, who, although still young, had
travelled in many countries, and had been through a period of
service in the American Army. Not long after the schoolroom
episode I found him employed in building a church; then in control of the municipal elevator at South Qu'Appelle. Later I heard
he had gone into real estate, and on the last occasion I met him
he was the managing director of an important financial house in
Regina. That is the charm of Canada, none of the doors are
closed – yet. The women teachers also do well, and school teaching in Canada offers a far better prospect than is usually known
in Britain. Nor is the law of certificated qualification quite as
rigorous and unyielding as its word. I know that a woman who
has been a school-teacher in Britain is permitted to teach in
Canada without obtaining this certificate, because I met one in
October 1911 at Sedgwick in Alberta. She had arrived in April,
and told me she had not the smallest intention of teaching when
she came out, but the opportunity came, and in the six months
she had already *saved* more money than she could have earned
in Britain – where she had taught for ten years – in a year.

On the last day at the farm I put my house in order. The wheat
had been sold and paid for, all but a hundred and sixty bushels
held in reserve for seed. I bought winter coats for the four

horses, and that winter I and my brother acquiesced in the great mistake of keeping them as warm as possible in the stables, instead of sending them out to seek warmth in exercise. The two cows were rapidly approaching the dry season; the farm at that time was unfenced, and the two calves had wandered off in search of others of their kind. There was no special friend to bid 'Good-bye' barring Dick, the gelding of the lighter team, who had something delightfully English and sportsmanlike about him, and always played up to our appreciation of his pace with fine intelligence, although he was too heavy for a hack, and one had to make friends with him by less usual methods than the ordinary medium of bridle and bit.

On the last night I started for the political meeting at Lipton by that far-reaching white light of the moon in which one's memory always cradles Canada. Lipton was across the Qu'Appelle valley, and fully sixteen miles distant, but not only the moon but all the stars smiled at distance, and the delicate but exhilarating ice-breath, which steels the nights of sun-blessed days in the Canadian November, delivers one out of reach of the adversary – whether armoured in terror, or shrouded in mystery, or clothed in the everyday garment of the humdrum.

The meeting was held in the implement shed of Messrs. Macdonald and Newth. As I drove past I noticed that the benches seemed packed – with men only! My friend Dick McGusty was hovering round, and in his usual happy manner sheltered the fact that I had arrived at the place where the presence of my sex was certainly not anticipated. He felt quite sure I should be more comfortable in Mr. Macdonald's office behind the scenes, and I, who would not for worlds have missed what such a number of men had gathered together to hear one man say, felt that I should be much more comfortable if another woman shared the doubtful honour of my seclusion. I had but one acquaintance of my own sex in Lipton, but her dwelling was within a hundred yards of the building, and with great good-nature she cancelled a previous appointment in order to 'stand by.'

A quality, implied in the statement 'that he has never spent a dollar of the public money,' is claimed for Mr. Haultain so frequently, and with such an air of holy exaltation not to say exclusion as to make one a little curious about Canadian politicians in general. The frankest information always leapt to the service of discreet inquiry, revealing the fact that, in the political development of a new and wealthy country, vulgar opportunity is set with the grace and glamour, and endowed with the special absolution usually reserved for traditional temptation. I gathered that from the seats of the mighty, reserved for politicians, one had only to stretch out the hand in a peculiar manner to grasp 'the cup of Tantalus,' and it seemed that some had more intelligence, others less resistance, whilst here and there one made 'the great refusal.' Inquiring into the ways and means of entry into the circle I heard so many queer stories that I came to the conclusion it was empty gossip, and asked a member of the Legislative Assembly of one of the Western Provinces if it was true that in Canada votes could be bought for half a crown.

'Where did you hear it?' he demanded with such real live interest as to send my mind in search of adequate apology. 'That's all right,' he answered consolingly, 'only I never got a vote yet for less than five dollars.'

In those days, too, one was always hearing that Mr. Haultain was the Rosebery of Canada. Both statesmen are endowed with most attractive qualities of voice, both possess the power to see and the courage *to look* round a question, and both seem subject to the possession of the larger vision which carries the man who dreams himself a party-politician far past that particular degree of distinction which, in the mind of mediocrity, bears the label of success; but here the resemblance seems to cease. Lord Rosebery is a perfect and complete medium of expression; the inspiration of his thought not only strikes home to the least complete and most languid of its relations through his voice and his word, but even through the newspaper columns of his reported argument. Mr. Haultain has not this gift; one collects the evidence of his greatness bit by bit in the development of the Prairie Provinces, in the lives as well as the hearts of his fellow men, those whom, in the old pioneer days, he pulled through hard times by sheer force of determined thought and prompt action. One divines that, in spite of unquestionable ease in speaking, with Mr. Haultain expression lags behind thought, but one feels that the British statesman might have thought so much further had his power of expression been less easily perfect. Lord Rosebery is great through what he has said: Mr. Haultain is great through what he has done.

On the night of the Lipton meeting he talked of the National School of Canada. An admirer who seemed to be located very near the platform, and to have drunk not wisely but too well, to the success of the meeting, punctuated the speech frequently, and a little informally, with the protest, 'Say, Haultain, old man! we ain't going to have no ca-clatachism.'

With the pioneer's fatal gift of sympathy and love of individual justice Mr. Haultain had granted to the territories the system of separate schools.

In his single-hearted devotion to tolerance he had failed to perceive the subtle danger of the tolerance of intolerance, which however he recognized long before it fell like a gyve on the freedom and future of the race in the form of the 'Ne Temere' canon of the Roman Catholic Church. That night he frankly acknowledged his error, and announced his intention of thinking and working for the one National School, in which all the children of the many sects and nations which pour into Canada might receive their education together. The announcement cost him the Roman Catholic vote in Saskatchewan. In making it he risked the honour of political leadership in the province which his genius had formed, and he lost. But when the day came that he passed quietly out of the Saskatchewan Chamber of Legislature to take up the office of Chief Justice of Saskatchewan, there was not a successful politician throughout the provincial or dominion parliaments that might not have envied the vanquished leader his dignity and reputation.

But as I said, it is in the history of the people of the provinces, and especially during the pioneer phase, that one finds the evidence of the power and accomplishment of Mr. Haultain. On the night of the Lipton meeting I am afraid I thought that, as he was so much finer than all the others, he ought to have been a great deal finer than himself. And driving home across the prairie I could only feel very bitter indeed against male monopoly in the kingdom of politics, because as I passed the windows of the hotel, in which on the night of my first arrival on the prairie I had been denied food, and tea or coffee because nine o'clock was too late an hour to expect such fare, I noticed that at 10.45 P.M. it was simply packed with men who were evidently under no difficulty in obtaining the particular form of refreshment they required. And it seemed so very hard that whilst men can so easily obtain everything that is bad for them, women may not have even the very few things that are good for them.

9

At home by the lake shore – of Canadian diversion

My first day at the Clyst was the 'day of rest.' At luncheon I found the two girls had returned from their convent to spend Sunday, and in the afternoon they took me out on the lake in their canoe. It was November 18, the sun was glorious, and even the water of the lake not really cold; but although in 1905 snow did not fall until mid-December, the night frost must have been strong, because on December 5 I walked across the ice-capped lake to my first glimpse of a charming but deserted bungalow in a curve of the shore. Afterwards I heard that it was built for his bride by an Englishman who endeavoured to raise horses on a section of prairie surrounded by grain-fields, and in time the intelligence of the horses drove their owners from their lovely, but not entirely waterproof, home on the lake shore to seek consolation in a house fitted with all manner of modern convenience in the wheat town of Indian Head.

Nearly every afternoon between four o'clock tea and seven o'clock supper I made my way across the sparkling ice-path towards the land of the setting sun and the veranda of that forsaken home among the shriven maples. Approached from the lake, it was a peculiarly arresting spot in the frozen wonderland – exquisitely still, yet remote as the lovely face of a dear friend in the abandonment of death; but in summer it is a jewel in the setting of the indescribably beautiful lake shore, which seems to hold fast the inspiration of colour in the caress of shadow and silence, as though, even whilst it worshipped, it withheld its best gift from the inexorable enchantment of the sun-god enthroned over hill and valley, wind and wave, in the clear compelling majesty of highest heaven.

At the Clyst we lived very simply. The seven o'clock breakfast-bell rang usually and most mercifully in the neighbourhood of half-past eight. When my host was at home he read and wrote through the greater part of the day in his study, and he always knew the English news according to the *Times*. I don't think I ever remember a house where people talked so much or gossiped less. My hostess assisted her lady-help in the household duties, as do the greater number of Canadian ladies. I made my bed and kept my room in order except for a weekly turn-out, but I was never permitted to do the smallest household duty outside the threshold of my own door. There was also a chore-boy, who eventually found a place in the early history of my farming experiment.

He arrived at 'the Clyst' about a week after me, and his name was Heriot Hylton-Cave. He had come out from England the preceding July armed with an introduction to some desirable English people, for whom he had worked through the harvest and threshing seasons. The son of a clergyman's widow of limited income, defective eyesight had prevented him following his brothers into the Service, and Canada had been selected for him as it is for so many younger sons, because it is generally considered to be the refuge of the destitute warmed by the sun of 'the land of Promise.'

Heriot Hylton-Cave was at first inclined to be somewhat home-sick, but as he bucked the wood for the kitchen stove, the hall stove, the dining-room, the drawing-room, the study, and two bedrooms, and hauled water from the lake, cleaned the stables, milked the cows, rode in for the mail every day, and on Mondays turned the washing machine, he passed quickly through the phase of home-sickness into the more permanent period of work-sickness. He was a philosopher about many things, and always kind and considerate to the lady-help. Whilst he found the chores – wood bucking and water hauling – distressing from the active point of view, they formed historically for him a theme of which he never tired and over which he could be graphic and amusing. One day I remember seeing my brother literally doubled up with laughter during the happy period after meal-time when men grow interesting to each other.

'Oh, heaven and earth! It's Hylton-Cave,' he explained. 'I wouldn't have missed him for a farm. He has just been reciting to us his list of so many thousand pails of water and ever so many more thousands of poles he bucked at the Millingtons'. I haven't met anything more refreshin' in Canada.'

Once a week Mrs. Millington was at home to her friends – a custom which is increasing in Canada, and is particularly convenient in a country where one's friends often have to drive for a long distance in order to keep the link of friendship and social order from hopeless rust. Occasionally they gave bridge parties, and on great occasions a dance. Bridge parties are in general the special form of entertainment, but where there are younger members of a family the evening usually ends with a dance.

I was included in the invitations which came to the Millingtons, but excused myself from social amenities on the plea of literary work, as I wasn't sufficiently devoted to diversion to care about driving or walking in the open with the temperature at anything below zero to the hospitality of a Canadian house, which on gala occasions is usually set at about 90° without any prospect of shade. But on a day in December Mr. and Mrs. Millington and the lady-help gave such an interesting account of the festivities of the night before that I found myself sharing Heriot Hylton-Cave's frankly expressed regret that he hadn't been there. The occasion had been a dance given by our nearest neighbour – a bachelor. An Englishman and his wife were keeping his house and farmstead in order just then, and the arrangement of the evening had been left entirely to the lady, who had not been long in the country.

The dance had been a success, but the supper a triumph absolutely supreme in the annals of dance suppers in the Qu'Appelle Valley, barring the fact that the shack was of very slender accommodations and none of the guests could get into convenient touch with the supper – stuffed turkey, galantines, Charlotte Russe, &c. &c. The expression on the face of my hostess, taken into consideration with her own dance suppers, which were perfect in every detail, convinced me that it must have been a truly great occasion and worthy of a drive in the open at 50 below.

Again and again Heriot Hylton-Cave returned to the topic of the supper, discussing it with Miss Lister, who seemed ever ready to produce an even yet more desirable detail from the historic menu.

'Ah!' he exclaimed with a deep sigh, 'I would have given a dollar to be there!'

'I am sure you would,' agreed Miss Lister.

'But mind you,' he added, 'I should have eaten my dollar's worth!'

The party was such a success that in a few weeks the bachelor gave another. I am not quite sure whether it was curiosity or greediness that drew me, but in spite of the prohibition of 'Progressive Bridge' in a corner of the card of invitation I went, and nearly came through the ordeal of the game with flying colours. But either the gods were at my elbow and basely deserted at half-time, or I grew unaccountably and miserably hungry, and towards ten o'clock began to do everything that one shouldn't in progressive bridge. I shall never forget the face of my partner, who was regarded as a kind of pillar of Fort Qu'Appelle and took bridge very solemnly indeed.

In its proper hour supper arrived, but this time we fared Canadian fashion. Tiny chicken salads, and many kinds of sandwiches with lemonade and coffee, and a choice of strawberries and cream and trifle were handed round, so that every one saw less but ate more than on the memorable occasion. When I came to know them well, I told the Englishwoman of the sensation her first supper had created.

'Shall I ever forget it!' she exclaimed. 'For days I worked hand in hand and egg for egg with Mrs. Beeton, and then they left it all – positively *all* for us to eat meal by meal, until at the end of ten days we thankfully returned to salt pork.'

Another diversion was the children's party at Fort Qu'Appelle. For this annual event the little town is canvassed and gives as though endowed with the beautiful gift of giving. A giant Christmas-tree is provided, and on this is hung a gift for every child attending school, from the collected fund, but anyone is permitted to hang a gift for another on the tree, so that whilst each small and big child gets some treasure, some get many. Beautiful toys, gloves, handkerchiefs, chocolates, candies, an occasional book form the interestingly wrapped parcels which grace the tree, and in addition from the subscription list is provided a highly diverting tea for the children and all who care to join the Christmas party. The ladies of Fort Qu'Appelle contribute cakes, the Hudson Bay Store lends the china, and the kind of people who do things prepare the feast. At the 1905 Christmas party after tea the tables were cleared and chairs and benches placed in the orthodox manner, the guests sat down, and from the platform the children presented their musical programme, which was strong evidence of the intelligence of themselves and their teachers; but as yet the Canadian children do not strike one as being fun-loving. They were ever so painstaking, but only two, and those of the tiniest, seemed to enter into the spirit of the thing. The dispensation of gifts was rather a solemn and silent proceeding, and when it was all over – there were no games! No games for those good-natured little martyrs who had toiled for weeks towards the programme and who, one could see, had to screw up the courage of war to deliver their lines and play their part to the audience. One simply longed to clear away those chairs and start a rollicking game of Musical Chairs or Blindman's Buff, Nuts in May, Kiss in the Ring, or Puss in the Corner, and make that prim town hall ring with the mirth of little children. Possibly the lack of laughter in Canadian children is owing to the fact that nurses, governesses, and other suitable guardians, whose most important business in life is to make children happy, are very hard to find in Canada. The children share the life of the grown-up members of the family and overworked mothers, only too thankful for their skilful aid in the tasks of the daily round, are apt to forget that in an age when the principal and by no means contemptible cry of the world is to be amused, the fun-loving side of a child's nature will make a wonderful return for care and kindness wisely bestowed. True, the reason may lie in the deeper cause that the Canadian child is born of endurance. The 'land of promise' has been won by those who held out against the odds, those who broke the trail of a new country and dug the foundations of its industrial development in the teeth of the north-west wind. When in digging through many feet of snow to find my well after a fierce blizzard from the west had successfully concealed it from woman and beast, I began to understand why the Canadians are silent and very patient and perhaps a little solemn, and it was also through this active form of understanding I arrived in time at the conclusion that if ever Canada strays into the reckless fury and folly of war, the endurance, which seems to claim the laughter of her children, will place to the credit of her account a magnificent army born of men and women not merely trained but bred to self-control.

Yet another function at which I was present in the town hall of Fort Qu'Appelle was the Agricultural Dance – 'Gentlemen's tickets a dollar – Ladies free.' It chanced that I was a little late, as I had to walk from the livery barn to the ball-room in the darkness, and had taken more than one plunge from the sidewalk to the snow *en route*. Dancing was in full swing when I entered, and with difficulty I dodged the dancers on my way to the cloakroom, which is found in a very small and curtained-off corner of the platform from which the musicians play, and supper is served, and the dowagers of Fort Qu'Appelle assemble to do honour to the occasion.

The crowd of dancers was positively dense. I wore a tall white muslin gown, but as it was not off the ground it tailed into ribbons after my second dance, 'the Military,' known in Britain as the Schottische. There were very few waltzes, many two-steps, fewer three-steps, and that most charming and graceful and delightful of Canadian dances, the 'Jersey.' Lastly, but chiefly, the Canadian dance which beggars all description and to be appreciated must be seen – the quadrille – which is stage-managed by a professional caller-off, who shouts his directions in language which is neither in rhyme nor blank verse nor glorified prose but a unique mingling of all three.

The caller-off is to be taken quite seriously, and woe to the man who fails to come up to public expectation. He must have nerve, vitality, originality, his own or another's humour, a voice that inspires and carries, and both discretion and philosophy in case of failure to please.

The caller-off on this occasion was called in from Indian Head. Each figure was explained to the enthusiastic dancers by the professional leader. One I remember ran:

Birdie in the centre and three hawks round,
Birdie fly out and hawk fly in,
Hawk fly out and give birdie a swing.

Another direction ran:

Ladies in the centre; gents take a walk.
Salute your own and pass her by. Don't be shy.
Balance to the next and all swing out;
Gents hook on, ladies bounce back;
Join your hands and circle a half; partners swing
Right and left back to the same old thing.

Another:

Around the hall, gents, take your partner for a promenade;
Stand her by and swing to the next;
Then bring her back with a half galopade.

The opening line of an historic direction completely absorbed my sense of wonder. It ran:

Ladies, cross your lily-white hand;
Gents, your black-and-tan.

I asked the man who works for me what he thought about it the next day, and he was contemptuous, not to say severe, in his judgment.

'"Twas poor callin'-off. He was hard to hear. Not much to say. It was no sort of calling-off. His ticket and supper was quite enough for the likes of him; they paid him three dollars, and he had no call to take the money.'

Christmas is an honoured and festive season in Canada, and was especially observed at the Millingtons'. The girls came back from their convent, and Christmas Eve was penetrated with that atmosphere of surprise without which no great occasion seems complete in Canada. The only son, a youth at college, was brought back for a week's holiday, smuggled into the house and carefully concealed until he popped up as a kind of Jack-in-the-box in the small hours of Christmas morning. At four o'clock I heard whispers in my dreams – at five shouts – at six I discovered a series of unexpected presents, a box of the most fascinating chocolates from my host and hostess, charming trifles from the girls, a monster blotting-pad from Miss Lister; and the respectable end of these early diversions was that the Clyst party was most unusually punctual at church.

In the evening the vicar dined with us. The table was charmingly decorated. The huge turkey was brought in by Heriot Hylton-Cave, looking a little bit cross in his immaculate evening suit, and followed by Miss Lister, who carried the vegetable dishes and the side dishes without the smallest shadow of consciousness of her pretty dinner-gown. Many interesting guests came to the Clyst that Christmas week, among them being a very pleasant Englishman of perfect manners who played bridge far and away better than anybody else, but who I noticed was always merciful and even kind to his partner; and, best of all, there was a man who knew music. He was the brother of my host, and I think the most truly musical man I have met outside Germany. We had both been students at the Royal Academy, which was a bond, but he was there in the days when it was under the directorship of Sir George Macfarren, before my time. He had gone out to Canada and was farming in the neighbourhood of Elkhorn. I don't think he was wealthy, and I am not sure that he had a piano in his own home; and pianos are sufficiently rare in Western Canada to be thoroughly appreciated. But he touched every note as though he loved it, and uttered every phrase as though he understood; and he had the delightful way of passing from one message to another, just making music without waiting for the interruption or encouragement of conventional thanks. The memory of that Christmas octave is set amidst familiar phrases of Beethoven, Weber, Schumann and Bach, with Chopin in between and all around, and strangely shadowed with that curiously alive bust of Chopin in the Luxembourg garden, a keepsake which seems to have caught the spirit of radiant vision, and passionate, reckless longing and tender acquiescence which reveals itself in the consolation and inspiration of the exquisite work of Chopin, as though the artist had been borne on the wings of the morning to see the heaven that needed his sweet service and had dropped lightly back to earth of his own free will to suffer and to wait.

And so we came to the altar-step of the New Year.

10

Nancy – the second payment – the first loss

I was due to make the second payment of a thousand dollars on January 1, 1906. In November I clearly saw that I could not pay the whole of it, in December that I could not pay any of it, and I had to send to England to ask for a further advance of two hundred pounds. At the time I had received three hundred and fifty pounds in addition to the sum I had taken for wheat. That year I was not due to pay interest. For the remaining six hundred and thirty pounds due on the land I gave my predecessor a mortgage charged with six per cent. interest; the bank-rate was just then standing at seven per cent., but a mortgage on easy terms is usually offered by the vendor for the greater part of the payment, as the sale of a farm in Canada is by no means an easy matter even to-day, although the purchase of ready-made farms for ready money would be good for the Canadian farmer, and good for the British newcomer to the farming conditions of Canada.

On January 6 my funds had not arrived. True, among my Christmas presents there had been the very useful one of twenty-five pounds, but that I had dedicated to the altar of pleasure. From my earliest schooldays I had carefully guarded my altar of pleasure – I believed in it then – and I believe in it now; and I had observed that whether it is good for you or bad for you the one thing the average pastor, or master, or creditor seeks to take from you is the thing which your soul loves. Long after I was old enough to know better I had been greedy about more *marrons* glacés and cream-filled chocolate cakes than were good for me, and vain about the possession of many more hats than I could wear; but I loved flowers most dearly and truly and always insisted upon having them near. When the particular person in authority to whom I invariably owed more than the full sum of my month's pocket in advance discussed the situation, I always noticed that neither my expensive greediness nor vanity provoked attack so much as the few pennyworths of violets that were always consoling, and kind, and silent, and *there* when the world went wrong. The soul expands with pleasure as the heart expands in giving, but the people who wait to give until they can afford to give *never* give. To return to the gift upon my own altar, it was reserved for the inspiration of a visit to New York, and to return to January 6, 1906, early in the afternoon my predecessor called on me for the payment of the thousand dollars already six days overdue.

I was in no enviable frame of mind. Jim, the most powerful of the four horses, was ailing, and my brother constantly complaining of the cold stables, lack of hay, shortage of oats, and things generally. He insisted that horses must be blanketed, and kept horses and cattle in the stable during the winter. Experience taught me never to keep them in a single day to obtain physical comfort through the rigour of the Canadian winter; the blood must be kept in swift circulation, which is only obtainable through physical motion. I was new enough to feel very worried over everything, and my predecessor naturally wanted his money. In those days I was totally unaccustomed to being without sufficient for the emergency of the hour, and by way of carrying my own grievance into the camp of the adversary produced the worn-out old argument of the hayrick, which I had ignorantly and foolishly, but quite freely, yielded at his request. It would have been more just and more dignified to have borne the burden of my own lack of foresight in silence, but it is not easy to bear the knowledge that your beasts are threatened with an insufficiency of food in winter weather. The old man was hurt and angry at the charge of injustice. He departed with a cheque for eight hundred dollars, for which I had obtained permission to overdraw my account, and he no doubt carried with it a sense of injury. On the 13th the money arrived from England. I sent the balance, and being set free from immediate worry, quickly forgot my grudge. But it is never wise to risk making an enemy where one may be glad to find friendship in an evil hour, and if I had suffered in silence I should have been spared some anxious days.

It was on a January Sunday that I first met Nancy. Her owner was a familiar friend of the Millingtons, who came and went as he pleased. As we were driving into church Nancy's charming red head came round the snow-clad corner of the hill, and seemed to belong at once to the little bunch of Britishers who own a very green field in my memory.

Later in the day I told her owner that I liked his chestnut filly better than anything I had seen in Canada.

'So do I – *nearly*,' he answered. 'How old do you suppose she is?'

I guessed her four off.

'Wrong,' he said, 'she's rising ten. But she is the very gamest, smartest little mare I have come across in all the years I have been in this country. I should have to be very hard up indeed to part with Nancy.'

In the afternoon I made love to her in the stables; but apart from being excellently well-mannered Nancy is not demonstrative to strangers. She adored her master, and suffered the adoration of others. Her owner's pleasure in my admiration was complete.

'You must ride her, you really must,' he suggested. 'The Millingtons have asked me for next week-end. I'll bring her along and we will go for a ride on the hills in the afternoon.'

I hadn't ridden anything but Charles Edward and my neighbour's bay mare Mabel since I left England. Mabel had a fine stride, and after Charles Edward seemed everything that a hack should seem. But in those days to be carried by Nancy was to ride on the wing of a bird. Her mouth, movement, manners, were in perfect poise, and as inspiring as a breath of mountain air. We cantered lightly along the lake-side trail until we came to Maple Grove, then up through that lovely gap of the hills best known as Maloney's *coulée*.

'Let us go and call on the Maloneys,' suggested Mr. Edwardes, as we reached the top, and away the horses flew on a straight swift gallop to their door.

The Maloneys' house, which is very seldom spoken of by its orthodox title of French Park, has I think the most beautiful site and prospect of any house on the hills of the Qu'Appelle Valley. Whichever way one looks is Nature in her inspiringly beautiful mood. The windows of the house face southward on to the West Lake and catch the full form of the noble lines of hills, from the heights of which miles and miles of prairie stretch away into the violet heart of the never-never land.

The house is a comfortable but unpretentious building, an extended rather than glorified shack. The main building is divided into three separate rooms each leading out of the other, behind is the inevitable lean-to kitchen flanked by a useful room which does duty for dairy, larder, and storehouse, and over the kitchen was the hired man's room. It is a proverb throughout the Qu'Appelle territory that there is always a meal in waiting at the Maloneys, and history also relates that on one occasion a party of three walked in very late one night, slept, took breakfast, lit the fire and departed without interviewing either host or hostess; and the only people who didn't seem just a little surprised at so much being taken for granted were the Maloneys. Irish, happy, hospitable, and kind they were always. Mrs. Maloney had come out to Canada as the bride of Captain John French, who was shot whilst in command of his detachment of Mounted Police which supported General's Middleton's column on the historic occasion of the Battle of Batoche, when the rebel troops were badly beaten although Louis Riel escaped.

If Nancy's pace has a superlative movement it is at pink sundown when the air is light and sharp as steel and she is homeward bound. I threw the bridle on her neck and slipped to the ground with that delightful feeling of elation which occasionally escapes from the seventh heaven to play round on Mother Earth usually through the four-footed channel of 'one of the best.'

'I think you ought to be perfectly happy to be her owner,' I said to Mr. Edwardes, 'I shall never find anything to quite please me in Canada now that I have ridden her.'

As January wore away the weather grew colder, but at no point of that marvellously lovely and temperate winter was it in the least unbearable on the hill-sheltered sides of the valley. About the 20th the Millingtons all went away. Miss Lister, Heriot Hylton-Cave and I took a great walk, climbing a *coulée* and running home across the lake trail, but on either side of the setting sun the golden sun-dogs threw their challenge of intense cold to those who dwell in the land of frost.

'We shall have a bitterly cold night,' said Miss Lister. 'Heriot, be sure you make up the hall stove the very last moment.'

When we got home she gave us each our choice for supper. She chose milk-toast and I chose caviare, and Heriot Hylton-Cave selected porridge; and whether the porridge wasn't the right sort of supper and our 'lord of creation' retired considerably earlier, or whether he failed to put on the usual number of logs I never knew, but about four o'clock I awoke to the fact that every bone in my body was rebelling against the low temperature. I think it was the only occasion on which I was uncomfortably cold during that first winter season, but I only rode about three times and seldom drove, and I walked a great deal. My weekly eight-mile journey to the farm I accomplished on foot without difficulty, and on one occasion I walked to the farm, sleighed fourteen miles to South Qu'Appelle and back with Dick in the cutter, then changed horses and got back to the Clyst all within eight hours. There is no path in all sorts and conditions of trails so light and easy as a thoroughly well-packed snow path.

Every day I looked just a little more gaily forward to my visit to New York. I had taken Canada and I expect myself much too seriously that winter, and instead of writing up this ordinary little everyday adventure on the prairie I wrote solemn articles on emigration which the literary agent who controls such mat-

ters for me returned at once with the frankest intimation that
they were unsaleable; and in the still franker interpretation of
time I easily recognized the truth in the saying that 'a little
knowledge is a dangerous thing,' and thanked the gods, and the
agent, that those special papers never reached the shame of
printer's ink. But I was a little sore to think that it was possible
my work could fall from quite a high price to 'unsaleable,' and I
felt that a breath of New York and the atmosphere of my fellow
craftsmen would put wrong right. So on the 7th of February I
packed a cabin-trunk and a hatbox, and on the 8th I sat waiting
at my writing-table for my brother to drive me in to catch the
transcontinental train. When I caught sight of him coming up
the stairs, I saw at once that he was in trouble, and my thoughts
flew to the horses.

'It's Jim,' I said; 'is he dead?'

'Not Jim,' he answered. 'Jess. She seemed quite all right when I
fed and watered them early this morning. I harnessed her twenty
minutes before I started, and I chose her because I thought it
would be a shorter stage for her, and Dick would be faster to take
us from the farm to South Qu'Appelle. Before we had come half
a mile she suddenly stopped, rolled over, and when I got to her
head she was dead.'

My brother was so entirely upset about the loss that I could
only feign to make light of it; but even on that day I felt a kind of
premonition that the shadow which I had refused to recognize
might dodge me – the shadow of bad luck which I had entirely
omitted to take into my calculations.

The misfortune brought us both to the face of affairs. My
brother told me that he had decided to return to his homestead,
and if we could possibly manage to get the money together he
would like to put up a roomy shack so that he might take on
'stoppers' – passengers on the trail. The Grand Trunk Railway
were grading through just then about seven miles north of his
· homestead, all the supplies were taken over the trail on the edge
of his land, and he considered there was quite a fortune in it. If I
could lend horses and seed from the farm he could crop the ten
acres with oats, break up the balance of the land required by the

law of homestead to be put in shape for crop, make enough to pay his way and repay me before the end of the season when he would sell up and go home. Eagerly I put my lips to the draught of enthusiasm, and swallowed the fresh responsibilities.

'I shall have to start almost at once, the weather is breaking,' he said; 'as I must use the horses to haul the building materials, I must get it over before you need them for seedin'. I thought perhaps you wouldn't mind coming back to the farm from New York.'

'I shan't go,' I said. 'I can't possibly afford it now that I must get another horse. I have told Heriot Hylton-Cave that I will have him as chore-boy directly the Millingtons can part with him, and I don't in the least mind staying alone at the farm whilst you are going backwards and forwards.'

When he had gone I thought it all over. I had bound myself to a responsibility with the bond of another's capital. The responsibility might demand a far larger capital than I in my ignorance had anticipated. That this increase of demand was certainly not anticipated in England my weekly mail never failed to impress upon me. The only thing possible seemed to be to cut all side lines and throw oneself right into the breach as a working farmer. When Destiny grasps you by the shoulders if you fall in with the idea, the burden of compulsion seems to cease.

The Millingtons were most kind and sympathetic about the loss, and Mr. Millington advised me to go over and look at the horses of Mr. Edwardes' brother-in-law who was leaving the neighbourhood. The next day Mr. Edwardes came over and persuaded me to go back with him and see the horses.

The loss of the mare, the unaccustomed weight of money worries, had blinded my judgment and unnerved me altogether, or I couldn't have missed the splendid chance I had of completing my list of implements, and securing one or two of Mr. Mayne's valuable Clydesdales at the astonishingly low prices for which he offered them. After sixteen years of hard pioneer work his careful judgment and splendid patience had supplied him with a perfect plant for working a three hundred and twenty acre farm, but in the process the farm had become mortgaged to the extent of a big interest; also that part of the valley seemed peculiarly susceptible to the attack of early frost, and the present industrial population of the cities had not then arrived to cause the demand for meat and dairy produce which places the commercial farmer in a very much more independent position than the pioneer farmer who had to count on wheat alone to produce money. So Mr. Mayne had resolved to sell his farm, and to use the balance that remained to purchase a livery-barn in a city about three hundred and fifty miles farther west. The sale of the horses for cash was urgent. He offered me a four-year-old grey Clydesdale expecting to foal within the month for a hundred and fifty dollars cash. She was not nearly as tall as the big team, but bigger than Dick, and I made that the excuse for refusing the offer; but I did not feel sure that the bank would allow me to increase my overdraft so far, and I knew that I could buy on the usual terms of deferred payment. It was my first really bad 'sin of omission,' and the law of 'no forgiveness' of course held good – no seed, no harvest.

There were times in Canada when you might be worth five thousand dollars yet not be able to raise five dollars. Mr. Edwardes was deputed to go to the city in which was the livery-barn. He needed ready money for the expenses of the journey, and they both needlessly feared that the horses would go for half nothing in an enforced sale. When I refused the offer of the mare Nancy was coupled to sell her, the price of the two being two hundred dollars. I felt I couldn't afford both, but remembered the money set aside on the altar of pleasure and tumbled to temptation by offering a bit of it. I hadn't the smallest idea that Mr. Edwardes would accept fifty dollars when I offered it, and I haven't any real excuse to offer for the wretched price except that the iron had entered into my soul over one or two other little deals where I had no doubt most easily earned the gibe of 'English green-horn.' I had a strong desire to offer to advance the sale-price and let him redeem Nancy when things mended, and an honest impulse to offer at least seventy-five dollars. But he was in a tight place, and he took my offer because he knew Nancy's well-being would be in safe keeping.

'Will she go in harness?' I inquired.

'I have never tried her,' he answered. 'She was the best cattle pony I ever rode in my life, and you can see by her brands what they thought of her in the Mounted Police. I had hoped never to part with her. The day you rode her I knew you understood about horses. I can't take her as things are, and I would rather let you have her at a low price than take chances about her future owner. And if at any time you have to part with her I feel sure you would be careful too.'

In the end Mr. Mayne's horses sold well. The mare fetched two hundred dollars cash, and all the rest were eagerly claimed. I was offered seventy-five dollars for Nancy at once, and later a hundred and twenty-five dollars; but, of course, we never parted, and to-day she credits my account with one fine five-year-old horse, three mares, and a colt, in addition to her own priceless self.

At the sale of implements I bought a second wagon and a set of bob-sleighs, but the sale went well and I had to pay a fair price. However, I could have got a seeder at twenty-five dollars, but I had already ordered one which cost a hundred and thirty.

It was in the drive back from Balcarres to the Clyst that I was so perished with the cold that I almost made a vow never to drive again in the winter in Canada, and I always found the best and in fact the only resource against the worst days of the Canadian winter to lie in physical exertion. My last day at the Clyst was like the first – Sunday. I had arranged for the wagon to go down for my baggage during the week, and on Monday, February 12, after four o'clock tea I bade the Millingtons good-bye and walked back to my post at the farm.

PART II: SPRING

'But to have lain upon the grass
One perfect day, one perfect hour,
Beholding all things mortal pass
Into the quiet of green grass.

'But to have lain and loved the sun
Under the shadow of the trees,
To have been found in unison
Once only, with the blessed sun.'

1

A daughter of the prairie –
the coming of Nancy

I went back to my farm determined to remain in personal charge
until it could be left to fulfil its rôle of a successful revenue-
producing investment in the hands of others. I had not the
remotest idea that I was entering on a phase of strenuous labour,
and had certainly no intention of sparing more than two years of
my life, into which I hoped to gather all that was worth while in
every corner of the globe, to the proving of agricultural or any
other kind of labour on the Canadian prairie. By way of temper-
ing the wind to the shorn lamb I constantly assured myself that I
would travel east or west through the coming winter, and that I
would make the cottage as beautiful as I could, since I had to live
in it.

The first days were not exactly inspiring. The temperature, it is
true, was often above zero; but an east wind raged, and the stove
pipes smoked. I scrubbed floors and cleaned out cupboards, but
the result simply grinned at my labour, and finally I lay down
with the worst headache on record.

My brother, returning from a journey to South Qu'Appelle,
where he had been to discover the possible cost of the lumber for
his stopping-house, was kind but not flattering.

'You will only wear yourself out if you rush your fences, and
cleanin' this house is no joke – I have tried it myself,' he said
with conviction. 'It is too cold to accomplish anything that you
cannot do within three feet of the kitchen stove. When you had

earned a warm, and a jolly good meal washin' out your bedroom, I have no doubt that you returned to the kitchen to find
the fire out; and in any case that east room is a refrigerator when
there is no fire downstairs. I cannot think why you like it.'

It was no use to explain that the walls were white instead of a
crude and angry blue, and the floor green instead of yellow; and
at that time I hadn't even discovered that the sun looked straight
into one's eyes as it came home from the east.

'One can attack things so much better if one's bedroom is all
right and restful,' I explained. 'But you are quite right, it is unbearably cold.'

'I will put up the little stove downstairs and set the drum in
here,' he promised. 'And to-morrow I shall go over to Mabel
Mazey and ask her to come along and scrub and polish the
whole show. She is a brick, and can do anything. Perhaps you
could induce her to come over once a week. If she can't come for
a whole day, she might for a half; and it is wonderful what
Canadians can get through in the shape of work. I shan't have to
go north for a week, as the man whom I want to build my shack
won't be in the neighbourhood before. I can get plenty of wood
bucked, and the stable in apple-pie order, so that you can get
along all right until I come back.'

Mabel Mazey arrived just after our midday meal on the next
day and went to work with a will. She scrubbed the floors,
polished grates, helped my brother set up the little heater, and
finally she washed out every cloth she could lay hands on. I was
lying down with the tail-end of the headache of the day before,
but conversation was general through the stove-pipes.

'Guess now I'm right down tired. And your sister, she will be
thinking it's supper-time.'

It is wonderful what effect the warmth of a Canadian stove will
have on the brain of a chilled and tired body. Of it came conquering moments luring one on to new efforts. I went down and got
supper in a twinkling. Mabel Mazey was the friendliest person,
with a well-shaped head set on a well-formed body, curly hair
growing in the prettiest way off a white brow, smiling eyes, and a

humorous, well-shaped mouth with perfect teeth, and a chin that just curled off a pillar-like throat; yet in those days one couldn't possibly describe her in any other way than rough and ready.

All her days she had worked in the open air and loved it. In herding cattle, tending young stock, ploughing, discing, harrowing, she was equally useful, happy, and at home; but she was a true daughter of the four winds of the prairie, and often have I listened to argument as to which is the most rousing way of the wind in Canada – north, south, east, or west. She didn't jump at the idea of coming over once a week to break the back of my domestic duties.

'I guess I might manage half a day to oblige you,' she said, 'but I shall have to stop coming directly the weather breaks and we can get on to the land; and it looks as though it would be good and early this year. But I'll come till then, seeing that you are a bit lonesome and green about things. And when I have to get on to the land there's Pearl – she's next to me. I guess she wouldn't mind obliging you if you asked her.'

I inquired as tactfully as I could of terms.

'Well, I guess the pay all round here is about the same, a dollar a day.'

'You will be quite content to take half a dollar for the half day?'

'That will suit me all right. Now I guess I must be getting back to round up the cattle.'

'How many cows shall you milk to-night, Miss Mazey?' inquired my brother.

'We have only got four milkers now, but none of the youngsters seems to care about the job. Ain't you milking? Well, I guess you will have a cow coming in soon; and if you are wanting butter, maybe mother would oblige you with some whilst you are waiting. We don't sell except to Roland Dennison. You see, the kids eat it all. Seven pounds last week. Guess I shall be late getting back.'

'I'll fetch your horse,' volunteered my brother.

'Now that will be real kind.'

The horse was of an order that a British M.F.H. might have ridden with pride, one of the noblest-looking brutes in my memory – tall, proud, powerful, generous, masterful, and kind. His name was Paul, and, like his mistress, he followed the call of the daily round without a murmur, and without ever losing a breath of his splendid pride. Chasing cattle in a round-up or racing across a straight mile of black loam, waiting for the seed, drawing the plough, the disc, or the harrows, hitched up with three others, distinctly not of his class, or carrying off the honours of the show ring, Paul took each separate detail as though it were the peculiar office which life had confided to his special care.

Mabel refused all aid and vaulted into the comfortable Canadian side-saddle which she has never forsaken. We watched them skim the stubble.

'I wish I had Paul under me over a line of British fences! She can sit a horse, can't she!' said my brother, on a note of admiration.

'And clean a house,' I added with true homage. And that night I undressed and fell asleep in comfort, and if the temperature ruled a swift accomplishment of one's toilet, the kitchen was the warmest haven even ten minutes after the stove had been lit.

There are but few duties on a Canadian farm in the winter. Watering and feeding the stock and cleaning the stables were the only ones just then, as neither of the cows was expecting a calf until March.

'What shall you do about milkin' if a calf comes whilst I am away, and before Hylton-Cave comes along?' inquired my brother.

'Don't suggest any such calamity,' I entreated. 'I think I would rather do without milk and butter for ever and ever than milk. Besides, there is Mabel Mazey. Since she rescued me from those household chores I feel within reach of a tower of strength.'

'What shall you do if anyone comes to the house and asks to sleep, or anything?' was the next question.

'I should tell them that I was living alone, and it wasn't convenient, and that there was a bachelor's shack and a hearty welcome at every other corner.'

'Well, they wouldn't think much of your sense of hospitality. It is considered very bad form to send people on to a neighbour if they want a meal or a night's lodging on the prairie. It's nothing to do with the "angels unaware" theory and that kind of thing, you know. And they are always quite prepared to pay for their meals. But you really can't refuse.'

'Very well,' I agreed, 'I will lock my door, and tell them to make the best of all the rest of the house and what they can find in it.'

'I have never known anyone come yet except a stray policeman,' he said consolingly. 'Only work-seekers will be about soon, so I thought I had better prepare you. "When you are in Rome," you know.'

On Sunday, February 25, the east wind was blowing hard, and my brother and I were discussing his stopping-house plans over our midday meal, when there was a great announcement of arrival from his dog.

'By Jove! there's a man and team leadin' a horse!' he exclaimed. 'And such a jolly little beast!'

'It's Nancy,' I said, 'and Mr. Edwardes!' and promptly flew out to meet them, forgetting hat and gloves and terror of frost-bitten flesh.

Nancy was installed in the fifth place in the stable, a single stall in the warmest corner, which the great Boaster and my brother had fitted up with care and attention to detail in the way of a deep manger and convenient oat box.

'I thought being newcomers you had probably omitted to put up any oat sheaves,' exclaimed Mr. Edwardes, 'and as Nancy is used to them I brought along a few. When she knows she is at home she will get round and find her own feed, but she is certain to feel a bit strange at first. This stable isn't very warm, is it? Have you a blanket?'

I flew for a set of travelling garments which had belonged to a dear dead four-footed friend of whom much too much had been expected in the racing world. Nancy submitted to her thick and comfortable blue and yellow coat as though she had never seen anything inferior, although the ragged remains of the four sets I had purchased at Fort Qu'Appelle in the preceding November were hanging like grey banners of battle from the rafters. However, they were the only sample of horse-clothing which I bought or used in Canada. Circulation by exercise, and also by plenty of the best of hay and oats, threshed and in the sheaf, became my method of fighting the climate; and even my brother allows that it is miles ahead of external wrappings.

Mr. Edwardes remained with us overnight. The experience he had put in through the many years he had spent in the country made him a most interesting companion, but I fear he found our many-windowed cottage unmercifully cold. He bade his faithful comrade good-bye with a tight-gripped lip. I offered there and then to let him have her back at the same price – I hope as though I meant it.

'Please don't think of anything of the kind,' he protested. 'We are off next week to Medicine Hat. I am quite content with the deal, since I know she will be well cared for and quite at home in a day or two.'

But Nancy was inconsolable for many a day. She has the prettiest way of making herself understood, and all the time one waited by her stall she didn't eat, but turned her head and made pathetic little whinnies of inquiry for her master. She is not demonstrative, and my ever-increasing affection throve without any marked return of devotion for many a day. Indeed, I think it was not until a year after, when Felicity, her first foal, came into the world and we shared the delight of her care, that Nancy acknowledged me as her true owner, but now her 'welcome home' is worth the ten days' journey.

Two days after my brother, having done everything possible to save me inconvenience during his absence, went off with Jim and Kit, the big team, on his forty-mile journey north to meet the architect of the stopping-house; and I spent the only lonely night of many a night alone at the farm.

2

The mirage of spring –
my first chore-boy –
a new horse and a new man – seeding

Just as the enchanting season known as the Indian summer usually precedes the severity of the Canadian winter, so does a twin-sister of enchantment, which is as a mirage of spring, frequently break into the monotony of winter temperature, sending zero and its baffling blizzards away on the wings of the four winds with just one soft breath of delicate and delicious sweetness. Sometimes the blessed break is as a tiny oasis in the desert, lasting but a day or so; sometimes it lingers on for two or three weeks. Snow melts, ice shutters abandon the window-panes with a crash, the glorious sun peers in and lies deliberately, and most soothingly, about winter never coming any more; snow tears drip – drip all day long from the stable roof; long stretches of golden stubble and islands of black loam emerge from the soft white wrappings of winter, or peer inquisitively at the sun through a mask of melting snow; in the gay sunlight and soft sweet air the plaintive note of the snow-bird seems to borrow a tone of the English thrush; and if it were not that the cautious bluffs are still bare and dark, that the prudent trees withhold their garment, and that the voice of the prairie is still silent, one might dream not only that spring is here, but summer nigh.

This fair and gracious season followed in Nancy's trail, warming one's heart and softening the last days of February and the early days of March so that one remembered that yellow daffodils were keeping company with pink tulips and English violets within the precincts of grey Westminster, and then rode at full gallop into the shimmering, glowing whiteness of the prairie snow, since rosemary is not for spring.

Together Nancy and I learned our neighbourhood. Barbed-wire fencing was not nearly as general then as now, and but for one solitary fenced enclosure, which held all the charm of the unexpected on either side, we could carve our line to Spring-brook as the crow flies. The delicate and exhilarating air that comes from the union of ice and sun in this sweet season goes to the head of mankind and beast, and with the brilliant sunshine mocks caution and all sombre virtues. We followed imaginary trails, and chased vivid and delightful and evasive bits of land-scape through glorious snow-clad spaces of the prairie, and more than once even sure-footed Nancy lost her fine sense of trail and plunged us both into an unexpected bath in a snow-drift.

It was Mabel Mazey who first took me to Wideawake, where we raced in earnest from end to end of a mile stretch of summer-fallowed seed-bed which cultivation and the action of frost and snow had rendered fine as garden soil. Paul and Nancy travelled over it neck and neck, but Paul's longer nose was in front at the finish. We saw the huge barns and the prim houses which mark the prosperity of the prosperous farmers who grow wheat by the mile from Wideawake to Indian Head. Mabel commented freely on all we saw, and especially the direct relation of the size and number of the granaries which dotted the fields, to the income, expenditure, and peculiar characteristics of the owners of the same; but her cheerful tongue fell silent at the bleached bones of more than one dead horse in the neighbourhood of these coffers of wealth.

'Many's the horse that's killed by getting at the wheat,' she explained. 'The land is all open like in the winter, and sometimes they get at a whole lot spilled under the straw piles, and some-times they get it out of a leaking granary. My, it's a cruel death!'

We ambled back to our bluff-clad neighbourhood and con-gratulated ourselves that, although there might be more profit for the farmers on the plains, the picturesque element of our own immediate environment was worth much.

The lovely sunset of that day recurs so often in one's memory! Beyond and above and all around the purple bluffs and shining sloughs, and violet hue of distance, the pale clear tints of the evening sky, aquamarine, shell-pink, and palest blue, lay resting on a sea of opal set in pure gold; and the prairie, which through all that glorious day had been yearning to sound the spring song and to burst into leaf, bowed to the hush of evensong and seemed for a moment to kneel at the altar of the setting sun. In face of the sky at sunset hour on the prairie it is so easy to understand why humanity's idea of eternal rest and sweetness points to the heavens as its best expression.

I put Nancy at the timber bars which did duty for a gate at the Mazeys', and she tucked her legs under her and rose in the air at the merest suggestion of a leap, so that I repeated the experiment at my neighbour's stouter bars, forgetting that my saddle was attached with one not perfectly sound British girth that had been through a Canadian winter. We cleared the timber, but the girth snapped, and the saddle went one way and I the other. Nancy, sniffing supper-time, promptly deserted, and went gaily home alone.

When my brother returned from his consultation with the architect, the plans for the stopping-house were frankly discussed. It was simplicity itself in design, and was to consist of one big living-room downstairs, its fellow bedchamber overhead, and a lean-to kitchen; but everything in the way of building is costly on the prairie. The old-timer put up his log-and-plaster shack himself; the newcomer usually has to buy lumber, which is extraordinarily dear, and hire labour, which is ruinous. We agreed that it would take all the fifty pounds that was coming through from England even to give it any sort of start; but the outlook seemed most promising since he said the solitary Touchwood trail was already alive with trailers on their way to Kutawa, the nearest point of the Grand Trunk Pacific Railway which was in process of construction between Winnipeg and Edmonton. He had already encountered the leader of the supply section of the outfit, who had promised to make the new stopping-house their stop-over point, since it marked half-way between Lipton and their head-quarters and was practically on the trail.

We agreed that I could easily dispense with the two huge bed-steads I had bought from Mrs. Creegan, and the big kitchen table, four of the eight chairs, and the bench and various other oddments.

'I shall make all my expenses and at least five hundred dollars over long before harvest,' said my brother; 'so that I can let you have the fifty pounds back just when you want it for wages and that kind of thing.'

'I wanted it for the new work-horse,' I said. 'But, as you say, one can buy horses on time, and it would be a pity to miss such a fine opportunity.'

As a matter of fact the stopping-house did not go at all badly, although I doubt if it ever had a genuine margin of profit. Occa-sionally there was quite an embarrassing number of guests, on one occasion I believe they totalled a score; but many of them claimed hospitality in a friendly way, which of course was against commercial success. My brother put in his time and his homestead duties, claimed his patent, and in the end sold his homestead and house for two hundred and twenty pounds! But in Ireland he had earned an income of five hundred pounds a year as a brewer, and his homestead experience and result prove the folly of men who can do well in more suitable openings in the industrial development of Canada falling back on the hun-dred and sixty acres of free land just because it is free land. Homestead land is usually far from a railway, and needs all that experience and a true vocation for agriculture can give towards its development. It is a godsend to the migrating agricultural labourer with a family, and it might be a godsend to some women-farmers if it were open to them, but the way it has been used by emigration agents and others merely as a bait to attract any sort of population to Canada has often been bad for the land, and sometimes worse for the man.

He left finally on March 6, and from then until the 19th I was alone. The big team went with him until I required them for seeding. Dick, the survivor of the light team, and Nancy became great comrades; and if Nancy refused to forget her absent master except when I was in the saddle, Dick adopted me from the first, and initiated me into the art of horse-feeding and stable-cleaning. Immediately after breakfast and grooming he took Nancy out to graze, but at sundown he brought her back and waited at the well for drinks, and then begged for oats in his own matchless manner.

On March 11 a tiny calf arrived. Molly, the mother, seemed to expect all sorts of things from me; but I was not at home with cows and didn't appreciate the task of cleaning out the cow stable. Mabel Mazey as usual came to my rescue. She bundled the newcomer into the five-stall stable, milked Molly, and gave her a bran mash, fed the little calf with her fingers, and every day for a week she rode over twice a day to milk. The matter of the feeding of the calf I accomplished easily enough.

'My, you're handy yourself!' she said one morning as she watched my method with the little thing. 'Guess it wouldn't take you long to milk either.'

'There are two things I haven't the smallest intention of doing in Canada or anywhere else,' I answered. 'Milking and making bread.'

On the 18th Heriot Hylton-Cave, released by the Millingtons, joined my forces as chore-boy. Owing to my ignorance in the art of hitching up, I had walked five miles down to the Fort for my mail and two miles on to the Clyst to find out the exact date of his arrival. I found that it was that same day, and after four-o'clock tea we set out on the seven-mile tramp home. Before we marked half-way I felt quite sure he was feeling a little tired, and, with a guilty feeling that my companion did not enjoy walking as much as I, longed for landmarks long before they were due to arrive. However, we reached home, and Mabel Mazey's daily visits and my stable-cleaning duties ceased for a while.

Without inquiring into the average wages of chore-boys of Mr. Millington or my neighbours, I had offered Heriot Hylton-Cave fifteen dollars a month. He was always up so very early at the Millingtons', the stables on the occasion of my visits had seemed particularly clean and tidy, and he had had the advantage of some months' experience on the big farm of the Englishman to whose immediate care he had been confided, and to whom from his own account he had rendered valuable service at harvesttime. Then he had made his own dressing-table at the Clyst, and my frankly expressed admiration of the neat and ingenious contrivance brought forth the history of his knowledge and experience of carpentering which sounded well, and I felt it would be invaluable and count for a lot in house and stable. Besides all this he could milk and hitch up, and he was just an English boy and I knew him.

The work went fairly well at the start, and I played my part well three times a day according to the sound and practical advice of Dick McGusty, but I could not help noticing that the stables did not seem quite so neat and tidy as at the Millingtons, and the particular and most necessary labour of shifting the winter manure from the stable and its environment distinctly hung fire. My new chore-boy too was occasionally a little melancholy, although he cheered up over the business of fetching three loads of hay which I was permitted to purchase from Guy Mazey as a great favour at five dollars a load; and when my brother returned for a few days at the end of the month his spirits reached top note. Then came his great and glorious day, which I signed with so scarlet a mark of appreciation that I fear it marked the beginning of the end.

I had purchased from Mr. Mayne's sale a set of bob-sleighs, a second wagon, and another bedstead for the stopping-house, and Heriot Hylton-Cave was deputed to fetch them from Balcarres, a distance of eighteen miles. I had arranged that he should bring back something for the Millingtons in the wagon and leave it at the Clyst in passing. Horses and man breakfasted well, and started on the journey, but at midday down came a heavy fall of snow, and even my brother and I, who had set out for the Fort in the teeth of the north-west wind, turned back half-way with the remark that for some journeys life was really too short.

The snow was still falling when we retired at the usual hour, without a thought of anxiety either for the horses or their Jehu, feeling confident that the Millingtons would have insisted on their remaining at the Clyst, especially as Heriot's sight was defective. At dawn my slumbers were disturbed with a shout – it might be described as a shout of triumph veiled in modesty.

'We have been out all night on the prairie. Couldn't see an inch,' shouted Heriot. 'I dropped the lines on the horses' necks and all that kind of thing, but even old Jim threw up the game. So I turned them into a bluff and stayed there all night.'

'What's all that, Heriot?' demanded my brother, rocking with mirth. 'Lost in the bluff! Out all night! Are Kit and Jim alive to take breakfast, or are you the sole survivor?'

'I expect you are very cold and hungry,' I said. 'Light the fire, and I'll come down and get you some breakfast. Only why didn't you stay at the Clyst?'

'Well, Mr. and Mrs. Millington both begged me to stay,' he answered, 'but I told them that, whether I got back or not, I knew you would expect me to go on to the end.'

Hoist on my own petard, the only way out of it was to get breakfast. Besides, it is no joke being out all night in a snowstorm on the prairie even in April, and the boy had come well through it, although it was a case for discretion rather than valour. However, I made him go to bed, said nice things, and felt kind and gratefully disposed over the whole matter.

But the daily round and common task hung fire badly after this splendid adventure, and as for manure heaps I will not say that they grew, but they certainly failed to decrease.

'He is a nice little chap and amusin',' said my brother as he took leave of me. 'But if you mean to get the seed in quickly, take my advice and get the best man you can find, and pay him good wages. But don't give top-hole salary to your chore-boy until you find out for yourself what he is made of. If you had offered seven dollars for the first month and promised to give a rise at the end if he was worth it, you could have got at least a month's good work out of Hylton-Cave. He can work if he likes. But none of us ever choose to work if we can see a way to avoid it.'

My neighbour, who had returned from a winter in England, also eyed the mountains of manure wrathfully.

'That chore-boy of yours is having a nice easy time,' he remarked. 'Are you going to keep him?'

'I haven't found a man, and I can't milk,' I said lamely. 'I must have somebody, but I am afraid that he and I are not particularly good for each other.'

'What are you paying him?'

'Fifteen dollars.'

'It is too much by two-thirds.'

'That's not the boy's fault – I offered it.'

'Well, he can work if he likes, but he wants a good Canadian hustler behind him. I have two boys coming out from the Old Country next week, and their father wants me to find them a job. One has been a pupil on an English farm for more than a year; he ought to know something. You had better take him for a while, and I'll keep the brother on my place. Danny McLeay would gladly give your lad a job for the seeding month, and keep him on after if he is any good. But he hasn't experience enough for you. By the way, have you decided on a fourth work-horse?'

'Not yet. Two men from Springbrook have been over about one, only one was a gelding and the other was old. I should so prefer a mare – big you know, and not too ancient.'

'Danny McLeay has a good beast,' he said. 'A fine match for Jim and Kit. He is not exactly young, but an infant in comparison to old Jim. He is about the same size, only well-covered; one foot turns in a bit, but that does not interfere with his work. He is asking one hundred and eighty dollars for him. He wants something down on the deal, but will wait till fall for the balance. If you don't buy him, I shall.'

Tommy was a big, white-faced, white-footed bay. I closed the deal the moment I saw him, agreeing to pay eighty dollars spot cash and sign a note for the balance at ten per cent. My neighbour bought the two-year-old polo pony, Skye, on the same day,

and Skye became the sire of Nancy's first foal. He was swift and
altogether a delightful hack, but my neighbour had no particular
use for him and sold him at a fair profit. Eventually he passed
into the possession of a racing man, for whom he won valuable
races.

'What are you going to do about a man?' inquired my neighbour one very hot day when hardly a scrap of snow remained on
the landscape.

'It's a serious problem,' I acknowledged. 'A person named
McEwan called on Saturday, and I engaged him at thirty dollars
a month, although I didn't exactly like him. He was to come in
on Monday. A much nicer man called later in the day, but I
couldn't close with him as I had already settled the matter, and
didn't even bother to take his address. And now neither word
nor sign of McEwan.'

'Nor ever will be,' he answered. 'Danny McLeay's cousin,
Roddy McMahon, is staying over there, and he will come along
for the seeding month, at any rate, only he won't hire on without his team.'

'What are his terms?'

'Three dollars a day, man and team, with board and forage.'

'It seems rather a lot just as I have bought a new horse,' I said
anxiously. 'What do you advise me to do?'

'They say he is a good man on the land. He should be too,
since he was born and bred on it and could plough before he
could read, I guess. You see, if you hire him and his team to seed
with Kit and Jim, you can put Hardwick on to the manure pile or
to do some stoning, or even harrowing. Your second team can
easily draw three sections. He should be able to manage horses
after being more than a year on an English farm. However, I'll
tell Roddy McMahon to come over and see you.'

He came later in the day. I was writing in my sitting-room
when there was a very loud knock at the door.

'You are Mr. McMahon, I expect?' I said.

'I guess,' said he. 'Pleased to meet you.'

I did my best to persuade him to work for me without the
team, but he was firm on the point. I was buying hay, and oats

were almost at vanishing-point. I foresaw an ever-increasing list of expenses attached to the actual three dollars a day.

I engaged him for the seeding and he arranged to come the next day, and I rode away to Springbrook to request that the new seeder might be sent over at once. Then I went on to Strathcarrol post office and had tea and poached eggs and maple syrup with the Carrols, and Ella rode home with me. In the distance the glow of prairie fires suggested care, but I refused fresh worry out of simple gratitude that my team was made up and a seeding-man secured, and that night I slept the sleep of the truly thankful. On the morrow there came no hired man. However, the next day, on April 10, he arrived, and, to borrow his own phrase, 'got right on the job.'

The first movement in the ceremony of seeding was the ploughing of a fireguard in order that one might fire the stubble of the eighty-acre field without danger to the country-side. The law insists on a thirty-foot guard all round the field, but the usual plan is to burn with the wind and save oneself as much trouble as possible. Prairie fires in those days were very common, destroying whole districts; but with the more complete settlement of the country the big patches of fallow land did much to check the running sea of flame, and in my neighbourhood the danger from prairie fire is nothing in comparison to what it was in 1906.

When the guard was ploughed to the extent governed by the conscience of Roddy McMahon, my two men drove off in a wagon to the straw pile and brought back load after load of dry straw to the skirt of the field, where they laid it in the stubble to give a good send-off to the fire. The heat of the sun had caused every breath of moisture to evaporate from the stubble, and the wind being in a favourable quarter it was decided to fire after noon of the second day. The straw piles went first and raised a splendid blaze, and all would have gone well had Roddy McMahon's conscience been just a little nearer the degree prescribed by the law on the north side of the fence. But at this point the fire leapt the guard and got into the bluff which adjoins the stack-yard and the stable. I had driven down to the Fort and didn't share the top notes of excitement, but a black-faced but triumphant hired man supported by all my neighbours greeted me as I came in at the gate with a tale of marvellous escape from a clean wipe-out with fire! Roddy McMahon, who, if he ploughed furrows before he could read, probably made prairie fires before he could walk, remembers this above all other fires, and always insists that Heriot Hylton-Cave shall share the remembrance.

'Do you mind, Heriot, that day when the fire got away on us and came into the bluff? I never see anyone so scared in my life. Off you rode for Roland Dennison, and by the time you come back I got it all beat out.'

The next phase in the preparation was the cleaning and pickling of the seed-grain. I was arranging to buy a fanning mill, but Roddy McMahon suggested that his uncle and my neighbour John McLeay 'might so well loan his.' He drove off for the mill, and there came down in its wake my good friend and neighbour John McLeay and his dog, and in the wake of both my predecessor and my brother.

'My, but there's lots of wild oats in that seed, Roddy!' said John McLeay.

'And is that the seed you'll be sowing?' demanded my predecessor with a hint of sarcasm. 'I guess it's only the English would sow good land with wild oats.'

'Well, a Canadian raised it,' retorted my brother.

'' Twas so fine a crop as has ever been raised in these parts. A few wild oats don't count in the reaping,' was the retort; 'but it's only a greenhorn would sow them!'

Wrath smouldered in my brother's eye, and I dropped into the argument.

'I don't know anything about wheat-raising,' I said. 'But if it is folly to sow that seed, just let us know a little more and advise me what seed to sow and where I can get it.'

'I guess my own wheat is a lot cleaner than that,' said John McLeay. 'I could smell the smut as I came within five feet of the granary. I'm not saying but I have a wild oat here and there, but I have not got them near so bad as that.'

In the end I agreed to buy seed-wheat from John McLeay, to be cleaned by my men in his own place at a cent above market price. The wild oats had seemingly neither discounted the weight nor lowered the grade at the elevators, therefore I reckoned I should only be a dollar out on the actual cost, plus of course the cost of hauling. On the other hand, between May and September the price of wheat is usually on the upward grade.

But when the sample of cleaned seed-grain came from John McLeay I was bitterly disappointed. It is true that there were not so many wild oats as in my own sample, but after the seed argument I felt that there were far too many for desirable seed, and said so to the man.

'I guess every one in these parts has got wild oats,' said Roddy McMahon, 'and there's bound to be more this year than last because of what's shelled on the land. Next year when eighty acres is due to summer-fallow that's the time, I guess, to clean 'em out.'

The process of pickling seemed simple enough. Heriot Hylton-Cave fetched several pails of water from the well whilst Roddy McMahon waited at his ease on the doorstep. When sufficient water had arrived, a big paper packet of bluestone was dissolved and poured over the load of grain as it lay on the granary floor. It was then well turned with the shovel in order that all the grain should get the benefit of the shower-bath. I learned that this bath was necessary to destroy the parasite smut which does much harm to grain, lowering the grade as can no other enemy except frost.

'I guess it will be all dried out by after dinner,' said Roddy McMahon. 'And we can start seeding.'

Easter had intervened, and these preparations had taken up three days, so that it was at midday on April 17 that I drove the wagon with ten bushels of seed-grain to the starting-point. Roddy McMahon followed with the seeder. He emptied the contents of a bag into the container, examined the feeders to see that the passage was clear, and drove away. As I watched the first seeds fall to the earth I had a great desire that I might sow Success. By success I meant something swift and brilliant. It all seemed straight sailing and absurdly easy, and I never dreamed that there lay between me and success years of arduous toil and seasons of bitter disappointment. It seemed to me as I walked back to the cottage that I had assisted at a ceremony and the ceremony was an inspiration. I wanted to do my level best, but I was perfectly sure the gods could do nothing less than theirs in order to stand by a woman-farmer. So I went in to prepare supper and attend to my household tasks, and Roddy McMahon went east and west with the seeder, and neither of us, I am sure, gave another thought to the fact that as the wheat-seed dropped from the seeder to the seed-bed there passed in here and there a wild oat.

3

Chore-boys – 'the beautiful necessity' – the story of a plough

Heriot Hylton-Cave received my decision concerning his exit with philosophy, and frankly acquiesced in the opinion that an experienced chore-boy would be better for me, and a farmer of experience better for him. He accepted the offer of Danny McLeay, and arranged to go at the end of the month.

On April 20 the Hardwicks arrived. They were a prepossessing pair of well-built, well-dressed, manly, healthy Britons. Hating to abandon British customs, and hating even more to cheapen the privilege of the using of front names, I distinguished them as Hardwick major and minor on the first evening my neighbour brought them round to the cottage, which they pronounced to be 'not at all a bad show.'

It was not quite convenient for Hylton-Cave to move on to his new job for a few days, so for a time he and Hardwick worked together. With three male beings to cater for I had to think quite seriously about meals, but beyond this I had little trouble. Hardwick major had put in more than a year with a farmer who had made his pupils work. He lit the fire, brought the water, milked quickly, and to the last drop, and did all without grumbling; but he banged the pails and the pots and the pans and the chairs, and everything he touched; and he shouted and whistled and sang at all times and seasons, until I wondered whether milking itself might not be less hard to endure.

It seems altogether contemptible not to have been above such trifles, but I wasn't above much, and I had no experience of the heavy toll hard work demands of mind and body, as even Hilaria had seemed to take it for granted that I was hopeless at skilled labour, and only fit to fetch and carry in domestic concerns. Noise I hated more than any evil thing, and would have cheerfully walked miles or lived with the dumb to avoid it, but it happens that one of the most attractive traits in average Canadians is that they speak quietly and work almost silently, so that I walked honestly into the pleasant belief that in manual labour gentleness always accompanies a fine intelligence. Certainly lack of gentleness lowers the grade of the finest intelligence. Hardwick shouted at the horses, threw on their collars and harness, threw it off, and always arrived on any scene of action with that irksome bang and clamour which must be wearing to the nerves of animals and is certainly wearing to implements, so that although I liked him and liked his work I found him very hard to bear in places. However, feeling that land and beasts and stable were in good hands I turned my attention to the beautiful necessity of the cottage.

The first thing I had observed within doors was that the kitchen was long, and had an air of space, and although the windows were guiltless of a solitary correct line, they were graceful. From the south one looked across the wheatland to the picturesque bluffland lying between the Touchwood trail and Springbrook, from the north, away across four miles of peaceful prairie towards the line of land on the far side of the Qu'Appelle valley, which from that distance looks like a friendly sea, blue as the Mediterranean. So I banished cookstove, pots and pans, and everything that wasn't in the picture to the smaller square room which had been my predecessor's cherished parlour, and had known the glories of an all-over carpet, an organ, a sofa, and a wall-paper – rare distinctions in prairie farm dwellings in those days. Then I bought white paint for many dollars, and the softest, brightest shade of green paper for less than two, little dreaming that I should have to paint every inch of the woodwork and paste on every scrap of paper myself. I didn't mind the painting so much, although I thought my own end must arrive before the end of the ship-lap ceiling; but the paper was a different matter. I procrastinated for weeks, and then in an evil hour it occurred to me that the two boys might be able to hang it since it was patternless.

Heriot Hylton-Cave jumped at the idea. He assured me that his mother frequently papered her drawing-room walls, and that he had often helped; and he talked so convincingly about care and method in cutting and fitting the strips that I believed him. I always believed in him when he spoke of his mother. He adored her, and she had the kind of face that made one want to be kind to her son. When he spoke of her I saw him in the splendid and heroic light of the night out, and forgot that the daily round and common task proclaimed his near relationship to the frail family of the Can-does.

Hardwick was even more cocksure than Heriot, though less convincing, since his only reason for confidence lay in the assurance that he 'could do anything.' However I gave the paper, the two-foot measure, and the scissors into Hylton-Cave's keeping, the paste and the brush to Hardwick, and went down to the Fort for everybody's mail, delighted to have got rid of an irksome task.

When I returned half the room was hung with paper, but it seemed a little unusual. I drew nearer to find that it had been pasted on from the outside.

'I thought it was a queer thing to do,' said Hylton-Cave, with his hands in his pockets, and a gleam in his eyes that I mistrusted, only that one never can be sure of anything that lurks behind spectacles. 'But you see you gave him the paste and brush, and it wasn't my business to interfere.'

'Not your business!' I said wrathfully. 'Didn't you tell me you had both seen and helped your mother put on paper a hundred times?'

'Yes, but Hardwick said he knew a professional bill-sticker and they always do it this way because it makes a better job.'

I made them pull every scrap of paper off the walls before supper, and the next day I rose to the occasion and attacked the job myself. It chanced that it was my birthday and the loveliest day in the world, but I had to stick to the foot-rule, the scissors, and the paste-pot, and the paper, long after the sun slipped down behind the horizon because I knew if I didn't remain with my task until the very end I should never return to it.

When it was finished I had the floor scrubbed, and I oiled and stained, varnished and polished it myself. I laid the offering of my only Indian rug in the centre, and hung the cool green curtains at the windows. I enamelled a packing-case writing-table, bestowed a picture here and there, placed my bits and pieces, and bought a comfortable chair, until it really seemed the place of *dolce far niente*. But it was ages before I could be properly idle in that room. My neck ached when I looked at the ceiling, my knees ached when I looked at the floor, and bitterness simply flooded my heart at the memory of chore-boys when my eyes rested on the cool, soft tint of the wall-paper.

In the nature of things *dolce far niente* is an open-air condition. This truth came to me on the day that Spring really came to the prairie. Spring comes in a day in Canada. There is none of the announcement of arrival with which she invites attention to her coming in England. One morning at sunrise you look dolefully at a white landscape, break thin ice with a grumble, and another firm repetition of your conviction that she never will come – but before sunset she is with you, actually sitting there in her petticoat of vivid, sunlit, delicate, caressing green; and in the spring of 1906 the prairie blossomed and bloomed as though love and life were one indeed. All the tints bright and subtle, kind and cool, dangerous, clear and gay, burst forth together. Palms innumerable, fragrant and exquisitely lovely; poplars drawn up in guardian groups dressed the landscape near and far; the purple petals of the sweet Pasque flower, tucked snugly in its cup of silvered silk, spread gay carpets for the fairies on the unbroken virgin soil. Spring cried: 'Awake!' and the voice of the prairie rang out of the heart of the earth sun-clear and strong. The croak of the hosts of the frog-world in full chorus, the thin high note of the gophers, the jest of the cat-bird, and the thirsty rattle of the bittern joined in the spring song led by the lark's gay, glad summons to hope; the grey-blue walls of the sloughs took on a lapis tinge at the ardent kiss of the sun and where tongues of fire had licked angry ways across the prairie, a new-born growth of tenderest emerald hue mocked the end of destruction in the triumph of life. Azure sky above, fragrant turf beneath, the magic of the dry, clear air, the precious glow of the sungod! The buzz and hum of growing, gathering life which throbbed from every blade, swayed in the wind, and whispered in the waters, charming song out of silence, flame out of ice, warmth out of snow – gay, glad, gracious, lovable, lovely life was awake at the call of Spring and cried out: 'The altar of labour, and the place of *dolce far niente* is the earth.'

Many an hour of sweet idleness did I lay upon the shrine, because even in that first season I realized that since I had to pay in full for the time of my hired man I must make full use of it. Breakfast I served punctually at six o'clock – early rising soon ceased to be a hardship – so that I had many hours of leisure between breakfast and the midday meal, which was always served at noon, and supper which was timed for 6.30. A teamster is supposed to put in ten full hours a day on the land in Canada, and to groom and feed his team of four horses. Meals are set in the unwritten law at 6 A.M., 12 noon, and 6 P.M.; but it is far better for beasts and men to delay the evening meal in order to allow at least an hour and a half for the midday rest.

The wheat-field was seeded in six days, and, following the advice of Roddy McMahon, I had the fifteen acres which had received some vague attention from the plough in the preceding year, spring-ploughed, disced, and harrowed, and there we sowed oats.

'The other twenty-five acres of that dirty land must be twice ploughed, I guess,' he continued. 'It should be ploughed shallow right now to give the surface seed a start, then when the weed comes up good and thick we can turn it all in with the plough. Guess you would like me to be getting on with some fresh breaking. There's some good chunks of land left to break up yet on this farm. Only I guess you will have to be sending Hardwick up with the pickaxe to get busy on the stones. It don't pay to keep stopping the plough to pick out those fellows!'

'I have found a patch of land on the far side of the pasture,' I said, 'and there I think you will get in more than twenty acres of level breaking. Of course, you mustn't stop to get out the stones; I quite understand. I'll come and show you the land I mean.'

'I guess it's quite a piece,' he agreed, as we examined a stretch of unbroken prairie immediately behind the forty-acre pasture. 'Maybe I had better get on to that first. If it comes rain it will be too sticky for the plough in the summer-fallow. I'll just get the breaking-plough right here, and then I can shift on to the breaking come rain. There's another five acres we can get in on the west – a tidy little bit of land; it will make a good field of that ten-acre stretch across the slough.'

I congratulated myself on having the right sort of man for the land in spite of his superiority to chores, of which he frankly informed me. At the same time I felt that I could not afford to pay a man at the rate of three dollars a day right through the working season, especially since I had to buy feed.

'You see how I am placed,' I exclaimed, when I paid him his salary for the seeding month. 'If I had plenty of oats and hay I shouldn't worry, or even if I hadn't bought the fourth horse, but as things are I feel I ought not to be hiring horses.'

'I guess you've no call to worry about any more hay; that last load we got wasn't much good to the horses anyway. I'll get on out after supper with the mower, and get in a load of prairie-wool.'

Orthodox hay consists of the long grasses cut from the sloughs of the prairie; prairie-wool is the shorter, finer herbage of the prairie proper. Cutting and gathering this would mean too much labour, but in spring-time, when feed has arrived at its vanishing-point, one is only too glad of the opportunity to gather prairie-wool, and horses appreciate and thrive on it wonderfully well.

In gathering the prairie-wool my helper blessed the mower and cursed the rake – implements I had purchased as a bargain for fifty dollars; but it was three days later when he came to me on the matter of the plough, for which he seemed to have no language in reserve.

'I've never been done over a plough I guess before, but I can't get this fellow to go nohow. I guess Dick McGusty should take her back all right, and give you another.'

'He won't do that,' I answered. 'My brother used it, although not much. But he is certain to say we have spoiled it.'

'He won't waste time saying that to me, I guess. Anyway I am going down to the Fort this evening. Guess you best write and tell him the plough won't work, and he must come up and set her right.'

But Dick McGusty wasn't in town. He had a valuable homestead in the neighbourhood of Loom Creek, and he had failed so far to put in time, or perform the duties attached to the true possession of the same. Any newcomer in search of a desirable homestead usually hunts around for these quarter-sections nominally attached to absent owners, and has no scruple about taking their place if possible. Roddy McMahon and I both knew of one who had an eye on this particular homestead.

''Twould take a better man than him to jump Dick McGusty's homestead,' he said, 'but I guess he has shifted him on from the Fort all right. Joe Salmon, he's down at the Massey-Harris shed now, but I guess they won't have implements down there much longer. All the land's settled round the Fort, and if Dick McGusty's going to Cupar he'll take all he can with him. Guess 'twas a pity you paid for that plough.'

'Well, I haven't paid for the mower and rake,' I said.

The Massey-Harris agent arrived the next day and solemnly assured me the plough would work.

'He don't know no more about ploughs than a baby,' gibed Roddy McMahon, after his departure. 'But I guess you've had to pay for it, and I must try and work it all right. It ain't so bad on the level, but get on to the hills and she won't cut an inch.'

I wrote to Mr. McGusty, and expressed my opinion clearly. A week after Roddy McMahon came back with the information that he had seen him in the Fort, and had given him his mind about it.

'And did you tell him that it was utterly useless to do decent work with, and that he must write to the Massey-Harris people about it at once?' I asked.

'I did that. And I told him what I thought myself, good and plain.'

'And what had he to say for himself?' I asked, fully prepared to enjoy the story of Dick McGusty's humiliation, and forgetting, I am afraid for the moment, the frequent friendliness and good advice I had received from him.

'He said: "I guess we have all of us had to learn in this country, Roddy. She'll learn."'

That year there were only twenty-five acres of summer-fallow to cultivate, and by hook or crook Roddy McMahon turned them twice. But the next year there was heavy work for the sulky plough, and the Englishman who was working for me asked me to come and prove for myself the utter impossibility of doing decent work with such an implement. It was then that I sent my complaint to the Massey-Harris office at Regina. They referred me to their nearest agent at South Qu'Appelle, telling me that he would put it in perfect order. It took a man and team a full day to take it in. The agent told me he knew the model which was brought out in such and such a year and had proved a failure. He had half a dozen of them on his hands, but had never risked losing a customer over them. 'It's no use saying I can make it work all right when I can't,' said he. 'Best buy a new one; there's a model that's doing fine work in this neighbourhood.'

By 'The Waters of Marah' the prophecy: 'She'll learn,' recurred in my brain, and also the fact that I had thrown away sixty-five dollars on a plough that had turned over twenty-five acres of summer-fallow after much persuasion, and then retired from active service. After a month's trial I bought a John Deere single-furrow plough of a neighbour, and was so well pleased with it that I bought the gang model of the same make from the agents of that Yankee firm at South Qu'Appelle.

4

Dairy-produce – fencing – milking – gardening – Victoria Day

Roddy McMahon agreed to work for me for a time at one dollar fifty a day and without horses. It was a great relief, as I had already bought two hundred bushels of oats at thirty cents a bushel, and had also started to realize the fundamental commercial law of remunerative farming, namely, that one must never buy anything in the way of food for stock, and very little for household need. Food for man and beast should be raised on the farm, groceries and fresh meat should be obtained in exchange for dairy produce, the great point being to avoid spending money, which in the nature of things is scarce and most valuable in a country whose natural resources are so great, yet to a certain extent locked up in the earth, and only to be delivered to the liberty of exchangeable value through the medium of capital and labour.

The two cows made excellent contribution to the revenue. I used all milk, cream, and butter necessary in the house, and then took several pounds of butter weekly to the Hudson Bay in exchange for household necessities. In those days they gave current price, or rather its value, without charging any sale commission; now like the majority of traders they get as much as they can and give as little as they need. I made my butter with cream scalded and turned Devonshire fashion, and seemed to obtain more in proportion to my milk than my neighbours; but it involved considerable care and work in scalding the milk, and the only dairy I had at my disposal was the unlined earthen cellar of the cottage. Often I bitterly regretted that the money spent on the veranda had not been invested in a small stone dairy with a cemented underground compartment where one's produce could have been secure from summer and winter temperature alike, for even in those days there was money to be made in dairy-farming in the North-West.

The breaking went well. The five acres on the west boundary were quickly turned, and this new field I dedicated to the purpose of raising clean seed. It was in settling the limit of this small corner that the orthodox place of my western boundary first invited discussion. At the time the farm was bounded north, east, and west by unsettled land, and I and all my neighbours made use of each other's trails as a matter of course, so that there was never the smallest difficulty in reaching the winding, picturesque, untidy, and by no means safe by-way known as the Touchwood Trail. But the fundamental law that governs Western Canada's most admirable plan of survey is that a road allowance sixty-six yards wide shall be set aside every mile north and south, and every two miles east and west for the building up of the highway of the country, which ensures egress to the national highway to every farmer of one hundred and sixty acres. But good roads in the urban district of Saskatchewan are still very few and far between, and not a few of the best throughout Canada are due to the national enthusiasm for motoring.

My neighbour assured me that the heap of stones supporting a lengthy but infirm pole marked the far side of the road allowance, and not the north-west corner of the farm; but Roddy McMahon contradicted him flatly, and also prophesied that in any case the surrounding land would never be settled, and the Touchwood Trail would never be abandoned. He carried his point, and the limit of the five acres across the road allowance. Within five years I was hemmed in on every side, and had literally to beg my way through a neighbour's crops to obtain an exit. It seemed the more unjust since taxes drawn from my half-section had contributed to the development of the country for over twenty years, and long before any of its environing land had been claimed for culture – but in 1913 the road was graded.

This making up of the urban highway is one of the most important and yet one of the most neglected of the factors which count in the development of Canada. From start to finish its construction should be in the power of experts only, and held high above the reach of the design of political intention or the self-interest of individuals which frequently hampers it.

The end of the discussion of the actual boundary was that I resolved to fence the half-section on every side. It was not indispensable, because the forty-acre pasture was sufficient to protect the cropland from my own stock; and from May to November herd law compels every one to keep stock within bounds. In those days also one could send cattle to graze on the lake-shore land in charge of the local herd for a dollar a head, which included their six months' run in good pasture, their collection and return. To-day the charge has increased to a dollar a month. But through February, March, and April bunches of vagabond horses and cattle had called at the door of the cottage and tramped round the veranda, in any hour of the twenty-four, and helped themselves to the greater share of the vanishing oat-straw stack. All this one might have forgiven or forgotten but Dick and Nancy had gone off with them on more than one occasion, and were by no means eager to return even to the loaves and fishes of an orthodox stable and generous supply of oats; and in consequence I made a two-strand three-mile barbed-wire fence round the farm when I could least afford it.

Fencing in Canada is usually done by half-breeds. They are peculiarly alert and clever in any task which brings one into direct touch with nature and elementary conditions. I sent Hardwick out to the bluffs to get pickets, and grew tired waiting for his return with less than a score. It seemed so long and endless a business that I gladly made a deal with Tom Klein to cut and point the pickets and to put up the fence.

The three miles of barbed wire cost about one hundred and sixty dollars, including pickets and Tom Klein's labour, but the cost now of a two-strand fence is higher and works out as follows:

8 rolls wire	$24.00
660 pickets	19.80
Labour	20.00

63.80 per mile

It made a big hole in one's shrinking capital, and when it was finished my neighbour consoled me with his opinion that it was quite the worst of the many bad fences he had seen in the country, and that it wouldn't keep in one's own horses, not to mention keeping out other people's cattle. However, although in learning the detail and method of fencing I became aware that the pickets should have been driven fully ten inches deeper, the corners strengthened, and the wire stretched absolutely taut, it certainly served to keep in horses, and where may the fence be found to keep out a steer who will go down on his forelegs, get his head neatly under the bottom strand, raise it on his back to pull his body through, and finally rise on his forelegs and squat on his haunches for his final roll to the other side? Also my own calves developed sporting instincts, and leaped barbed wire as lightly as a hunter leaps a hurdle, and frequently chose to pasture on the wrong side of the fence.

Before the fence was an accomplished fact Hardwick had passed into the service and tuition of Guy Mazey. I don't think we should have parted quite so soon, as his work was really good in places, and I was getting accustomed to his noise. But one afternoon I was bound for the Fort and the Hudson Bay Store with seven pounds of butter to trade for groceries. I had washed the dinner dishes, packed the butter, made my own toilette, and the time limit for Hardwick's half-hour, for digestion, had expired twice over. I called, but there was no answer, no sign of a buggy. I went to the stable to see if Nancy was harnessed, and tumbled over Hardwick sleeping sweetly. It was a hot day and a pardonable offence, but there had fallen from his mouth a half-consumed cigarette, still alight, within a yard of Nancy's bedding. I said all that flashed in my mind at the moment, which is seldom wise on any occasion. Hardwick made use of the opportunity to inform me that certain men in the neighbourhood were coming to him daily to beg for his service, and that the lowest offer he had received was fifteen dollars a month, and that as others seemed to think so much better of his qualifications than I did, he thought he had better go at the end of the month.

I instantly agreed, and not altogether in the heat of the moment. I knew that he was good enough to be much better, and under no circumstances would I have consented to bar the way to his advance. Some days after, when we had agreed to forget the word, and honour in deed the fact that I considered smoking in stables a criminal offence utterly unworthy of a sportsman, he asked my advice as to which of his offers he should select. I could have cried: 'Iscariot!' at more than one name on the list of his would-be employers, but I revenged myself on them all by advising him to go over and hire on with Guy Mazey. I told him he would get there the lowest salary, the hardest work, the biggest family, unending chores, an endless procession of toil actually bridging dawn and darkness, and a really fine experience from one of the finest workers in Canada. He took my advice, Guy Mazey hired him, and I let him go at once. He remained there three months, giving satisfaction and learning much, and within quite a short time he went on to his own land and did well. He was quite perturbed about who would buck the wood and milk for me. I didn't mind about the wood as I had learned to do it myself, but I was in a dilemma about the milking and not at all sure that Roddy McMahon would help me over the difficulty, when I remembered the occasion on which I had heard Hardwick ask him to milk the hard cow.

'Milking, wood-bucking, water-hauling, and the biggest part of stable-cleaning is chore-boy's work,' he had answered. 'I wouldn't do chore-boy's work for forty dollars a month.'

On the morning after Hardwick's departure he stood in the doorway: 'Guess you want me to milk them cattle,' he said, on the note of accusation.

'I don't know who, if not,' I replied. 'You know that I can't milk.'

'Well, I guess I'll milk till a new chore-boy comes along. But if a man needs to get through his ten hours a day on the land he ain't got no time for chores.'

But on Saturday nights he always returned to the Fort to the bosom of his family, and on Sunday morning I attacked the business of milking. Hardwick had given me one lesson, but I was so thoroughly helpless on that occasion that I thought it would be wiser to wait and worry it out alone, and on that Sunday morning I sat through two hours pulling and pressing, and squeezing and giving vent to my feelings. At the end of that time I had about a quart of Molly's milk in the pail, and I hadn't even looked at the hard cow. I got up for a moment to ease my cramped limbs, and Molly, thoroughly fed up from the prolonged ceremony, walked off gaily, kicking over the pail in her exit!

As I turned into the cottage with rage and rebellion in my heart, Hardwick minor came across the wheat-field. 'My brother asked me to come over and milk for you,' he said. 'He couldn't get away himself because of the chores at Guy's. He said he knew you would be alone, and in difficulty over the milk.'

I told him the story of the morning.

'I'll go and catch her and finish her off now before I milk the other one,' he said, 'and as it's late they will be all right until to-morrow,' he added consolingly.

It is not a scrap of use to pretend because one can record delightful bits of chivalry, now and then, that as a rule my chore-boys did their duty. They didn't and they don't. The newcomer is immediately taught by the old soldier – in chore-boys – to make as much as he can and do as little as he possibly can for his money. But if I had much to forgive I had also much to be grateful for, and undoubtedly much was forgiven me.

Later on that Sabbath day there was a sound of wheels, a well-filled democrat stopped at my gate, and I recognized the Creegans.

It was the first time they had seen the farm and they were awfully nice about everything. They praised the lines of green wheat, the jolly view, the two new granaries, and everything within my green sitting-room, but especially the oiled and polished floor. Indeed I felt as though the mountain had at last approached Mahomet when Mrs. Creegan asked me if I would tell her by what process I obtained such excellent result, and I think this was the only occasion on which I have been asked for a hint concerning any detail in housekeeping. Meantime another member of the party who accompanied them had been introduced to me as Mr. Rossiter, a fellow traveller of the Creegans, who had just returned from a visit to England. He was in search of a job; he thought as manager of a farm.

He had been in the merchant service, and with one's usual habit of taking a great deal for granted, I reminded him that a sailor, of course, was always at home in any kind of work, and he acquiesced without any token of the embarrassment of modesty.

He told me that he had no actual knowledge of farming or farm implements, but it would be simply a matter of watching another do it, and he would be quite all right.

'We thought perhaps you would be able to offer Mr. Rossiter an opening,' said Mrs. Creegan, 'and that if you liked his work, he and Mrs. Rossiter would be so useful to you here.'

'I am sorry,' I answered. 'But the Canadian who is working the land for me suits me so well, because he knows everything and I know nothing. I want a chore-boy. But chores, of course, are worse than tiresome: milking, stable-cleaning, wood-bucking, water-carrying, and stoning the land on the breaking. And the salary, of course, is not much. I only pay ten dollars.'

Before they left Mrs. Creegan confided to me that she was more than disappointed that I had not been able to offer him some kind of work: 'He has been with us since he came,' she exclaimed, 'and we have neither work nor room for a third man. I shouldn't recommend him to you only that I really think he would be useful, he is quite a good carpenter. And all sailors are handy men!'

'I have a lot of painting and whitewashing to get through in-doors and out,' I said. 'I meant to do it myself, but now that I have the chores on my hands time seems to shrink. In any case I'll think it over, and consider if it is possible to offer him a little more money. But I had made up my mind to learn to milk; it would make one so independent of chore-boys, and I doubt if I shall ever do it myself as long as some one is round to do it for me.'

Usually I spent my hours of idleness on the shelving, sweet-scented bank of a sheltered slough, dreaming of the things that I would do on the day after to-morrow, or watching the sky or the flora and fauna of the prairie. The ducks made a kind of nursery of this particular slough; they were most fascinating, the parent birds were so fussy and the long families so foolish – the art of living should be learned from young ducks. And the gophers! Crouched on their haunches with their dainty little forepaws dropped in a most convincing attitude of supplication, they seemed, like those shallow but interesting Pharisees of old, to have walked off with the star parts of virtue without even pay-ing the orthodox price of a sense of sin. But Fate is presenting her bill to the gophers; they do not merely pilfer the grain, but in filling their subterranean granaries with winter's keep they rob crops by the acre. The Government is now in hot pursuit, armed with a package of 'kill-'em-quick' and the sharp sword of the righteous wrath of the farmers. Yet the dying cry of the gopher is not a pleasant sound to carry in one's heart, and one always hopes that the earliest specimens of the species did not make that attitude of prayer their very own in vain.

But, alas, the altar, so truly worthy of the thank-offering of sweet idleness, was a full half-mile from the kitchen in which it was my daily task to prepare the food of to-day, and the green sitting-room in which it was my daily duty to take thought for the food of to-morrow, and as one new chore after another en-croached on my hours of pleasure I resolved to raise an altar to *dolce far niente* at my door. Beautiful as were the flowers of the prairie, in the vicinity of the cottage none had planted flowers. It had something attractive in the way of form, but the veranda and the colour of the turf were marred by all sorts and conditions of weed. So I said there should be eight flower-beds around my accommodating veranda, but in the end I threw in the corners and so there were four big ones, and at north, south, east, and west the turf still clung to the veranda, affording the convenience of a comparatively clear approach, and also dividing the really arduous work of digging into sprints. Roddy McMahon had initiated me in the Canadian method of planting potatoes, but there was no digging attached to that or any form of his agricultural labour. He believed in implements, and was most anxious to attack my flower-beds with the plough. He ploughed, disced, and harrowed the potato-patch, and then he made a very deep furrow with the plough and I ran behind and dropped in the potatoes; the second time round we covered one row and prepared the seed-bed for the next and so on until the plot was seeded. Then the surface was harrowed again, and my leader and guide said that we had fixed the potatoes all right and returned to the breaking, whilst I returned to my spade. By the afternoon of May 23 I had got through about a quarter of my task when I went in to get supper for him and for Mabel Mazey, who was spending her last afternoon with me, her duties on the land having recommenced in earnest. Being the eve of my *first* Victoria Day on the prairie it is excusable that my sense of the holiday question was undeveloped. I had made an ignoble compact with the man that holidays should be ignored until the dream of the breaking of fifty acres was an accomplished fact. I served the meal on the veranda, and shared it with him and my neighbour's daughter, who had so often played the Good Samaritan in piloting me through the weekly half-day of more violent exertions upon which the order of my house depended.

'You ain't comin' down to the picnic to-morrow! My, but that's too bad!' I heard the Good Samaritan exclaim, as I turned the corner, with the chief supper-dish of poached eggs and fried potatoes.

'No,' he answered. 'I didn't make out to take no holiday before we was through with the breakin'. Good Friday we sowed, and Arbour Day I never reckon to count for much. A man may as well sow oats for work as plant trees an' call it holiday. But I guess Victoria Day is gettin' to be something pretty good.'

'Of course,' I said. 'You keep her birthday for one of your holidays, don't you? I remember passing through Toronto last year on Victoria Day.'

'We don't set much store by kings and queens in this country, but I guess that Queen Victoria was a real good woman,' observed the Good Samaritan.

'So they tell,' agreed the teamster. 'And not a bit stuck up on herself neither, for all she was the first woman in the world, an' dollars enough to buy out the whole outfit! Victoria Day is gettin' to be pretty middlin' good holiday all right! If it wasn't for the breakin' I guess I'd be going down to the picnic myself.'

'Well, I guess it ain't often you've missed a holiday or a picnic neither. My, you bet there'll be a crowd! Dave and Danny've got up a horse-racin' match – ten dollars aside. Twenty dollars collected up to yesterday four o'clock for the kids' sports! And the Indians bringin' in their ponies for the races this three days. They are all camped out by the lake side.'

'Is Danny going to run his sorrel mare 'gainst Dave's pinto? I guess my Charley horse could knock 'em both out,' said Roddy, with his heart in his eyes, and eyes and heart many miles away from my upturned acres.

'You had better go,' I suggested. 'A holiday will do the horses good and I don't mind doing the chores.'

'Guess a day off won't do 'em any harm. I'll hitch up and get right on down as soon as I've fed oats.'

'But ain't *you* going to the picnic?' fairly screamed the Good Samaritan.

I explained that I ought to be going to Mrs. Millington's Victoria dance, and that I didn't want Nancy to make the two journeys.

'Shame you should miss it, though! It will keep us guessin' to pack our kids in the buggy or I'd ask you to go down with us. Why don't you ride down horseback? Is it because you've got nothing to take? We all take something; cakes or cream or butter or sandwiches. It's all put on the table together, and you take what you like. Mother could help you out with two jelly cakes, I guess. Or take a pound of butter. My, but your butter is all right!'

It was a warm, sweet-scented, glowing, growing, Victoria Day. There was no cooking. I measured up oats all round, took a sun-bath on the veranda with my morning tea, and dallied with the decision of the dance. To keep the horses in all day was out of the question. Yet if they had their honest share in holiday joy which beckoned from the forty-acre pasture, I should have to bring them in, feed them, round up the two cows, milk them, catch Nancy by hook or crook, harness her, get into an evening gown, drive seven miles, in an open buggy, to the hospitable house on the lake shore, where for several hours, one would breath again the atmosphere and charm of gaiety unflecked with hint of hon-est toil! Then the seven-mile drive home, and the task, while still embarrassed by the skirts of diversion and by the shadows of the dawn, of divesting Nancy of her harness. Finally the ordinary routine of the day's work after a night of dancing. Everything was against the dance, but the supreme consideration for the honour of Victoria Day. If the Canadian wife of an Englishman could rise to the occasion in the giving of a dance it was clearly an Englishwoman's duty to be there – I decided to go.

Delighted with the effects of my efforts with dandy-brush and curry-comb, a mischievous dweller in the air compelled me, dur-ing the second feed of oats, to the disentanglement of the love-locks on Dick's heels. I heard the sound of a blow, and can just remember wondering who was hurt. It seemed ages after that I picked myself up from the far side of the stable door and crawled into the house with a grinding ache under my left jaw. It wasn't Dick. Dick was the most chivalrous as well as the gamest brute that ever bent brave shoulders to the plough or pulled a cutter across Canadian snow. He had sniffed at Kitty's oats. Kitty had promptly struck out at him and I had caught the blow. Luckily her hoofs were unshod, but it settled the question of the dance.

'I don't want to frighten you,' said the sister of the Good Samaritan, who had come over to borrow my saddle, 'but it was on Victoria Day that little Jack Macandrew got a kick in the jaw just like you. He took sick of lock-jaw, and died in the hospital the very next holiday.'

The blessed sun went on smiling and healing.

There were voices on the trail before nine o'clock. I was at my end of the veranda and remained there. It happens that one's presence is not always welcome on a holiday, but on that night Roddy McMahon made a great point of coming my way, so I knew that all was well.

'I brought along this feller. He was lookin' for work. I guess he'll do all right. He knows he's got to do the chores.'

'Did you have a good time?' I inquired.

'Pretty middlin'! The Fort fellers ain't up to much. They got scared over losin' their dollars and the race was off. There was some good pony racin' with the Indians, though. My, but I lost a chance! There was a breed down there with as nice a little horse as I ever see. An' he sold him for thirteen dollars! Worth a hundred if he was worth a cent!'

'Thirteen dollars! He must have been mad.'

'That was it. Mad-drunk, wasn't he, Pat? My missus guessed I ought to buy him for you, but I hadn't got the dollars with me.'

'But you don't suppose that I would buy a valuable horse of a drunken man for half nothing!' I protested. And then knew I had been horribly tactless, superior, and ungrateful.

'It's different with you, I know,' I exclaimed in contrition. 'We don't see the thing in the same light. Honesty is our one national decency. It has eaten its way into our bones. We can't help it any more than you can help your accent; that is to say, than *we* can help *our* accent. To have bought that horse would have been all right from your point of view, but out of the question for an English person. You know what I mean, don't you, Pat?'

'I am an Oirishman, lady,' said Pat, on the solemn side of ambiguity. But I felt rather than heard arrested mirth.

'Who bought it?' I asked.

'I guess 'twas the little Englishman. I don't mind his name. He came out last fall with his wife and kids.'

There was a tiny silence, followed by shrieks of Irish and Canadian laughter, in which I only failed to join because of my aching jaw. But the reason of my silence was misconstrued.

'I shouldn't have said, only you asked me straight out,' said the Canadian. 'I guess there's good and bad in all alike. 'Twill all come out in the wash!'

From the granary came music. All the stars drew near to listen:

Scatther his enemies,
Confound their knavish thricks –

'I guess we had enough of that comin' along the trail, Pat. Quit singin' them King songs. 'Tis Queen Victoria's Day.'

5

An Irishman's fortune – stoning the land

On the morning after Victoria Day Roddy McMahon introduced me formally to the Irishman, whom he addressed as 'Pat.'

'I guess he must be pretty badly broke,' he explained. 'He come up to me just as I was leaving the picnic and asked me to ask Jack Leader if he could sleep in his barn. I said, "I guess you must want a job all right." "I do that," said he. "I can put you straight on to the trail," said I, "if you come along back with me right now." I told him I guessed you would be willing to give five dollars for the first week certain, and a better offer if he was worth it at the end. I guess he's a good man all right on the land, and come July I must be getting some hay up for the winter. Maybe he would stay on here then and do your chores and get up the hay. I'll come along and run the binder through harvest, and he can stook.'

I cheerfully assented to the proposal, and the two went off together.

At the end of the first day Roddy McMahon came in to supper first, and in most cheerful spirits.

'Pat's worked fine,' he said. 'I can't think why a chap like that should be taking a job at twenty dollars a month. I guess I'll go down and fetch my team, and to-morrow he can get on to the summer-fallow with my team and Dick, and I'll keep to the breaking with the three big horses. I guess he's too good a man to waste his time doing chores and getting out stones.'

I was deeply interested in the increase of the land under cultivation, and eagerly assented to the suggestion that he should go down with Nancy and bring back the team at once. 'I'll do the chores I promised. 'Twas a piece of luck finding him!' he said.

I liked the Irishman well. As a rule when I have more than one man working for me I don't share their meal, partly because I couldn't help noticing that they ate much more when I wasn't there, and also in those days I often used to dash in from my outdoor chores at 10.30, light the fire, peel the potatoes, and make the pudding, and serve it on the first stroke of 12, and by the last stroke I was thankful to flop into the armchair in my own room with the solace of an 'individual' teapot and bread and butter.

But Pat was witty and most willing as a raconteur, and on one or two occasions – to my cost as it proved – I shared meals. On Wednesday and Thursday the work simply raced ahead, you could positively see the new fields forming from the distance of my bedroom window, and my flower-beds expanded too. On the Tuesday night Pat insisted on taking the spade out of my hand so that I might learn to dig like an Irishman, the principal point being to disperse the sod with a hard bang from the back of the spade after turning it. It was delightful to see him dig, and he seemed mightily pleased to hear it said, although I begged him to take his ease and look at the papers on the veranda or elsewhere, after his long day on the land.

But on Thursday down came the rains of June, a day or so in advance, and in sheets, and with the rain came ten tiny pigs in the open. Both men brought in their teams, which I knew meant that the rain would last. Roddy McMahon knows every move in the game of shelter and will find it anywhere – under a horse, or a bush, or a wagon, but he only comes in when it's all up.

'I guess I'd best go down to the Fort and buck wood for my missus,' he said. 'Pat here can do all the chores.'

Pat rescued the small pigs and induced the mother to follow him into a warm corner of the middle stable. He showed me how to mix her food, and then he put on his sheepskin coat and returned to the digging of the flower-beds in spite of the drenching rain.

'Begorra, and isn't it just the rain itself that will be getting it into the order of a fine seed-bed,' he explained.

Steadily it fell for thirty-six hours, and I don't know whether it was due to the long moist interval between the acts, but when work was resumed on Saturday things didn't seem to move so easily.

'Pat and me best change teams this afternoon,' said Roddy McMahon. 'Pat, he don't like Dick. The work is a bit hard on Dick, and he won't go for everybody, I guess.'

I felt a little disappointed. There was something so awfully engaging about Dick. Only a few days before I had driven him in Roddy McMahon's buggy, which is usually a death-trap, across the prairie towards the Fort and missed my way. Suddenly a line snapped, and I remembered that Dick was supposed to be only four years old – as a matter of fact he was only three. We were nearing the valley, and the noisy rattle of the old buggy plus the sense of liberty that comes with the sudden snapping of a line was quite enough to go to the head of an older horse than the long-legged baby, who just kept to his swift, strong pace between the shafts as though nothing had happened, until I coaxed him to obey my summons to halt. Many men murmured against Dick's ways on the land, but he was too young to have worked with the three heavy horses on the implements, and I think he gradually grew to connect men with the work he hated and women with his oats and the work he liked. He was always obedient and kind and helpful, and seemed to know when the others were trying one's patience, and did his best to make things easy all round.

On Tuesday night Roddy McMahon came in with an air of regret.

'I guess Pat's off to-night, or leastways tomorrow,' he said. 'He says he owes you an extra day 'count of the rain.'

'But why off?' I exclaimed. 'You say his work is excellent, and of course I will pay him its proper value. Say a dollar a day until you go, and then thirty dollars a month until harvest, and through harvest – harvest money.'

He went out with the information. But Pat was unyielding – his heart was on the trail. I gave him a cheque for the week's work in the morning, but remembering that he was very poor and would probably walk to South Qu'Appelle, I collected all my small change and borrowed a little more from Roddy McMahon to make up a dollar in cash, in case he wanted to buy anything on the road, and I asked Roddy McMahon to take it out for me.

'Best stay another week anyway, Pat,' I heard him say. 'It will be another five dollars for you, and I guess it will be more. She's that stuck on her flower garden.'

'It's not you nor her that should be advisin' me about five dollars, Roddy. I'm thinking I've more in the pocket of my old coat than you've ever seen, and more than she'll make on her farm for many a day.'

Roddy McMahon returned in the most subdued frame of mind I have ever seen him in. 'I knew there was something wrong,' said he, 'when a chap like that feeds on a five-cent bag of biscuit and looks to put in the night in an old barn with the horses. He dragged out his roll of dollar bills right there. "Roddy," he says, "I ain't much good at 'rithmetic, just see if it counts out all right. Should be a thousand dollars." And every dollar of it was in the roll all right.'

'But why did he come and work?' I asked. 'After all, he has worked splendidly.'

'Yes; and I guess he would have stuck to the job if it wasn't for something you said.'

'Something I said! What can you mean?' I asked.

'You mind that day you was having dinner with us and telling us about Old Country ways you said, "Get hold of a good English workman and you can't beat him the world through"? Well, when we got outside, Pat says, "So it's an Englishman will be the first workman, in her way of thinking. Well, there may be room here for a Canadian Roddy," he says, "but after that an Irishman will be after taking the trail."'

I had mastered milking and become quite independent about wood and water, but I had found out in some indefinable sort of way that Roddy McMahon hated working alone. It was true that every evening after work was over he went off to his uncle or his cousin, whose farms were within easy reach; but all the men who came along voted him good company, and men who are good company seldom care about being much alone. I remembered the Creegans' visitor, and went down the next day to offer him the job of second man, as I was particularly anxious not to risk any hindrance to the work on the land. I could see the work was going ahead, and I didn't want to part with the man, who seemed always a bit of the land.

'I was recommended a man who has just come out, the other day,' I told him at dinner-time. 'I'll go down this afternoon and see if he is still disengaged. Next year's seed-bed, I see, is the first consideration, and you shan't have the smallest interruption if I can avoid it.'

'Breaking land and leaving the stones ain't right,' he agreed. 'I tried getting off the plough and turning up the biggest fellows myself. But it ain't any sort of job, an' makes a man mad. Pat he ought to have stopped on. Hardwick got out a few, but he wasn't much good. You couldn't tell him anything. He had too much courage.'

'Too much!' I exclaimed. 'But one can't have.'

'Well, he always got his answer back, and was looking to teach me to work the land all over again, I guess.'

'Ah! We call it cheek,' I explained.

'That's it. He was well fixed with cheek all right. I'll milk the cattle for you. Guess it may be late before you get back,' he said magnanimously.

I offered Mr. Rossiter twenty dollars for a month's work. I told him he must milk, and that I should probably want him to do house painting and a little carpentering, but that his principal duty would be the monotonous work of stoning the land in front of the breaking plough; but that Roddy McMahon was good-natured, and knew the land and its implements from A to Z, and, I felt sure, would teach him anything he wanted to learn.

Afterwards I heard that he had said, 'If I am expected to do carpenter's work, why of course I shall want carpenter's money.' I think he was not at all anxious to move away from the hospitality of the Creegans, and that it was a very special effort on the part of Mrs. Creegan that induced the move. However, I carried him off in triumph, and to me he was courtesy itself, so that I didn't even resent his rather blatant note of self-confidence.

'I can do anything when I make up my mind,' he said. 'Don't trouble about that. I am not one of those who talk a great deal about what they can do. But I have no doubt when I have been a day or so on the place you will see that others can do just as well as this man McMahon.'

I saw I was up against a strong sense of the comparative, and inquired about his wife and child.

When we got home I found that Roddy McMahon had finished work, cooked his own supper, and gone on to his cousin's for the night.

I prepared supper and took it with the new man, thinking he might be lonely, as undoubtedly he was.

'Ah, how different it all is!' he said with a deep sigh after he had thrown a most unflattering glance around the kitchen. 'At home you should have seen my house. My dining-room – a carpet, armchairs, sideboard and all.'

In the morning milking was a slow process. Roddy McMahon, always kind to newcomers, helped him out with the hard cow, and then took him off with the team and pick, crowbar, and stone-boat to learn the meaning of stoning the land.

At the end of the morning he returned looking so very tired that I said that I would go along and help in the afternoon, and he enjoyed himself thoroughly when I spent a full ten minutes getting together all the little stones that don't matter. Roddy McMahon got off the plough and took me to a big fellow in the neighbourhood of the plough, and showed me how to test its depth and raise it if possible by inserting the crowbar as a lever, and when it was too tightly set to move in this manner to free it from the imprisoning earth with the pick; and all without a word, barring the usual phrase of encouragement at the end, 'I guess you'll get them out all right – but it ain't no work for a woman.'

I stayed out until it was time to go along and prepare supper. It is hard work stoning the land, and when the sun is on one's back almost exhausting; but if you don't dissipate the best of your strength trying to do the work of ten minutes in one, and take it in a firm and easy way, it is not altogether disagreeable, since one works in particularly close contact with the soil, and at least one can go home from the half-day's work with the consolation that the seed-bed is free from a few of the monsters which occupy a great deal of valuable space, obstruct and destroy implements. The insect population seeks the shelter of a stone as the natural centre for industrial development, and verily every 'big fellow' that is rolled off in triumph means disaster for a miniature city on its site.

At the end of the second morning the new man was obviously done.

'Rest this afternoon,' I advised. 'I'll go on with the stoning, and when you are sufficiently fit I shall be glad if you will go on with my work on the flower-beds instead.'

My garden bed had not, however, advanced when I got in.

'Well, how did you get on?' he inquired.

'Oh, I got out quite a few,' I said. 'Do you feel well enough to milk? It's Sunday to-morrow, take a long rest, and perhaps by Monday you will be fit again.'

But on Monday he complained that the land work was beyond his strength. He was downhearted, disappointed, homesick. And one never really knows whether people who appear to have an extraordinary opinion of their own power are not putting it on just to hide the weakness of which they are really conscious.

He wanted to go back to the Creegans, but I suggested he should put in the month doing odd and light jobs such as whitewashing and painting, and give himself a chance of growing physically stronger before he abandoned the idea of life on the land.

He started on the roof. I always helped him on to the veranda, and about every fifteen minutes he used to call me to pass my opinion on his work with all the manner of a portrait-painter. When we were not yet through one-half the roof the paint gave out, so I said I would send for some more, and he could go on with the work in the house whilst we were waiting for it. He painted the kitchen ceiling, and did it well, but spoilt my pleasure in it entirely by insisting on mixing that wretched pigment which produces putty colour instead of white. He also distempered two of the bedrooms.

'What do you think of it all, Mac?' he demanded of Roddy McMahon with the pride which at least made no pretence to ape humility.

'I guess it takes a mortal long time,' was the withering answer. 'If my work took me so long time as yours, guess we should be seeding when the wheat was ready for the binder!'

'I guess that feller ain't feeling good,' he told me after. 'He was offering Bert Mazey a dollar a week to come and milk the hard cow. His sort is best back in the Old Country.'

It was early one morning that he flatly refused to continue distempering, but the climax came on a day when I drove off to South Qu'Appelle directly I had served dinner, and returned somewhat late in the evening.

My brother, who had come down for a day or so, met me at the gate. 'I can't stand talking about another chap's work,' he said, 'but that new man is no good, and you ought to get rid of him. He grumbles about everything, and the moment you had driven off to-day he turned into his room and said he had finished work for the day, and he advised Roddy and me to do the same.'

'I am sorry you won't work,' I said to him the next morning. 'You know I have tried everything that could possibly make things easier for you; but I can't have anyone round who refuses to work except through illness. It isn't fair to the others.'

'Pay me my month's wages and I will go at once,' was the answer.

'Your month's wages?' I inquired.

'Certainly. You engaged me for a month, and you will pay me for a month, or the law shall make you.'

'When the law makes me, most certainly I will pay,' I answered. 'Until then you have worked so many days and so many half-days. A month's pay in Canada is due to twenty-six working days. My brother will give you a lift to the Fort, and here is your cheque.'

'How am I to know that it is any good?'

'By inquiring at the bank. I never keep dollar bills in the house.'

Other insults, led by the well-worn invitation to search his boxes, followed. This particular man had received nothing but consideration from me. I was unutterably sorry for him and honestly tried to do everything I could to cheer him along. He might have been a particularly useful member of society had he chosen. As it was he deliberately added helplessness to hopelessness, and he was the only person with whom I had a stormy passage or with whom I agreed to differ in Canada and in whose conduct I failed to discover my share of the blame. And one's share in the blame is always just a little consoling.

'You're best quit on him,' said Roddy McMahon. 'I never see anyone yet to do so little and to want so much praise for it. 'Twas a fright!'

6

The rains of June –
haying – harvest

On the Canadian prairie the harvest depends on the 'rains of June.' In 1906 these 'rains of June' fell in floods, and one saw the grain literally leap up from the earth to meet them. Mabel Mazey hardly ever came over just then, but her sister Pearl kept the weekly tryst with my household chores, which, however, only occasionally included the washing. From her I learned that Mabel was busy on the farm with disc and harrows, and even with the breaking plough, and every week used to hear how much work had been done on Guy Mazey's land.

At my neighbour's advice I left a bridle-path through the wheat-field. 'It won't hurt for a time,' he said; 'indeed, the wheat just there will be the thicker for the packing.'

Pearl arrived one sun-warmed afternoon that had come in the trail of days of rain. 'My, the rain has brought on the crops fine!' she said. 'But I guess you are going to have rare trouble with the weed – it's a fright! Stinkweed and mustard and shepherd's purse. I've never seen any so bad; though they do say you can't see the wheat for stink-weed on the trail to the Head.'

'Do show me which is which,' said I, 'and I'll go out and weed.'

'My! but you could never weed out that great field. And there's wild oats, too, I guess. Father says there always has been wild oats on this farm. I guess you had better wait and let the grain knock the weed out this year, and next year you'll be

summer-fallowing the field. But if you should do any weeding –
why, take out a grain-bag and take the weed right off the land
and burn it. It's no use to leave it lying round in heaps. Father
says stinkweed comes up to seed every month.'

I did a little weeding, not much, as it seemed to make no impression. As a direct result of that afternoon's conversation I
blocked my end of the bridle-path through the field, under the
impression that if I was to be disgraced by weed, the eye should
not be allowed to see what the tongue should not carry.

I worked hard through June at the stoning, and started to harrow, at first with only three sections drawn by Dick and Nancy.
From the beginning I was perfectly happy working on the land,
only I wished it was some one else's turn to get those tiresome
three meals a day. I had conquered milking after a fashion. That
is to say, I could extract every drop of milk even from the hard
cow, but it still took a very long time; forty minutes for two
cows, and Mabel Mazey could milk Molly dry in five. I never
overcame the difficulty of milking with the left hand, and to this
day get at least seven-eighths of the milk with the right hand
only, to the horror of some of the ardent disciples of method
who have sojourned at my farm from time to time. But even the
worst kicker submits to my method, so it has its points.

It was early in June that a letter came from my eldest brother
to say that he was coming out. His intention was to start a brewery. I hoped that he would find the water of Fort Qu'Appelle
good enough for anything. He intended, however, to put in a
month on the land with me, and he wished to spend that month
precisely as he would spend it were he one of a thousand immigrants tailed off to work for any farmer. I was delighted. He had
justly earned the reputation of doing things thoroughly. Great
interests had often been placed in his care with a sigh of relief,
and the more difficult the task the greater pleasure he had
always seemed to take in ploughing his way through. He was
due to arrive about the third week in June, and when day after
day passed and there was no news of him I got most horribly anxious. Besides, the haying season was approaching, and at last in
despair I engaged Hardwick minor for a month, so that he might

help Roddy McMahon put up a few loads in case my brother had wandered up another trail, although I began to feel quite certain he was dead.

I walked over to my neighbour one Sunday afternoon and confided to him that I was most wretched because all through the night a spider had ticked the death-watch on my bedroom wall. He led me into three corners of his shack, and I heard the same funeral march in each; and then he advised me to spend a couple of hours weeding the mustard in my wheat-field by way of a nerve tonic.

On the next day Roddy McMahon's father came to see me, and he always came to stay. He had the pleasantest way with him, and must have poached on the preserve of the Irishman's blarney-stone. He had the deplorable misfortune to lose both legs in a fifty-below-zero night out on the prairie. I always admired him for the pluck and resource with which he endured the blight of such a misfortune, but I think even still more because he was such a fine shot. He sat up in his old buggy, which had a very vagabond air even beside my own, and with the lines gripped between his stumps he brought down duck or rabbit and everything that flew or ran as though by magic. He often talked to me about the days of his youth in Scotland, and his aunts, who must have been gentle-mannered, kindly women of the well-to-do order, and he was always regretting he should never see the old land again.

'Oh, but you will some day,' I told him. 'If you want a thing so very badly, you can always get it; only of course you have always to pay, and sometimes to wait.' In my heart I didn't feel quite so sure about it, because I knew his land was mortgaged right up to the margin of its loan valuation, and only that day he had been entreating me to find some one who would give him nine hundred dollars for it. But I don't think he had ever been a very careful farmer, and his entire quarter section was dirtier than the dirtiest bit of my bad field.

'But if I sold it for five thousand dollars I should never go back home again,' he said with a sigh. 'I was a fine brae lad when I left. I would never have my aunties see me without my legs.'

I was in bitter trouble that day about the loss of a calf, and it was harder to bear because I felt it was in a measure due to my carelessness. I had tethered my two small beasts in the garden as usual, and immediately after breakfast had gone out picking stones. I had to scramble to prepare dinner in time, and when I went out after the men were served I found the younger calf lying down and obviously sick. Roddy McMahon said it was sunstroke, and acting on his advice, I bathed it frequently with cold well water; but all in vain, at sunset the little thing died. It sent a gloomier shadow over my deep anxiety about my brother, until my neighbour came along with a wire which told me he had arrived safely but had been detained in Montreal.

On the evening he came we walked all round the farm. The mosquitoes were out in furious swarms, but he said he did not mind a bite or so. He was full of admiration for the oats, which were really very beautiful: strong and healthy and thick enough to conceal all weed. He thought, too, that the wheat-fields looked beautiful, but not as thick as in England, where, however, I believe grain is never sown on stubble. He raised my spirits almost to the point of rapture by saying the farm surpassed his expectations, and that in England such a place might be worth three hundred pounds a year. Nearly all the land in my immediate neighbourhood was uncultivated, and one of the first visits we paid was to one of the model farms of the further neighbourhood, owned by Mr. Thomas Grigg, who came up from Eastern Canada with less than two hundred pounds capital, but had bought and sold pigs and horses and steers and dairy produce all the time, so that he made enough money to cultivate his grain land really well. His wheat-fields were two hundred acres and even more in extent and as even as a lawn, and his house was the pleasantest villa that I can think of on the land in Canada, with a cement cellar and bathroom and every convenience under the sun. His barn and stables, too, were great, and the little block of buildings was set on the side of a big, beautiful gully which on the other side stretched away over miles and miles of wheat land.

Mr. Grigg had then been farming in the North-West for over twelve years, and he had very little to learn when he came up from the east. I admired his farm more than I can say, and so did my brother, who occasionally made of it a channel through which to talk at me of the relation of admirable method to excellent result.

I thought I let my brother down very gently. I had taken quite easily to the habit of rising with the sun, sometimes even at dawn, and I took him tea and that kind of thing before I even mentioned the time. When my brother Lal had brought me tea in the morning I had felt that I had no claim to a single growl throughout the day. The fact is, new-comers make rather a mistake charging everything as though it were easy, then they hate it when they find it isn't. For instance, my newly arrived brother said, 'I have never milked, but of course I can milk. Give me the pail.'

'The hard cow is rather a test,' I warned him.

'Well, if *you* can milk her, I suppose *I* can,' he said with dignity. How he grew to loathe and detest that cow, and the curses he wasted on her! But the worst of it was I didn't know much about the laws that govern the generation of stock, and as he had once spent two months studying with a veterinary surgeon I took it for granted he knew all there was to know. He solemnly assured me she was not going to have a calf, that she was as old as the farm itself, and he most strongly advised me to get rid of her. In the bitter end I traded with Roddy McMahon for a four-year-old heifer which drank its own milk. As her calf was supposed to be coming shortly, I didn't find this out for a long time, because as a matter of fact the calf failed to arrive until nearly a year after, and just a month before the hard cow, who had passed into the possession of Danny McLeay, produced a heifer, and another and another as the seasons passed by. Five years later I wanted to buy her back, for she gave the richest milk I have ever seen in Canada, but he asked me forty-five dollars without the calf, and I had only paid my predecessor forty-five dollars for her including the calf.

Just about that time my brother Lal arrived, bringing with him a sheaf of oats in bloom and four feet high, grown on the ten acres of his homestead which he had broken during my resi-

dence the year before. He came to borrow the mower and rake
for a few days, and it was arranged that my elder brother should
go to Lipton with the wagon at the end of the fourth day from
the departure of the mower and rake, and bring them back.

Remembering how the trails had bothered me when I first
knew the prairie, I volunteered to pilot him on Nancy. My habit
was dripping and dry again long before we reached Lipton, but
by the time we had bidden Lal good-bye and turned on the
homestead route a July edition of the rains of June had set in,
and when we reached Troy Hill it was a miniature Niagara, and
I saw that the safe conveyance of the rake hitched on to the
mower hitched on to the wagon was going to be a problem sufficient to tax the ingenuity and experience of Roddy McMahon
himself.

At the hip of the hill we decided to take off the rake and push
it back into the wide wayside. Relieved of the tail of the outfit,
Tommy and Jim persevered gamely until they came to the neck
of the hill, which, however, really defied footing, and there was
nothing for it but to get rid of the mower and pull the team and
wagon along in sprints. Sheets of rain poured down on us, darkness was falling, thunder rumbled all around and in and out of
the hills. My poor brother! And poor Canada! But the next day
he was so nice about the adventure and so sorry about his ex-
pressive expressions, which I really hadn't noticed, and in any
case should have considered he was quite justified in using. But
when he said, 'I wish I had your patience,' I was so flattered that
I really had to tell the truth. 'You wouldn't,' I said, 'if it had been
a wind storm. I rather like rain.'

To the hay harvest he was quite a godsend. Never since the
days of his sojourn have I seen such marvellous loads. The few
Canadians who saw them stared in amazement, and indeed on
one occasion there was nearly a tragedy. With Hardwick minor's
help he had already pitched and packed two loads on my advice.
I had not seen the size of the loads, and Roddy McMahon had
assured me that three in the morning and two in the afternoon
was a fair average. They had gone out for the third. Twelve
o'clock came, half-past, one o'clock, and no sign of hayrack or

men. I climbed on to the stable roof, but could see no glimpse of them, and as my brother was born on the keynote of punctuality, I made up my mind that they had met with an accident, and set out on the side-trail to seek their remains. I met them a short distance up the trail. My brother wore his best expression of resignation. Hardwick minor was a little flushed.

'Where have you been?' I shouted. 'I felt sure you were dead, or something of the kind. What a ripping load!'

'Load!' said my brother bitterly. 'It was a respectable load when we turned to come home. I cleared out that big slough near John McLeay's pasture fence, and, fool that I was, I trusted the lines to Hardwick for a moment as we pulled out of the slough, and the horses wouldn't have made a mistake had he left them alone, but as it was just as we came up the incline the whole outfit pitched over.'

I couldn't help laughing, and Hardwick joined in the mirth.

'It's all very well for you who weren't there,' said my brother, 'or for Hardwick, who saw what was coming, and fell clear on the right side; but it is no joke being buried under a ton and a half of hay within an inch of the pitch-fork.'

'Beastly experience,' I acknowledged. 'Come and dine.' It takes an Englishman to put up a ton and a half load of hay on the Canadian prairie, and if a Canadian had been looking on he would have qualified his Englishman with the usual colouring.

'It was such a splendid load!' he murmured. 'And of course the steak is dried to a chip.'

'It was,' I acknowledged. 'But I remembered how you hated it, so I gave it to Pax, and put ready some more. By the time you have unhitched and watered the horses the meal will be just ready.'

Throughout that pleasant summer I rode much. I didn't appreciate men of method then as I do now, but it was delightful to have one's horse saddled for one again, and the saddle and bridle and iron and things all polished and shining and as they should be. My brother wouldn't take Nancy, but Charles Edward paid us a short visit in exchange for Dick, and although he certainly was not an inspiring mount, he saw much of the country in the beautiful Qu'Appelle valley. We usually rode between 6 and 11 P.M., and one Sunday night we lost our way hopelessly, and it was certainly Charles Edward who led us back in safety to the gate of the new fence.

Acting on my neighbour's advice, I engaged a man who was breaking seventy-five acres for him to break twenty-five for me. He was to break, disc, and harrow, in short put in shape for crop, twenty-five acres, and the charge was to be five dollars an acre. He found his team of four horses in fodder, and I agreed to board and lodge him; and I found this by far the cheapest way of breaking up the land. The name of the breaker was Si Booth, and in common with most of the other Canadians with whom I seemed to come in contact he was distinctly more individual than typical. He was very tall, lean, with a sunburnt, well-formed face and those far-seeing blue eyes that always seem on the lookout beyond the horizon. He hated that his work should be ruled by the clock, or even the sun. 'If I work by the piece when I'm in the mind and horses feeling good I can break three acres a day easy. And when I feel like quitting work for a day or so, why, I'm free to quit.'

He had a perfect way of handling young horses, and reduced all the 'frights' in the neighbourhood to a lamb-like docility and to do him cheerful service, either as one of his team of four on the land or even in single harness. He had a delicate digestion, which I never failed to bear in mind. He was always friendly and kind, and my brother and I used to love watching him at his work. Everything went with such tranquil ease as he walked untiringly behind his team of four horses, two out of which were usually unmanageable bronchos with whom no other man could afford to have dealings.

I reckoned that the addition of this twenty-five acres would bring my 1906 seed-bed up to seventy-five acres breaking, in addition to thirty acres summer fallow and the arms of the eighty-acre field, which would be seeded with oats after spring ploughing. In addition there were the five acres for the seed garden, which I stoned heroically. I knew I couldn't afford the extra breaking, as it was already clear to me that my stubble crops from the eighty acres wasn't going to produce anything near the result of the first year's crop gathered from a summer-fallowed seed-bed. But I couldn't afford anything, so I kept my mind's eye front and positively refused to turn to the right or the left where the comforters of Job are always in ambush.

My brother was very busy cultivating the thirty acres of summer fallow, which he assured me was still in very rough condition, and that in his opinion Roddy McMahon got over the ground too quickly. However that may have been, it is certain that he got through more work in that first season than in any succeeding year; but my own idea is that the weed of two years' seeding choked the land, and hindered the miserable plough. Here and there it just scratched the undulating land in the dips, leaving the seed-bed shallow in places, and a lot of extra work for disc and harrows. In constant accompaniment to some excellent work, my brother grumbled. He confounded the disc, the harrows, the horses, the mosquitoes all in a breath, but to the furthest of all possible limits under the sun he confounded my cooking.

I didn't condescend to stand up for myself about the cooking, but I said that Roddy McMahon, who at least knew his business, did awfully good work on the implements, and considered the horses the best team in the neighbourhood.

'Mac could plough with an old nail and disc with a hairpin,' he said scathingly. 'Not an implement, not a solitary thing, on the whole place is complete. Where there should be well-fitting bolts and nuts I find bits of wire, hairpins, bits of string! Anything does for Mac.'

'Well then he has resource, you must allow,' I claimed.

'Resource! There is such a thing as too much resource. Sometimes I think I almost dislike resourceful people. It is all very well to be able to fall back on an alternative, but your resourceful people always seem to *select* the alternative. I don't profess to know anything about implements, and I can tell you it is not easy to learn on Roddy's implements. And you do things yourself in exactly the same way. I take the trouble to get up at dawn, or go out after work, so that there my be birds at least for the table. And instead of taking the trouble to pick them you skin them. Yesterday I shot a couple of canvas-backs that might have almost resigned one to life on the prairie, and you skinned them and tossed them into a stew. A positive sin! I shot a snipe this afternoon and I picked it for your supper. If you eat it yourself, you may understand the difference.'

I wondered if my brother would fall back on alternatives or if he would continue to pick the feathers off small birds if he had to prepare food for the three meals for three men day by day, week in week out, not to mention washing up; but I wasn't altogether indignant.

After all he was married, and so many wives make of the dining-table an altar of propitiation that it isn't to be wondered at that quite a number of husbands and others seek their best moments of life in the hour and at the place of meat-offering. Besides, although I never felt quite so inferior as in glancing at my reflection in his correct mind, I managed to score sometimes; seldom in the satisfactory form of word, it is true, since life among 'the lords of creation' was teaching me the force of discretion, but occasionally in deed.

The memory of one Sunday morning sends a glow of victory through me to this day. It was over the water question. The water question in nineteen cases out of twenty is a little difficult on the prairie. Broken in on a homestead where I lived through three months of appalling discomfort on the top-note of health without any other than slough water, I had developed an unconcern as to colour, flavour, and convenience, which seemed to arouse nothing less than exasperation in the mind of others in any special time of stress. My well is quite the best in my neighbourhood from the greatest number of points of consideration. If it sometimes is overfull, it is never empty. All through the winter, when many of my neighbours were melting ice and snow to supply their stock, I had enough and to spare of pure and sparkling quality. But before the spring flood dries out of the slough the well is a little difficult of access. The usual method of bringing the water to the house is by means of a barrel set on a stone-boat drawn by a horse to a point as near the kitchen entrance as possible. I used Dick and Nancy on these excursions, and never had the smallest difficulty with Dick. Occasionally Nancy wandered off into the slough with the barrel whilst I was occupied with the pail and the well, and now and then she objected to the weight of the load, but she could always be coaxed home.

On the occasion of which I write the colour and quality of the water were excellent, but the well still a little difficult of access. The water had only just dried out of the slough; the pathway across was beset with pitfalls for the uninitiated, and even under the best of conditions it is wisdom to haul the water barrel in patience and good temper.

Suddenly through the pleasant Sabbath atmosphere shot the fierce breath of wrath, reproach, regret, recrimination, curses! My brother came round the little group of poplars that guards the open-air pigsty alone.

'What's wrong?' I inquired.

'That obstinate devil won't budge an inch although the barrel is only three parts filled! Look at the state of my clothes! On this place one has literally to go to Hades for water. Of all the –'

'Oh, hush! *I'll* come,' I said indiscreetly in the stress of the moment.

'And you may come! But I'll lay you a five-pound note to this miserable farm, which I should think you would be glad to get rid of at any price, that you will not get that obstinate beggar to haul in the barrel.'

Dick and I knew and liked each other better than anyone in those early days on the farm. It was during the first temporary absence of the big team that I learned through him how to clean stables, groom horses, feed and water them. I knew that if I couldn't compel him to bring the barrel to its destination, at least I could induce him to try, and in two minutes back we were with our splashing load. The same kind of tragedy occasionally occurred with Nancy, who was an angel in the saddle, but only submitted to harness, and now and then didn't fail to let me as well as others know how very far she was born above it. On one occasion, before I understood her, we were half way up Troy Hill when she suddenly started to travel backwards, and then stopped. I felt that only physical pain or weakness could cause such behaviour, and at once got out and led her to the top. To this day she frequently stops at the foot of Troy Hill and turns her head with the unmistakable request to me to get out and walk, but an appeal to her vanity in the form of a compliment always saves the situation. My brother wouldn't condescend to cajolery, and occasionally there was a scene. He grew a little bitter, and I am afraid so did I. Nancy was one with the beautiful bits of the prairie.

August came: one walked in shimmering, friendly, gossiping green oats up to one's eyes. The green of the stately and more self-possessed wheat was turning to pale gold at the tips, and in places deepening to the hue of amber, so that one might have dreamed it full harvest time but for the wind which waved it here and there to prove to the watching, waiting farmer that the surface of gold was still flecked and lined with lingering green. A hayrick weighing about fifteen tons, taller than is usual on the prairie, but not particularly orthodox in form and altogether unthatched, graced the stackyard. It is claimed in this land of heavy work and scarce labour that the winter veil of snow provides all protection necessary for hay; but much is wasted through rot caused by autumn and spring rain, and now that the dawn of the day of commercial farming is really come to the prairie, and all farm produce is consequently on the ascending scale of value, it is probable that much more labour will be expended on the cultivation of grass and protection of hay.

We saw much of our neighbour John McLeay, whom we all liked well, and who told us plain, unvarnished tales of the rebellion; of the good money that was made by the land settlers through the hire of their wagons and teams to bring in the stores and ammunition for General Middleton's forces. He showed us the repeater with which they were armed, and he might well have presented it with a tall tale of heroism, as it was of the kind that made one feel ready to meet all Europe; but he frankly acknowledged that he and most of the neighbours lived in fear of the Indians, and that at the first word of their possible presence owner and repeater sought refuge under the bed. For my effort in agriculture he had the kindliest encouragement and most soothing flattery. He wouldn't see any wild oats nor smell any smut in my fields or granaries after that first occasion, and always had his finest word of praise ready for the pigs and the cows and the horses. When I needed advice and a little reassurance I always walked along the pleasant side-trail and talked to him in the shack which he built and which he has lived in for over twenty years, and which is quite the most primitive prairie home in the Qu'Appelle neighbourhood. Up John McLeay's trail went also both my brothers when feeling fed up with the ache of toil and the pain of mosquito bites and the stress of things in general on the prairie; and our kind host had always a soothing word for our ills and a pleasant yarn of the days when he took three months to come out from Scotland in a sailing-boat, or the days he cleared his homestead down east, and the crops they gathered from just an acre or so to hoard as gold; and then the splendid day, already more than twenty years old, when he came West to select his homestead and choose the loveliest half-section in the Qu'Appelle valley because a prudent adviser begged him to make wood and water his first consideration; and how he had selected homesteads here and there for one and another member of his family until it seemed quite a McLeay settlement. Once or twice I had tea in the shack – tea without milk, because although he had about half a dozen milch cows he never bothered to milk – and bacon of his own curing, and bannock of his own baking. And for me the cups and plate went through the infrequent ceremony of regeneration by water. For hours have I listened to his yarns, and never was an unkind word spoken of friend or neighbour or stranger. He is first favourite with the elevator men, and always imagines he gets a pull with them in grade and price, but on that point I have my doubts.

So on the second Sunday in August John McLeay and Lorna, his faithful dog, came along the trail to inspect the crops. As usual his judgment was flattering.

'It's the finest stubble crop in these parts, I guess, and you'll be getting a great harvest. But say now, dinna be in a hurry to cut. You should be a good eight days behind me with the binder, and I'll not be cutting till next Thursday.'

He took his drink of milk, which is the only form of hospitality which we can persuade him to accept, and when he had rested awhile and the sun was going west he got on to the trail again.

'So-long,' said he as we parted at the gate. 'I guess I'll go and have a look at your breaking, and get home by Danny's. Maybe I'll be seeing you again before the binder gets to work.'

On August 17 Roddy McMahon took the binder into the wheat, and my brother and I did our best to keep up with it as stookers. None but those who have followed the binder day after day can realized the monotony of this labour of stooking. I did a fair share between the preparation of meals, but, heartily as I disliked the form of indoor labour, it broke the monotony; to my brother it must have been almost unbearably irksome. I stooked on the left wing of the field, and after supper I worked by moonlight to endeavour to keep up with my fair share, and in the cool reviving air of evening the entire character of the work changed as though some monotonous measure of duty had suddenly softened to a soothing chant. The desire to growl ceased to pursue me. All one's irritating angles and corners seemed to round off in some soft and silent process of the early night. But the stooking of that eighty-acre field of stubble crop, and the sight of a wide and totally unexpected area of wild oats, brought my brother's dismal experience of a prairie farm to its final summing-up.

'If we had plenty of capital and could buy a decent place with a decent house, and a decent barn, and a decent bathroom like the Griggs', and could afford to get out trained English labourers to work it properly as we do in England, there might be something in it,' he said, 'but as it is, Lal is quite right, it is a convict's life. I am afraid you have taken on something you will never see out. And I am very sorry for you,' he added with due solemnity. 'I determined to see you through the harvest, and I am afraid it will be far below your expectation owing to these wild oats.'

'You must allow that the feed oats are splendid, and the hay is good, and at least I have learned to live economically and to do without things,' I said in the energy of self-defence. 'And if I don't see it out, at least it shall never see me out. Next year I shall have all that newly broken virgin seed-bed, and although expenses will be a long way outside the value of the crop, I can draw on my other enterprise to meet the difference, and that at any rate is a commercial success.'

'You want eight good horses and two good men to get this place into anything approaching successful commercial enterprise,' he insisted. 'However, I must move on east to see what prospect Canada holds out for a brewery. It should be good considering one pays a shilling here for a bottle of stout that is sold for twopence in Ireland.'

On September 12 he left, and was obviously not sorry to go, although kind if a little inclined to be angry about what he no doubt considered to be my obstinate determination to pull through. If he worked as a martyr all the time, at least his work was stamped with that quality of excellence with which genuine martyrs sign their work; and the fact is I wasn't in the mood to be generous to men just then. Always at the back of my mind had been the belief that they had a genuine title to the splendid term which has come to be a byword, 'lord of creation.' To make life possible one drank at the fountain of the thought of men, not women; but through the shoulder-to-shoulder rub of everyday working-life in Canada it grew clear that although more giants had issued from the male division, within the crowd men have hoisted their pretension to superior power not on the rock of superior work, but on the sands of superior wages – the misappropriation and unfair division of money. Had my brother been a little more sympathetic about the fact that I had to wash towels which were called upon to perform the united service of sponge, loofah, and occasionally of soap and water for the man on the land, I might have been a little more sympathetic about his having to use the towels I washed. As it was, he sat on the edge of the veranda with a face like a boot and washed out his own towels in Hudson's soap, used strictly according to the directions on the wrapper; and I heartily wished that it had been the fate of a great many more men to wash towels all their lives. But I admired him immensely in many ways and envied his order and method, as I did every one who came to the farm armed with these fine weapons. The truth is that, like Nancy, and, according to Browning, even the good Lord, both of us were badly in need of a little praise. When he had gone I looked about me, and in view of the many stooks in the wheatfield which bore the wild oat crest, I knew the result of the year must be a financial failure, so I tossed my hope and faith to the next. I saw that the ten and four acre arms of the big field were clean and free from wild oats, and I determined to use them for oats in the following year, so that I might reserve every acre of the land of the new seed-bed for wheat. Roddy McMahon agreed.

'It would be a good act all right,' he said. 'I guess we must try and get in a threshing outfit good and early, so that you can get threshed out, and we can plough up that much easy this fall. There ain't nothing doing between now and threshing, so I guess I'll quit. You can do the chores all right and don't need to be paying a man. Alan Redcliffe he'll be threshing out John McLeay and Danny and Dick Ryan and that bunch, so I guess it will be wise to get him to come on in here same time. I'll take a team for you on the round, and they'll all come back and help you out.'

'Do,' I assented. 'Make the usual arrangements and tell me what they are, only be sure and let me know a day or so before when the threshers are coming.'

'That's all right. I guess I shall bring back the team most nights. Old horses want good stable this time of year, the nights begin to get cold.'

He brought me a load of wood before he went, and that afternoon I was again alone, but this time in tune with things in general and absolutely independent. I could hitch up a team, haul water, buck wood, harrow. I could milk the hard cow with patience and Molly with ease. My cooking chore was at an end; I need no more wrestle with the washing of towels. I was most easefully and blessedly and thankfully alone. A soft sweet rain came sweeping up from the West. I sat in a deckchair on the veranda and watched in sweetest idleness as it dripped on to my flower beds, in which nasturtiums, mignonette, and love-in-a-mist already flourished amazingly. And there came to me with the silence and the softly falling rain of that restful afternoon a deep and abiding love of solitude which, like the consoling breath of the soil, cleanses the channels of one's understanding to sun-clear vision, discovering all the arrogance and unkindness in criticism, revealing the illusion of difficulty, proving one's anger and wrath and righteous indignation and clamour for justice occasionally funny and always unworth while. Like rain falling softly on the parched bed of thristy flowers, solitude revives one's energy of life; in its atmosphere there comes the bird of peace with its reassurance of the hourly vanishing waters of the flood of things temporal, the tendril of truth gathered from the tree of knowledge, which is the eternal centre of the homeland of the soul.

7

The harvest of
my first seeding

It is recorded in my diary that within the first week of my release
from the service of men many weak spots revealed themselves in
the armour which the daily round and common task forged
upon me in my first season on the farm. On the first day I met
with bad luck. I was due to fetch barley chop from Guy Mazey
for the well-being of my pigs, but Nancy burst her halter and
made off, and refused to be caught until after sunset. It is registered that I failed to milk that night. On the following day comes
the entry, 'Stayed in bed until 7:30, being deeply interested in
"The Marriage of William Ashe," but remembered my duties
suddenly and got out on the stroke of remembrance.' On the
next, 'An awful morning, intensely hot. Severe headache, and
took at least two hours to find the cows, who had got right away.
Lost my temper and blasphemed badly and loudly and bitterly. I
haven't the common sense to lay hold of method to prevent
these happenings, nor the self-control to bear the natural result.'
Later in the week, 'Rose with the sun. Went out and did my
chores one by one thinking of the thing I was doing all the time,
or at least remembering to try to. Kept my temper when Molly
kicked over the pail of milk which had taken me forty-five minutes to extract from the hard cow.'

From the twenty-first of September through three whole days
the rains descended, and as usual miniature floods came down
the chimney, and in through the cellar shaft, to which one of my

newly made flower beds had discovered an entrance for all things that should not be found in cellars – flies and gophers, and rain and dust, and on one occasion I found there a family of lizards. Guy Mazey passed through one day on his way to the Fort, and he prophesied that when the rain cleared the wind would blow the stooks 'good and dry,' but he added that the rain was most penetrating, and that he feared it would both discolour and soften the grain, and maybe lower it a grade. It is marvellous how its tiny leaf envelope protects the wheat-kernel; but it is in the season when the grain doesn't need protection, when it is caught dead ripe by the reaper-binder under the top-note of the harvest sun, and stands for twenty-one days at ease in stook, sun-drying through the day, and hardening to the kiss of the early frost by night, and finally passes through the threshing process into a sound granary without having once known the contact of moisture since harvest, that the Canadian prairie provinces send into the world's market wheat for which the world can find no match, red-gold and hard as bone.

Tempest followed the heavy rain. The wind-storm is the one mood to which Nature is subject on the prairie in which I found it hard to find a part. The very power of thought as well as action seems to desert one, and even when you remain in the house it is physically exhausting, and nerve racking; and the sense of rest and relief when the wind storm has passed over is inexpressible. However, on this occasion my sense of relief was short-lived, since I perceived that in the force of its passing the greater number of the stooks had come to grief. Some had blown hither and thither at the sport of the wind, others had merely collapsed, but I knew in my heart that I ought to restook every one, and to begin that very hour.

But one does not tumble into the chore-boy's and every other duty on a farm without paying the penalty in physical fatigue. In those early days even milking tired me, but cleaning out stables reduced me to something too limp even to grumble; and in stooking but a small share of the harvest sheaves I had become fully aware that this is one of the strenuous tasks in the life of an agriculturist, a task requiring sharp attack and sustained resolution to pull it through. A day of blazing sunshine followed rain and wind. I procrastinated for two days.

'I am afraid your wheat may be injured if you don't get your stooks together,' my neighbour warned me.

That day, the next, and the next I stooked and bitterly I reproached myself for the delay when here and there I found a bonny yellow sheaf with some of its members already in tendril on the rain-softened bosom of Mother Earth, discoloured and at first sight almost mildewed. But, like most ills that befall from without, the appearance of injury was greater than the actual damage, although stooks should never be permitted to lie on the ground but should be replaced on the earliest possible occasion when storm has dispersed them, since in spite of the special care provided in its natural envelope the grain will soften even if it doesn't discolour or burst into growth. For two days I restooked rather grimly, passing from row to row without daring to look more than twice a day at all the rows behind. I finished at four o'clock on Saturday, and went into the cottage and flopped upon my bed and remained there some hours over Sabbath sunrise, so the cows must have had another night off.

Nature grew tired of her vagaries, and the avenging brightness of the fall set in. The Qu'Appelle valley lay like an irregular trail of blazing gold beneath the Indian Summer sun, and on either side the grey-green, sun-tanned tint of the prairie seemed to gaze with a little weariness, and just a little wistfully at colour. Colour that had but to come and lay in laziest loveliness by the lake-side watching the sky to draw throbs of worship from those who passed through the valley. Colour that had done nothing, whilst the prairie-land which had thought, and energised, and brought forth richest offerings for man, and had grown weary sharing the burden of toil seemed to become a little more faded, and was almost disregarded – except in its special gift patches of amber stooks – because Beauty chose to save her supreme gift for the hills and coulées of the lake-side. Colour, 'the soul's bridegroom,' was in the happy valley drawing all that was glad, and sad, and best worth having from the soul of man! And in the Indian Summer even the monster wind goes off for a holiday, or goes to sleep, so there is none to whisper to the prairie that the winter snowfall will soon cover the features and face, and almost change the form of the Great Mother; that after all hill and valley, lake and *coulée* are just bits of her, and that its own gay, glad, new day of spring is always coming.

Nancy and I spent delightful hours along the more silent and unfrequented paths of the prairie which stretch and wind along the hills east and west of Fort Qu'Appelle, and between Le Bret and Katepwa and on the western side to that paradise of sportsmen known as the Head of the Lakes. Returning from such an excursion one evening my neighbour tossed me into a fever of anxiety by hinting that in all probability I shouldn't get threshed out at all, as Guy Mazey was threshing his crop and then moving south to a bigger job; and that no outfit would come out of its way to do my solitary wheat-field, especially when they saw the wild oats in the corner!

But on the Sabbath morrow came John McLeay to say all was well. The threshing outfit of one Alan Redcliffe, a farmer who owned many acres on the wheat plain of Wideawake, had promised to come to our corner directly he had threshed out his own crop. The outfit was to move into Danny McLeay's on the evening of the next day, from him it would go to John McLeay, then to me if I were willing. If!

No words can make clear how much I owed to John and Danny McLeay in my first seasons. It is true they were relations of Roddy McMahon, who had a quiet way of going after them in every untoward or impossible occasion connected with the well-being of the beasts or the moving of granaries. In late years in London sometimes I have felt inclined to add a note to the jeer that greets the threadbare argument that women must not be allowed the privilege of a voice in the selection of their lawmakers lest chivalry, which has held for so long such a comfortable armchair in the hall of tradition, might be heard of no more. But although to whatever degree generosity may enhance the quality of justice, it must never be allowed to take its most sacred place, I can't say chivalry hasn't any real existence when I remember how often those three men came across the prairie to do me service in time of need; when I think of their simple courtesy and kindness, their word of sympathy and advice when things went wrong. To deny that the advantage of careful breeding, and training, and culture is each in its measure a factor in the creation of the completely gentle man is ridiculous, the thorough-bred is as unmistakable in the human as in the equine order of beings; but the Canadian gentlemen begins indeed on the prairie, and the development of manner is as interesting and full of promise as the development of character and the material prosperity of this great nation which is so sure of a leading place in the history of the world.

In the morning came Roddy McMahon to claim my sheaf-rack and team for Danny McLeay's use, and towards evening I heard the hum of arrival. I rode over to see the wheat; it was of a most beautiful sun-kissed colour, and clean and hard, but not quite so hard as it had been in the previous year. Wheat in stook cannot stand such rain as fell in that September. Heriot Hylton-Cave had assured me that Danny McLeay must be contemplating matrimony as he was sowing lawn grass in front of the shack, and he added that after the ceremony had taken place the shack would hardly continue to be free quarters for bachelors, nor would ducks be any longer cooked in butter. Roddy McMahon's sister was cooking for the threshers, because Danny McLeay didn't marry until the next year, when the shack grew to a four-roomed cottage and became the cleanest, neatest, and most comfortable prairie home I saw in Canada.

'It's good wheat all right,' he said, as we leaned over the top-bar of his roofless granary, 'but I should have been away ahead if I had stacked before the rain came. But it's going to be a better yield than I looked for!'

The outfit came on to me a few days later, just twenty-four hours before I expected them. At three-thirty Nancy was objecting to carry sausages, roasting meat, and the crockery which in those days the Hudson Bay Company, under the chief factorship of Mr. Archibald Macdonald, made a sportsmanlike practice, worthy of the business enterprise and tradition of the 'Adventurers of England,' of lending to their customers for the festival

of threshing without charge, and at six-thirty I had to feed fifteen hungry men.

'My! and no woman to help you. But I would have come myself only that I have been away from home helping John and
Danny these three days,' said Roddy McMahon's sister, who
sometimes came with her three boys to pay me a visit.

'It's all right,' I said, 'Miss Ryan has promised to come. Hazel
said Mrs. Ryan would have come herself only she had to go
down to the Fort to attend the Woman's Aid Meeting.'

Hazel, who was one of the brightest, kindest children I remember in Canada, had offered to stop herself. But I always envy
Canadians the power of getting through their household duties
as easily as one puts on one's clothes. If I hadn't learned to
achieve mine with glory, at least I could get through without
shame – in silence. But if conversation was expected of me there
was no end to *contretemps*; baking-powder went into the gravy
instead of flour, salt was in the place where sugar should have
been, and everything in need of the temporary process of the
oven was completely forgotten until the perfume of its ashes told
the tale; and the teapot could never be found.

Miss Ryan came in before the dishwashing hour, but she had
come from assisting some bachelors through their threshing,
and was obviously suffering from severe headache caused by
overwork. I dispatched her to my room for rest and sleep, having
served the meal of beefsteak and potatoes, scones and stewed
apples without mishap. Utterly weary and worn out my guest
slept until morning. I had told Roddy McMahon to tell the men
on the outfit that they could use the two remaining bedrooms as
they had no caboose and sleeping in granaries is cold and uncomfortable when once frost has set in; but I hadn't bargained
for a guest in my own room. However, the training in my
brother's homesteader's shack and its attendant tent has often
made difficult matters easier to deal with, and I spent the night
on my bedroom floor covered with a travelling-rug and an evening coat, and a dressing-case for a pillow. It says something for
prairie chores as well as prairie air that I did sleep, to wake with
the first shadow of dawn, and I served my fifteen guests with

porridge, sausages, and fried potato, scones, and treacle on the stroke of 6 A.M.

My kind 'aide,' however, was no better; I thought she was on the verge of illness, and insisted on her going home before noon. Through two days I roasted joints, and occasionally dropped them, fried beef-steak and bacon, peeled potatoes, made scones and puddings, served my guests and washed up without daring to pause for a moment. The men of the outfit were wonderfully pleasant and considerate as they always are, and Roddy McMahon milked, hauled water, bucked wood, made the tea and poured it out, and proved that his power of resource did not begin and end on the land.

The harvest was not encouraging, although distributed in three granaries it looked a great deal more than it proved itself eventually at the elevators. I paid for the threshing of one thousand two hundred bushels, but it yielded only seven hundred and eighty bushels at the elevators, where all but the first four loads was heavily docked in grade and in weight for smut and wild oats – and, of course, my seed grain. Over and above the seed grain I used was forty bushels which I had cleaned and did not need. I sold this at South Qu'Appelle in August as No. 1 Northern for a dollar a bushel without dockage, precisely the same wheat as the bulk which had just passed as No. 2 Northern with, I should think, the heaviest dockage within the experience of the elevator men of South Qu'Appelle. I determined to sell no more wheat at the local elevator, though there are times when this is practically unavoidable, but I always contend that in justice to the farmer, who is the chief corner-stone in the foundation of the prosperity of the country, in every town marked by an elevator, Government weights and an expert grader appointed by the Government should stand sentinel by its side. In his first hand-to-hand struggle with the land the farmer of little or no capital has often far less to weary and dishearten him than when he arrives at the stage where his dealings with banker and trader set in until he passes through their difficult way to the place of prosperity where he is no longer at the mercy of either.

wild oats. At the end of the second day Roddy McMahon asked me to let him off the hauling job, and gave such excellent reasons for the request that I couldn't refuse. The four loads settled the threshing expenses and the balance of the wages due to my helper. I owed no money to the trading people, only a very tall note to the Union Bank which included all such payments, with the exception of the hardware store bill, which at that time included binder twine as well as general repairs. My land payment was not due until January 1, 1907, and I had long foreseen it would have to come out from England. Full of thought and anxiety for the coming season, which I felt sure must bring down the scale of event to the credit of my side, I refused to worry about dollars, and just in time, since Jack Douglas returned from South Qu'Appelle that night with the news that the price of wheat had fallen locally, owing to a hopeless blockade at the elevator, and the next day he ploughed the garden as a preliminary canter, before attacking the important work of the four and ten-acre arms of the big field.

No sooner had my new man attacked the plough than I understood the wisdom of Roddy McMahon's advice to pay only fifteen dollars a month. Jack Douglas got well on to his work, and stuck to it grimly in spite of the unfriendliness of the weather and severity of the wind. But he neither understood the implement nor had he any practice in ploughing. He took the greater part of two days to plough, disc, and harrow three-quarters of an acre of garden, and ten days to plough ten acres of land. But I liked him. He was quiet and obliging and trustworthy, and I felt sure that beyond all, he was really fond of beasts. He had walked the horses home most carefully after disposing of his load, no matter how forbidding the weather, and he always tucked them up must snugly at night, sparing neither time nor trouble over plenty of hay in the manger and ample bedding. It seemed a real pleasure to him to make them comfortable. He rebuilt the manger and put in a window. It is true he won my assent to pulling the heavy but expensive hayrack to pieces to provide the lumber, but at the time we had already entered into an arrangement by which he undertook to remain for his board and the sum of fifty dollars through the winter, and the seeding time, and possibly through the next season up to harvest, for twenty-five dollars a month; so that when he assured me that in the spring I could get the lumber and he could then replace what he was borrowing from the hayrack, I assented at once and I thought I was particularly fortunate to have come across him. I drew water and bucked wood no more. I remember one day I was paying a call in Springbrook and had most carelessly left Nancy untied at the gate. When I came out to get into the buggy I found that she had already left, and, in consequence, I had to walk home four miles. Half-way across the wheat-field I met Jack Douglas coming to look for my remains in great distress. Nancy had arrived quite safely, but the empty buggy had aroused his anxiety. Nothing can ever cancel my debt to Roddy McMahon for having bestowed upon me the gift of independence through his own hatred of chores, but I was not the less grateful for the attention and consideration of the British newcomer.

When ploughing was over, I started to look for winter fuel. On the adjoining section which at that time was virgin prairie, and the property of the C.P.R., there was any amount of green poplar, but very little dry wood, but my neighbour, Richard Ryan, was a first-rate fuel man and he most kindly suggested that Jack Douglas should work with him in the bluffs.

Meantime I started out myself with Dick and the stone-boat to clean my favourite bluff in the pasture of many loads of young and very dry poplar, which had been killed through the passing of prairie fires, and which had, beyond all other fuel, the power of producing immediate and intense heat. Provided with this, one can prepare breakfast in fifteen minutes, and on a forty below zero morning the kitchen will be glowingly hot in ten.

Two gloriously happy days I spent in the heart of this bluff dragging out contributions to the various piles which Dick hauled home on the stone-boat. He was absolutely happy, nosing round for the choice scraps of pasture outside the bluff, whilst I worked within, and no other horse could have taken home the load quite so cleanly, or so cleverly have avoided the snares which beset his path.

But after noon had passed on the second day the wind which had blown bleak and chill in the face of a brilliant sun, fell softly and abruptly almost as though it had turned back in sudden fear; a sombre veil dropped between earth and the golden sun, the little snow-birds started to chant their haunting note of requiem, delicate snowflakes fell here and there, heralds of the thin white sheet of the first snowstorm which came sweeping out of the north. When snow is coming to the prairie, there precedes it that strange and indefinable melancholy hush that is felt at sea when the fog swoops down. The winter pall drops softly with tenderness and with beauty upon the face of the great mother, yet sadly, and with relentless intention to divide. The end of the working year is come, so very soon the kindly generous, consoling earth that is still at hand, awake to the touch of her children, will be far away in stone-like sleep. Dicky's bright bay coat, and whinny of triumph and greeting to the other horses, as we sighted them bringing home their load, were the only cheerful notes to break the complete and saddest silence. It was in removing my glove to fasten the barbed wire that I discovered the loss of a cherished treasure in a strange familiar stone which had dropped from its place in a marquise ring that I had worn from my schooldays. On a background of soft green stone, sensitive to all change in the weather, had been carved with perfect art the slender, exquisite form and delicate head of a woman. Somehow time and association had given her a place in the consolation which is so often hurled as a threat from the pulpit, that 'God sees all.' Anything would have seemed eventful and significant that afternoon, but a scrap of one's cherished life seemed to have vanished with her, completing the sense of abandonment which the coming of the snow always brings about one. I had an almost overpowering impulse to break through my armour of philosophy, and go back and seek the thing that I cared about. But the snow had already obliterated the marks of our passing; the row of guardian poplars by the bluff seemed to stand with arms uplifted to a vanished heaven. In the intense silence, in the atmosphere of profound sadness which has its sacred place in the heart of the solitude of separation, winter swept into possession of the prairie.

PART III: WINTER

'Yet in despite of all disquietudes
...
In spite of doubt, despondency, and death
Though lacking knowledge alway, lacking faith
Sometimes, and hope; with no sure trust in aught
Except a kind of impetus within,
Whose sole credentials were that trust itself;
Yet, in despite of much, in lack of more,
Life has been beautiful to me ...'

1

Of fuel and fear – the end of the year

In winter my cottage could not be described as cosy, although now and then, when men have been in residence, I have sometimes had to fly from the Scylla of a burning fiery furnace within, to the Charybdis of the temperature outside, no matter to what degree below zero it may have chosen to fall.

Jack Douglas curled up at the first breath of winter, but many newcomers curl and uncurl. Within a few hours of its first appearance, the snow lay very deep in the bluffs, and only the slenderest instalment of fuel had been felled and brought in. My heart sank as I observed my helper stepping gingerly out to his chores, with his collar pulled up to his eyes, his head hidden between his shoulders, his uncovered hands in his pockets, and a general air of being prepared to go under to winter, who, like all bullies, is a coward, and delights in the special torment of those who fail to look her straight in the eyes. Ominous also was the fact that he loved to watch the fire; I thoroughly understood the temptation, but I would not have dared to give it place in Canada. Directly his night duties in the stable were over he put out the kitchen lamp, opened the stove door and watched the fire until after 11 P.M. ... fire that was consuming winter's fuel, nine-tenths of which he had still to fell, clean, and haul. In the morning came the natural result of the night-watch, and it seemed as though he could not get up to feed the horses at sunrise, so that in spite of his obvious love of animals and what I feel sure was a fine sense of duty I grew anxious concerning the prospect of the horses through the frozen months. Oats late or oats early are always *oats*, but all stock should be patiently and faithfully watered until each has fully satisfied the craving thirst of winter, which is no less severe than the parching thirst of summer. The well was quite a hundred yards from the house, in the open, and even in February and March when the days grow long and bright, the icy wind can cut and sting through every moment of a water-chore.

I resolved to be peremptory over the matter of fuel. My *aide* considered himself an excellent woodsman. I thought him fair. I asked my neighbour how many poplar poles a man should fell in an hour and he said the half-breeds brought down a hundred easily. I took the information home to Jack Douglas, who refused to believe it, and affirmed that if by any outside chance it could be accomplished it would certainly not be with the axe with which I supplied him. Within the week he felled about three loads; at the end of each day they were gathered together, piled in a neat heap, and counted, so that there might be no dangerous optimism in any calculation concerning the sum of one's ammunition. But having presented the standard of a hundred poles an hour the woodsman used it to dwarf all other considerations. He slashed north and south, right and left, omitting to stop either to clean or to collect, with the result that the tall indignant poplars fell over one another like men on a battle-field, root and branch interlaced, and it was plain that a heavy fall of snow would render their rescue a most arduous, if not hopeless task.

'I have a great favour to ask you,' he said one day at dinner, 'will you promise to grant it?'

'Not until I hear what it is,' I answered, 'but I'll do my best.'

'May I have a half-holiday this afternoon to go to the Fort, and buy a new axe? I'll pay for it.'

The final clause annoyed me badly. 'I have told you that a certain amount of fuel must be felled, cleaned, packed, and ready to haul before the next snowfall,' I answered. 'It may come at any moment, and if so it will be impossible to work in the bluffs within a few hours. The fuel *must* be gathered. If the axe is difficult I am sorry, but it has brought down so much that it can bring down a little more, and a half-holiday, with snow already here, and more coming, is ridiculous.'

'But I don't mind working in the snow,' he objected, 'and after all it isn't your affair. You won't be here through the winter. It's my own look-out.'

'Is it!' I said in exasperation. 'Where would you of all people be without sufficient fuel! A person who dreams for hours on end by the fireside at night, and has to be driven to gather fuel by day, is not the person to find his way into prairie bluffs in mid-winter. A nice story would go round the world if you happened to be laid up here without fuel. Your well-being is my direct responsibility up to a point, so just get back at once to the bluff, and presently I will come along with the hatchet, and clean for you.'

All the afternoon he sulked. He was so slow in getting down the poles that he had time to muse a hundred grievances. At supper-time he gave me a week's notice.

It was rather trying. Over our six months' arrangement, providing he took fair care of my stock and belongings as I believe he would have done, both of us would score. But if he left at the moment I had to pay him at an excellent rate of wages for the work of an amateur, and a very slow although a very promising amateur.

In the anger of the moment I said I would not pay him according to the higher, but the average rate; and, in his anger of the moment, he said it was exactly the thing that every one had prophesied would happen if he hired on with a woman.

'You have been gossiping about me,' I said. 'That concludes the argument. You leave tomorrow morning.'

'Oh, but I couldn't,' he protested. 'I'll stay on a week or until you are suited if you can't easily find anyone. But you can't possibly be left alone with all the winter chores to do. What would every one say!'

'That is the last thing that matters,' I replied. 'You leave tomorrow morning. Not to-night, because of the snow.'

In the morning I paid the full extent of his claim at the full rate and he left. The story probably proves me arbitrary and severe;

but I was still very inexperienced, and still rebelling against the newly acquired knowledge that in everyday shoulder-to-shoulder life men take so much kindness and consideration from women for granted but calculate the value of every scrap of their own service; and then, in their veneration for the world's opinion, demand that woman shall also fill in the blank space, or erase the blot on the record which every man is still under the illusion he keeps with the wellnigh exhausted tradition of chivalry.

I have always felt sore about the matter, at the time because he was my fellow countryman and he hadn't been out long, and because in behaving as a schoolboy about the half-holiday he had forced me into the unattractive rôle of schoolmarm, which I played with ease; and also because, although reason and justice were on my side in the wages argument, I wished with all my heart I had said no word, but paid with a tight lip; but later on, most of all because in the second year of his stay in Canada, where in time he did excellent work for one of the best farmers and straightest men in my neighbourhood, and in spite of occasional moods, won the respect and goodwill of his comrades, he died from the kick of a horse.

When I parted from my hired man I had every intention of engaging another to fill his place, and of carrying out my intention to spend the winter in England. But after a further snowfall the weather cleared. I fed the stock at 7 A.M. and found the mornings amazingly brilliant and inspiring. One day, as I crossed from the oat granary to the stable with breakfast, two prairie wolves sprang up and galloped away from the door of the hen-roost. Pax, my dog, started off in pursuit with a yell of desire, and for the first time I wished I had been any sort of shot. I owe so much of the joy of life on the prairie and elsewhere to living things, that the very sight of a gun seems the symbol of treachery to a friend; but the prairie wolf does incredible mischief in the poultry yard, and threatens the prosperity of the country to such an extent that in most districts of Saskatchewan the Government still pays a dollar a head bounty. As anything from four to six dollars may be obtained for a good skin, wolf-hunting may be described as the commercial sport of the prairie.

The sight of those two hungry faces, the note of desire in the yell of Pax, suggested wolf-hunting and that a winter with the stock should prove an experience with delightful points. I felt confident that I could never again be poorer than I was at.the moment and reckoned that in putting in the winter myself I could save at least twenty pounds over the wages and winter's keep of a hired man, in addition to my travelling and personal expenditure; so I resolved on a winter alone.

Far more than the strenuous work attending the care of stock and culture of land, the prospect of solitude seems appalling to many women for whom the active pursuit of farming offers strong attraction, and material inducement. Often women have talked to me with a flattering little hush of awe in their voice about what they term one's courage in relation to this winter spent on a prairie farm with one's stock for company; but surely the true definition of courage is to do the thing you are afraid to do. For instance, only the year before I came out to Canada I was spending the summer in Paris in the pleasantest *atelier-apparte-ment* I can remember. It was quite at the top of a very long stone staircase of a tall house just behind the shops of the Avenue des Ternes. From the window of stained glass around which inquisitive bits of ivy fluttered one looked across some lower buildings into a lovely garden with tall trees, and sniffed in the perfume of the limes in the Bois which, once you have spent a whole day with them, will float to the altar of the imagination at any point in Paris. The household gods in this artist's home were few in number, and this, together with the delicately polished floor, gave it an air of space. An old oak-chest, a book-case, a lounge by day which became a bed by night, two chairs and a writing-table found a place on the floor, and on the walls glowing bits of landscape, the work of my friends who owned the flat, and just by the glass-panelled door which led into the atelier there was the unsigned portrait of a cavalier which cried out, 'I am a child of the genius of Hyacinth Rigaud.' One was never alone, or unwatched, or dull with the portrait in the room. 'Life is sweet *we* know,' said the cavalier at dawn, at noon, in the softening light of eventime, and even when he grew a little sad in the light of the one lamp which was kinder to all else in the room than to him. 'Life is sweet *we* know,' echoed the spirit of joy which some poverty-stricken genius had arrested in a fly-smudged terra-cotta bust of a boy which I had bought in one of those shops, peculiar to certain quarters of Paris, where for a few francs treasures may be reclaimed from a dust-heap. But at night there was another presence in the place, and neither the *concierge*, nor the *femme de ménage*, nor the cavalier, nor the boy, nor my friend the owner of the apartment who had moved across the Seine to live in the Rue de Val-de-Grace, would explain. It is true she allowed that the Cambridge don, who had been its tenant through the long vacation in the year before, had also felt, but not seen, the thing she *saw* because she was endowed with the gift of unveiled sight, which is usually named clairvoyance. She assured me that people endowed with this gift felt no fear, meantime I need have none, since, although she could not tell me all, she could at least assure me that *It* of the shadows would not harm me. From that day in order to curtail June's short hours of darkness I sat in the two-franc seats of the Opera-House or elsewhere night after night, and walked home as slowly as possible, and quite unmolested, through the 'dangerous' streets and boulevards of Paris; but although the cavalier simply shouted 'Life is sweet and nothing matters' as I opened the doors as noisily as possible so that I might not hear the beating of my heart, and although my smiling boy pleaded that he loved the pleasant, peaceful room better even than the home where his creator had snatched a wandering sunbeam, and hidden the treasure in his eyes; and although my friend of the unveiled sight said I could take it on at the end of her lease for the beguiling rent of sixteen pounds a year, I left before my tenancy expired because I simply couldn't stand it any longer. I ran away from the indefinable, haunting, suffocating something I was afraid of. I know about fear, and it isn't on the prairie; on the contrary solitude here seems always healing and soothing to the mind, just as the reviving air of evening seems to refresh the toil-worn body after the very hottest and most arduous day spent under the sun.

I found my stable-chores strenuous, but in fair weather not severe. I wore felt boots, and thick woollen mitts covered with leather pull-overs, but a thick coat was not necessary, and was usually discarded after ten minutes of stable-cleaning had set one physically aglow. A thousand bushels of grain had been threshed within two hundred yards of the stable. When the wind was down bucking straw across to the stable for bedding was pleasant exercise, when wind was up it was purgatorial penance, and when a blizzard raged it was impossible.

At first I continued to rise with the sun in spite of its late winter hours, and lit the kitchen fire, and warmed up before feeding the stock; but as I had five horses and six head of cattle, besides the pigs, to serve with breakfast, I usually found my wood-fire rather low on my return, so when the need for economy in the matter of fuel became obvious, I abandoned the practice as a luxury, and lit the fire on my return from the stables.

After I had taken my own breakfast I returned to the stable, and as neither of the cows was in milking form, I watered all who required water, and they went on their way for the day. When a storm was before us they usually remained very near home, and looked with threatening envy over the stack-yard fence, which had been put up by my predecessor and had started to show the strain of time. After they had gone on their way I cleaned the stable, fed the pigs, who are late risers, bucked wood for fuel, passed my time usually in reading and writing until half-past three, when I made tea, and prepared for about two hours work among the beasts, who usually came home at sunset in a bee-line led by Nancy.

My neighbour was obviously perturbed concerning my determination to stay on through the winter without help. He tried every warning and argument in turn, and I couldn't help thinking that I caught a glimpse of something I had seen before in the eyes of hunting men when women take chances at the particular phase of a run where the claim of chivalry would be hard to bear, and harder to obey.

I refused all idea of difficulty, and set my intention tight against help. I said I had several loads of wood cut, and I had only to gather it. He was anxious to gather at least one load for me as he was going down to the Fort to stay with friends, and considered I ran a most dangerous risk. However I determined not to run the risk of exposing the nakedness of the land by setting him on the trail of my own fuel store, and, remembering that John McLeay had offered me a load of dry wood from his fine store if I would send for it, I said if he would fetch that for me I should be most grateful. The greater part of my own store, I explained, was neither cleared nor piled, and as I very specially wished to reserve that exercise for myself I shouldn't have it hauled for the present.

He was obviously resentful about the whole matter, but he went off and fetched the wood; and throughout the winter when he was at home he often came across to see how I fared, and his man came through on several occasions and always insisted on doing something or bringing something; but that year the snow was very deep, and it took nearly an hour instead of the usual twenty minutes, to walk from the shack to my cottage.

As the cold grew stronger I found that my most difficult chore was in getting hay from the rick built Canadian fashion. The snow packs the hay tightly, and the frost freezes the snow into a kind of invincible thatching. If one can get it off in sheets hay-feeding is comparatively easy, but to pack the mangers tightly full for the night makes a great demand on time and energy. When the weather was kind I rather enjoyed it, but when a wind raged or the mercury dropped badly below zero, one had to draw on the outside notes of patience and endurance.

Quite the pleasantest duty of the day was the 8 P.M. feed of oats. To begin with it was usually preceded with two hours reading by the pleasant warmth of the stove, and one can nearly always arrive at the 'heights of one's own heart' via the ladder and lamplight of another's. Afterwards I climbed the rickety ladder which led to the big store of oat-sheaves on the stable roof and from that point I dropped them all overboard, and then descended to distribute this favourite form of feed among my four-footed family. The cattle seldom used their stable, and I always tried to encourage a love of liberty; but they had no honour about seizing on the oat-sheaves as they fell from the roof, and sometimes the evening feed was performed in anything but the silence of the night. The stable roof, too, had its weak points, and one night my leg went through a thin place in the roof and then set so tight that I endured all the torments of the legless in ten seconds. Sometimes the wind blew so hard that one had to set one's teeth to climb the ladder, search for the binder-twine of the sheaves by sense of touch, because snow falling on the warm glass of the storm-lantern meant grave destruction to fifteen-cent chimneys in bad times. But in average weather the chore of the last feed was altogether delightful, one could see the white landscape for miles around by light of the moon, the wind seldom stirred, the cattle lay around, gazing in restful content at the heavens, or munching big caverns in the oat-straw stack. None could possibly feel lonely within sound of the friendly, flattering greetings that are heard from the stable at the first sound of your footstep until the last gallon of oats has been deposited in the last empty box, and the day's work is really over. One walked back to the cottage under a world of stars and the drawn swords of the glorious legions known as the Northern Lights, a regiment which the archangels might have provided as a Royal Guard to guide all strangers through the new land, where Fear the gaoler cannot breathe.

Early in December I was confronted with trouble. With great care I had kept my own cattle out of the stack-yard, except for one defiant steer who leaped a barbed-wire fence as a chaser leaps a hurdle. Tom Klein had completed my ring-fence, but being in a hurry to attend a fair, had gone off without making a gate. With the optimistic intention of putting up an orthodox English-looking gate I had failed to insist on his return, with the result that a very second-rate imitation of the Canadian barbed-wire gate had been thrust into a position it was powerless to hold. The cattle of my neighbour Richard Ryan simply breathed on it and it fell over, and they proceeded at once to the stack-yard and laid siege to the hayrick.

It is not what cattle eat in a stack-yard that raises Cain in one's heart, but what they render useless, and from that day through many weeks of the winter a certain portion of the day was spent in hounding them out. Pax was a good cattle-dog and we could always get rid of them, although never without the prospect of return, but the loss of time and annoyance and physical exhaustion attached to this daily warfare were altogether trying.

Then too I had to face the fact that I was desperately short of money. On January 1 I was due to pay one thousand one hundred and sixty dollars to my predecessor, one thousand dollars being the third instalment of my five payments of one thousand dollars each, plus one hundred and sixty dollars, the agreed rate of interest at six per cent. The blockade at the elevators was likely to last, but this was more or less a relief as the bankers knew one really could not sell and settle, and it would have been awkward at that period to get my wheat hauled fifteen miles to the elevators. The working expenses that year were very heavy: the fence, the breaking, the balance of one hundred and eighty-six dollars for the horse Tommy, had overdrawn my balance at the bank considerably, and the note came in every month to remind me that I was in the Bank's debt for a sum considerably in excess of one thousand dollars, plus a monthly increasing interest. I had done very well indeed with my butter, eggs, and salt pork, selling sometimes as much as eight pounds a week of butter to the Hudson Bay Store in exchange for provisions, and had also disposed of a great deal of all sorts of food-produce to my neighbour in trade for oats. My pigs were not in condition for sale; John McLeay brought his friend David Chambers to look at the eldest family, but he offered less by a dollar each than I asked, and the second family were very late comers indeed; but I should probably have made the deal with Mr. Chambers had I not been well supplied with wild oats for feed. Pigs won't go outside if they can avoid it in the winter, and they throve wonderfully well on the oats in sheaf, also the straw kept them warm and comfortably bedded. As the manure was always burned there was no danger of the wild oats regerminating over the land, and I knew the pigs would render me a useful contribution towards expenses in the spring. It did not occur to me that there could be any difficulty about bank loans; money had seemed almost to walk towards one from the bank counters at first, and eight per cent. has such an attractive sound in the way of interest, that I always considered that the Bank held the weightier end of the obligation, and that they certainly would not wish to lose so valuable a customer. But the fact remained that the two hundred and thirty pounds I was expecting from England would be entirely absorbed by the land payment and its interest, and that a few hundred bushels of wheat liable to fall in grade and certain to be docked in weight for its measure of wild oats was all I could rely on to settle my bank bill and to meet the working expenses of spring and of summer, as my neighbour insisted that this year there could no longer be any doubt about the fact that I *must* plough the big field shallow in early June and deep at the end of July.

The only economy I could put in practice at the moment was to save on myself. I dispensed with storm-windows and all superfluous food. Guy Mazey had sold me the forequarter of a steer for something just over or just under eleven dollars, but hacking off joints with an axe was a toil so I passed it on to my brother for the use of his guests at the stopping-house, and used the few remaining joints of the pig which Roddy McMahon had killed for me just before threshing. There were two legs and they lasted each about three weeks; with the frost well in one could not have distinguished this pork from cold turkey, and it became no more monotonous than the tea and coffee and bread and sultana cakes which completed the menu. I had learned to make bread as I found it was much cheaper to buy flour than bread. I had neither milk nor butter nor eggs through December and January, but I was really being nourished on the air, which suited me amazingly as long as I lived this rather unusual life of outdoor service. Directly I attempt to pass the winter between the contrasting temperature of the orthodox heat within and the average cold without, I feel both extremes to be almost unbearable. It was the outdoor interest that made things not only possible but even delightful, and often have I looked back regretfully on those mornings of exhilarating work and healing solitude when a breakfast of sugarless, milkless, but newly made coffee, and bread thawed in the oven, seemed truly a feast for the gods.

Just before Christmas I drove into the Fort to get a fresh supply of necessaries, and the delicacy I resolved on was a pound of butter. It cost forty cents, and when I got home I was so cold that I forgot it was in the sleigh and only remembered it in the morning when I saw a piece of grocery paper by the door. Roddy McMahon's dog Rover and several of his friends had followed us home and evidently devoured the spoil. Butter is a great luxury at Christmas-time, while eggs cannot be had either for love or money, but my friend Mrs. McDougall received a pound of butter, I think as a Christmas gift, and shared it with me.

On Christmas Day I drove in to service at the Anglican Church. A biting wind blew a fierce pain between my eyes, so, declining various invitations, I spent the greater part of the feast day in my stack-yard and, I am afraid, made Christmas night anything but a time of peace and good tidings for my neighbour who came to seek his marauding cattle. But I had been tried in the fire and found wanting all through the day, and as a climax, in chasing the beasts out of the yard, I lost one of the pretty earrings that had been among the Christmas gifts sent to me from England. When you have never a moment to examine your own reflection except when the mirror is frozen over, when if you do catch an unexpected glimpse of yourself you wish you hadn't, earrings are a refuge of the destitute, for if matters are past improvement at least they effect a change. By the time I had ended my attempt to impress upon my neighbour the depth and breadth of the value of the gift of which his wretched cattle had robbed me, I believed it all myself, and went to bed on Christmas night a very injured person indeed.

The morning found the temperature set forty below zero, and the wind biting. I went out and worked at the fence and the gate, but in sprints of ten minutes only. I was vainly endeavouring to staple barbed wire into place when I saw Mrs. McDougall driving up the trail with a holiday guest.

'I guess I could make you a gate in no time' she said. I did not doubt it, because she really could do anything.

We had a long and pleasant gossip about English people and things as we sat around my stove, but I think she was the first and last of my visitors that winter, barring my neighbour and the Vicar. The cold settled in badly, the thermometer spending its time anywhere between forty and fifty below zero. In the last days of the old year I went in to tell my predecessor that my bank draft from England might be late, so that if it did not reach him by the first he would understand.

To my intense surprise he expressed himself perfectly content to wait as long as I pleased, not only for the principal, but for the interest.

I thanked him and was greatly relieved, but declined the offer to postpone payment of the interest, having heard once that compound interest would break the Bank of England. However, he told me he had great confidence in the value of the security, and I was only too thankful to have the opportunity of falling back on the capital to settle my bank overdraft for the year. I had tea by the bright stove in the pleasant house from which one looks out on both lakes, delicious tea with cream, which clearly hailed from a relation of Molly, and the jolliest cakes.

I drove home with an easier mind, and the year of 1906 passed into its very last day ... the day of the spirit of farewell. It dawned in brilliant winter glory, but grew silent and solemn after the hour of noon was passed. From the south window of my green room I saw the string of beasts returning for drinks. It was my duty to prepare for their coming at the well, but on that last day of the year I tumbled to the temptation of thinking back. For a moment I remembered ungenerously that some of the hours of the dying year had been sad and many almost unbearably weary. 'But many were glad and none were bitter' smiled the pale gold sun, as it slipped behind the shore-like line of grey which veiled the horizon. It seemed like the last word of a friend. I did my chores the better for it. If you have to water horses, pigs, and chickens, all anxious to drink from the same pail at the same moment, all born in the faith of the survival of the fittest, you must take with you as your weapon the temper of a devil, or, as your shield, the patience of an angel.

2

Preparing seed-grain –
newcomers

Heavy snowstorms fell in the first weeks of the New Year, but I pursued my programme with the horses, who in all kinds of weather spent some hours of each day in the open. I forsook the green room and spent my days in the kitchen, since the wood pile visibly decreased, and I knew that in the North-West lack of fuel is not a case of Spartan endurance but a matter of life or death. But January 10 was bright and clear, and I attempted a journey to Fort Qu'Appelle. Not caring to take the wagon-box and team through the unbeaten track, I borrowed my neighbour's cutter, but before we had made a mile of the road Nancy pitched me head foremost into a snowdrift, and then made off towards Mr. Ryan's house fully a mile west. By the time I had caught her and we had ploughed our way through the snow to the trail it was too late to dream of going down into the town, and I returned to my neighbour's with the cutter and shared the excellent beefsteak which formed the *pièce de résistance* of the midday meal.

On the next morning I counted my remaining poles, and later in the day went off with an axe in the direction of the bluff where John Douglas had been right and left, north and south, in order to arrive at the standard which my neighbour had set up. The poles had become deeply imbedded in the snow, but many of them had been robbed of the sap through the prairie fires and were in fine condition for warmth-giving fuel; others were green, but desperately intertwined and closely packed by three feet of frozen snow, and the difficulty of getting them out was greater even than it appeared. To free one tree and clean it and get it away was out of the question. One found the base, chopped off each branch as it occurred on the way to the summit, and when eight or nine branches had been chopped the tree had to be raised to gauge the possibility of getting it out. Sometimes by great good luck I struck the last that had fallen, which simplified the matter of rescue; but many of the first to fall had gone down head foremost with the trunk in the air. However, disentanglement was almost interesting; at least, it always had the flavour of the unexpected. Pax begged so hard to come with me, and felt the cold so bitterly when he came to the place where he had to rest during my labour, that for his sake rather than my own I limited the time to an hour; for, once I had crossed the bleak quarter of a mile of stubble, it was impossible to fail in getting warm between the axe and the cleaning and emancipation of six poplar poles. It is just at such times as this that evil may happen, for the body being roused into unusual warmth, the mind loosens its hold of the fact that the temperature is still fraught with danger. One day, deeply interested in the head and shoulders of my last pole, I allowed my leg to remain for a moment or so in the hole into which it had slipped. Victor over the tree, I turned to draw out my leg and found it fixed as in a vice. The ghastly fate of the lower limbs of Roddy McMahon's father flashed to my brain, and I had a bad moment. Most thankfully I made the passage home on two sound limbs, and resolved never to take chances concerning my most useful extremities, and kept the vow.

In the intervals between stable and feeding chores and the emancipation of felled trees it was almost unbearably cold. On Monday, January 14, I learned from my neighbour that the temperature had dropped to fifty-five below. I begged that he would not tell me of any further descent, and felt thankful that I didn't possess a thermometer. Nevertheless, the following notes in my diary bear witness to the fact that one is physically in thrall to the inexorable hold of extreme cold.

'January 16 – Chored, and made good progress with the wood pile. Bitterly, almost unbearably, cold.

'January 17 – Sleepless nights and feeling the cold badly. Could do nothing worth doing to-day. Getting up late and going to bed early to economize fuel.

'January 18 – An appreciable shade warmer. Small addition to wood pile, as poor Pax feels the cold terribly and whined to come home early.

'January 19 – Mr. Green (my neighbour's hired man) brought me a loaf of excellent bread and did a splendid morning's work for me. Temperature considerably easier but the wind bitter, and every sign of a blizzard. Felt bad and sad. My lesser ills are so trying. Chilblains and occasional rheumatism, and even the horses can be rather exasperating, especially Jim, at the well. Cannot get in to the Fort to collect my mail, but post it through Tommy Johnson.

'January 21 – Glorious day. Many shades warmer. Cleaned stables. Baked. Worked at the wood pile. Attacked a short story. I haven't dared to start writing before, the fire goes out in two minutes, and the ink is usually frozen solid. The Vicar called, and we had tea in the most untidy kitchen. He seemed frightfully perturbed because I bucked wood. If that were all! Reading Plutarch's 'Lives' again. Excellent company in these days.

'January 22 – Wild night and morning, but temperature decidedly easier in spite of bitter wind. Cleaned pots and pans and sawed one of the big logs. Unfortunately they don't seem to throw out as much warmth as one might think. Still, anything to get back to my own room and the inkpot again. The kitchen is dreary and depressing with frost-bound windows and everything packed on the stove to thaw out. Pax much better.

'January 26 – The very loveliest day in spite of piercing wind. Felt well and worked well and wrote well. Mr. Green came over under the impression that it was Sunday. But it must be to-morrow; I can't have lost the schooldays' instinct for the extra hour of the day of rest.

'January 27 – Sunday.'

On Monday I was walking across the wheat-field *en route* for the stage-coach to post my mail. Tommy Johnson was not always in command through that winter, but each Jehu in turn was friendly and kind about taking in my letters. Half-way across the field I met Roddy McMahon.

'I guess you'll likely let me have a couple of loads of oat-straw in trade for a load of wood,' said he. 'I'm right clean out of hay for my horses, and I know you got lots, and more oat-straw I guess than you'll get through. I'll bring along a good load of wood in a day or two.'

I closed the deal eagerly and thankfully, and told him of my difficulty in getting the wood out of the snow.

'It's a nasty job that anyhow. The snow is good and deep all right in the bluffs. There's quite a few of us got a permit to get down wood on the other side the valley. I'll be along with a load by time you're ready I guess, an' I'll just get along with the sleigh and haul in what you got ready before I load up the straw-rack. Just show me where to find it.'

I posted my mail, and when I got back there was the wood of my gathering piled in the vicinity of the kitchen door. Roddy McMahon had bucked about as much in five minutes as I could get through in an hour; so that night Pax and I and the frost-bitten cat who had adopted us kept royal cheer by the hearth.

January's last day but one brought a terrible blizzard. I had great difficulty in watering and getting sufficient hay for the night's feed, and for the last feed of all I had to fall back on the inspiration of Caesar and the Rubicon in order to climb on to the stable roof and gather my sheaves in the howl of the storm; but by morning the weather had cleared. Mabel Mazey came over and brought me a pound of butter from their first churning. The last entry of my diary for January reads: 'Thanks be, to-morrow is February 1!'

Blowing and snowing came February. Then frost hard and obstinate, even in the shining face of the sun, which contrived to win its way through the storm-clouds from time to time. One night just as I had watered the last beast I heard the sound of sleigh-bells, and Roddy McMahon came in view hauling a simply ripping load of wood. My diary contains an entry concerning this occasion which should have been in scarlet letters: 'I have been WARM all day! It seems that it is quite easy to keep warm if one has plenty of the right kind of fuel.' I finished my baking, got through all the outside chores, and came in for a cup of tea and a lazy, restful evening. It was so perfectly delightful to be comfortable again. Pax revelled in the warmth and wouldn't move from the stove even at the music of the preparation for tea.

On February 5 I went to South Qu'Appelle on financial business, and as I drove back I hardly dared believe it true, but there was an impression that the oasis of the mirage of spring was waiting round the very next corner. My neighbour, who was very kind when he forgot to be furious about a woman doing everything he considered she shouldn't, was busy with the buck-saw. He had put the stable in apple-pie order, filled the mangers with hay, cut a reserve supply with a hay-knife he borrowed from another neighbour, lit the kitchen fire and boiled the kettle, and after the warmth-producing power of all this physical exertion he was absolutely cocksure that the mirage was at hand and spring itself just behind her own illusion. We had tea in my pleasant sitting-room, and told each other the heat of the stove was almost unendurable after the unusual heat of the sun; and we discussed our seeding plans, and he told me of the wonderful year in which seeding had been finished by the last day of March, and I believed him. That night the temperature eased off, there was a complete thaw, the mirage cheered us for just three days, then back we fell into the clutch of zero. But it did cheer one, how completely none can quite explain.

On February 9 I walked into the cow stable to find a small heifer. My neighbour came over and milked Molly for her first milking, but she was perfectly quiet, and although absolutely inconsolable for a day or two after he took Julia into the horse stable, she was able to take all the consolation I could offer in the form of oats and salt and bran mash, and before long she cheered up, resigned herself to the inevitable, and rejoined the bunch. Julia was perfectly content in her warm nest in the horse stable just behind Dick, who was immensely interested in the frequent attention shown the newcomer, with whom he always remained good friends.

On February 14 I made my first butter of the year, and that season I sold a considerable quantity at the excellent price of thirty-five cents a pound, which was maintained until July, and I think did not fall below twenty-five cents through that year. Milking and attention to Julia must have increased my work, as just past the middle of the month I find these notes in my diary:

'February 17 – Up with the sun. Milked and chored before breakfast. Had a long morning in an initial effort to clean out the cattle stable. One shouldn't let these things get behind. Very tired and stiff. The wind grew very strong towards evening and all the beasts came home early – significant of storm.

'February 22 – Very cold again. Three eggs. Read 'David Harum.'

'February 23 – Made three pounds of butter.

'February 24, Sunday – Mr. Green came over with a loaf, as usual much better than mine. Wind very cold, but able to use green room again. Feeling rather out of sorts. No time for reading or writing; no easy time. Not much sun in these days, but the spring is coming!

'February 25 – Weather growing colder. Pax hates it badly.

'February 26 – Breath freezing on the blankets again. Reading Plutarch and Emerson and Wilberforce – "Romulus," "Fate," and "The Awakening."

'February 27 – Very cold. Wood very low. Read "Lycurgus and Power."

'February 28 – The last day of February and bitterly cold. Everything frozen in the kitchen. Anxious and depressed over news from England. The low state of fuel means spending one's days in the kitchen again. Reading Wilberforce, and Meredith's verse.

'March 1 – The third month. Very much warmer, and fresh load of fuel arrived with Roddy McMahon. Now I really have no excuse and must try to get to work again.'

I had vowed that I would not sow a wild oat in the land which I had broken, and as at the time I knew of no grain-fanner which would separate wild oats from wheat, I determined to clean my seed by hand. I took a two-bushel sack into the kitchen and filled it in four half-bushel journeys from the granary, and by daylight and lamplight I stuck to my task. Of course it was quite absurd to have contemplated or even to have hoped to clean over sixty sacks of seed-grain in this way, and I don't know that I was ever under the impression I could finish; but I didn't leave off, and when three filled bags were facts accomplished, standing side by side against the kitchen wall, the pride I felt in showing the contents to anyone who came along as a sample of my 1907 seed-grain, absolutely free from smut, wild oats, or any sort of weed-seed, baffled qualification.

My method was to throw a basinful of grain on the kitchen table, which was covered with white linoleum, and separate the good from the evil with the blade of a knife. If the good was beautiful, the evil was profoundly interesting. None could imagine that half a dozen cupfuls of smut and weed-seed in a sack of seed-grain could be so dangerous to the growth and financial value of a crop, or that it could be so varied, strange, and vividly vile in appearance and powerful in its evil purpose. Of all grain and flowers of the field, I think wild oats seem most strikingly full of life in the seed – it is like a vegetable grasshopper; whilst a ball of smut gives one the same kind of expression of its place in the vegetable world as does the Watts portrait of *Mammon* in the human race. The accomplishment of cleaning all the grain was practically hopeless, but it had the tremendous incentive of being complete in detail; every basinful of wheat that went into the grain bag, every teacupful of weed that went into the fire, meant health and strength for the crop of 1907 and its ensuing crops. Of course there were moments when I had to acknowledge that it was absolutely impossible to get through, when my back and head and hands and heart ached, but deliverance came in the middle of March.

My brother arrived from his homestead on the 6th and remained until the 10th. He told me that a man had passed the night at his stopping-house who held the agency for a fanning mill which he guaranteed would separate wild oats from wheat. He promised to write to ask him to call on me with a specimen of the mill, and said he should tell him no better sample of grain could be found in the country for the advertisement of the purpose of the mill.

The man and the mill arrived in due course. He remained overnight, and the next day he set up the mill in the granary and extracted the wild oats from the wheat in a manner which seemed amazing as it practically removed every wild oat from the seed-grain. Freely I gave the twenty-six dollars which he demanded for the treasure, and through two seasons it did good although very slow service; but always there was a great deal of waste, partly through the milled wheat which fell under, but also of an important percentage of the very finest grain, which passed out at the back of the mill with the wild oats. Later it became slower and more wasteful, and it was then that the lack of judgment in buying farm implements from a travelling agent was brought home to me. I wrote to Chatham complaining of the changing mood and time of the mill, and received several neatly typed sheets of argument and copies of unsolicited testimonials in reply, chiefly in testimony of the immense satisfaction the Chatham separator had given to every one else in the North-West. The unsolicited testimonials included one from the Minister of Agriculture in the province of Saskatchewan, and was evidently intended as the final proof of my personal lack of intelligence, or veracity. Of information, or in answer to my suggestion to trade for another mill, neither ink nor paper nor the valuable moments of working hours of a stenographer were thrown away, and, swallowing another expensive lesson from experience, I purchased another model from Messrs. Morgan and Vicars of South Qu'Appelle. This operated as a fanning mill in addition to its special purpose as a wild-oat separator, and although it cost more it was well worth the difference in price.

From the time of the arrival of the mill I cleaned many bushels of grain in the forbidding temperature of the granary, instead of a few bushels in the comfortable warmth of the kitchen; but the cleaned seed-grain was soon ahead of my stock of grain bags, which vanish from the prairie far more surely and certainly than illusion itself. So I fell back on an empty bedroom as a seed-grain store, and before the end of March I had eighty bushels ready for seeding, including eight bushels I had cleaned by hand and which I reserved for the five-acre seed garden I had broken on the north-west boundary.

One Sunday in March the Mazey girls came over and helped me do my evening chores. They pronounced the horses to be looking just splendid, and really they were a jolly group. Jim and Tommy looked so huge and powerful in their big coats, which were starting to come off by yards with the curry-comb; and Ricky who, in spite of his love of wild gallops with the jolly bands of old and young horses who at that time spent the winter in the unrestricted freedom of the prairie, always seemed glad to get home again, and who thrust his soft nose in one's hand and left the well a little laggingly in the trail of the others – just enough to convey a tiny consoling impression of regret that one couldn't come too. Nancy was looking brilliant and younger than ever. She always led the band, and her dainty, elastic movement seemed in friendliest contrast to the slow, deliberate intention of the huge cart-horses to follow in her wake.

Quite early in March I drove into the Fort to see the Macdougalls, and for the first time I was aware of the effect of the solitude of the winter. My voice seemed deep and strange, but it was delightful to be with one's friends again. Later in the month I drove back to Fort Qu'Appelle with my brother on his way to his homestead, and went into church for morning service, then walked across the lake and lunched at Crow's Nest, and back to tea at the Mound. I had to leave early because of my evening chores, so Mrs. Macdougall walked back with me as far as John McLeay's gate. But, pleasant as were such days as this, my diary throws a light on the sharp and constant contrast of the weather in that altogether exceptional year of 1907:

'March 17 – Lovely day, very warm. Felt inclined to sit on the stable roof among the sheaves and read, but cleaned the cow stable and stuck to my guns generally. Found a stolen nest with fourteen eggs.

'March 18 – Awoke to a terrible morning. Blinding blizzard and heavy snowdrifts here and there.

'March 19 – Bright fair day with very cold north wind, but snow melting in the sun, which cancels a good deal of anxiety about the beasts. The well has gone well through the winter, but now there is trouble. I most carelessly left it uncovered and the snow got in. Mr. Robb came over to ask me to exchange cockerels for hens for his daughter's wedding-breakfast. He mended my stove-pipe, for which I was most truly thankful.'

But in March, although storms may blow, the warm rays of the sun pierce the clouds in the intervals of the warfare of the elements and the snow melts at its magic. Towards the end of the winter my task of watering the stock had become a severe test of patience. The spring still flowed as generously as before, but the ice at the base of the wooden casing had thickened, and the water gathered daily in the ice-basin. Sometimes one pail took six journeys to fill its comrade, and occasionally two horses would attack the half-filled pail and spill the hard-won water. Often exasperation got the better of reason on such occasions, and one realized how easy it might be to become brute-like in the service of the very brutes that make life so well worth living, and when one got back again to the precincts of the stove, and skirts and temper thawed out together, wrath seemed so unutterably silly. So that when the thaw brought shining pools and none bothered any longer to fight for first drink, it was an extraordinary relief. But although after a blizzard I have had to dig through twelve feet of snow to get to the place where I must dig twelve feet down for the well, I really never dare grumble, because whilst many other wells give out from drought, or frost, my good spring gurgles in through all seasons, and at least I have been spared the ache of sending a thirsty beast away without its full measure of water.

By the end of March the weather became loaded with the intense anxiety attached to the coming of the seeding month. All wheat should be in its seed-bed by May 1. Oats may be sown as late as May 20, and the very last seeding day of the species of barley warranted to mature and ripen in sixty days is June 15; but much can be done towards wheat seeding in the matter of perfect preparation, and I did all I could to reduce worry by work, the object being that Roddy McMahon should not be kept waiting one moment for cleaned and pickled seed. Seeding, harvest, and threshing times are his strongest points, and I always found him a rock of defence in these very critical periods of the short farming season on the prairie.

The end of March had its days of promise, or I should not have agreed with him to return as early as April 8, except that it is the very best time possible to clear off big stone which has been got out but not taken off the seed-bed. The following notes in my diary close the season, and should have closed the natural period of winter, but the year 1907 from start to finish was exceptional, not typical. It proved such a ruling factor in the history of my experiment, occurring as it did at the critical moment, that it is essential it should be faithfully recorded. It is seldom, however, that the entire wheat crop raised in the prairie provinces escapes without a scratch of early frost here or there; this is hardly to be wondered at considering the enormous expanse of land included in these provinces. The failure of the 1907 crop was not caused by early frost but through the belated spring and lack of sun in July and August. The whole season was in strongest contrast to the sun-blessed perfect seasons of 1905 and 1906, which years caused a leap in the development of Canada's prosperity, proving again that the farmer is the god in the car of this nation of most brilliant promise. To return to the closing days of March 1907, the record of my diary reads:

'March 29 – Good Friday. A bright but bitterly cold day, the wind seeming to blow from every quarter and absolutely piercing. Two men called in search of a job. Spent most of the day as I spent Christmas Day, trying to keep the cattle off the remnant of hay which with care will easily pull us through the seeding month. Temper distinctly milder on these occasions, but horribly tired and rather down-hearted. The weather is trying one just now far more than in the worst of winter days, when at least nothing mattered but oneself.

'March 30 – Cleaned seed. Very cold. Hard frost and wind.

'March 31 – Bitter piercing wind. Hard frost and Easter Sunday – the greyest Easter I have ever spent, but the sun went down in vivid gold. Bert Mazey wasted my whole morning discussing the price of my pigs of the future in connexion with his hayrack of the past. I haven't the smallest intention of selling the pigs, and wish I had gone to church. Miss Lister and Mr. Smith came to tea. Towards evening the wind softened, and March went out more or less as the proverbial lamb.'

3

The seeding month –
the coming of Felicity

April came, my very own month, and I forgot it. I lay in bed long after my friend the sun had risen, and positively without excuse since it was a fine and gracious morning, warm and exquisitely bright, with that indescribable quality of exhilaration in the air which we name the joy of life and in our hearts prize more truly than any other gift. When I had worked my way through chores that couldn't be avoided, I claimed the first of April's days as holiday, and walked over to John McLeay's with Pax, whose unbounded delight was good to see. John McLeay was out, but we rested at his door and walked home again, carefully selecting our path by guidance of the herbage, whose earth-bed had already claimed its measure of sun, yet for all our care occasionally I sank with startling suddenness knee-deep into a drift.

The next day I returned to the wheel of the grain separator, but poor Pax, who seemed so fit and well and kept me company the whole day in the granary in spite of his strong dislike of the music of the mill, had a very bad fit towards evening, and I wondered if I really ought to follow my neighbour's advice to have him destroyed. But all beasts of the prairie love life with their very last breath; they seem to thank you for the final effort to save, and to hope on with you all the time. The hardest thing required of one in the circumstance and event of farm life is to kill.

On April 3 came a blinding snowstorm. On the 4th I sold two pigs to the local butcher for the sum of twenty-five dollars, but the bargain was immediately followed by a fierce hurricane, with another fall of snow and the wildest weather. The sudden reverse was evidently too much for my newly acquired patience, since, following an account of the day, and in spite of the deal with the butcher which was always for ready money, I read in my diary the following words of a mood of despair: 'Clothesless, bootless, penniless, wretched!'

The fact is that the winter in Canada demands a very special outfit for the protection of hands and feet: felt boots and leather-covered woollen mitts made in the form of a baby's glove. Both hand and footwear are useless directly winter is fairly away, because the softening snow at once penetrates the felt boots, and the mitts are in the way when one requires full use of the fingers. There is nothing in the wardrobe scheme that one is so thankful to buy or so glad to burn as these particular symbols of the Canadian winter. I had probably burned mine all too soon, and the return of winter found me minus armour. However, the mood seems to have been as transitory as the weather, since the record of April 6 reads:

'Woke at sunrise to a perfect day. Fed oats without hat or coat. Milled seed-wheat with door and window open. Softest, warmest sunshine. Good day's work.'

On April 8 Roddy McMahon returned for the seeding month. It was cold and stormy, but he wasn't afraid of the weather, and talked with much energy about the stones, although eventually I removed the greater number of these myself, stoning not being among his strong points. We were both very anxious to get in the seed early, and he was mightily pleased that it was so clean and good to look at and to show other people. He promptly volunteered to take his turn at the mill-handle, although he criticized my new purchase as 'good and slow all right.' In my heart I was afraid he might not be quite so careful as I was in picking out any stray wild oats when bagging up; but I had determined to pickle every grain myself, and reserved that occasion for the final capture of those strange, dark, creeping vampires of the grain world which, when they once obtain entrance, take possession of the soil with swiftest power, and cannot only take the place of the wheat but suck health and strength from the few blades here and there that fight through its thrall into a puny existence. Wild oats can knock off three-fourths of the value of a wheat crop almost before the farmer has time to realize that the enemy is within the field.

The second day after the return of Roddy McMahon I awoke to a heavy snowfall, and fell back on a heavy heart.

That time I was utterly, completely rebellious. Through the winter weeks I had got up on time and done my chores more or less cheerfully, but the moment I had no choice and had to cook breakfast for another I simply longed to sulk, to refuse to do a single thing, and to remain in bed until the winter had really and truly gone on its way. However, the porridge was cooked, and the bacon and potatoes, when Roddy McMahon came in like a big hurricane, covered with snowflakes and his face alight with good tidings.

'You've got a new horse,' said he.

If anyone had reason to sulk that day it was the new horse, Nancy's first foal. Nancy didn't seem to possess all the knowledge mothers are supposed to have on these occasions, but she was simply bubbling over with pride and pleasure and maternal anxiety at the curious creature at her side. And Felicity *was* curious. Skye, the two-year-old pinto pony that my neighbour had bought of Danny McLeay when I bought Tommy, was her sire; and Felicity was a pinto too, with one wicked Skye-like grey eye and another most lovable Nancy-like velvet brown eye; but in form she was absolutely perfect, and life on the prairie brought her glorious health and strength.

'Do you know what I should do with that brute in the stable if it was mine?' said my neighbour after the first glimpse at her.

'What brute?' I asked.

'Nancy's foal. I should wring the creature's neck before anyone could see it.'

'Nancy adores her,' I answered, 'and so do I.'

Nancy from the first allowed me a big share in the care of the baby, who was the happiest thing in the world; and in spite of all the ills that blow in with wind and weather the name Felicity became her, since life to her seemed just joy itself, and every fresh surprise brought a new delight. The other horses were most deeply interested in the newcomer, and so were all their many bands of friends. On the Sunday afternoon after her birthday I heard the tramp of hoofs and the rush of a four-footed host in full gallop, and across the wheat-field through the falling snow I saw Nancy racing at top speed with Felicity at her side, and about fifty horses of all sizes, age, and colour, gentle and simple, in hot pursuit. Fearing that too much sport might affect the milk, I went to the rescue and found Nancy fearfully perturbed, but Felicity was greeting them all in the equine form of Canadian 'pleased to meet you,' and obviously enjoying the fun without a touch of fear. If she didn't succeed in changing the face of the weather in that most unpromising seeding month, she at any rate made one forget the anxiety with which it was loaded; and she also brought good luck in her trail, since two brothers and two sisters complete the family of Nancy up to date.

Three days after her advent, a big white sow, one of the litter born in the rains of the preceding June, produced ten small pigs; but one was suffocated within a few hours. I had also three sows of the same tribe from whom I hoped for families of ten or more; and in addition there were eight small pigs born in October, being the final contribution from the sow which I had bought for ten dollars of my predecessor; but these latecomers had not thriven so well as the June family and were not nearly ready for market. I was offered twenty-five dollars each for my three sows, which was an excellent price at that time; but through the folly of counting my pigs before they were born, I refused to part. Even had all gone well I had not sufficient food for them, and the farmer should never, or only at the outset, or in emergency, buy food for her stock; she must grow it. Had I sold all for seventy-five dollars and spent half the money on weaned pigs at two dollars fifty, and the other half in my emergency on barley-chop for their food, I should have made over cent. per cent. in the deal at food price within six months; but pigs were the one corner of my proposition which had always seemed to be there in time of urgent need of food or money, and I foolishly staked all on the chance of number, without even taking due consideration for every point of the chance. As it was I had bad luck with each of them, partly through allowing them to stray round the straw piles and make their own nest of welcome, and the end of it was that the united families of the three numbered but ten in survival, and never throve quite as well as the nine which arrived in the snow.

The weather being quite hopeless, Roddy McMahon returned to the Fort, and did not come back again until April 22. In the interval I had the misfortune to lose Pax. I had to go into South Qu'Appelle on business, and he begged so hard to be allowed to come that I took him, only I didn't like to take him into the hotel dining-room, so I bought him some meat at the butcher's and left him outside whilst I took my meal. Through the dining-room window I caught a glimpse of him walking up and down looking a little frightened and forlorn, and from that hour he vanished. I went to every livery-barn, advertised, offered a reward, and returned to South Qu'Appelle on the following Sunday, but all in vain; I never saw my faithful comrade of the winter any more, and for several months remained dogless; but the pigs made such onslaught on the potatoes that, in hope of settling the matter, I accepted Bobs from a mutual friend in exchange for sixteen pounds of butter.

When Roddy McMahon returned from the first day's stoning on April 22 he said that the surface of the summer-fallow was in fairly good trim, and that we should seed with good luck on the next day but one. However, there came hard frost and bitter wind, and it was the first week in May before we started to seed the summer-fallowed land. In despair I started preparation for the pickling of my seed-grain, although it is not wise to give the seed its bath until within a few hours of seeding.

For the cleansing and disinfecting process nearly all farmers who once used blue-stone now use formalin, the quantity being about two pounds to sixty bushels of grain. The main object is to get every seed bathed so that it becomes proof against the infection and attack of smut; and also in this the last procedure before passing under the pressure of the soil, much smut-ball and weed-seed of the lighter kind will rise to the surface of the water, and can be skimmed off and burned. Guy Mazey, who had over two hundred acres to seed that year, and never risks loss of time, plunged his two-bushel sacks into the pickle, left them immersed for ten minutes, and withdrew them, allowing the grain to dry in the sack. This process saves time all round and is quite permissible with perfectly clean seed; although even perfectly clean seed affords some work for the skimmer in the open bath. I might have used this method for my six bags of hand-cleaned seed, but was confronted with the difficulty of hauling the heavy grain-bags in and out of the barrel; besides, I enjoyed looking at it. The Creegans used the bath I bought from Eaton's, and that was quite the nearest approach to the model of the latest pickling bath which that year was to be seen at Mr. Dillon's hardware store, and was purchased and greatly appreciated by many of the wealthier farmers. The greater number of my neighbours used two barrels, plunging loose wheat into the pickle in the top barrel, and when they considered the immersion sufficient they withdrew the cork and let the pickle run out into the second barrel, threw out the pickled seed to dry, carefully covering the heap with sacks in order to prevent the escape of the fumes of the formalin, and then repeated the process until all the seed-grain had been through the ceremony of the bath. The most primitive and least effective of all methods is the one I quoted in my account of the seeding of 1906; and my own process is slow and unusual, but excellent in result.

I turn a bag of grain into a barrel of pickle, and after three editions of stirring and skimming I remove the grain from the barrel in a half-gallon milk-strainer and toss it into a corner to drain, being careful to cover to keep in the fumes of formalin. Of course if I could have afforded to purchase Mr. Dillon's orthodox seed-bath, which revolved, and stirred, shook, and drained forty bushels of grain at one immersion, I should have saved much time; but hours are usually more plentiful than dollars through the first few years of a farmer's proceeding. When the pile of bathed grain is dry, I bag, pouring the grain rather slowly into the bag in order to seize on any wild oat that has escaped annihilation. I had sown dirty seed and reaped its harvest in 1906, but I think I can truthfully say no farmer sowed cleaner wheat than I in the years that followed. That year, 1907, my grain was pronounced the cleanest that went into the town; and it chanced that in 1910 seed-cleaning and pickling was the first form of farm labour into which I initiated some Englishwomen who came out to me as pupils. It is always a test of patience, almost of endurance; but the result again was excellent, my 1910 crop scored No. 1 Northern and was declared to be the cleanest and best sample of grain threshed in the neighbourhood. I sold a quantity of it for seed, and about seven hundred bushels in the following May at a dollar a bushel. But of course clean seed is only half the battle; the land also must be clean, and that is a far more difficult matter to deal with.

To return to 1906. My pickling process can be very cold, and it was not possible to do a great quantity at a time in the granary as the water froze in the barrel and the pickled grains froze together in the heap, and my hands were painfully numb and helpless; so with a little persuasion I got a barrel into the kitchen, and there I pickled seed-grain in comfort, if I cooked in more or less disorder.

In all I cleaned nearly two hundred bushels of my 1906 crop, but not nearly so much was used for seed. I had many bags of tailings for the pigs, and also forty bushels over, which I sold the following September in South Qu'Appelle at a dollar a bushel net. My seed-oats I bought from Mr. John A. Macdonald, for some years the member for North Qu'Appelle and eldest son of the last of the chief factors of the Hudson Bay Company, who is a keen agriculturist and who at that time owned a quarter section at the foot of the hills which skirt South Qu'Appelle on its southern side. This land is now divided up into building sites, but at that time oats were raised from corner to corner of the one hundred and sixty acres. The big field was quite a centre of local interest, and Mr. Macdonald used to sell every grain of its produce as seed, usually at double the average price of oats.

This seed I sowed in the ten- and four-acred arms of the big field, which had been full ploughed after bearing its two crops of wheat. Barley was sowed in twelve acres of the forty-acre field. Roddy McMahon disced and harrowed it directly we got on the land, in order to give the surface seed a bed to rise through; and when he had finished wheat and oat-seeding he ploughed in all this voluntary growth and sowed barley. Barley matures so quickly that it should be harvest-ripe before any voluntary accompaniment of wheat or wild or tare oats can arrive at generating point, so that it all comes down together without danger of wasting good in spreading evil seed.

In the eighteen acres of summer-fallow, the twenty-five acres of breaking Si Booth had broken, and the thirty acres Roddy McMahon had broken, we sowed wheat; but the last five acres to be sown in the wheat-seeding was the seed-garden on the northwest boundary, and therein went my hand-cleaned seed.

When seeding was over I looked out upon the new fields, newly sown with grain which I had cleaned with my best effort, and felt that I had done all I could towards the harvest of 1907. In my diary I find this entry:

'The most difficult time of the first year is over; another has its fair start. It was a year of much toil and a certain amount of hardship, disappointment, and worry; but always there was the inspiration and consolation of the beasts. In spite of failures and my many failings, especially a habit of occasionally doing my work in a rebellious sort of way – one may just as well do the inevitable amiably – I have made a step forward in my work and got on terms with the daily round. I am going strong – absolutely independent of people and circumstances!'

Here the record of my diary ceases for some months, as if the arrogance of the last phrase had bared itself to invite annihilation from the arrows which were lurking in the future. Yet with truth and without offence against the spirit of humility I might have written: 'When all my sins great and small stand up to claim me, let it stand for my defence against the sin of omission that in those frozen months which waylaid spring in 1907 I cleaned seed-grain with *all* my power.'

4

The land and the man

At the end of the seeding month I had to find a new hired man. My shrunken capital absolutely forbade me to hire a man and team, no matter how strong was the argument for the land's sake. But if only I had been strong enough to take that special chance, I should have saved myself eventually much anxiety, worry, disappointment, grave financial loss, and possibly the life of a horse.

Nothing need trouble any farmer but this matter of working expense, since for labour one can train oneself to fill all emergency. But horse power or steam power is imperative, and none can insure against occasional casualty. Over and over again I have known the traditional run of bad luck with horses confront the newcomer, and occasionally the old-timer, on a prairie farm. For this reason mares should always be purchased when possible in preference to geldings; the years go by so quickly, and in case of loss or mishap none can realize the relief of going out to the pasture to select a horse to fill the vacancy, in place of going to one's banker for an eight per cent. ticket to the market, where even now good horses are more easily sold than bought. The newcomer, too, should invest a generous margin of capital in cattle: steers and heifers grow into money so quickly, and from two years old upward steers stand in emergency for substantial and immediate contribution to the imperative purchase of horses, or implements, or hire of labour; and these three occasions can be at any unexpected moment absolutely essential for the successful working of the land on which one's net profit and ultimate prosperity depend.

The cost of living on five acres or five hundred is entirely a matter of choice, when the degree of necessity is left behind. The degree of necessity demanded from me in the winter of 1906-1907 an expenditure of twenty-two dollars seventy from November 1 to April 13. Incidentally, it included flour, tea, coffee, sugar, lamp-oil, marmalade, raisins, currants, baking-powder, yeast-cakes, matches, salt, tapioca, jam, and for other food I had my turkey-like pork. After the middle of February, too, I had a good supply of butter, eggs, milk, and cream from the stock; and also a contribution from the sale of such produce to set against my twenty-two dollars seventy. It is wisdom to pay cash down for one's land, and to break no more of it than one has capital to work; but a living can always be obtained in farming on the prairie, and the life of a woman-farmer is very different from the life of a farmer's wife on the prairie. Some may prefer one, some the other; but the one is an entirely different proposition from the other.

Roddy McMahon was, I think, sorry to leave, and might have also waived his objection to hiring on without his team, but he had an offer to break land near Lipton at the rate of five dollars an acre. This sounds well, and comes out well under the satisfactory conditions of board and residence for man and horses, barring oats. But he told me afterwards that he had a rough and uncomfortable time, and found there was little if anything in it; and I have always found it to be the cheapest way of breaking new land, and getting it put in shape for crops, providing you have a breaker who really knows the work – one who has won the knowledge through much experience.

On the last day but one I drove over to Indian Head to look for a man. I had left it until rather late, and in the end I had to drive the eighteen miles in a gale. A gale at this season of the year means that you hold on to your seat and the lines, and trust yourself to the discretion of your horse, with eyes shut fast against a merciless cloud of soil, blown by the wind from the

seed-beds which line the way on either side of every road allowance between Wideawake and Indian Head. I arrived in the
spick-and-span little wheat town with a face that was literally,
but so completely, black that it marked one as hailing from
another race, rather than as being a member of the great un-
washed. I had to decline the printed invitation to take a bath at
the Imperial Hotel for the sum of fifty cents, because of the message of the clock, and immediately after the midday meal I set
out to find a man. I could hear of none anywhere. At the livery
barns, in the hotels and stores there was the same tale of the
numbers who had been work-seeking yesterday, and the other
numbers who would most certainly come off the work-seeker's
train on the morrow. I had given up the quest as hopeless, when
I caught sight of Sergeant-Major Dubuque in the High Street,
and turned back to ask him if he could help me.

It chanced that a young man was doing a wood-bucking chore
for him at the moment whom he thought might be useful to me.
He had just returned from a sojourn in Regina, where he had
been a guest of the Government; but the Sergeant assured me
that the part he had played in a horse deal was certainly not the
leading part, although it had carried off the penalty, and that he
could honestly advise me to give him a trial. Also he recommended me to offer him fifteen dollars a month, and what he
was worth at the end of it.

I had expected to pay at least twenty-five or thirty dollars, and
I engaged the man, whom I will call Adam, on the spot. He
dropped the bucksaw, put his coat over his overalls, and got into
the buggy after he had fetched a small brown-paper parcel from
the house. On the way home he sat at the extreme edge of the
seat, which must have been most uncomfortable, and at the half-
way point of our journey he carefully unfastened the brown-
paper parcel, and refreshed himself from its contents of dry
bread which was keeping company with a collar, a tie, and a
brush and comb.

'They give it to me when I left the jail yesterday morning,' he
explained. 'But that Sergeant – what's his name? Dubuque?
Well, he's a good man all right. A man needn't go hungry there.'

I shouldn't refer to his visit to Regina only that from the first he discussed it so frankly himself, his chief topic of conversation was of life within walls of the house with the barred door, and the usual word of his defence of any act or habit with which I found fault, 'Well, I guess you know what you want, but, Boys Alive! that's how we did it in jail.' He was full of the kindest sentiment and good feeling towards his caretakers, and couldn't say enough in praise of the kindness of Sergeant Dubuque; in fact every detail of prison life had his strong commendation. It seems that prisoners in Regina are comfortably lodged, well fed, and have liberty in the intervals of work to read, write, and talk to each other; and there was a bathroom, not reserved for the ordeal of that first baptism of humiliation, but for the regular care and cleansing of the body which most surely is of aid in the refreshment of the energy of the soul. Judging from his personal experience the entire prison system of Regina seemed formed on the basis of a generous, wholesome desire for the uplifting, rather than the down-treading, of those human beings who lose their footing in the mire.

I listened with deep interest, and was so glad to think that I was at last in a country, and a British colony, where, since there was clearly no *mauvaise honte* about doing time, a system of justice had been thought out, altogether ahead of that which condemns the fallen to pass out of the unhealthy and demoralizing atmosphere of the sacred frying-pan of the Scribes into the even more debasing period of torture in the sanctimonious fire of the Pharisees. One day, in talking to a mutual acquaintance, I expressed my satisfaction at Adam's service as hired man, and also my admiration for the system of justice which encouraged a young nation to stand up for the fact, that once a transgressor against the common law had paid its penalty, he stands among his fellow men a really free man – free to live and love and work as any other man. But the Canadian was silent, only the suspicion in the eye said far more plainly than words, 'Birds of a feather.'

As we drove through the beautiful grain-lands of the Indian Head trail the comments of Adam were altogether inspiring to his new employer.

'My, that's as pretty a piece of breaking as ever I see down East! But I don't care to see so many stones. Those fellows should be cleared I guess. And that land is too much on the ridge like. Boys Alive! Give me breaking turned right flat on to its back.'

Just as we turned into the bluff and slough land of my own neighbourhood Dick cut off across an old trail that we had used in the early spring, and the farmer came out to us in great wrath for driving over his newly sown breaking.

Canadians are most casual about such matters as a rule, and I have never been called to order before or since on this point, and was rather ridiculed by Mr. Grigg for picking my road most carefully round his big crops before the road between us was graded. However I apologized most sincerely, and explained that I was a farmer too, and wouldn't do mischief for worlds; and in the end I was graciously permitted to continue on my way across the new breaking instead of being compelled to turn back.

Adam worked well the next day harrowing with three sections behind the seeder, but on the morning after I had said good-bye for that season to Roddy McMahon I nearly lost his successor.

I think he felt lonely, and on second thoughts was not sure that he cared about a woman 'boss'; but the reason he gave was that my terms were far too low for his service.

He walked across the field to my neighbour's, and I thought I had seen the last of him, but he came back within half an hour.

'Well there! Boys Alive! Guess I'll stay my month. The fellow over yonder says maybe I'll have to go back to Regina if the Sergeant hears I've quit.'

He assured me he was bred on a farm in Eastern Canada, and I concluded that he was perfectly at home in the use of all implements, and farm work generally. He rose literally at daybreak, and sang long before the lark. At any moment after 3 A.M. one might hear him descending the stairs, and his invitation to the cows to attend the ceremony of milking might be heard across the valley. He was a very slow milker, and I do not think a good one, as Molly developed warts and a general soreness which usually may be traced to a rough or misunderstanding hand.

Neither was he kind on the surface of things. 'There ain't a beast on this here place as minds,' was his constant complaint. 'You've got to make a beast mind,' his verdict on my happy family, until at last I sharply requested him to mind his own business. But he could be thoroughly trusted in the matter of their food and water, and I came to the conclusion that there was more love of noise than any ill-feeling about his constant abuse.

I had complete confidence in his power as a ploughman, drawn I must confess from his most able criticism of the land-work we had passed on our way from Indian Head. One day I left him to strike a furrow on a piece of land which I intended to add to the big wheat-field beneath its left arm.

When I returned about an hour later shouts and shrieks guided me to the place where he stood raving at the horses. I followed his furrow which, barring the fact that here and there the plough had slipped out allowing the soil to remain unbroken, reminded one of a winding, curling, English stream, bent in reaching a river some day in its own particular time and place.

'I thought you told me you had ploughed before, Adam,' I said.

'Quite a bit down East,' he answered without turning a hair.

'Take the horses in now. Supper will be ready in an hour.'

I was within a few yards of my neighbour's gate, and I thought it wisdom to ask his advice. He came back with me to see the furrow and laughed until he reached its end. 'By Jove! you had better stick to the chap,' he said. 'He is certainly not lacking in perseverance. I heard a great noise going on, and thought you must be killing pigs. His quarter of a mile furrow stretched out would measure a mile from point to point, and by the look of it the shear is blunt as a board. Well, I'll swear the greenest Englishman that ever ploughed with horse or ox has never left a furrow on the Canadian prairie to beat that.'

'But what am I to do?' I said wrathfully. 'I can't afford to hire a man with horses, so I couldn't keep on Roddy McMahon, and men are as usual scarce and expensive.'

'You have no business to be breaking in any case,' he said. 'You have all you can do to get through the ploughing and cultivation of the big field with your limited horse power. I should put him right into that. Begin on my corner where the wild oats are thickest, and then if you haven't time to plough the whole field twice over, you can get through the worst part of it. I have a plough here I can lend you until I need it myself, and if you will bring the chap over to-morrow morning I'll start him on.'

On the morrow Adam and I crossed the field with Jim, Kit, and Tommy, and took the first lesson in ploughing. At the time I hadn't the smallest idea of tooling any of the implements but the harrows, which I found perfectly simple to deal with, and for a good walker, pleasant exercise made interesting through the presence of horses. But I waited to see Adam take his lesson that morning and digested it. My neighbour cut the leading furrow, turned and brought back the horses; put us into line with the next, and went on his way leaving us to worry it out. Of course I knew the 'Gee' to the right, and 'Haw' to the left rule of the road, and the mechanism of the levers, but it seemed to me that the fundamental rule of the furrow in process was to keep Kitty always safely in the furrow, more especially as she had a distinct inclination to reconnoitre to the right or left. I turned a few furrows, and at the end of the time Kitty knew the meaning of the command 'Furrow, Kitty,' and obeyed it.

At Adam's turn he slipped out badly more than once, the sod of course remaining uncut, and unturned in consequence.

'How careless you are, Adam,' I exclaimed. 'Didn't I tell you to keep Kitty in the furrow? Try to say "Furrow, Kitty"; she will keep to it.'

'The fellow didn't teach you that,' he answered. 'Boys Alive! I guess I know more about ploughing than any woman.'

'If you dare to answer me again,' I said, 'I will immediately send you back to Sergeant Dubuque. And now you can get on the plough, and make the best of your difficulties without my help.'

'No offence! No offence!' he insisted. 'Only I guess I know all about a plough.'

In the course of an hour he had caught on to the principle, and, although slow does not describe the pace, had I governed

my ploughing after the moral of the fable I should probably have
come through that season's work with the triumph of the tor-
toise. Adam loved his new accomplishment. I yelled myself
hoarse over calling him in to dinner, and actually voiceless in
calling him for supper; and in the end I had to walk across by the
last glow of sunset to induce him to unhitch. During the day his
work had steadily improved, and although he had accomplished
no more than Roddy McMahon would have got through in half
a day, it was carefully done with no untrimmed patches, and
neat, with most respectable turns. The horses, too, in spite of
their long day were cool and comfortable, without any trace of
fatigue. I slept with a lightened heart, but the self-satisfaction of
Adam in the knowledge of his increasing experience and power
found vent in a freedom of habit which I couldn't endure.

'Adam,' I said one day, at the end of my tether, 'understand
that I will not have you give way to that disgusting habit in the
house.'

'Which? Chewin'?'

'No, spitting; but either is disgusting.'

'If a fellow chews he's got to do the other, I guess. Boys Alive!
Can't quit chewin'.'

'You can go outside when you require to do the other.'

From that hour he left the table several times during a meal
with the preface of 'Scuse me.' 'Boys Alive! Handy things them
verandeys,' was always his tribute on his return.

Before he had been with me a week, my brother came down to
borrow Kitty and Jim to put in his crop of oats. I knew I ought
not to spare them, but there were none that we could hire, and
there was no way out of it. Adam was by way of sulking at the
horses being taken away, and I sharply reprimanded him for a
remark he had made over it. 'No offence,' said he. 'I was only
having a laugh. Boys Alive! I guess a fellow's got to put up with
a lot from a woman boss.'

I thought that the time of my brother's visit would be an excellent opportunity to kill a pig. It was already getting late because
they should never be killed during the season of thunderstorm
or in excessive heat, as it is most difficult, even with the greatest

care, to get through the pickling process in time to avoid any risk of loss of meat. My brother never hesitated to refuse to kill himself, but he said if Adam could do the act, and the pig wasn't so very big he could assist.

'Can you kill a pig, Adam?' I inquired. 'If not, it must be sent to the butcher. But I don't like sending them to the butcher, because although I think an expert can probably get through the business much more swiftly and humanely than the average man, I am sure a pig would rather die ten swift deaths than be caught and hoisted into a wagon, and taken on a long, strange, jolting journey to a place of dread.'

'Kill a pig! Boys Alive!' said Adam. 'Kill a dozen. Kill a hundred. Butcherin's my trade. I learned the knife with a butcher down East. Kill pigs! Boys Alive! You have me there, and cattle too. Butcherin'! That's my job of all the lot. If you want to give me a job to suit me fine and good, just show me the knife, hold him down, and one, two –'

'Be quiet at once,' I said, hating him I think more than I had ever hated human being before. His eyes had a ferocious, bloodthirsty look, and his face, with the Friday chin of those who use a razor once a week, looked like the face of one who killed with glee. 'See that everything is ready, so that it is got over as quickly and quietly as possible, and come and tell me when it is done.'

All the winter through I had fed those pigs, who were friendly creatures, not very big, and pigs can be so human. I waited in the granary for the wail of the announcement of the end. Two or three unusually feeble editions came at intervals of about ten minutes, and I felt my poor beast was going through the hateful business over and over again. At last I heard my brother call me.

'Is it over?' I asked.

'That bragging, bouncing, cowardly fool,' he said, 'and after all his yarns about butchering down East! He can no more kill a pig than I can. He shook like a woman the moment I had everything fixed so that we could get it over in a second, and then he wanted me to do it.'

'And didn't you?'

'No, but I admitted I couldn't. If I had known about it, I would have brought along my gun. Of course, if it was a matter of starvation I could do it, I have no doubt.'

I was furious with them both, but especially Adam, as he took the whole proceeding as a fine joke, and wasn't in the least concerned at being caught out in lying bounce.

'Boys Alive! Two nice pairs of greenhorns you got on that butcherin' job. Couldn't kill a pig, not both the two of us.'

The poor little pigs were cowering in a corner with frightened eyes, and didn't die for a further six weeks, and the occurrence brought about one excellent rule on the farm, which is never broken. Every pig has to be shot through the head before it is butchered in the usual fashion; it makes very little difference to the meat, and all the difference left in this world to the pig, who, instead of dying a hundred deaths through terror, is dead before it knows it has to die.

One morning going in from work within an hour of dinnertime I found a tall and very athletic-looking Englishman waiting on the veranda. I recognized him as a man who had been recommended to me by some friends in South Qu'Appelle. I explained that I had already engaged a man, but he dined with us, and when I heard a glowing description of the two years he had passed on a Manitoba farm, of the acres he had ploughed, disced, and harrowed; of the horses and cattle he had taken two miles to water through that dire winter, and finally of his positive preference for the use of a walking-plough – and John McLeay, and Sandy Stewart, and David Chambers all swore by walking ploughs – I began to think it would be wisdom to strain a last point, and pay him the thirty-five dollars a month he required until the ploughing was through which, with his experience, should not be more than six weeks, and keep Adam on for chores and stone-gathering, haymaking, and carrying. The plough only required three horses, leaving Dick and Nancy for lighter but most necessary work; and before Mr. Oliver left it was decided that he should come back a week from that day, when the horses would be ready for him.

I walked across the field to put him on the line for the stage, and we met my neighbour.

'He has had excellent experience in Manitoba,' I explained, as we watched him swing across towards the coming stage, 'and if there is anything he doesn't quite understand you'll advise him, won't you?'

'A man asking thirty-five dollars a month has no business to need advice on his job from anyone, and you should have hired horses instead of letting yours go north. You haven't nearly enough horse power for three hundred and twenty acres, and how can you expect to run five hundred with them. Adam started on his work well, and you could have got on to the harrowing in his trail with Dick and Nancy, and I think you might have pulled through. This man may be all right, up to his work, but you never can tell! Any man who has been in the country five minutes will swear to experience.'

My brother was later on his return than he anticipated, and my new helper had no team.

'But, of course, with your experience, you can fence,' I suggested. 'Please get the four corner-posts in for the garden, and then go to the bluff, cut and point the necessary pickets, and begin to fence the house between the posts.'

When I returned from the Fort I saw at once that fencing was distinctly outside his experience. 'I know it requires practice,' I said, 'but you see it is impossible for me to pay two men, and also a half-breed, to do this kind of work.'

As a matter of fact fencing is very simple; it is, like most work in Canada, monotonous, and requires patience and perseverance, but the reason of the failure of the average white man to fence is that he is too lazy to prepare with the crow-bar sufficiently deep holes for his pickets. Every picket should be at least eighteen inches in the ground – twenty-four is better. If one examines the fence, and even the fence repair of the average hired man, it will be found that the pickets are put in anyhow, with a blunt end, and from six to ten inches in the ground; yet it is not only easy work for a man, but quite possible work for a woman. It is straining taut the barbed wire that is the real difficulty, although the sound picketing is the test of the fence. But it is far cheaper to employ expert labour, and pay from sixteen to twenty dollars a mile to get it thoroughly done by half-breeds, than feed white men and pay them by day or week for the same job. The best fence I have seen in Canada was in the Sedgwick Colony of the Shaughnessy Ready-Made Farms prepared for the settlers of 1912, and I think only white labour was employed for this.

'My work has been entirely on the land,' Mr. Oliver explained. 'I might begin a little breaking to-morrow with the two horses, as I really don't seem to make much headway with this kind of thing.'

Adam was looking on, first at the fence and then at the fence-maker, his hands in his pockets, and there was no mistaking the look in his eyes for disappointment or sympathy.

The next day Mr. Oliver attacked a patch of scrub-like land just outside the garden fence. It wasn't exactly successful, but I knew it must be difficult to accomplish with just Dick and Nancy to pull the plough, to say nothing of an ancient rubbish heap en route, which kept guard over a pot and pan pit at its side, and which I should think had been in use a dozen years. But in the evening my brother and the team returned.

'Boys Alive! Lal. Seen his fence?' I heard Adam inquire of my brother.

'Whose fence?'

'The other green Englishman's.'

'Look here, Adam,' was the wrathful reply. 'I never hit a chap beneath my own size, but if I ever hear that word "green Englishman" from you again I'll give you a bath in the slough.'

'Boys Alive! No offence! An' I guess I'm so clean as any man on the land come Sundays, though I don't go in for style.'

'Ah! and you can kill a pig can't you?'

'Boys Alive! So well as any green –'

My brother drew just a little nearer.

'Say it, Adam, say it, and back you come to Regina if I have to drag you there in the stone-boat myself.'

'Boys Alive! That's all right. No offence! No offence.'

In spite of the dialogue Adam was as wax in my hands before the advent of Mr. Oliver, then he sulked, and was as unmanageable as an untamed broncho. He rose at his usual hour – rather earlier – and milked the cows, and then sat on the veranda and talked to himself, and sang dirges until I called him in to breakfast.

'Why aren't you helping in the stable?' I inquired. 'I won't have men sitting round doing nothing before breakfast.'

'I ain't going to do the Englishman's work for him. Guess it's his team now, not mine. And I ain't going to work in the stable whilst he's there.'

'What has he done to you? He doesn't interfere with you in your work in any way,' I said angrily.

'Boys Alive! Didn't he take away my ploughing after the other feller up north had taken my team? Still *he's* all right, I have not a word against him, but this other greenhorn, he's too fond of chewing the rag.'

We should probably have parted at that moment, without further exchange of sentiments, but one of my neighbours appeared at the gate.

'Good morning, Adam,' he said. 'I guess you haven't seen my cow round.'

'I see a cow so thin as a razor,' said Adam.

'That's my cow.'

'Boys Alive! I shut her in the pasture long with our bunch. Guess I'll come along and give you a hand.'

'That's real kind, if it won't be taking you off your job.'

'Got no job. She's handed over my team to a green Englishman.'

The ploughing seemed to go well the first day or so and then between my many chores and household duties I failed to go and examine the work every day. Hoping and believing it was going well I arranged that Mr. Oliver should have every other Saturday afternoon off to go down to the Fort for tennis. But every day there was a bad quarter of an hour at the start. Between Roddy McMahon and Adam I had become the champion early bird of the neighbourhood, and to see the new man play with his five o'clock breakfast when I knew he wouldn't get another meal till twelve, made me perfectly wretched.

At the end of his month Adam passed into the domain of Danny McLeay. I was awfully sorry to part with him but I didn't like living in a quarrelsome atmosphere; and I felt sure that when Mr. Oliver realized that he was entirely responsible for the work, he would rise to the occasion. Besides, it is the greatest mistake to imagine that because you are paying a man a low salary you can't lose much by him in Canada where labour is so expensive and so scarce. An extra hand outdoors always increases the indoor work, and no man is kept for nothing. The cheapest labour is the best labour and the best system of all for the woman-farmer is to train herself to do all her own chores and hire her field labourer at special seasons by the day even if she has to pay the very highest market price. In Britain we grow up with the idea that kitchens and bedrooms are born clean and remain in that state without labour; none can make clear the labour and energy which women distribute, looking after the personal need of men who never give a thought to the work they are creating, but will spend hours meditating on the work they can evade.

5

Shadow and scythe
beneath the sword

It was about this time that divers members of a party of British immigrants who had come over to work on the main line of the Grand Trunk Pacific Railway between Winnipeg and Edmonton found fault with their work and left it, I believe in several cases long before they had worked out the balance of their fares, according to arrangement with the British shipping authorities who had sent them out.

On their way down from Kutawa they passed my brother's stopping-house, and it appears that he told them that I should probably be able to recommend them work in my neighbour-hood, and that certainly they would not be allowed to continue on their way to South Qu'Appelle without an opportunity of restoring the body after the fatigue of sixty miles on foot.

The first to claim my hospitality was a party of four or five, but as they only asked for bread and boiling water to make their tea by the wayside, it was easily given. The next was a very famished and miserable-looking person named Thomas. He pitched the sorriest tale of woe and hardship in the railway camp, to say nothing of the torture of fatigue and hunger on the sixty miles' walk with the sole sustenance of half a loaf of bread given him by my brother. That he was really half starved his phenomenal increase in size within the conditions of peace and plenty which fell to his lot proved indisputably. It was the day of Pearl Mazey's weekly visit, and we gave him the best meal we could collect, and

Pearl said that never within all the years of her recollection of the annual visit of threshers had she seen a man so hungry. I sent for my neighbour, who was looking for a man who could cook and look after the house, and who could be left in full charge during his occasional absence.

'Adam can work splendidly, as we both know,' I said, 'but his cooking would be dire, and I don't think it would be wise to leave him. This man looks sensible and comes off a bad time. Why not give him a trial?'

'Si Booth is round doing some more breaking,' he said, 'and it's a cook and house-help I am wanting. It takes a great deal too much of my time. I'll give him a month's trial.'

So Thomas departed in my neighbour's wake engaged as hired man at twenty dollars a month.

Such numbers came off the trail to call on me after this that I left off meals and gave advice instead; and also I began to make pointed inquiries as to how much of their contract for fare they had settled before deserting their post, and not in one single case did I find that the game had been played out to the end.

In defence they pleaded that the hardships had been unbearable: irregular work, poor food. But in their eyes the cruellest wrong of all was the compulsory subscription to the medical fund. 'And never an ache or a pain in my body these twenty years, and they call this a free country! Give me England!' said one.

'Well, it's something to have made that discovery,' I reminded him.

'And I assure you the snow blew into the tent, and it was positively an inch deep under the mattress. And they've got the impudence to call it Eden!' said another.

'A mattress!' I exclaimed. 'You don't mean to tell me they allowed you that luxury?'

'And if you could have felt it, miss, you might well call it by that name,' he said in derision.

'How much were you earning in the Old Country?' I inquired of each, and the answer of nearly all of them was to the effect that they were earning good wages when they could get work; but this average worked out at about one day and a half in seven.

'And you contrived to get over to this country – where you can get good wages six days out of seven – because Canadians have been reared in the tradition that our word is as good as our bond,' I said; 'and the first thing you have done in the new country is to break contract and raise reproach and ill-feeling against England. Don't talk woman's twaddle about hard mattresses and weak tea to me! Who cared about comfort, do you suppose, at the Front the other day? And what of our history in the Crimea? How many of your wives haven't pawned your clothes for your meals? No matter what were the conditions of discomfort of your camp, you couldn't have got out without signing that contract. I don't think much of the people who sent you out on those lines; but the point is that, having taken it on, the least you could do was to see the thing through.'

Whether the news spread that I was no longer sympathetic or 'agin the Government,' or that Thomas was in control of my neighbour's kitchen, I don't know, but my cottage was no longer the selected stopping-house. One morning in passing through the precincts of my neighbour's shack, on my way to the Mazeys', I saw a son of Erin in the doorway, and when I returned my neighbour said he thought among the visitors of Thomas there was one who might suit me as hired man.

Patrick O'Hara had a shock of auburn curls, blue eyes, and eyelashes which he fluttered in a heart-softening manner.

'I followed the plough as a boy in Ireland, lady, and, faith! though the farmer would not have me milk because he caught me having just one drink out of the can on a thirsty morning, shure it'll all be coming back to me.'

'I have a teamster,' I explained, 'and your work would be chores for the first month at least; and I want the stable roof returfed, and the stables kept clean and comfortable. Also there is a great deal of stoning to be done, and fencing; in fact, you would have to do anything I required, and the pay is only fifteen dollars for the first month. If you suit me later, you might take the teamster's place; and I want a really reliable man as caretaker for the winter. Mr. Dennison tells me you have a wife and child whom you are anxious to bring out.'

Patrick O'Hara crossed the field with me, and that afternoon the yard was indescribably neat and tidy, and all the mangers were well filled for the incoming of the horses; and the next day he started sodding the stable roof. In the afternoon he requested me to come to his aid in order that he might make quicker progress. I had seen something of sod-work in the summer I had spent among Hungarian settlers in my brother's homestead, but then I had only collected the turf and looked on; on this occasion I pitched sods from the wagon, and Patrick O'Hara caught them on his fork on the roof, until some gigantic sods fell by the wayside, and I followed them in sheer exhaustion.

I am afraid that the 'all things to all men' trait was very strong in Patrick O'Hara, but undoubtedly he was a good man on the land or anywhere else when he chose to work. Mr. Oliver called him into all the difficulties in the matter of ploughing with excellent result, and long before the month of trial had expired Patrick was fluttering his eyelids and murmuring much of his loyal and unwavering intention of fulfilling his contract, while he mourned the absurd inadequacy of a salary of fifteen dollars a month to the need and merit of a brilliant Irishman.

Just at this time my attention was drawn to certain portions of the ploughed land which the plough had barely scraped in its passing. But long before that, and in many ways, I had realized that both Mr. Oliver and I had exaggerated the value of his experience in Manitoba. He was looking ill and worn. The very early hours, which are so healthful to the strong, are more than trying to the men and women of weaker physical stamina; and my horses, with but half their work of the season half done, were all looking wretched – harassed and spiritless and worn as I had never seen them look before.

'I am sure you are not strong enough for the work,' I told Mr. Oliver, 'but I can't take chances over the ploughing. Better stay on as my guest for a while and rest. I'm sorry, but Patrick must take over the plough and the care of the team from to-day.'

Patrick had agreed to remain with me through the season for twenty-six dollars a month, and harvest wages through harvest days. On the departure of Mr. Oliver his wages were raised to thirty-five dollars, of course on the understanding of remaining to the end of the working year, and that there would be no other man. Winter terms we had not discussed, but it was understood that his wife and child would come out; and meanwhile I had at his request instructed an agent to pay her ten dollars a month on account of his wages.

Mr. Oliver stayed on for a day or so, and shortly after he left he returned to tell me he had found work which suited him ever so much better – brick-laying on the new cathedral at South Qu'Appelle. 'Two and a half dollars a day,' he said; 'but of course I have to find my own board. But presently we are going to build a big house for a rich farmer in the neighbour-hood, and then we shall get our board thrown in. It is quite near the Fort, and I shall try and get down for tennis on Saturday afternoons.'

He was the son of an English clergyman, the patron of whose living had secured for his son an opening in one of the most important shipping offices in London. But although in his heart he didn't love the plough, he never hated it as he hated the pen. I heard with great regret a year later or so that my suspicion concerning his health had been only too well founded, and that he was lying seriously ill in a hospital many miles west.

That there must have been a few isolated days of the typical sunshine of the prairie during May and June I am sure, because I have always in the smiling corner of my memory a picture of Julia and Felicity lying on a manure heap under the blazing sun, and ever so many small pigs running in and out their legs and sniffing round their ears, and then bolting like an army of cowards when Julia flicked her friendly tail or Felicity raised her inquisitive head; but when the rains of June started to fall it was obvious that the shadow of 1907 which had veiled the way of spring was lingering on the prairie. Cold, wild days were with us still although no hint of frost, and the well-advanced grain had leaped into long luxuriant growth. The prairie was an oasis of deep green, waiting in coolest patience for the harvest sun. I looked thankfully and hopefully at the crops, but disconsolately at the big field, from end to end of which the plough still made its slow but strenuous way. Before the exit of Mr. Oliver I had abandoned hope of a second ploughing, with the exception of the few acres Adam had ploughed first, and which now bore a growth far and away thicker than any seeding. These acres lay in the south-west corner, catching every sunbeam that strayed from threatening clouds, a brilliant sheet of emerald grain threatening to fulfil the natural law of its maturity long before the plough could get to the place in time to stop the catastrophe.

Had I known more all would have been better; but, knowing very little, I was face to face with the severest test in farming on the prairie – knocking out the wild oats. Had I retained the service of Roddy McMahon that year I might have done better in 1908 and got entirely rid of them more quickly, although I should have learned less; but the wild oats were right in the land, and the only way to get them out was to encourage them to grow out. That the difficulty is not confined to the newcomer or incompetent farmer I proved in the season of 1908 and 1909. One day, riding in the neighbourhood of Springbrook, I passed a very perfect seed-bed. It ran, I think, over a hundred acres, and was quite even, and as far as cultivation went it might have been an immense market garden prepared for an expensive system to be worked on a colossal scale. I hadn't seen the implement the farmer was using, so I rode over and learned that it was a cultivator; also that its owner, Mr. George Robb, had been plagued and pauperized with wild oats through more than one season, but he thought he had knocked them safely out of his 1908 seed-bed. 'I shall go through once more with the cultivator,' he said, 'that will make the fourth time; then as many more strokes of the harrows as I can get in before freeze-up.' I was not in Canada in 1909, but in 1910 he was my neighbour at the hotel dinner-table in South Qu'Appelle, and reminded me of our meeting.

'How did the crop on that field turn out?' I inquired.

'I seeded it down with my best wheat,' he answered, 'and when it was well up it was the thickest crop in Springbrook, only you couldn't tell whether it was wheat or wild oats that had been seeded. So I ploughed a good fire-guard and fired the lot. I guess they are right out of the land now.'

I think they must have been too, because this year Mr. George Robb is putting up quite the biggest and most modern of any of the many modern houses in Springbrook.

But to return to the field which was destined to be the strength or the weakness of my own proposition. It was certain that by double discing, followed immediately by continual harrowing, I might have produced, and immediately killed, the greater part of the surface weed-seed which had fallen through the crops of the seasons of 1905 and 1906. The very deep ploughing of 1907 not only turned up the wild oats which my predecessor had deliberately buried out of the way of the average turning of seed-bed soil, but it retained all the surface seed shed from the two crops I had harvested, laying up a fresh edition of disappointment, loss, and toil. Meantime I faithfully practised the good methods I knew of. Patrick O'Hara made clear to me the excellent work and time-saving that is accomplished by immediately following newly ploughed land with a stroke of the harrows. In this way the soil has no time to cake in chunks, a great deal of weed is pulled out of root to the surface, and pulverization is accomplished in the end with far less work. Every day at four o'clock I went out with the harrows and relieved Pat so that he was able to get well on with the chores before supper and in this way the harrows kept close in the trail of the plough.

But the fence of the forty-acre pasture was giving out badly, and we not only had wandering calves occasionally, but we couldn't be quite sure of keeping horses within bounds through 'the day of rest.' To this I owed my first regular experience of ploughing which stood me in such good stead in a day of need which was not far on in the future. Patrick constantly called me to put in a half-day 'following the plough' whilst he mended the fence. I learned to manage it fairly well considering how much more difficult it is when weeds have grown so rank and strong that even very deep ploughing will seldom bury them and will not always quite turn over those of deeply penetrating root; so that, desirable as my deeply ploughed acres looked, and soft as was this seed-bed prepared for 1908, I knew, when I cared to face the truth, that many strange seeds were there; but I looked right and left and saw the dark green crops gracious and glorious as they swayed with the wind or stood up straight and strong through the heavy rain, and I said in my heart, 'With the harvest I shall pull through in spite of things.'

On the strength of my faith and their promise I commissioned Si Booth to break and put in shape for crop a further twenty-four acres for 1908. Four he added to the big field, sixteen he broke east and west, taking a difficult hill in his passing, and four he added to the original six on the east boundary. I begrudged the four and said so almost complainingly.

'The land in that corner is sandy, it hardly seems worth while to risk twenty dollars there,' I said. 'Did you notice how thin the wheat is compared even with the other breaking? I'm not sure that there isn't even alkali at the far end.'

'Your summer-fallow crop is the finest I ever buried head and shoulders in, and should yield forty bushels to the acre if I ever saw it in this country. But it isn't headed out yet. The grain on the east fence is in full head. You'll not be sorry, I guess, you broke up that land.'

'Is your wheat in head yet?' inquired my neighbour.

'Only here and there,' I answered. 'But the barley looks almost ready for the reaper.'

'Take care of it then, it's about the only crop you'll get this year.'

'Oh, do be quiet!' I answered. 'You invite disaster with your eternal prophecies of bad luck.'

'It's July 23,' he answered, 'and sunshine – nowhere! Wheat should be in head by July 12. I reckon we are a good three weeks behind, with the indispensable condition of sunshine dead against us.'

'The sun will blaze for us presently,' I prophesied, 'and we shall have the most bountiful harvest on record.'

'It will need to blaze soon or it will be an unrecorded harvest.'

On Sunday, July 28, the sun shone in amazing brilliancy. I walked through the pasture into the twenty-five acres beyond to find the wheat in full head and in its most delicate and exquisite stage of flower. It was absolute in its beauty, so alive, so strong, so glorious – just a living, breathing blessing; and in that gleaming, silent day of rest, as I stood in the heart of the field with the lovely thing around me I was glad to think that because I came to Canada that specially clean and beautiful field of wheat was there; and when every event and circumstance of the harvest of 1907 has faded in my memory I shall still see its glorious prophecy, still watch the tall mass of living loveliness sway towards me from every side, still be glad with the sunbeams playing in and out among the delicate green shades of the waving grain, still remember how it seemed to thank one for having helped it into its kingdom of clean, sweet life.

But after that day there was so little sun, so little progress. Nancy and I, with Felicity in tow, made our way east and west through the wheat-plains of Wideawake, Indian Head, and Springbrook, and the lovely environment of wheat-lands that line the banks of the strange creek which runs up through Springbrook from Fort Qu'Appelle. Never had the promise of life been so glorious in our special part of the prairie provinces. Walls of green grain rose in surpassing fullness and beauty on either side of everywhere, and although there had been much rain there was but little wind and tempest, and in consequence very little had lodged. It seemed as though Providence couldn't fail it, not so much because of fear of financial loss, or even the care and labour that those miles and miles of grain stood for, but because of hope and the best kind of faith – it was life itself, a phase of Providence incarnate.

It was just at this time that Ricky first showed signs of that most evil of all disorders to which horses are subject in the, generally speaking, health-giving and health-preserving condition of life on the prairie – swamp-fever. I noticed him flinch at weight, and shrink back from his work one day when he was called upon to take fourth place on the disc, and it was obvious that he couldn't pull. I told Patrick to take him off and put him in the pasture.

'Ye canna get through without the disc, and three horses canna draw it. Dick can pull if he chooses,' said Pat.

'Take him off,' I repeated. 'I must get another.'

My neighbour Richard Ryan the elder was breaking with two bronchos and an old horse on his side of the west fence. He had a fine way with horses, and was always gentle and careful and kind. These old-timers seem to get through quite as much work as the modern hustlers, and they are nearly always gentle and clever with horses. I admired the man and his work immensely, and especially the patient way he walked so quietly through a run of bad luck till the gods cried 'Enough!' and he slept in the acre on the hill. He gave me a day's trial of the old gelding, whom he strongly recommended and on the point of whose age he was perfectly frank. The price was a hundred and fifty dollars cash, and I was glad to think that if I had to part with a hundred and fifty dollars just then, it would be to him. The manager of the Union Bank at South Qu'Appelle advanced me the money in spite of his pessimism over the weather; and nearly all bank loans depend on the weather between June and September 1. Ricky went into the pasture, and from that day did no more work except that now and then I took him a short distance in the buggy. It was on such an occasion that I first heard the fear which had been hovering in my mind put into words by another. 'Dick's failing,' said a woman who had been born and bred on the prairie and knew every phase and turn of that dread disease of the equine race, swamp-fever. 'Dick's failing'! In that moment I knew that life held more in the balance than a hundred harvests, and realized the full meaning of the difference in animal and vegetable life. Dick, who had been swift as a sunbeam as he pulled the cutter across the snow, strong as a young lion, and gentle as a child as he lent his brave shoulder to the disc or harrows, or scampered with the buggy over the trail – Ricky, who had never omitted to whinny forth a friendly greeting even when oats were almost under his nose, was *failing*! Out of the clear intelligence of his eyes he made one understand that it was no good, that something in the very centre of him had given way and he couldn't go on; that even to draw me just a mile or so across the prairie was too much.

My neighbours came to see him. Guy Mazey, who had lost six horses through swamp-fever in less than as many months, another neighbour who had lost twelve. All of them were of the same opinion that Ricky was smitten with the dread disease in which the victim first shows unmistakable signs of failing energy, then passes into that stage where life seems gradually consumed through internal fire, and the horse fades slowly away like a human being in the last stage of consumption. Happily this terrifying form of sickness seems to be passing away from the settled parts of the prairie, and I never felt quite sure that the illness of my poor horse was due, or entirely due, to this disease. With generous workers, human or equine, there is always the danger of overwork. It was Father Hugenard, one of the leaders of the giants among the workers of Canada, who, when he found himself stricken with sudden physical failing, said to me, 'No, I have not done well; had I done well I should not now be unable to work. To be imprudent is not to do well.' In taking full measure of the splendid swiftness, the great heart, the generous nature of one of the noblest and most lovable horses I can remember, amongst many in the Old Country and the new, undoubtedly there had been imprudence. I was so proud of his speed and the splendid way he charged Troy Hill. Felicity takes it in just the same way, only Dick was so young, younger than I knew; and in any case one should never take all a three-year-old will give. I sent for Dr. Creamer the well-known horse-surgeon of South Qu'Appelle, and he thought rest and special food and tonic might pull him through, and that it was altogether best for him to be out. So he remained with his favourite Nancy and Felicity in the pasture; but although Felicity was kind, Nancy, to whom he had always been so good, was cool. Horses are selfish in their affection for each other; the old and the sick usually walk alone. But although through the end of the summer and the early fall Ricky was happy 'in the quiet of green grass,' and eating voraciously of the luxuriant herbage of the slough, he became thinner and thinner, and the shadow came nearer in the depths of his kind eyes.

6

Summer diversion –
law and labour –
Patrick O'Hara and Si Booth

Tennis and dancing were the favourite forms of diversion in the historic village of Fort Qu'Appelle, which since the coming of the Grand Trunk Pacific Railway has developed the plain and useful features of a town without losing any of the attraction of its exquisite environment which blesses the trail of the Qu'Appelle valley all the way.

One cannot dance through the summer months even in the cool region of the Qu'Appelle lakes; but the tennis club of Fort Qu'Appelle has all the distinction of tradition defended by the force of exclusion. At one time, to be known as a member of the club gave much the same *cachet* in the district as presentation at Court during the Victorian era. Also, in common with many of the great persons of the Victorian era, face value went for little. None would guess from a glance at the club enclosure with its distinctly primitive pavilion the important part it played in the creation and preservation of a social atmosphere in the little village that grew round the Hudson Bay fort in the centre of the valley wherein the Indians love to dwell.

On Saturday afternoons the members of the club take it in turn to provide tea. At one time it was *tennis* and tea, the very simplest affair; but gradually tea was threatened with symptoms of an attack of the comparative degree, and some one whispered that the powers had ordained that there were never to be more than two kinds of cake, lest the humiliating suspicion of *tea* and tennis should fall upon this gala day of an association of the North-West Territory which marked the manner of things social according to the tradition of the Mother Country. However, whether it was because of, or in spite of, tradition and exclusion, some very delightful people were to be found among the members of the club from time to time; and although I very rarely had time to get down to the Fort even to collect the necessaries of life, I appreciated the privilege of admission to the club and faithfully kept my day for tea.

That year it chanced to fall in July. Patrick O'Hara packed me, and the tea-things, and the rolls and the rock cakes and the big cake, which I greatly feared was still uncooked in the middle, and Molly's cream, which is the very nicest cream in the Qu'Appelle valley, into the wagon. In fact nothing was forgotten except the indispensable items of tea and water, and drawn by Jim and Nancy, with Felicity in the rear, we came, in Jim's time, to the enclosure, which is an odd corner of one of the loveliest bits of hill and lake scenery in the world. A friendly man dashed off for a pound of tea at the Hudson Bay Store, and the Macdougall girls, with all the other friendly men in tow, went off for water by the short cut to the Mound, which always saves a lot of time providing you are sufficiently agile to make the passing of the creek without mishap.

My tea was quite a success, and no doubt I must have arrived home with an air of triumph, or at least unusual enjoyment, since Patrick O'Hara made use of the occasion to impress on me that a holiday did every one a power of good and it was 'aisy to see it's yerself that's the better already.' Later I heard that the South Qu'Appelle fair was to fall on a day in the following week, and Fort Qu'Appelle fair a week after; and although Thomas and Si Booth and the first division of the Mazeys and all the neighbours were going, Pat himself was not even dreaming of a wish to go.

Every one went to South Qu'Appelle, and he gave me its history in all the glory of fact and fiction, adorned with many expressions of thankfulness to exalted representatives of supreme wisdom

who had decreed that Patrick O'Hara should have a natural preference for duty, in the form of the plough, on those special days
on which the other ninety-nine chased special pleasures. We had
reached the last section of the ploughing at the near end of the
big field, but it ran into several acres, and when it was finished
there were still the brilliant acres which Adam had turned, with
wild oats of all lengths and sorts and sizes rushing into more life
unless the means of annihilation could catch up in time. On
every possible occasion I encouraged horses and cows to feed
from the volunteer crop on the principle that every little helps;
but a field of tame oats and my cherished seed-garden were close
at hand, so I never dared to turn all the beasts on to it, although
that has since become the most effectual method of checking
wild oats' scourge in this neighbourhood.

On the afternoon before the fair at the Fort, as I went out to
relieve Pat of his team at harrowing-time, I saw Thomas walk
away from the plough.

'They're that set on having me with them to-morrow,' said
Pat. 'They'll likely be having a race. Mr. Dennison has lent them
the buggy, Si Booth will drive the baulky mare, and Thomas says
he will be riding. "Ye're throwin' away boot-leather and your
throuble, Thomas, coming over," I tould him, "for, faith, ye'll
not be seeing me at Fort Qu'Appelle fair."'

'Pat, I know you must be wanting to go with them all,' I said.
'It's very plain-sailing just here, I can finish quite a piece of the
section during the afternoon, and next week we can get on to the
last, and maybe we can catch out those oats after all.'

After a few orthodox protestations, not quite up to his usual
form, Pat yielded to my suggestion, and the next day after dinner
he vanished across the field in his Sunday clothes.

On the morning after the fair I awoke with a sense of vexation
and walked to the window. At the gateway of the pasture the
horse which Si Booth had ridden stood bridled, but without any
hint of an owner.

Pat's room was empty, the bed had not been slept in. I caught
the horse easily and put him in a stable, and after breakfast I

harnessed the team and waited until I could nurse my wrath no longer, and walked over to my neighbour's dwelling, expecting to find them all there with a penitent Pat.

But there was no sign of life within the shack. I climbed the difficult way to the sleeping apartment. It was exactly as they had left it. I turned home determined to waste no more valuable time, but to hitch up the team and get on to the ploughing, whilst my sentiments of Pat searched space in vain for adequate terms of expression.

At eleven o'clock Thomas came limping across the ploughed land, and he dared to come with a laugh – a shamefaced smile, it was true, but it was distinctly intended to show mirth. So I told him he was a living disgrace to the British Empire, and brought other truths to the wrong side of discretion. Thomas resented my sentiments, my words, and my interference, and reminded me that we were in a free country. I forswore magnanimity and asked him how free he had been in the free country on the first day of our acquaintance. To my surprise he became contrite. 'But you say too much,' he added. 'A fellow don't care to be told he is a disgrace to his country.'

'And what is a Briton but a disgrace when he puts in a night in jail for drunkenness?' I said, drawing my bow at a venture.

'We wasn't the only ones. Every man round town was full, and six of us was in the coop! Mr. Dennison came and bailed us out this morning. Paid the fine. Pat hopes you will advance his wages to repay it.'

'If it wasn't for Pat's work I wouldn't advance a single dollar. Six men finish their holiday in Fort Qu'Appelle jail, and all British, I suppose!'

'No, there was one half-breed; and all the Canadians was drunker than any of us.'

'Quite so, but not so silly!'

'It was Pat's fault, he got quarrelsome. We was all comfortable in the bar, and I said, "Pat, I'll go and get the mare and hitch up, and we can get back easy like." Says he: "All right, Thomas, I'll wait here." I found Dolly and put her in the buggy, but when I got back, Pat he had taken more. "Be damned to you!" he says. (Excuse me, miss.) "I'll fight you!"

'"Pat," says I, "you're drunk, man. Come on home now, and I give you my word I'll fight you in the morning."

'"It's drunk I am!" says he. "I'll fight any man in the room!" But nobody offered. "I'll fight any man in the Dominion!" said he, encouraged like. And the half-breed he started up and there was no stopping them. I came out of it all and sat on the sidewalk to think what was best, and the police-sergeant took me for doing nothing. And it cost a lot.

'This morning Mr. Dennison came and bailed us out, and we started to come home with Dolly, and just as we got to John McLeay's gate she bolted. Pat jumped out of the back of the buggy, but I sat tight until she started to jump the fence. Then I fell out. The mare's cut herself mortal bad and the buggy is in splints, and you bet Pat's afraid to come back!'

In the afternoon Mr. Macdonald's little daughter came to see me, and I left the plough to get some tea. My neighbour had been staying with her people for the fair, and she knew all about the escapade.

'Shall you keep Pat, or send him away?' she asked, as I searched for cream in the cellar of what I thought was my empty house.

'Oh, I shall keep him,' I answered. 'It's of no use to pay a man full wages up to harvest just to secure his service through harvest, and let him go at the very time you need him.'

'Is he a very good man?' she asked.

'Yes, he is a good all-round man when he chooses – very – only he is like most newcomers in this country, very slow.'

Meantime Pat had returned and heard my verdict from his room. My wrath had burnt itself out over Thomas. I was prepared to behave to Pat as though nothing had happened. Undoubtedly an old temptation had overtaken him, and I could not forget that in the several weeks through which he had worked for me there had been no sign of such a weakness, and that the simple Irish labourer had behaved as a gentleman.

'Have you had food to-day, Pat?' I inquired.

'Not a crumb.'

I cooked him some beefsteak and made him some strong tea; it inspired confidence.

'You'll be giving me the dollars to pay back Mr. Dennison the fine?' he ventured. 'Fifteen dollars.'

'Yes, I'll let you have it at once. It was rather an expensive adventure, wasn't it?'

'Faith, miss, it's cruel! An' not a scrap of breakfast. I'll say that for them in the auld country jails, they'll always be giving you your breakfast.'

Shortly after I met my neighbour and he spoke of the affair.

'I suppose you know he is talking of quitting you,' he said. 'It seems that he heard you say he was slow.'

Not for a moment did I believe that he really thought of leaving; but whether it was the result of wounded vanity or of reaction after his adventure I know not, certain it was that Patrick O'Hara's work began to flag. Si Booth was busy on the breaking, and the barley crop being ripe he undertook to take it off with my binder and team. Pat left following the plough, which seemed to be moving more slowly than ever, and he and I stooked before noon, but at dinner-time he said the old wound on his leg was giving him great pain, and in the afternoon I finished the barley stooking, leaving him to prepare supper and attend to the stock.

I didn't get back until eight o'clock. I was hungry and very tired, and greatly enraged to see the calves outside the fence and Pat looking as though it did not matter.

'It's divil a bit of use thryin' to keep thim in. Faith, I've done my livil best!'

'Then you must lock them up. You know as well as I do that they will spend the night in the oats.'

The next day we returned to the ploughing. I relieved Pat at four o'clock with the harrows, and as usual he had a place here and there to point out to me where I had carelessly allowed the seed-bed to escape the harrow – but these landmarks were never allowed to escape the observation of my tutor. One can't help noticing that those who stand most in need of a little charity for themselves in the judgment of others seldom fail to carry round the eye for eye and tooth for tooth measure in their judgment of others.

He came to me in the evening. 'Since it seems my work's no longer suiting you, maybe it's better I should be going at the end of my month.'

'Your work suits me well when it's good work. I can't risk the cattle getting into my neighbours' crops, and I intend to say what I think when you are inclined to let things slide,' I answered. 'My engagement with you is through harvest. If you leave, I pay you the original wage agreed upon before you took Mr. Oliver's place and not a cent more.'

'I have done my work well. You've said so yourself more than once.'

'I could get any number of men to work well for me at a dollar a day between June and September. If you leave before harvest, you will get that rate, no more.'

I knew the fifteen dollars' fine must have been a hard hit, and he had asked for money more than once to send home. I quite concluded that the discussion had put an end to his intention.

On September 3 I met my neighbour in his gateway. 'What are you going to do about harvest help?' he inquired.

'It will depend on the weather. If we escape the frost, I shall hire stookers; if not, I shall stook myself.'

'Who is to drive the binder?'

'Pat. He is awfully keen about it. Si Booth showed him exactly how it worked at barley-harvest, and his bad leg gives out stooking.'

'But Pat is leaving you and comes to me tomorrow to stook for me through harvest.'

'Impossible!' I said. 'I have heard no word of it. A week or so ago when I spoke to him about slacking he hinted he would like to be off, but when I showed him I should use my privilege over the wages there was an end to it.'

'Well, he came over to me and said he was quitting then; that you had found fault with him, not because of the jail episode but because he was slow. He has been round nearly every day since, and said that whether I gave him a job or not, he should quit. I didn't know you weren't fully aware of the whole thing. Men being scarce, I told him he could come on.'

'But I raised his wages to the end of season on the sole condition of his remaining,' I said; 'and he is caretaking through the winter for me, and his wife and child are to come out in the spring.'

'I think you will find he is leaving you,' said my neighbour.

I called Pat. 'What is this that I hear about your going on to Mr. Dennison and leaving me on the eve of harvest?'

'Dennison needn't make too sure of getting me there. Plenty of others round is wanting men.'

'You have been bothering Mr. Dennison for days to engage you. You want to get there simply because you think you will get an easy time and because amongst men you are free more or less to disgrace yourself, as you did the other day. Understand that if you leave me without notice *you* will pay for it. *I* shan't. I need not pay you a farthing for breaking your contract. I shall consult a magistrate and let you know exactly what I shall do in the matter.'

'I've earned my money.'

'You've done nothing of the kind. Had you remained until the end of the season you might have earned the full sum on the average of the higher rate of wages after August; and until the day of Fort Qu'Appelle fair I thought I should be leaving a trustworthy man with my beasts. Had you left at the end of your first month you would have drawn just fifteen dollars. I should have hired Roddy McMahon and his team to finish the ploughing and it would have been finished weeks ago. If I were you, for very shame I could not leave that worn-out job for another.'

'I've earned my money.'

'If the magistrate decides that it is so, I shall obey the law of the country.'

I consulted Mr. Thompson, postmaster and justice of the peace at Fort Qu'Appelle, and he said it was the worst case of the treachery of a farm-hand that had ever come under his notice. 'Dock him a fortnight's wages,' he advised, 'and if he insists on his claim let him sue you. As you have no written evidence it would be a little difficult to judge exactly how you stand over the change of wages. But a man that leaves his employer on the eve of harvest engaged at a scale of wages to carry him over harvest will not go unpunished in this country.'

I docked the two weeks' wages, but as I had advanced his wife two pounds through an agent in England the fine was considerably curtailed. He put his shoulder to his work on the last day as he had done on the first and left my yard in perfect order. He came in just before he crossed the field to my neighbour's shack.

'Shall you pay me my wages, miss?'

'Less a fortnight for your dishonesty in leaving me at this time. If you still think you are entitled to the full amount you must sue me.'

'I shall not do that, miss, I'm no believer in the law.'

'I can quite believe it.'

'I've worked well for you.'

'You have played the meanest trick that a workman can possibly play, and – not that I consider it makes the matter better or worse – you have played it on a woman.'

So on September 4 I was in the midst of a hundred acres of grain, which the frost might attack any night, and I had hay to cut and carry, and six acres of my field still to plough.

Si Booth returned with his team that afternoon to disc and harrow the acres he had broken. He was a man of few words. 'That's the meanest trick I've known any man play in this country,' he said. 'He's been after Roland Dennison to hire on ever since the day of the fair. It's too bad.'

However, I was too busy to worry. I wasted no time in words, but mowed and raked and got right down to the ploughing, which was none the easier because I knew that my ex-professor and hired man was watching me finish my bits and pieces which were very near the windows of his new abode; and even now I do not finish the bits and pieces in good style, but I never leave an inch unturned. I finished late on Saturday night, the sun had gone beyond the horizon a full hour, there was just a pink glow in the west as I walked home behind my team across the seedbed of 1908, and again I consoled myself with the old illusion that the gods would set everything right which was wrong with that seed-bed because they knew so exactly how things had been. But it is only the half-gods who spare in the making.

No words can make clear the intense anxiety that gripped the heart of the people of the prairie provinces in that first week of September 1907. It was true that the year was preceded by two years of perfect weather and of the most bountiful crops on record. But this had but increased the general desire to extend possession. Thousands of acres had been bought on the system of extended payment at from six to eight per cent. interest, implements had been bought to work it, and increased horse power. But in 1907 the September moon arose on a green and unripe crop; only a miracle of the weather could save the situation, but the general hope was that the spring having been so late in coming, frost also might keep off a week or so.

On Sunday evening, September 5, I called at the house of my neighbour Richard Ryan, and there I found several people who know every phase and symptom of the fates that wait on harvest. Mr. William Nicoll was there, and he owned several sections of wheat that year; among them was a thousand acres which he had raised in partnership with Mr. Ryan's eldest son.

'Shall you start, or wait?' I inquired of him.

'We start to-morrow morning.'

'But do you think I ought to start?' I asked. 'My wheat has barely turned in places, and since we have had winter nearly all the summer, mightn't we reasonably expect a dash of the saving grace of summer now?'

'We shall get it,' he answered with a rather weary smile. 'The Indian summer – after the frost.'

'But it seems so unreal – Harvest! and I haven't seen a solitary yellow field!'

'And you won't see one this year,' he said, 'it will be a green harvest all right. George Seymour cut a week ago; it was always his father's plan. He is making huge stooks so that it can ripen good and slow in stook, and I guess he'll get the pull of us all. It's all up – don't wait. No farmer can afford to wait in this country when once September is in.'

'Well, you should all know better than I. If you are intending to cut immediately, I ought not to wait,' I said; 'only it seems to me that the sun cannot fail this glorious crop.'

On the following day I made arrangements with a man to come that night and start on the oats the following morning. He failed to appear. I waited until nine o'clock. It was a glorious day, perfect harvest weather, and the oats at any rate were just ready for the reaper. I walked over the newly broken field on which Si Booth was finishing his last stroke of the harrows.

'What will you charge me to take off the crops?' I asked him. 'I can't afford to hire horses, as you know, with an expensive season behind me and with this awful uncertainty in the air. But I won't risk the grain, and I am entirely in your hands about the charge.'

'I can't very well work without my own team I guess,' he answered. 'But if you will find them in feed I'll take off your crops with three of my horses at four dollars a day.'

At that time the greenest stooker was asking and getting two dollars a day. I had expected a demand of anything from six dollars a day upwards.

I thanked him. You can't gush in Canada, it seems almost as bad form in the freedom of service on the prairie as a breath of patronage; only it was the kind of thing that makes one want to stand up for all Canadians for ever and ever.

'If you will go straight across to the four-acre oat-field with the binder,' I said, 'I will hitch up my own team and start discing the big field. I would rather not start stooking until you have got several rows down.'

The sun shone on one's back in kindliest fashion, and oh, it was healing-sweet after all those days of work and worry and suspense. And the disc never demands much of one's intelligence. I grew rested and refreshed and hopeful; the hum of the binder was as 'Consolation' by Liszt. Long before I went to dinner I was hoping again – believing. But by three o'clock the wind had turned bitterly cold. Now and then I had to get off the disc and walk. Suddenly there blew from the north a storm of cold and penetrating rain. Si Booth unhitched his team and went in;

it is not wise to bind wet grain even at the point of the sword of frost. An hour later I followed.

For four days it stormed, then cleared two hours before sunset – fatal hour! That night of September 9 marked the end of suspense, the frost came – twelve degrees.

7

The frozen harvest of 1907

In a way the actual coming of the frost was a positive relief. The strain of suspense was over, the sword had fallen and hope was dead.

On the morning following the frost I stooked oats and I hoped Si Booth would go out with the binder, but he told me the heavy wheels would not turn over the sodden ground, and that he doubted that he would be able to start even on the morrow. However, on the next afternoon I called him in triumph to hear the hum of my neighbour's binder; but it ceased almost as suddenly as it had started.

'Couldn't travel I guess; but it should be going all right after to-day,' said he.

'It's Sunday to-morrow,' I said regretfully. 'Have you any conscientious objection to harvesting on Sunday?'

'No,' said he, 'I've no conscientious objection to it I guess.'

'Neither have I,' I agreed hopefully. 'It is preposterous to think that it is not the truest and highest service to make every possible effort to save the wheat of the world; and after all, it is the teaching of the One in whose honour the day is kept, isn't it? The beasts of the field had to be helped, and for the hungry wheat was gathered, wasn't it? So we will take the binder out to-morrow, and if anyone has to do time, why I will do it – after harvest.'

He looked a little surprised, but quite determined. 'I ain't got any conscientious objections – 'tisn't that! And I think what you say is the thing. But I wouldn't be the first to do what none of the neighbours do.'

'If you won't, then there's an end to the matter; but I think that in a year like this people should be commanded by priest and parliament to go out into the fields and save the harvest.'

'It sounds all right,' he agreed.

A killing frost should have supported my theory, but the Sabbath night was exquisitely soft and soothing and the new day dawned warm and fair. We started on the six acres I had despised because of the sandy element in the soil. I had decided that I couldn't afford a stooker and must do it myself. Si Booth shook his head ominously, but I hoped by stooking by moonlight, when he wasn't there, to convey the impression that I could keep up with the binding. As I had to walk half a mile to the field and then leave it an hour ahead of him, to prepare meals, I knew I should have to feel my way through, since I couldn't possibly see it.

'This six acres is good and ripe,' said he, as I fell on a line of sheaves. 'If it was only all as ready to cut as this it would be all right. It's hardly frozen; with another day's sun on it, it would have been shelling out. You got a bit of the best wheat of the country just here.'

By the time I had washed up the dinner things he had crossed the adjoining stretch of prairie and was reaping the twenty-five-acre field. I was rather thankful to be out of his watchful and somewhat disapproving eye. The monotony of stooking ceased to bother me after my first season, but it is rather exhausting physically, and that year exceptionally so, owing to the bulk of the sheaves being green and in consequence very heavy to lift and difficult to place. I hadn't finished six acres when I had to leave to prepare supper, but I returned and completed the field by moonlight, and walking home round twenty-five, stooked the rows of fallen sheaves that lay in the way, and felt that I had considerably lightened the task of to-morrow.

On Tuesday the same programme exactly. On Wednesday afternoon twenty-five was nearly down when the binder came sharply against a stone and snapped a small but most important member. 'I'll get into town for the repair right now,' said Si Booth, 'but it's vexing, and all going so well. I guess I'll bring back a stooker if I can find one.'

'Perhaps it would be as well,' I allowed, 'although I have enjoyed it immensely so far. But you are getting rather far ahead, aren't you? Still, I shall pick up this afternoon.'

I worked east and west along the rows of the twenty-five-acre field until the stars came out. It wasn't possible to finish, but as I was alone at least there was no supper to get. I could milk and go at once to bed. As I walked across the pasture bitterness threatened me; I was deadly tired, the sheaves had been greener and heavier than usual, and it seemed to me hopelessly unripe. I came within an ace of the suffocating conviction of utter failure when suddenly out of the dusk came a friendly whinny, and Felicity galloped up to welcome me, with Nancy in close attendance, and my poor old Ricky plodding along in the rear. The three horsers walked with me to the gate, and I remembered that grain was not the only produce on a prairie farm, and that one who knew things had said that every situation had its compensation. And the beasts did make up for a lot and were always there. The cloud lifted. I determined to work my way over the rock of difficulty gamely.

The light of a lamp shone from my bedroom window. I thought that perhaps my brother had come along from his homestead to help me through, but I found Marjorie McDougall, who had come up on the mail to stay a day or two with me to help me with my chores.

The house already bore the McDougall mark of a house in order. The kitchen was warm and bright, supper was ready, and an air of good cheer pervaded the whole.

Si Booth did not get back till the next evening, and the next day we finished the reaping of the breaking. That night a very severe run of frost set in, and after that the forty-nine acres of summer-fallow blackened day by day in the rays of a blazing sun.

The new stooker had not long been out from England. He was the son of a tailor, living in the neighbourhood of London, and had been apprenticed to his father. He knew nothing whatever of life or work on the land. On Saturday night a gale blew, and on Sunday morning just twelve stooks stood for the four dollars due for his pay.

I restooked the greater part of his beat with Sabbath patience, and told him as nicely as I could that in stooking I must find my superior, and that he wouldn't do. I heard months after that he went on to Regina to follow his own trade, and a year ago that he was doing wonderfully well, and had already been back to England to spend a winter with his own people. I drove him into Fort Qu'Appelle, and went on to a house on the lake shore where I heard an Englishman and his wife were to be found who had farmed in the Mother Country. They were looking for work, and would possibly be glad to become my caretakers for the winter.

The English woman was fair and beautifully neat and clean. A fluffy-haired, fairy-like little girl was running about in a scarlet dressing-gown, just out of her bath. The house was spotlessly clean. The mother told me that her husband was away on the hill, stooking for some people that I knew, but that her brother-in-law had just arrived and might possibly care to come and stook for me. I drove up and recognized the young Englishman who had lately arrived from New Zealand through his likeness to the little girl. I told him my business and that I was prepared to pay twenty cents an hour – two dollars a day, but that I required his services immediately. He stopped at the house to get his bag, and drove home with me in the wagon to the farm. I undertook to finish twenty-five acres, and he crossed over at once to the farther breaking. He stooked from dawn to dark without a hint of waning energy, and he asked me if twenty cents an hour held good if he could get in an hour extra.

'That's a great man you found,' Si Booth said to me two days later. 'He's the first stooker that ever made me get an extra hustle on the binder.'

The Wiltons arranged to come to me. I agreed to pay a dollar a day wages till freeze-up, and to board them with their two children. Through the winter they were to receive ten dollars a month wages and plain board, consisting of meat, meal, potatoes, tea, sugar, rice, evaporated fruit, and dairy produce, and what butter and eggs they did not need in the winter had to be bartered in exchange for groceries. I made it quite clear that any more luxurious fare they might require for themselves and their children they had to provide for themselves; but subsequent events proved that I failed to make it quite clear that although I undertook to pay for adequate fuel from Hudson Bay Reserve or elsewhere I expected him to fell it and have it home ready for use.

I was still busy stooking when Mrs. Wilton came up to see what my house offered as a comfortable home for the winter, and we concluded arrangements for them to come in on Thursday, October 3.

Meanwhile, my stooker had justly earned my very highest opinion, backed by Si Booth. He was the most energetic, intelligent, and conscientious workman I met in Canada. He had trained as a chartered accountant in England, but his health obliged him to seek a less sedentary occupation, and he had gone to New Zealand, and from there he came on to Canada, to compare the possibilities of the two countries, before advising his brother which to select from the points of view of farming and family consideration.

His fame spread, and my neighbour George Hart, who is a born hustler himself and loves another, offered him three dollars a day to finish the season. However, he was anxious to remain with his people and asked me if I could arrange to let him work at the stacking, discing, and fencing with his brother until he received a summons he was expecting from Chicago. He said if it could be arranged he would gladly accept a dollar a day as the rate of remuneration.

I wasn't in a position to afford an extra dollar a month for labour just then, and, in fact, was marshalling all my force and power of resource to meet the day of the year's settlement, but it

seemed unwise as well as ungracious to refuse the labour of so
excellent a workman at such a rate of wages, and in stacking oats
I reckoned I should be preserving good spring feed, and also that
I should evade the cost of threshing at least five hundred bushels
which would balance his month's wages. He did some fencing,
which could not be described as excellent, but in any case it is far
cheaper to get this fencing done by experts; and at least he completed a very useful small pasture for the horses, and meantime
my bunch of cattle held fine bean-feasts many hours a day round
the stooks of frozen wheat which marked the sacred five acres
sown with my hand-cleaned seed. Fate had decreed that these
acres should be left until the last, the grain was frozen black –
even the pigs looked at it with a discontented air; Nature, bless
her, seldom provides a moral to adorn a tale, she hasn't time. All
the grain that I reaped which was worth having, and it was the
best in the neighbourhood, I drew from the six acres I had
despised because of the light soil, and I thankfully used every
grain of it for seed in 1908.

Before the threshers arrived my excellent Englishman had departed to a lucrative but temporary post at Chicago, but the bogey
of the frozen crop frightened these useful people and valuable settlers off farming on the prairie, and the co-operative system and
more temperate climate of New Zealand had all the attraction of
the 'distant drum.' Before the younger brother left they had absolutely decided to move on to New Zealand in the spring.

Again that year the Redcliffe outfit threshed for me and my
neighbours, and for once I presided over my threshing with enjoyment and peace since at leisure from my household chores.
Mrs. Wilton was an excellent housekeeper, and marvellously
quick. My party of eighteen was fed thoroughly well three times
a day, and in the afternoon she found time to take the children
out to watch the engine. Every one had a word of praise for her,
and they were acknowledged throughout the neighbourhood as
'real good people all right,' although he never shared her gift of
speed, nor she his grace of tact.

No threshing outfit would work on the usual terms that year,
although I think had they done so it would have come out all

right for the owner of the outfit, as it is in the weight far more than in bulk that frost sets its seal of damage in the gathered grain. Mr. Redcliffe's terms that year were forty dollars a day, and I think I had to find five stook teams. The threshing of the crop took two days and cost eighty dollars.

During June Mr. Oliver and Adam had hauled my wild-oat wheat crop to the elevators at South Qu'Appelle and I had been badly hit and very indignant over the sales. That one should be docked in weight for wild oats on a fair scale is perfectly reasonable; to be docked in the grade of your wheat because another grain is mixed with it is grossly unfair. The same wheat which was graded No. 2 Northern and docked unmercifully was graded No. 1 Northern when I had cleaned it, and bought without dockage also at South Qu'Appelle. The moral seems why not clean all, and retain the tailings for pig-feed; but this would take up very much valuable time, whereas the fanning mills at the elevators are so speedy and so perfect that the wheat is cleaned almost as easily as it is shifted from the grain-wagon into the elevator-bin. I determined never again to sell on the street in my wheat town; but I hadn't the slightest hesitation in lodging a thousand bushels at the Municipal Elevator whilst waiting for my car, because the man whom I had first met as school-teacher of Springbrook was managing that elevator in 1907, and I knew I should get a fair and square deal. The depot-master takes all applications for cars, and applicants are served in rotation; one farmer one car is supposed to be the order of service. Only twenty-four hours are allowed for loading, and therefore it is impossible when hauling grain from a distance to get it all in without lodging it at its starting-point. It was satisfactory from all points of view that I had perfect confidence in the holder of the scales of justice that year, the difference in the value of frozen and sound grain cannot be truly gauged until it arrives in the scale and then it is startling. I expected to fill my thousand-bushel carload easily from my two granaries, and also to have a few loads over, – hope seldom left my side for long. The end of the reckoning was that I had to borrow a wagon-load from Mr. George Seymour to complete my thousand bushels, which went in due course to Fort William, after being sighted and graded at Winnipeg, and which netted thirty-five cents a bushel after freight and attendant expenses had been settled.

Mr. Wilton hauled carefully and well, and he subscribed to the absolute need for economy with good feeling and intelligence. It is the custom when hauling grain to stable one's horses for at least two hours at the end of the journey. A gallon of oats for each horse goes on the load, and a feed of hay is due to them from the proprietor of the livery-barn. The livery charge for team is twenty-five cents, and the charge for the teamster's dinner at either of the hotels or the restaurant was, at the time, also twenty-five cents. I had to arrange that year that my team took their rest and feed unhitched by the roadside, and Mrs. Wilton suggested that she should cut her husband sandwiches for his midday fare, which he could eat with a five-cent cup of coffee at the restaurant, and have his principal meal of the day on his return in the evening. I am afraid my armour wasn't proof against such enforced economies; it didn't hurt either horses or man, but the fact was I was within constant sight of the day of reckoning; I grew impatient and irritable and hardly ever stopped to laugh at the absurdity of being either. Also here and there, during 1907, I had been a little imprudent about work, and not only was horribly worried about affairs, but tortured with the sight of my poor sick horse, who, in spite of Dr. Creamer's strongest tonic, and boiled oats, and perfect rest, and the sweet air of the prairie, looked every day more like 'a shadow in the grass.' Altogether it is quite certain that I was difficult just then, and I think the English are always exacting and inclined to be fussy and hysterical over trifles when they first come out; and the end of it was I nearly lost my excellent caretakers, and they nearly lost comfortable winter quarters, and quite a useful sum of money.

A 'little rift' crept in over the subject of the children's noise, but the bottom fell out of the lute over the matter of the winter fuel.

Within my limited experience my countrymen are not clever woodsmen. Even Mr. Wilton's brother had gone to seek poplar poles with the box on the wagon, and had then brought home the tops instead of the poles of the poplars, in all the green glory of trimmings. Then again they are as a rule over-anxious about fuel, and never by any chance can find it; nor are they quick to discriminate between the heat-producing property of poles in different stages of qualification for fuel according to the evaporation of sap. They set a huge kettle of water on a stove packed with green poplar, and go away to wash their hands whilst they leave the frying-pan set in an open stove lit with the lightest of fuel burned match-dry through the passing of a prairie fire.

One dazzling November morning Mr. Wilton was shovelling the wheat into the wagon from the granary, and I was shovelling back to the far corners; I think it must have been one Monday morning and that there had probably been tea and conversation after church the day before.

'Have you ordered the fuel for the winter?' he asked.

'Ordered the fuel! What do you mean?'

'Our arrangement was that you should find me winter fuel, and I must see it all in before you leave. The neighbours tell me that I shall require seventeen loads.'

'Do they! Then it is certain that I had better abandon my intention of going since I don't see you felling, cleaning, and hauling seventeen loads of wood in seventeen centuries of Sundays unless a miracle arrives to your method. I used six, but that's outside the argument. I am perfectly willing to pay for seventeen or twenty-seven loads for you if necessary, but you must understand that you have to fell it, and to clean, and to haul it with my horses. I have arranged to pay the Hudson Bay Company a dollar a load to cut from their reserve. Roddy McMahon says you can go along with him when he is out with the others felling and packing, and you can haul it home as you need it.'

'I am sorry, but I must have the whole of the winter's fuel before you go. The neighbours tell me that it is a matter of life and death – that the risks of the winter are terrible indeed.'

'You and your family have been better housed and fed and cared for since it has been more or less my responsibility than the family of any neighbour in the district, – and yet you find it necessary to go to them for advice concerning my obligation to you!' I said angrily, and, in short, lost my temper badly, whilst he kept his with the same careful and deliberate precision that he kept his spectacles.

When I had said everything that I shouldn't, he shook his head sadly, 'You can't be expected to understand a man's duty to his family,' he said, and that was the beginning and end and the sum of his argument.

'I understand perfectly,' I contended. 'Don't I know and love to do my duty to my beasts? Through that alone I not only understand but appreciate your anxiety about your family; it is not that, but your lack of confidence in me which I resent. I am just as anxious about the comfort of my beasts during the winter as you are about the comfort of your children, but I don't insult you by discussing your ability to carry out your responsibility with the neighbours, and I don't even worry you to hurry on your stable preparations a little, although I sometimes fear winter will be through the chinks before you have finished the plaster chore. I worried myself, and worried a very good man last year about the fuel, although he was altogether too inclined to let the whole thing slide, but I didn't then know that I could pay five dollars for a permit to cut on the Hudson Bay Reserve, and that the men at the Fort usually cut in gangs, and many of them make their living in the winter by supplying people who have no convenience for obtaining it themselves. Besides there are half a dozen good loads left on the place, and in the immediate neighbourhood, if you take the trouble to go and look for it. However, to-morrow I will take out the wheat, and you will go out and get fuel and see what you can do in a day towards the felling and cleaning and packing and hauling of your seventeen loads.'

I walked back to the cottage, but couldn't get back to even terms with myself, and writing or reading was out of the question. I took up the little hatchet which I had used to clean my hidden fuel in the frozen months, and went down to the bluffs of the unclaimed land on the far side of the west fence, and there I started to fell trees. I had felled a stray one here and there before, but nothing approaching a load. At first I only got down about twelve to the hour, but they were good poles, big and sound, yet thoroughly dried out, with an excellent promise of warmth-giving fuel. I cleaned at an interval of four poles, and gradually the work got into my blood and I liked it. There was interest in seeking and keenest satisfaction in finding a little group of sap-dried trees, and getting them down was the nearest approach to sport at which I ever arrived on foot. By three o'clock I had sixty stout poles neatly packed, and I determined not to say a word until I had doubled my quantity. It is unnecessary to add that the satisfactory result of my labour did not soften my feelings towards Mr. Wilton. We loaded the grainwagon as usual on the following day and I drove off on the fourteen-mile haul to South Qu'Appelle. Mr. Rogers showed me exactly what to do at the elevator; it was quite simple. I did my shopping whilst the horses fed, and got home just before dark.

I had enjoyed the day immensely, and said so, although I have no doubt I should have found the prospect of many such days on end distinctly monotonous.

The shadow of event was in the atmosphere as I took my supper. Over my last cup of tea, hand in hand they broke the news to me they were not happy, and that they should go.

I was furious! I had paid him good wages for slow work, as except for the hauling and stacking Mr. Wilton's work at that time was too slow to be valuable in the actual land-work of a Canadian farm, and just as we were entering into the place where I should score – because I knew they would be honest, conscientious, kind, and careful caretakers – they were going! I told them what I thought in few words, adding, 'I am fifty dollars out of pocket.'

'And what are we?' said Mr. Wilton. 'We smashed thirty dollars' worth of furniture coming up the hill.'

'Heaven and earth!' said I. 'Do you dare sit there and quote the natural result of your own lack of foresight and common sense, and charge it up against *me*. That is quite enough; if you are going the sooner the better, and also the less said the better.'

In the two days' interval I went on with my wood-gathering, and always with increasing success. The hard work and the satisfaction I got out of it, and the anger I had got rid of at the moment left no place for malice.

'My wife and I would like to walk into the Fort to-morrow to look at houses,' said Mr. Wilton.

'There is no occasion to walk,' I said. 'Take the wagon, only it must go out first without the box to haul in the load of wood.'

He hauled it in looking just a little below his average degree of self-respect, which was always an honest self-respect without a hint of complacency. 'It is an excellent load of wood,' he said. He was always just.

'There are two more beyond. Try and get them in to-morrow.' They looked at each other, and at the wood, and at me, and I tried to look as unlike a person crowned with unusual honours as possible, although victory was positively sitting on every note of exaltation which time and event had failed to break in my everyday heart.

In the evening they returned. Both were very quiet, and obviously down-hearted. I learned about everything in due course. Houses were appalling dear – fuel at least four dollars a load. I held every card.

'I expect you would like to reconsider your decision to leave me,' I said.

'If you are able to get fuel I certainly ought to be able to do so,' allowed Mr. Wilton. 'You say very sharp things when you are out of temper,' he added, 'but even then you allowed that on the whole we gave you satisfaction and that you trusted us. If matters could be arranged –'

It was my very own moment and I could have backed out of the salary. I was far poorer than I had dreamed possible on the day I engaged them, the country was badly hit over the frozen crop, the storekeepers had followed the lead of the Bank; nothing could be obtained except for ready money. Free quarters and free board was that year a fair return for the winter's service, but a tear was running down the woman's cheek, and it hardly seemed worth while.

'Don't let us say anything more about it,' I suggested. 'We will forget everything but your claim of my share in the ruin of your household gods coming up Troy Hill – I shall never be able to forget that.'

I never gave Mrs. Wilton the opportunity to tell me much about myself, but she didn't altogether share her husband's grace of tact, and one day she seized it. I thought it would be good for her to remember that at least I did not take the smallest advantage of other people and reminded her of my lost opportunity.

'Yes, but it must have suited your purpose or you would never have done it,' she said in a tone of profound conviction, which also convinced me that I had not been the only one to notice the lost opportunity.

The snow fell early in 1907, the musk-rats had raised many huts in the sloughs, and there was every prospect of a long but pleasant winter. Although the snow was on the ground the sun was brilliant, and there was hardly any wind. The Wiltons had bodies of reasonable requirements, and hated overheated rooms even more than I did, the house was kept at a reasonable temperature, and I never remember being quite so comfortable in the cottage. The wood-box in my room was always filled, the house was spotlessly clean, my breakfast and four o'clock tea were served in simple, dainty fashion, and in the main I knew that I was in great good luck to have found such estimable people.

One morning I looked out of my bedroom window and saw Ricky standing in the shelter of the granary where he might catch the gleam if not the warmth of the brilliant winter sun. I went down and tucked him in the English horse-blanket, but he seemed so cold and frail, and so obviously beyond the liberty of the law of my outdoor theory, that I led him back to a box that I had caused to be railed off in the middle stable, and then I took in piles and piles of straw, and fed him with scalded oats and chilled water; but his eyes were very close to the horizon. I dared not think of him through the winter, but the thought of a bullet was hard to bear.

On that afternoon I drove down to the Fort, and when I returned I learnt that he had contrived to get out again, and had fallen over. Mr. Wilton had gone at once for Danny McLeay, and they had managed to get him up, and back into the stable, and thought even then that he might pull through, and they were all awfully good and kind about him.

But two days later I found him at the well, just half an hour after I had fed and watered him. He turned with his odd little greeting and fell over again, and that day Mr. Wilton had gone into South Qu'Appelle, and so had every one else but Patrick O'Hara, who came over and did all he could to help us raise him. When Mr. Wilton got back, we all tried again, until poor Ricky's eyes were glittering like the multitude of stars and the lovely moon which seemed to be shining down all too soon that night on the place where he lay in the open.

It was seven o'clock, when the first chorus of wolves came across the snow, bringing the curious dread from which death itself seems a gateway of deliverance, although it is always claimed that wolves will not attack a horse as long as a spark of life remains in the body. To the last he welcomed his oats, with the same appreciation as in the preceding winter when he had been the healthiest, kindest, happiest member of my bonny bunch, and it almost seemed as if his intelligence grew brighter as strength forsook the poor emaciated body. There was no longer the smallest doubt in my heart as to what ought to be done, the wail of the wolves had voiced decision. Just before nine o'clock some one fetched Patrick O'Hara with his gun. Pat was for the better part a sportsman and an unerring shot. Only those die who are forgotten. Presently the report came through my open window ... Ricky's spark of life had sped home to life's centre.

8

The day of reckoning –
auf wiedersehen

I had turned the corner of 1906 with a big deficit on the account of my working expenses. In 1907 I took less than five hundred dollars for my wheat, pigs, and butter in cash; but I had sold a great deal of meat and butter and eggs to my neighbour, although I had to purchase of him oats for my horses as I was insufficiently supplied. My working expenses for 1907 amounted to just over one thousand and fifty dollars. It must not be forgotten that this is the story of an individual working out an experiment with very little knowledge and insufficient capital. Had I, instead of breaking up more land, put every cent of available money into cattle and pigs and a good poultry-house, I should have made much money in a comparatively short space of time. But I arrived in Canada in one of its most glorious wheat seasons; cattle and pigs were scorned as money-makers in 1905 and 1906; to-day it is difficult to buy them for money. Again, although in 1906 I did badly owing to the unprepared seed-bed and the harvest of wild oats, it was, generally speaking, a brilliant season in the prairie provinces; and if the disastrous season of 1907 was badly felt, its lesson was very badly needed.

The list of my working expenses for 1907 reads:

Feed and seed	$64.90
Breaking twenty-five acres	100.00
Wages	260.70

Taxes	15.00
Fencing	9.50
Fanning mill	26.00
Binder-twine	27.00
Hail insurance	19.50
Horse	150.00
Grocery, flour, and meat, repairs, veterinary attendance	245.00
Threshing and teams	133.00
Total	$1050.60

In an average year this should be less by almost half. Wages have of course almost doubled since 1907; but my grocery and repairs bill is far too high. The finest form of insurance against hail or any other catastrophe affecting the wheat crop is to put the stakes into stock; but threshing expenses, binder-twine, wages, and taxes are standing expenses which must be provided for year by year through one means or another; and a good poultry-house, netted in with poultry-wire, should never be omitted in the beginning of a farming experiment. Turkeys are easy to rear, and average from three to five dollars in price. There is an excellent market for all kinds of food in the present phase of development in Canada, which is marked by a great increase in population and an admirable improvement in building accommodation not only in the cities but on the prairies. The shack-phase was very attractive in many ways, and one would not have missed the experience; but, 'for the good of all,' the well-being of the rising generation of the Canadian nation, the farmhouse of adequate accommodation for the average household of the farmer and his wife is a very real necessity, even if the building, as is frequently the case, should cost more than three hundred and twenty acres of land.

The two years' reverse might have seen the end of my experiment, and I should probably have left the prairies with just a wider experience of life and work at the end of 1907, and content to accept the offer of my predecessor to buy back the greatly improved farm he had sold in 1905 for the same price in 1907, but land had gone up in price and held its own in spite of the frozen harvest. The price of the adjoining section, without an acre of it turned and with its timber-value decreasing steadily, had risen from five to seven dollars an acre. Even the price of my money back offered by my predecessor was something of a compliment, because he sold with a crop harvest-ripe that yielded a thousand dollars, although all the world of Fort Qu'Appelle wondered at the time that even ever-green England could produce anyone green enough to give fifteen dollars an acre for the place. But although things were bad, it was no small thing to have learnt the worst, and if I had very little available capital to draw on for future intention I had a considerable amount of practical knowledge. I had learnt that wheat should stand for net profit, chargeable only with the cost of its seed and threshing; and that much, even in the season of 1907, the proceeds of the crop at its worst supplied. Food and wages and all expenses that do not definitely increase the value of capital in land, stock, and working plant, ought to be supplied through annual sales of stock and dairy produce. It was too late to establish those lines, more especially as the income I drew from a share in a business-concern in London had already shrunk considerably since my absence from England. But one should not only insure against the loss of one's wheat crop by making, but by saving. I knew that in future years I could save on wages, and determined to hire expert labour for seeding and harvest seasons and for a certain amount of ploughing, but to do all cultivation myself. Discing and harrowing, mowing and raking are easy work; one drives the whole time, and except that in mowing the vibration of the mower is occasionally jarring to the nerves of some people, one can return from a day's work on either of these implements with energy practically untaxed. A hired man and woman constitute a luxury to be recommended to all those who can afford it. Married couples are usually seekers of home and capital; the average hired man seeks wages, and some of them bring more work into the house than they succeed in putting on to the land. The woman who can hitch up her team and go quietly off to the cultivation of her land not only saves her purse the expenditure of the average wage of five shillings a day plus board, but she saves on herself – she conserves her energy.

The distribution of the sum left at my disposal required thought and care. It was hopeless even to think of the land payment of a thousand dollars, and even its interest was a matter of almost painful calculation. I had always faithfully paid to the credit of my account at the Union Bank all moneys that came to me from British sources or as payment for produce; in consequence my credit was on the stronger side. But the banks had shut down loans at the first rumour of frost, and were demanding payment of outstanding money wherever there was the smallest chance of obtaining it. I had not many creditors as I had made a point of paying ready money, even when I had to pay eight per cent. for the use of it; and it is far and away the best plan. A current account often pins you to the dearest market, and always persuades you to think lightly of necessary and unnecessary expenditure. The interest of my land-payment account, my repairs and binder-twine, the balance of my threshing account, the greater part of the breaking, were still unpaid. The market was practically flooded with grain of a low grade, and although good prices were being asked and paid for it in Liverpool, sales on the street of the average wheat-town were at below zero prices, and many of my neighbours were forced to accept these prices in order to meet interest due on land payments and implement accounts and the necessities of life. One did not see the heartbreaking, degrading signs of poverty as seen in England; there was a sufficiency of meal and potatoes and bacon and necessaries, there was fuel, and sufficient clothing – for the men at any rate, who could not do their winter work without it. But worry was on the face of every man, and the knowledge that the year of 1908 must be a year of redoubled toil charged with the unpaid bill of 1907 was still within the coming of the spring. I cleared thirty-five cents net a bushel for my wheat at Fort William after paying for my car. My neighbours the Collinsons had less than a thousand bushels, and were forced to sell on the street at South Qu'Appelle. It was practically the same sample as mine, and they had to take anything between twenty-five and thirty cents net. For wheat of practically the same grade, certainly not varying more than one degree, John McLeay obtained from sixty to seventy cents a bushel in the following spring.

I have said that bank loans were practically unobtainable. It is to be remembered that the frozen harvest of 1907 occurred in the same moment as the financial panic in the States, and although it seemed unjust and unfair that in the time of dire necessity the farmers, whose labour is the rock-bottom of all Canadian values, could obtain little or no aid from the banks of Canada, I found when I reached the States that my friends had to give considerable notice before they could withdraw small sums of the money lying to their credit. I complained bitterly to a wealthy neighbour that when I came to the country and hadn't particularly needed it money had been positively placed in my way, and now that I would have offered almost any reasonable price for it to settle outstanding debts without the sacrifice of my grain crop, I couldn't get a cent.

'Hold on! It will all come out in the wash,' was his advice; but he told me that even he had the same difficulty in obtaining money, and that he had heard on excellent authority that the banks had issued an order to all branches that no money was to be loaned to any client whose realizable security did not mark at least five thousand dollars.

I tell the tale as it was told to me, but whether an absolute fact or not, it is most certainly a fact that the small farmer is not aided as he should be either by the Government or the financial authorities in Canada. He seldom has one thousand bushels to sell in the early years of his wrestle with the land, usually weighted with the full charges for implements and horses and lumber, plus heavy interest. The rich farmer can command labour at the critical moment; the small farmer has to break his heart doing the labour of three men in order to get the one thing into the land which a few years ago was the only farm produce to command market and money.

It is the farmer in Canada, the man on the land, who has made those astonishing land-values which are being shouted to-day in every country in Europe, and in a time of stress things go harder with this man on the land, the producer, than with any member of those sections of society who depend on the foundation established and sustained by him to maintain their values.

It is claimed that the banks of Canada are admirable in the basis of their system and working principle, but the fact remains that they exist mainly for merchants of considerable capital and the farmer whose realizable security exceeds x; also the law of the price of bank money in the North-West is nothing under eight per cent. The finest gilt-edged security which British capital could obtain in Canada, one of the soundest and most promising and most effectual links of Empire, would lie in the establishment of a farmers' bank for the financial aid of farmers whose realizable capital does *not* exceed x, and the law of the price of money loaned should rule the highest price not to exceed five per cent.

My predecessor was both just and kind about my land payment and its interest, and his wife kinder; but he pointed out to me that of course the money rate was very high, and that he could easily obtain eight per cent. for that for which I was paying only six. I suggested that in future it should be held at seven, and he assented, and told me not to bother, for he was quite sure I should send it to him before long. He advised me to be sure and not fail to go and see his son-in-law, who was owner of the hardware store, and whose bill I was also not prepared to pay at the moment. There too I always obtained consideration, and when I offered to pay interest on an overdue account it was not taken.

The Union Bank would make no advance on wheat in the granary, or even lodged at the elevator. This was hardly to be wondered at since South Qu'Appelle was literally choked with low-grade grain. Mr. Donald H. Macdonald, the second son of the chief factor of the Hudson Bay Company, ran a bank at the time in connexion with his land business at Fort Qu'Appelle, and he lent me two hundred and fifty dollars on my carload, and just at the time thirty-six pounds fell due from London. I settled everything I possibly could, took a twenty-five-dollar excursion

ticket to New York, and forswore sleepers, and got out my baggage, which was rusty and dusty from its two and a half years'
sojourn on the prairie.

On the last day my brother came down from his homestead
and invited my dog back for the winter. So on the very last night
of all I made my round after the last feed, and saw all the beasts
tucked up comfortably with bedding up to their knees and
mangers full of the hay they love so well. This is the saving grace
in chief of farming on the Canadian prairie; the frost may seize
your marketable grain, but there is always food for beasts and
men. I knew that every four-footed friend would have plenty of
provender and be well cared for during my absence. Things still
jarred at times between me and my caretakers, who had many of
the failings of their many virtues, but the give-and-take theory is
in everyday practice in Canada, and they proved entirely equal
to their undertaking, and no words can convey one's appreciation of their care and thoughtfulness and general trustworthi-
ness through that winter. Mr. Wilton nursed the new horse
night and day after he had badly staked himself; and when I got
back in the spring everything was in perfect order, and the bill
from the Hudson Bay Store for the groceries supplied in excess of
the sum credited to the farm for eggs and butter was *five cents*.
Through them it has always seemed to me that, although the
British have much to learn from Canadians in their method of
active work on the land, they are most valuable and desirable as
general caretakers and overseers. These people, who were in
every way worthy of British tradition, and amongst those who
have gained for the British the homage revealed in the term 'salt
of the earth,' went on to New Zealand in the spring, and New
Zealand was the richer. They would have done exceedingly well
in Canada had they remained to take part in the more commercial farming of the present phase of development.

On the last night of my two and a half years' sojourn in Canada I find this entry in my diary:

'December 10 – My last day for the present. Drove into the Fort
with Lal. Cashed cheque, paid taxes, &c. Breakfast with the D.H.

Macdonalds. Walked up Baker Hill to say good-bye to the Griggs and the Seymours at Springbrook, then home. Horribly downcast. Felt a miserable failure – financial situation appalling – temper abominable. What will these years bring forth? They seem strange seed as one watches them lying in the soil tonight – roses must always "unfold within the mould," but seed doesn't always mean roses. I tried to do my best, but one can't do that from day to day, one's level best comes out in occasional throbs. One thing I have learned – to criticize myself without flinching. "Know thyself." One can't do that everywhere! Oh, the hardship, the hope, the trials, the sweetness and the sadness of these two years! How I have loved the beasts, and how heartily I have hated people and things here and there, and the end of it is for the present that I have to go off with a pen to save the plough, and that by to-morrow this time I shall be on my way to New York travelling in front of the dining-car minus a sleeper, certainly uncomfortable, probably hungry, and doing my level best to assure myself that – nothing matters!'

The next day I left by the stage for South Qu'Appelle and New York.

PART IV: THE TURN OF THE TIDE

'But noon beheld a larger heaven.'

1

The seed – the passing of
a prairie fire

I got back to South Qu'Appelle by the early train on April 14, 1908. Things had gone well with me. All the world was interested in Canada; I was possessed of practical and first-hand information. Offers of work from various magazines approached my pen, and although I was by no means out of the wood, many of the brambles which beset the way within were rendered removable. But on the morning I got back and fell off the train in the usual place and manner, which is always very far in the rear of the platform at South Qu'Appelle, gloom was in the air. Snow was falling, and I knew at once that I should have to drive through the fifteen miles which lay between me and anything that might have occurred within a two weeks' journey without any mail, in the teeth of the north wind. Whilst I waited for the democrat I took breakfast in Mrs. Walker's excellent restaurant, and there I learned that many farmers had already made use of the few fair days in the preceding week to get in the seed, and with all my heart I wished I had hurried on before, although April 15 is usually in excellent time for seeding anything under a hundred and fifty acres.

At the farm a delightful surprise awaited me. Mr. Wilton had communicated with me most regularly in my absence, and in one letter he told me that he had forwarded a sample of the seed-grain to the Government Seed Commissioner to undergo the germination test. I had read the result as forty-six germinative with a heavy heart, as it meant that I really ought not to sow the seed at all; but if I did sow, it would need a great deal more than the average one bushel two pecks to the acre. But instead of forty-six it proved to be ninety-six per cent. germinative, so that I was provided with some of the best seed in the country which, having been grown on newly broken land, had been, even before winnowing, almost entirely free from weed-seed. Mr. Wilton had done all the cleaning through the winter, and got on as far as possible with the usual preparations for seeding. His charge concluded with my arrival, and he and his family set out almost immediately for Vancouver *en route* for New Zealand.

I had arranged with Roddy McMahon to come to me that season for seeding, spring-ploughing, mowing if necessary, and harvest. The next day but one, warmest sunshine having followed on the trail of the snowstorm, the seeder started on its way across the big field. Good Friday fell in that week, and on Easter Eve the thermometer stood at seventy in the shade, and to all appearance the land was as dry as a biscuit.

It was after dinner that some well-disposed dweller in the air compelled my attention to one of the granaries which had not yet been brought in from the twenty-five-acre field. I scanned it from a distance. There was a faint smell of fire in the air. Clouds of smoke rose here and there from sixteen to twenty-four miles distant on the far side of the Qu'Appelle lakes, and, turning to the north-west, I perceived a further cloud which seemed ominously near. It was a spur to my procrastinating sense of caution, and I called to my brother, who was smoking the after-dinner pipe of peace with Roddy McMahon, and who vowed that on such a day it was killing work to remove a granary with four horses.

'Get two stout poplar poles to raise it,' I suggested. 'Once out of the rut, it is quite a short pull to the pasture trail, and then, bar stones, it will run as easily as a bathing-machine.'

Thirty-five minutes later the neat little granary was grouped with its near relatives among the somewhat unconventional farm buildings, and my conscience was eased of a load.

The long absence from active outdoor and domestic work had unsettled my attitude towards 'the daily round and common task.' There was bread to bake, butter to make, flower seeds to sow, stables to clean, it would have been wise to pickle Monday's seed and rest through Sunday; in short, there was a great deal more work than one could possibly get through under a brilliant sun set in a blue heaven, so I gave ear to the voice of the charmer and drove away towards tea and tennis at Fort Qu'Appelle.

Two miles up the trail Nancy cocked her ears and laid hold of the bit. The smell of fire which had hovered in the air for three days was suddenly suffocatingly near. We topped the little hill that marks half-way; hot air fanned my left cheek, and we were almost abreast of the long, thin scarlet line which ate its way across the biscuit-tinted prairie and left in its wake stretching away back to the southern hills of Fort Qu'Appelle a coal-black waste, grim and lifeless save for a smouldering bluff here and there where the fire had found food for its tarrying.

I remembered with relief that my nearest neighbours on that side of the trail, who were Canadians, had insured their homes against the danger of prairie fire by firing the wide outskirt of their own land, so that there was no necessity to turn back on their account. I hurried along my way to encounter smouldering and charred remains of fallen telegraph posts barring my line. The single wire which runs from South Qu'Appelle station to Prince Albert was down. I stopped to consider.

Not a breath of air stirred. The trees had only just started to bud, but the golden sun blazed down from a summer sky. Across the hills from the valley below one caught a glimpse of the lake, with ice-bound bosom still offering dumb resistance to the challenge of the sun. The contrast was specially unusual and fascinating to an Englishwoman. I longed to draw nearer. My only danger lay in the chance of the fire leaping the trail, and the odds of that chance with the wind right down lay at a hundred to one against. I went on.

On the top of the hill I perceived with dismay that the fire had leapt the trail and was travelling backwards towards the cemetery. I hurried on my way to carry the news of the danger to Fort

Qu'Appelle, but it proved to be no news to the usually sleepy little town that dozes in the heart of the valley of lakes. Fort Qu'Appelle was alive with anxiety. It appeared that for twenty-four hours the fire had played in and out of both lines of poplar and maple-clad hills which guard the valley on the southern side, and ill-tidings of distress and disaster fallen and feared were on every tongue. As I stood at the door of the post office a man was brought into the town in appalling agony. He had been badly burned in endeavouring at the last moment to plough up a guard. The fire, it seemed, had cut round and caught him out on the last furrow. Three of the horses had got off with a singeing, but one had been moved to the veterinary hospital at South Qu'Appelle severely injured; and the man had been brought down to the Fort – to die, said some; others that he would never open his eyes again. Happily none of these sad prophecies was fulfilled; patient and painstaking medical treatment combined with careful nursing pulled him through, and he was about again before seeding was finished, but the faithful horse had earned the long rest and went under.

Homeward-bound I climbed the long steep hill with a heavy heart. On the brow a democrat passed me in which were men of the North-West Mounted Police and men of Fort Qu'Appelle on their way to fight the flames from God's acre on the hill.

The hill behind us, we raced along, and this time on either side of the trail lay the black waste, but in less than a quarter of a mile we arrived at the scarlet line on the near side. It was eating its way very slowly due east and not perceptibly gaining ground south. For a moment I had both intuition and intention to get out and put it out. I could have done so in ten minutes, but I found on examination that the foot-mat of the buggy was missing, and experience had already taught me that one runs a foolhardy risk in attempting to tramp out fire on dry prairie. I consoled myself with the reflection that it must be starved out at the side-trail in the east, and feeling anything but comfortably conscience-clear, I turned the searchlight of judgment off myself and on to the men who had driven promptly to the rescue of the gravestones of the dead and as promptly and thoughtlessly away from the rescue of the lands and possibly lives of the living. I drove towards home fully determined to have my fire-guard ploughed – the first thing on Monday morning! At the gate I met Roddy McMahon going home for Sunday, and told him of the havoc the fire was working. He seemed to think we lay safely out of its reach, since it could not travel far with the wind right down; but we agreed together that in spite of the hold of the night-frosts the guard must be ploughed – the first thing on Monday morning!

I had no easy mind. Those creeping scarlet lines were reflected on my brain, and as the sun went down and the swift Canadian twilight passed into nightfall the lurid light in the north seemed to grow brighter and to draw nearer. My brother and I agreed that every beast should be turned loose, and that we would keep watch in turn. At the coming of each hour one or the other of us scanned the outlook. At dawn the red glow seemed to fade, at sunrise to die. Still smoke was rising and the wind had freshened, but it is in the nature of fear to fade with the daylight, and I turned in and slept soundly until there came a shrill whistle from my brother and the announcement that it was a quarter to nine and the kettle boiling.

Breakfast was laid in the veranda – Sunday breakfast: tea and toast and Crosse and Blackwell's marmalade, to be taken at the hour one pleases, which is a contrast to the working-day six-o'clock farm-hour breakfast consisting of porridge and fried bacon and potatoes, that can only be thoroughly appreciated by the man or woman who prepares both. I sat down in the sun's warmth and gazed on the sunlit landscape with a feeling of intense pleasure at being back once more to breathe the clear exhilarating air of the prairie. Suddenly the dweller in the air was at my elbow. Without any conscious motive I forsook my teacup and walked around to the north side of the veranda, and from there more sharply out beyond the garden-fence to the place where the side-trail lies in view. From the distance of a mile I saw a wave of flame rolling in towards us as the incoming tide rolls in on the seashore. On the east side of the trail a dense cloud of smoke, and on the west a gleam of scarlet announced the approach of other links in a literal chain of fire, and I knew there was but one way out of a clean sweep – 'on the prairie fight fire with fire.'

I went back to my brother. 'The fire is just on us,' I said. 'We are all right south and west, as the summer-fallow runs a guard, but unless we can burn off the overgrown guard that runs from the east to the west corner of the fallow we are straight in a line with the fire and –'

But he was already scanning the outlook. 'I understand,' he said. 'We have from fifteen to twenty minutes at the outside to get through with the job, and if we fail it's a finish. Come on!'

The wind was towards us, the stable-yard still covered with litter of threshing straw which had lain under the snow during the winter but was now all too dry and inflammable as shaving. It was a desperate and most dangerous resource but the only chance. The sound and solid English grain-bags I had brought out with me, and which Canadians refuse to handle as a rule on account of their weight, did good service that morning. Armed with one each and a bucket of water, we started in at our task, I working east, my brother west. For a short space there was silence save for the muffled roar of the oncoming enemy and the banging of the damp bags with which we quenched our several fires as the flames reached the limit we ruled.

As long as it was concerned with the old guard only our task was comparatively easy. The snow-cured and sun-dried herbage blazed up as swiftly as straw and as swiftly perished to the fine dust of flame. But further east the ploughing of the original guard had been less effective. The fire just frolicked into the straw-belittered yard, and three times I had to call my brother to aid me as the flame seemed to be beyond my power to extinguish. The third time he came his face was blackened with smoke and his lips set tight. 'Don't call again,' he said, 'if you can possibly avoid it; the last time I came round I only just stopped my fire from getting into the bluff, and if it gets there it's a finish.' So I set my teeth and made fresh flames, and beat them out until my hands and throat and eyes were as red-hot cinders caught in a whirlwind.

I had nearly reached the potato-patch, which would form another and considerable link in the guard, and would give the flames at any rate a roundabout trail to the house and the two-thousand-bushel granary, which still contained seed and feed grain of considerable value, when a growth of extra-dry grass gave a sudden impulse to the flame. It leaped into the air and raced along on its way towards the stable-door. I plunged my sack into the water and went for it with a desperate effort, which was successful, but my last for the time being. To my horror I found that energy had played out completely! For a moment there was neither a bang nor a yell left in me, and between the burnt-out guard and the potato-patch there still stretched a patch of dry herbage. I looked towards the flaming prairie to measure time. Between the scarlet flames, now no longer steadily but audaciously advancing along the fireproof trail, there came running towards me the figure of a man I knew, and in a few seconds he was at my side. He took up the sack and went on with my task, and I made my way round to the other side to find that my brother had succeeded in linking his guard with the guard of fallow land, so that we were comparatively safe on that side from the big fire, though still in serious danger from our own as the ever-freshening wind rekindled dying sparks to vigorous life, and from half a dozen places flame was creeping with the swiftness of a serpent to the invasion of the bluff. But my strength had come back and we fought them one by one.

Then came the sound of wheels. A buggy drawn by a little Canadian pony, prairie-bred and fearless as fast, flew on its way between the fences of flame until it reached the black waste of our own making which no flame could leap. It was Roddy McMahon, and his wife was with him, and her baby in her arms and two small children in the bottom of the buggy.

'So you burned the old guard,' he commented. ''Twas a wise act. You've saved a burn-out all right.'

'The fires will meet in the dip by the gateway and extinguish each other,' I answered, 'but there is still a wide opening to the worst danger. If it makes its way up the hill through the little pasture field it will catch us by the gateway of the big pasture –

close to the oat-rick, where we dare not fire a guard with the wind facing. If the rick fires we must still be burnt out.'

'Guess that's right enough,' said he. 'There's Joe Collinson. Here, Joe, give me a hand to get the team on plough. Guess we have got to plough up some sort guard round the oat-stack rick 'fore the fire can get round.'

The sulky plough was away on the land, the shear of the hand plough blunt as a board; the frost was only just out of the surface of the land, and the newly broken guard made but a poor show as a defence to the giant straw-rick which loomed behind it. The little gathering had grown to the number of a dozen, neighbours who, realizing that I was straight in a line with the danger that menaced us all, but for which Canadians and old-timers are usually prepared, had come to offer a helping hand.

An angrier note in the roar of the fire gave warning that the two blazes were approaching each other. I turned to see the main fire dash wrathfully down the hill to devour the lesser flame we had sent out to meet it. For a second the flames leaped high as they closed in a throttling embrace only to find mutual extinction. But the eastern arm came on as I had surmised it would, not with the mad menace of the flame that had found death in another, but with quiet indomitable purpose and wide-eyed for prey.

There was nothing more to be done. We stood by the inadequately guarded corner, within twenty yards of the oat-straw rick, each armed with a sack and ready to do battle with the flame-wave if it challenged, but each of us knew in our heart that if the flame continued to get within fighting distance the whole place was doomed. What could be done at the last moment had been done, the rest was with the Power that works behind phenomena.

The increasing roar announced the surviving flame to be gaining strength and power. With eyes set straight for the fatal corner from which it must approach, I suddenly remembered that I was not insured. I had fully intended taking out a policy before leaving Canada the preceding winter, but the frozen harvest had indefinitely postponed my intentions, luxurious and utilitarian. That was the one absolutely bitter moment of my life on the Canadian prairie, for then, and I think only then, through all the ups and downs of my farming experiment, did I doubt that my comrade 'the Power that works behind phenomena' was playing the game. The well-worn path through the pasture reminded me of the arduous toil of the previous harvest which I had steadily refused to acknowledge at the time. The icy hours of the winter of 1906-1907 recurred to my brain, with the serious personal disappointment of the sum total of my wild-oats harvest of 1906, and the far more serious because general calamity of the frozen harvest of 1907 – big reverses these – but with my fresh flow of capital and experience I knew I could force a way through. Only the fire would wipe away everything: seedwheat, seed-oats, house and granaries and barn. True, the most precious of my possessions – my four-footed friends – would be left to me; but the black and dreary waste grinned down even this touch of consolation, whilst a mocker in the air whispered: 'To sell or to starve!'

It was the last straw. Involuntarily my eyes quitted their post to glance their way. There they were, racing away towards safety in a slough, driven by a scarlet line of flame which was literally sweeping the pasture out of recognition and had contrived to leave my house and the unorthodox farm buildings, the granaries, the seed-grain, the feed-grain and my goods and chattels in the safeguard of a black unbroken circular fence. The hill and the north-west wind had fought against each other; the wind was with the flames, but 'the Power that works behind phenomena' was posted on the hill.

'Gee! but it's cut round in the bottom.'

'Well, say now, ain't that right down lucky! And the wind driving it along too! Seemed sure thing.'

'Can't come back on you now, anyway. You're safe enough. But I never see closer thing to a burn-out. Sure thing! Sure thing!'

I went forward in the wake of my beasts, who with unerring intuition were making for the fireproof seed-bed, or the sloughs which were as islands set in the midst of the blood-red sea of flame which was devouring all that lay in its way to the south-east.

When I got back the little gathering had dispersed, all save the teamster and his family.

'Guess the missus and the children best stay along with you while your brother and me should go along and see if they wants any help over yonder,' said Roddy McMahon, with his eyes following the danger to which his heart was evidently in tow.

In the gratitude of the moment I guessed the missus and the children might stay for ever.

Towards sunset I walked across the outskirts of the land and from the distance gazed upon my farmstead, a strangely isolated irregular patch of life and colour set in the black and lifeless waste. At the gate of the fence I met Guy Mazey.

'My! Things looked bad for you this morning though! I was coming across, but I had to plough up my own guard a bit; and then there was Roland Dennison. The fire seemed every bit like coming in on him, an' he away down at the Fort. And so you lost that good granary. Say now! Too bad!'

I gratefully murmured that I had lost nothing.

'But I see the granary in the twenty-five-acre patch yesterday forenoon,' he replied incredulously.

'But not yesterday afternoon,' I explained, and was conscious of the first faint symptom of returning self-respect.

'My! But I guess you struck it lucky that time all right!'

I think the escape from the threat of grave loss and danger did me much good at the time. There is always a temptation to put off the duty of to-day until to-morrow on a Canadian farm, not altogether through sloth but through over-work, aggravated by lack of method. The fire-guards around the buildings and the granaries would have taken but half a day of fall-ploughing, and not only would one have been secure against loss through fire, but in the event of such a fire rushing over the land one could have reaped the benefit of its passing with very little tax in the way of loss. It would have burnt off the stubble – always a day's work – cleaned out old sloughs, making clear way for young and tender herb, and in the shortest space of time replaced the dusky hue of the prairie with a coat of emerald green. Fire has always been welcome to the well-prepared as an excellent time-saver in the seeding month; yet danger there is and always will be as long as the unprepared are among the others; and it is good for the country that the danger of prairie fire in completely settled districts has almost passed away. At the time of the danger which beset me I was almost completely surrounded by unbroken prairie. Nearly all the land of the neighbourhood is now under cultivation, and there is no fire-guard or exterminator of superior efficiency to a stretch of ploughed land.

The fire was followed by the last snowstorm of the season; it checked seeding for six days, and then spring really came. After finishing the big field we sowed the newly broken twenty-five acres, then burned off the stubble of the preceding year's breaking crop and sowed that. Wheat-seeding was then finished. Afterwards we ploughed eighteen acres of stubble belonging to the summer-fallow crop of the preceding year, and sowed oats. Rain arrived to delay the barley-seeding, and it was not in the land until June 15, which, in spite of all proverbs, is fully ten days too late unless one is prepared for a very grave risk of frozen grain.

In the last week of April, on a day of snow and wind and my birthday, Nancy brought me the dearest of gifts in the form of a second colt, whom I named Jupiter, because in spite of all orthodox arrangements for his paternity he had selected his sire by some means or another, and it always remained a mystery. He was a beautiful bay colt, and took two first prizes on his only appearance in the show-ring. Felicity nearly lost her self-possession between delight and jealousy at his coming. When I half dragged, half carried him into the stable from the huge snow-covered straw-pile where he had come into the world, she came too, and when shut out from the place which sheltered mother and son she returned at regular intervals to kick in impatient and jealous anger at their door. All through the summer she insisted on sharing the milk, and one had to be always most tactful about giving her the largest and first share of attention. But left alone they were devoted friends, and Jupiter grew up

with all the dear ways of Ricky and a quite unaccountable likeness to him, and every beast of every species seemed to find in
him a prince of playmates.

The three steers and Julia had thriven well during the winter,
and so had the small steer who arrived in the middle of a grain-
field in the preceding August. Blacky, his mother, was the cow
who drank her own milk, and her efforts to steal her own calf
were amazingly original. Mr. Wilton, after having tried every de-
vice to secure her milk for the household, had eventually decided
that she might reserve for her offspring what she stole from her
owner, and let them run together. This probably accounted for
the unusual size and strength of her young steer. John McLeay
always allowed his calves to have all the milk until they ran dry;
and undoubtedly in cattle-raising, quite apart from the toil and
profit of dairy-farming, this is the best method of raising good
beasts for food.

The only disappointment in connexion with Mr. Wilton's
charge was the pigs. Out of thirty-three born in April only three
survived, and the other three sows did not farrow until June, too
late for November markets. It is possible, with excellent feeding,
to sell April sows at a good profit in the fall of the year; but one
ought not to have to keep spring-born pigs through the winter,
and it is only wise to encourage the coming of the second family
where winter accommodation is perfect. But at the end of the
seeding month of 1908 the stock and grain had an air of promise.
There was very little work to be done. Under thirty acres to
plough, and the hay to make, which in one of Canada's brilliant
working seasons is neither a hard nor a lengthy business. I had
to buy seed-oats and barley as my own were not sufficiently
clean, but the clouds were clearing off, and I had leisure to read
and to do a great deal of writing; and although I had no saddle-
horse, as Nancy was far too busy in the nursery except for an
occasional jaunt to Fort Qu'Appelle in search of things indispensable, yet the nursery had its own particular attraction for
one's hours of leisure, and already in the lovely limbs of Felicity
was the promise of the lightness and brightness and pace of an
ideal saddle-mare.

2

The blade – the ear –
the full corn

It was on the twenty-second day from sowing that I paused in some gardening one evening to notice that my summer-fallow field was flecked with bright green wheat-blades; then came early rain, and it raced ahead. Only here and there the regular lines were inclined to run out of form – in places it was strangely over-luxuriant.

'Your wheat is well forward,' said my neighbour, 'but very over-thick here and there. It seems to me that the seeder has been playing you false. It looks as though it had become choked, and then discharged the blocked seed with a flush directly the tube was clear. That, or other seed sprouting which wasn't sown this year.'

Guy Mazey passed by: 'The wheat's coming up fine,' he said, 'but some of it has been sowed too thick I guess. I always have one or two of my youngsters walk behind the seeder all the time. Then if a tube gets choked we clean it straight away.'

I was trying to work the farm with as little help as possible that year; all the land was sown, there were only about thirty acres of summer-fallow land to plough, which would not take Roddy McMahon more than ten days. This I disced and harrowed for all surface seed to spring, and it was settled that it should not be ploughed until it was well up. He came along one day to see how things were going, and I anxiously inquired his opinion concerning the wheat in the blade.

'The seeder don't ever clog,' he assured me. 'I see that everything is clear at the end of each furrow and I look in the seed-box pretty frequent, and get off to see what's wrong if the seed don't appear to be shrinking even like. None's perfect I guess. But 'twould take a better man than any round these parts to learn me my work on the land. And your wheat is the best about, way ahead of any other.'

'It's the most forward,' I allowed. 'But you can't deny that those over-thick patches are out of order. I was hoping you might be able to explain them away with some irregularity of the seeder. As you can't we may just as well look the only explanation in the eye – wild oats!'

'Well, maybe. That field can stand a few.'

'There is no wheat-tract in any country that can stand wild oats, and you know it,' I replied. 'It is not only that they can cause excellent wheat to be rejected from its own grade, but sooner or later it is annihilation to the wheat. It is of no use attempting to cross your bridge before you come to it, but it is foolish to deny the existence of a bridge which is already within sight.'

'Wild oats have been in that patch this ten years and they've got them all round in these parts. It's shame that the fellows you had to plough last year didn't know their work better. 'Twould have been a good act to plough twice, it would have got the best part of the weeds under and the oats too I guess. The breakin' and stubble is comin' along fine. Guess you'll be having a sight better harvest than any of the rest, anyway –'

'The comparative degree is the refuge of the second-rate,' I replied bitterly.

'What's that you said?' said he.

By the end of June I saw clearly that my beautiful field, which was the picture of health and coming wealth to the untrained eye, was to let me down badly. In the preceding season an additional thirty-foot patch had been broken at the skirt of the field nearest the house bringing the field right up to the garden-fence. Within the patch of newly broken land the wheat was perfectly clean and luxuriant and beautiful beyond description; and I was not only spared much criticism and condolence, but congratulations were showered upon me, which I accepted graciously and found soothing in spite of my own complete knowledge of the inner leaves and chapters of the field with the lovely margin. After all one should enjoy everything possible in this world. In the nature of things those who scoff at castles in the air, and the pleasure of anticipation, and the fool's paradise, can never gauge the sum of the dweller's debt to the dreamer in this world. A pleasure anticipated is pleasure still. I got all the pleasure possible out of the margin of joy, but by July 1 I saw that it was absolutely necessary to make hay of many acres behind it on the south-west side of the field, which had the appearance of a patch of degenerate oats with a wheat-ear here and there. Nor was the affliction confined to the outskirts of the field; one couldn't walk a hundred feet anywhere without coming across yards and even roods of them. A good way out of the problem would have been to make hay of the whole field, bar the margin; but the best way would have been to have waited until the sap had dried right out, and, like Mr. George Robb, of Springbrook, to have ploughed a good fire-guard, and made a cleansing bonfire of the lot. But I was in the place where one cannot choose, the place of a great responsibility. I was bound on one side of the Atlantic with another's capital, and on the other with a big land payment still to make in the future, of which at least a thousand dollars plus the interest of the whole would certainly have to be met in the fall; there was still a much overdrawn banking account; wages and the housekeeping account were being kept down, but in time the threshing bill would have to be met. On the other hand stock was growing into money. The two steers I had bought of my predecessor were ready for prompt sale in emergency, or, if harvest turned out well, we could afford to reserve one-half for household use, and sell the other to a neighbour at a cent or so above the price one would obtain from the butcher. I had hoped to make at least three hundred dollars in pigs, but I saw that little more than a hundred could be anticipated owing to the bad luck in the birthday month. For years I had argued loftily that poverty should never be permitted to matter; it threw down the glove to me again and again in fighting my way through the proposition of farming three hundred and twenty acres of land on the Canadian prairie with insufficient capital and only a growing experience, which always seemed to arrive at the spot just too late to be of use. Whether it was that I had to think hard for thirty-five cents to sharpen a ploughshare or to think hard for a hundred and thirty-five dollars to settle indisputable claims for indispensable service of horse or implement or man, I had to think hard all the time. But the little bunch of cattle was growing. Molly was at the time mother of two steers and two heifers, and the eldest steer was certainly worth the price I paid for him and herself together – forty-five dollars. Blacky had also placed two steers to my credit, and there was the other big steer who had hailed from 'the hard cow.' Best of all, there was always in view cheering me on to 'the heights of one's heart' Nancy with Felicity and Jupiter in tow.

That year too I had a lovely garden. Countess Spencer sweet peas, the seed of which had hailed from Covent Garden, and masses of Shirley poppy brought a mass of lovely colour to the flower-beds which I had dug in 1906, and when colour had basely deserted at the earliest attacks of Jack Frost, mignonette, and love-in-a-mist, which had lain almost concealed among the poppies, lived on fighting the frost-fiend with the last breath of fragrance and kindness. None can tell how much a garden contributes to the joy of life on the prairie. The season of flowers is so short, and toil is so long that the place of *dolce far niente* often smiled with me over the old dream of sweet idleness, but it never mocked, and the refreshment of the lovely flash and fragrance of that flower-bed perhaps could only be truly appreciated by a very tired person.

Every year the Agricultural Show is held at Fort Qu'Appelle. It is quite an event because the very smallest excuse is always sufficient to summon the whole world and his wife to the town between the lovely lakes. I was intending to show Nancy and Jupiter. Mr. Ray Dale and Kelsdon were to be my guests overnight. Mr. Ray Dale is one of the men to whom quite a wide area of Saskatchewan owes an uncommon debt. A great lover of horses he gave all his time and energy and every cent he earned to the improvement of horse-breeding in the Qu'Appelle neighbourhood. His horse Kelsdon had taken medals and prizes and championships from coast to coast. I made the best preparations possible for my distinguished guest. We cleaned out the coolest and lightest end of the log-stable and got up a load of the mintiest hay, but Kelsdon brought his own oats and seemed quite pleased and content with his surroundings. The next day he and Nancy and little Jupiter were brushed and polished, and prepared for the show-ring. Of course Kelsdon carried off everything that lay in his way, but Jupiter to my surprise and delight took off first prize in both the classes in which he was shown and a kind word and compliment from the judge to boot. No pen can paint the pleasure for which those two first-prize certificates stand.

Meantime the ears of wheat arrived to share the outlook, and the centres and east-end acres of growing grain fanned the inextinguishable spark of hope. There was a very little smut in the stubble crop, but the wheat itself was buoyant in spite of the fact that we looked in vain for our usual thunder-showers, and rain was badly needed. I missed the croak and criticism of my neighbour that year, and I missed his kindness too. His people arrived from England; there were tents and disorder around the peaceful shack, and presently a kind of miniature elevator towered on its other side; and when the disorder of the process of new buildings had cleared off, where peace had reigned order ruled. Not that the shack had ever been set in anything but the pink of neatness, and the fields of my neighbour's homestead were deep ploughed and clean, but capital and labour can accomplish so much more in a short time than just the land and the man – and very soon the little shack was the picturesque old friend rather than the centre of a model farm on which everything was just as my neighbour and critic and friend had always grumbled that it ought to be, and he was farming miles away on the far side of the valley.

It had been a glorious summer with the only drawback of a lack of July showers. On August 12 we awoke to a steady downpour of rain which ceased at midday, when the swollen clouds made way for the August sun. But at eventime the clouds had floated all too far away, and the sun went down in royal scarlet. In Canada we make everyday use of our senses – the sun is my clock, my body a faithful thermometer. Before dawn it had registered freezing-point; at sunrise I saw Jack Frost had called and left his mark. However, my poppies and sweet peas reassured me; they seemed even fresher and more lovely than before, but a line of potatoes on the south of the garden and on a line with the wheat drooped and blackened at the ordeal of the sun, although a quarter of an acre of a branch of their family fifty yards north escaped unscathed. I had arranged to go that day to visit the experimental farm run by the Government at Indian Head, and was glad of the drive as a means of distraction, and also as an opportunity of examining how far the frost might affect the harvest.

The horses caught the whiff of Jack Frost in the air. Tossing head and heel they flew across the prairie, jubilant no doubt in the consciousness that the day of their tormenting enemy the mosquito had fled once more, and good pasture would again be an undisturbed delight. On my way I passed a man driving a hayrack.

'Four degrees only,' was the reply to my question; but the next moment in passing a garden I noticed that the vegetable-marrow plants had gone under, and not a solitary potato plant had escaped. Onward we raced across the prairie trail towards Wide-awake, where to the left started those wonderful miles of wheat plain. Here, in the wheat season, miles and miles of unfenced grain line the trail on either side, unbroken save for the road allowance and an occasional patch of summer-fallow land, and through the avenue of standing grain one drives to the very border of the main street of the wheat town of Indian Head. Had the frost worked mischief? I asked myself the question many times during the eighteen-mile drive. The oats denied injury. The dusky tint of many a square-mile patch already invited the binder. I noticed that the wisdom of old-timers had decided to save on oats after the lesson of 1907, and bitterly I regretted that I had not been strong enough to live down to my own theory in this matter, for in my judgment the wheat would not be ready for the binder full ten days and their complement of treacherous nights.

I found that only two degrees had been registered at the experimental farm and at South Qu'Appelle. All the grain crops at the farm were harvest-ripe, and there was not the slightest fear of injury. I drove home determined to hope for the best.

The rain of August 12 brought more rain, but the sun was on the side of the wheat and shone with all its glorious might between the storms, and the green wheat-fields quickly turned to gold. The summer-fallow crop is usually the last to ripen, and therefore the newly broken frill of my summer-fallow patch led me to believe that it was ripe before the entire field was ready. My old neighbour John McLeay warned me against cutting too early. A well-known scientific farmer wrote a special article to the *Manitoba Free Press* urging the farmer to wait the full time in spite of the frost scare. Generally speaking, he considered the crop was sufficiently advanced to hold its own. He argued that if cut on the green side the grain was sure to shrink, and he maintained that in its very near degree towards maturity, loss on weight would exceed loss on grade, and injure the harvest more deeply than even a touch of frost.

On Sunday Roddy McMahon came along with the news that David Chambers had decided not to waste binder-twine nor harvest labour on his biggest field of wheat.

'The frost cut right up through Springbrook, but Dave Chambers he would have been all right if he hadn't been late getting in his seed. His nephews came out from the Old Country. I guess he put them on the seeder before they had time to know much, and he was a bit short-handed and nigh three weeks behind in getting it in. The frost has knocked one or two about, but we were in good and early, and I guess you're all right.'

I could only remember that in the preceding year a neighbour in Springbrook and the son of an old-timer had cut his wheat absolutely green three days before the fatal frost. He had built it into huge stooks and let it ripen in the sheaf. It graded No. 2 Northern, and sold at seventy-five cents when all the wheat in the neighbourhood was fetching between twenty-five and thirty-five cents. Every night the thermometer fell almost to freezing-point. The anxiety was too keen. I resolved to cut, and cut about four days too soon, and undoubtedly lost some bushels by weight in so doing. The crop of 1908 was altogether a different problem from the crop of 1907. Frost hardly touches harvest-ripe grain, but for every grain that it stands on the near side of har-vest-ripe so much the nearer it is to the destroying power of the frost, and in an average year three parts of the battle with the frost may be fought in early seeding. Here the service of Roddy McMahon stood by me so strongly. 'None is perfect I guess,' was one of his most frequent sayings, but truly at seed-time and harvest and threshing this man of the land would be hard to beat. Strength and speed were his strong points, and at all times and seasons he was full of resource. Much ill-fortune I might have avoided had he worked for me right through the season of 1907, and much that was excellent in the harvests of 1908 and 1910 I owed to his insistence of 'getting it in good and quick all right.'

It was fated to be a difficult year. I had some trouble in getting in the threshers, my corner having relied on the return of Alan Redcliffe's outfit, but he failed us. Then Danny McLeay secured an awfully good outfit which had agreed to take him and John McLeay in its line on the way to David Chambers. John McLeay felt sure Mr. Chambers would stand aside another day that I might be included in the grace, but although I begged hard he wouldn't give an inch. But two years later he most kindly allowed another outfit to come to me first, and the bad end of that good turn left him with his grain in stook through the winter, for the snow fell early, and threshing became difficult and indeed impossible.

However the kindness of 1911 cannot possibly be foreseen through the resolution of 1908, and I felt that he was ungener-ous and almost unjust about excluding me from the grace to which he admitted John and Danny McLeay; because although many an outfit would have crossed a mile or so to do our triple job, either alone was no particular catch. In my dilemma I drove straight to Guy Mazey, and he promised to help me out of the difficulty and to come in directly his own job was over.

On the following Saturday evening I heard the engine puffing along its way through the stooks. It was a steel-bright night, and I hadn't a shadow of regret for the loss of my day of rest, but just hugged to myself the consolation that the last act of 1908 would soon be over. In the morning the rain poured down in torrents and for twenty-four hours on end.

It hadn't been too profitable a threshing season for the men on the gangs. Wages are high, but when they cannot work they are not paid, and also when they are not working they are liable to discontent. The weather was growing cold, the men up for the harvest job from the east were anxious to get home, and inclined to kick at the smallest delay. I heard their sentiments freely expressed through Sunday, and knew that Guy Mazey would have his work cut out to hold them over a prolonged wait, but I was absolutely determined that not one bushel of my grain should be threshed until it was bone-dry. On the stubble and breaking crops the wheat was of fine grade, and perfectly clean and free from any kind of weed, but there was a tiny touch of smut here and there. To have threshed it on the finest shade of the damp side would have been a grave risk of tagged grain. I knew Guy Mazey was far too good a farmer to thresh before grain was thoroughly dry as a rule, but it would take an iron will to hold his gang together, and he couldn't thresh without his men.

Mabel rode over on Monday morning, she had promised to help me over my household chores.

'But it is utterly impossible to thresh to-day,' I said to her as we watched the soaked land steaming in the sun.

'I guess they'll be able to start up at noon,' she said. 'Father will be round by then all right.'

I walked out to the granary directly I saw that Guy Mazey had arrived. 'Did you think of starting to-day?' I inquired.

'Well, I guess we may be able to start up after dinner.'

'It's out of the question,' I said. 'That grain looks perfectly clean at sight, but there is smut here and there, and to thresh it to-day or even to-morrow without the strongest wind and sun to dry it out would be fatal. I know your gang are kicking badly, and I am afraid they are going to be harder to hold than you think. I'll keep the outfit round gladly if I have to keep them a month, but I won't have a solitary stook threshed until it is absolutely fit and dry. It's the first sound good crop I have raised. I am not going to take any chances.'

'The men are very hard to hold indeed,' he agreed, 'and I should be glad to pay them all off. But what shall you do? You see the others round are threshed out, and maybe you would find it difficult to get an outfit to put in for one small crop.'

'I must risk that. I met Mr. Redcliffe and he said he would come in on his way home; it will probably be late, but anything is better than a crop spoiled after harvest. You think it over and if you can't hold the men I shall understand, and any expenses concerned with the incoming of course I will pay.'

Fort Qu'Appelle, like all small towns, has a tendency to gossip. The different reports that got on to the four winds and other tongues concerning the entrance and rapid exit of Guy Mazey's threshing outfit from my threshing job that year were many, varied, and unflattering to both of us. But I had always found him one of the very best of my friends and neighbours. I knew none who worked so quickly and quietly and with such dogged, splendid determination. He took reverse in silence and good fortune thankfully, and he was always ready to help a lame dog over a stile. He knew about wheat, too, and how I felt about that particular crop, and if I stretched reason taut it was good reason, and I am sure he forgave me. It is certain he did not send in a bill for coming over with the engine and separator in vain.

After I left him I went down to the Fort to get provisions, and when I got back every vestige of the threshing outfit had vanished.

The hired man, who had been stooking and had remained on for fall-ploughing, met me at the gate speechful with amazement.

'A pretty thing you have done! Never have I seen such a thing as a threshing outfit sent off a place before, and not a stook threshed. And a woman too! You'll be keeping Christmas with your stooks.'

'That needn't concern you, since your wages will be paid in any case. Get back to your own business on the plough,' I said, without a sign of the anger that was blazing in my heart. The man was very valuable, quiet with horses, thorough in his ploughing, and he *knew* his work.

Every day I sought threshers in vain, but on Friday I found the gang on which Roddy McMahon was working.

'David Chambers ought to have let them come on to you I guess. It wouldn't have put him out none either. 'Twasn't like him neither. Guess this outfit will come on and thresh you out all right soon as we've finished up here. About Monday night I guess.'

Roddy McMahon has always a pull with a threshing outfit. The boss values him because he can put in the work of two without getting disagreeable. Through threshing he works in the same sort of spirit in which Englishmen put in every minute of a hunting run, so that all the gang like him too, even pitchers who rest so frequently upon their fork. He is never too tired to see that the women in the house have plenty of water and wood to engineer those three heavy meals, and whilst half a dozen are bewailing the chore of milking, or having a lively discussion as to whose turn it is *not* to milk, he has planted the milk upon the kitchen table and driven the cows back to pasture. Roddy McMahon at his best is a good type of Canada's most valuable specimen of the man on the land, and as he is always in his best form through threshing I knew I should get threshed out all right while such a friend remained at court.

''Twould be a good act if you were to see the boss and get it fixed right now I guess,' he said; and I rode across to the place where the manager was talking to Sandy Stuart, whom I hadn't met before, only we both claimed Mr. Brodie as a mutual friend.

'Too bad of David not to have let them come on to you from John McLeay,' he said. 'You should have come to me.'

Too bad it might have been, but it was quite right all the same, as he proved when he gave way for others and blocked his own passage in 1911. It is a concession that should not be required of any neighbour after the first week in October. The point is to hustle round and make your threshing arrangements the moment the binder comes in from the harvest-field.

In some way or another I had offended my stooker, or he visited the gangs stationed round about us, and began to regret the fact that he had asked to stay on with me at a dollar a day when other men were earning two dollars and two-fifty a day on the outfits. None was more staggered than I at his suggestion to remain on after stooking. He told me that my cooking suited him, but that was in the month of custard and stewed plums; when we came down to solid joints a change came over the spirit of his dream, and he didn't hesitate to abuse even as he had praised; but he was backsetting the hill field, which is the most difficult piece of ploughing on the farm, and every furrow was perfectly turned and not a horse turned a hair or ever looked tired.

One Sunday afternoon I was digging potatoes in preparation for my visitors and he came across.

'If my work ain't suiting you any longer, why, hand out the dollars.'

'It suits me perfectly,' I answered. 'I haven't the smallest intention of breaking our two months' contract.'

The threshers came in that week and he worked well enough, but evidently society was distracting and not exactly elevating. He forsook the armour of silence and I paid him off, leaving the hill field for the time being a study in brown and gold, and an unaccomplished fact as a seed-bed.

'You didn't pay him?' said Roddy McMahon hopefully, when I met him on the trail, and told him that he had gone.

'Of course I paid him,' I said. 'His work was excellent, but he refused to go on with it, and I paid him off.'

'He owed me five dollars,' he said. 'Guess we shall never see that bird in these parts again.'

'It was very foolish of you to lend it at all,' I said, 'but why not have told me, and I could have kept it back for you.'

'I guessed the fellow was all right, though he had some queer ways,' he explained.

The outfit had proved to be the quickest and most satisfactory that had yet threshed out for me, and to prove that Roddy McMahon's law of 'getting in the seed good and quick all right' is three-fourths of the battle with the frost, the crop that year, in spite of the frost of August 12, was entirely uninjured. The wheat from the summer-fallow was of perfect quality, very large, plump, hard, and bright gold. But it was heavily sprinkled with wild oats although I had mowed down ten acres, and had cast out the worst sheaves also from patches of wild oats which had gained complete possession here and there leaving yield of wheat practically nil. The wheat from the breaking was wonderfully good, and came out far and away above the threshers' estimate in weight, which is the supreme test. From the stubble crop of my breaking of 1906 I also got an excellent return of good grain; there was some smut, but we had threshed in the best of weather, and being bone-dry there was no suspicion of tag about it. Eight teams fed the machine and they finished the business in a day and three-quarters, and had I put on ten teams the engine would have kept up to the power, and would have easily got through in a day and a half. My threshing bill amounted to a hundred and twenty dollars including hire of three teams.

My total receipts that year amounted to one thousand one hundred and ninety-one dollars, the wages for the year I had kept down to two hundred and three dollars, seed oats and barley had cost me fifty dollars. My stores amounted to a hundred dollars, but I had visitors which increased the number of my household for some weeks. Binder-twine, machine-oil, and repairs came out at about a hundred dollars, giving me a profit of nearly seven hundred dollars on the year's working.

It was not good, but the profit was made in a year distinctly below the average in harvest return. Most farms reckoned that they drew two-thirds of the average crop that year. Also I was working down, 'lying low,' I had not enough horses, not enough labour, also not enough capital; I had to move very gently. It was, however, just possible to pay the interest of the mortgage, and five hundred dollars of the capital, and it was enough to prove to me that farming on the prairie properly done is farming easily done, and that, worked out on a well-thought-out plan, it is a practical and should be a highly profitable means of independence and wealth for women as it has always proved for men. But on every side my neighbours had obtained their land as a gift from the Government, or at least one hundred and sixty acres of it, and a further hundred and sixty had been added on the condition of pre-emption, which is by payment of three dollars an acre in addition to the performance of the homestead duties; in this way a farm in every way equal to the one which had cost me five thousand dollars was to be obtained by any man for nine hundred and seventy dollars. So that even allowing that a woman farmer is at a slight disadvantage in working out a farm proposition, she has the killing weight of extra payment thrust on her at the very outset. She may be the best farmer in Canada, she may buy land, work it, take prizes for seed and stock, but she is denied the right to claim from the Government the hundred and sixty acres of land held out as a bait to every man.

I talked to every man about it, and almost to a man they said: 'Too bad!'

3

Sales, mortgage –
'a larger heaven'

Three reasons contributed towards the expensive mistake I made
in again selling 'on the street,' but the last weighed down both
the others. My crop was naturally divided into three grades as it
was drawn from new breaking, stubble crop sown on breaking,
and a certain amount from dirty land, so that it was impossible
to fill a carload without mixing. Secondly, I had omitted to order
my car until there were very many names on the railway list;
lastly, I had to meet a promissory note for a sum of over five
hundred dollars. I discussed financial affairs with my friend the
bank manager, especially the matter of obtaining a new loan to
make my land payment if I first settled the note in full.

'Better get through your sales and settle quickly, wipe off the
old account and obtain a new loan,' was the advice I received,
and I am sure it was given in good faith. So I sold on the street,
but with a sick heart and an uneasy conscience; I loathed the
smallest offence against the wheat itself.

My first few loads from the breaking fetched seventy-seven
and seventy-eight cents and graded No. 2 Northern. I was disappointed at not getting No. 1, but it had been cut on the green
side, and the grain was not sufficiently uniform. But when I
heard that Mr. Hockly of Wideawake was getting the same price
net for slightly frozen grain grading No. 4 Northern, which he
had shipped to Fort William via Winnipeg, I sent samples to
Thompson and Co. of Winnipeg, who advised me that its value

was from ninety-five to ninety-seven cents per bushel – that is, allowing for freight to the East, eighty-four to eighty-six cents per bushel. So that, after allowing for freight, elevator storage and commission, I lost over a hundred dollars on the sale of thirteen hundred bushels of my cleaner grain, whilst that infested with wild oats was docked at the rate of 12 per cent. against the average standard of 2 per cent.

The farmer – the producer – is the indispensable factor in the development of Canada, but he is at the mercy of every wave of every ill-tide. There are times and seasons when the beginner, or the farmer without a sufficient margin of capital for defence, must sell on the street. Even if she or he has sufficient grain to fill a car, there may be a blockade at the elevators, or cars may run short, and in any case, when living at a distance of over ten miles from a railway-station, it is by far the easier matter to take in a load at one's convenience and dump it into an elevator than to haul in twenty loads within twenty days when wheat may be daily dropping in the market. It is to be remembered that the small farmer is invariably pressed for small money. The load goes in and the elevator man knows that it has to be sold; it is a case of leave it at the price or take it back. Wherever an elevator marks a wheat town the Government scale and the Government grader should be in the centre of its market-place. Whenever a charter is granted to a Bank it should be on the condition that a certain sum of money is to be kept strictly for the service of the producer at a fair and acceptable degree of interest. Much has lately been written against freight charges. I lived for some months twenty-six miles from the nearest bi-weekly railway service, and then through four years found it necessary to haul grain fifteen miles to the nearest railway-station; but since the coming of the Grand Trunk Pacific Railway from Winnipeg to Regina via Fort Qu'Appelle, within four and a half miles of my farm, I can appreciate the blessing of being able to fill a car within forty-eight hours, or even twenty-four if necessary. Many of my neighbours this year threshed their grain into the wagon and hauled directly to the railway-car, which was loaded and dispatched within twelve hours, and two-thirds of its value was obtainable on sight if dispatched through the elevator at Fort Qu'Appelle. For this inestimable boon one paid exactly the same freight charge as in the pioneer days, when it sometimes meant a three weeks' journey to sell a wagon-load, or in the days of my own experience, when it took from fifteen to twenty days to fill a car. Yet it is the farmers within the belt of convenience who kick at the freight charge, not those who are still depending on the railway development to make life easier. Of the freight charges I can only speak as a grain farmer. There seems to be some just ground for complaint of lack of organization between the producer and the would-be consumer of fruit and vegetables in Canada; but, given justice in weight and grade, I can well afford to pay ten cents a bushel for the transport of my grain, and I know that if I pay less it will not be at the cost of shareholders' profits, but at the cost of the inconvenience and delayed prosperity of the pioneer and the homesteader, whose experience I have endured.

To return to my story, I paid the Bank since it was too late to draw back, but there was no further loan forthcoming. The chasm between the receipts of 1908 and the accumulated payments of 1907 and 1908 had to be bridged. At this critical moment my predecessor appeared on the scene to announce that it was necessary to apply not only for the deferred payment of 1907, but the payment of the current year in addition – two thousand dollars plus one year's interest at 7 per cent. My predecessor and I had become the best of friends, but it appeared that a near relative was in great financial distress, and there was nothing for it but to demand my land payments; so we resolved to do the best we could for each other on the cheapest possible terms.

I turned at once to the banker who had advanced me money when the Union Bank had refused it in 1907. In difficulty it is wise to place one's confidence in brain. Donald H. Macdonald, the second son of the last of the chief factors of the Hudson Bay Company, has the reputation of being one of the shrewdest as well as one of the wealthiest men in Western Canada, and he never failed to help me when I went to him for counsel or financial service. In affairs he is not to be described as hard or lenient – the moment he gets inside a business proposition every fact jumps to its proper place, and not the smallest attendant detail is permitted to remain in the shadow. A financial service is none the less in Canada because you pay a higher rate of interest than in England. At the particular time I went to him every one was wanting money, and almost at any price. He arranged to pay off my predecessor and replace the mortgage. I had, of course, to pay the current rate of interest, 8 per cent., and all expenses incidental to the charge, and insurance against fire. I paid five hundred dollars off the original mortgage, and it was arranged that I should pay off that amount yearly and not attempt to make the greater payment of a thousand dollars. He advanced a minor and temporary loan for the settlement of various payments, and pushed my ship into smoother waters, so that I left in peace, if not in plenty, for England via Ottawa, where I had been promised an interview with the Hon. Frank Oliver, Minister of the Interior in the last Liberal Government, concerning the claim of Woman to her fair share in the homestead lands of Canada.

Manual labour gives one time for thought. I had an intimate knowledge of the life of the educated working woman in Germany, Paris, and in England. I knew that marriage was accepted by many women as the sole resource against labour in a world governed by laws made by men for men, where there is but the scantest justice and scant wages for the labour of women, because I had lived with and amongst women-workers who had also to wake up from their dream of resource and set to work for the living of two or three more in place of the original one; but I also knew that, happily for the race, there is another and increasing group of women who, if they cannot have marriage as an inspiration in their lives, refuse it as a mere resource. I met women forced by circumstance into business or industrial life the monotony and routine of which starved those very faculties which would have found full scope in the care of grateful animals and the varied labours on the land, and, having arrived myself at the place where I knew how to succeed, through having learned what to avoid, in farming on the prairie, it seemed to me that, through the untidy gap I had made in scrambling through a blind fence to get that knowledge, others would make a gate if they once realized that what men had done for themselves in agricultural pursuits on the prairie, women could also do for themselves. Woman can earn for herself independence and in time wealth. The minimum sum of independence I defined then, as now, in the sum of £5000, and I consider that a woman should be able to command that amount at least after twenty years' work on the land, providing she has a fair start.

It is impossible in a world practically governed by 'the symbol of Caesar' to avoid individual registration of one's direct relation to money. If you cannot control it it will control you. In the past it is an open secret that conditions have driven Woman into the bondage of money; the symbol must be forced to serve, or sooner or later it rules, and it rules with a rod of red-hot iron. The strongest point pressing forward the coming of Women's Suffrage lies in one of the remarkably few indiscretions among laws made by men for men – Woman's compulsory contribution of money towards the support of the State, because it is a definite acknowledgment of Woman's direct relation to money, which, always the chief factor, has become, through the power of laws tainted with the self-interest of the wealth-possessed sex, the ruling force of civilization. The solid argument which delays equal suffrage is the fact that man has the full force of wealth on his side of the scale.

The colossal fortunes of a handful of American women arrived at a crisis to bestow a new lease of life upon the superb condition of our English life, which was just then threatened with decay, if not extinction; but the sum of the private fortune of every wealthy woman in our land would hardly make any impression towards bringing the weight of wealth to that poise which would mark the control of the law of equity between the sexes.

To bring about this condition woman must make wealth; she cannot afford to ignore its force, and only by means of combination and co-operation can she hope to control it. The opportunities for wealth-making are greater than they have ever been before; from every colony they beckon to the woman capitalist as well as the woman labourer, and in the Colonies a combination of capital and labour is a wealth-compelling power.

The faithful chronicle of one's own difficulties may at first thought appear but a poor foundation for one's hope and firm belief that agriculture will prove to be the high-road and foundation of wealth and independence for Woman, but the strength of a chain is in its weakest link. To command complete and uninterrupted success for an agricultural experiment on the Canadian prairie or anywhere else, a certain amount of training in the theory and practice of agriculture is necessary, and also some knowledge of stock-raising, capital in adequate relation to one's proposition whether it is to be worked out on five or five hundred acres of land, a commercial instinct and a true vocation for life on the land, an innate love and understanding of animal and vegetable life. I had no training, inadequate capital, and my commercial instinct, though strong in theory, is weak in practice – I fail to hold my own in buying or selling, and should never discuss price except on paper. But in spite of this, and the fact that I am still behind my conviction that three hundred and twenty acres of good land in Canada can be worked to produce a net profit of £500 per annum to its owner, my weak link is very much stronger than at the time I set out for Ottawa to claim the right of women to their share in the homestead land of Canada.

On my way from the West I gathered news and considerable encouragement from the press-women of Winnipeg and Fort William. At Winnipeg I met Miss Cora Hind, who is the editor of the commercial page of the most powerful organ of Western Canada – the *Manitoba Free Press*. To her is entrusted the responsibility of first voice in the opinion, and report and publication of information which concerns the agricultural side of the industrial development of that section of the British Empire which attracts the interest of the world. It is hardly necessary to add that she has no parliamentary vote. The strongest weapon she holds in her professional equipment is her instinct for the weak link in the chain, and this is backed by excellent mental balance, wide experience, and impregnable honesty. I found her enthusiastic about everything connected with the expansion of resource for women, and kindly and deeply interested in the prospect of agriculture, in which she was theoretically well up.

From her and Mrs. Lilian Graham, and Mrs. Sherk of Fort William, I learned that Canadian women had already taken up the matter of Homesteads for Women with a deep sense of the injustice of a law which, whilst seeking to secure the prosperity of the country in enriching the stranger, ignores the claim of the sex which bore the brunt of the battle in those early and difficult days when every inch of our great wheat-garden of the North-West had to be won with courage and held with endurance. No pen can depict the fine part that Woman played in the spade work of expansion in Canada, although history throws many a search-light over the past, which discovers her claim to an equal share in the land which over a hundred years ago she helped to win by travail and hold by toil.

It is still among the pleasing traits of Canada that 'men in great place' are easy of access; throughout the Dominion there rules between man and man a common respect for Time. When I reached Ottawa Mr. Scott, the Commissioner of Immigration, received me at once, told me his full mind on some facts and conditions of immigrants and immigration, and listened to all I had to say about women-farmers and homestead land. I learned with regret that the Hon. Frank Oliver had left Ottawa that day for the Christmas recess, but Mr. Scott advised me to see the Deputy-Minister – Mr. Cory, with whom he fixed an appointment for the following morning.

Mr. Cory was kind and wore the anxious-to-please air of the professional politician which is always soothing, but I think he knew rather less of the practical side of agriculture than I of Blue books, and, just as I had anticipated, firstly, lastly, and all the time came the argument, 'She can't.' However, there was also a promise to place the matter before the Minister of the Interior on his return. But I never discussed the matter personally with Mr. Oliver. Not long before the fall of the Liberal party I heard that Miss Cora Hind had seen him on the matter, and that he had arrived at a decision to refuse to recommend the expansion of the homestead law in order to permit women to homestead because he considered it would be against the main interest of the country. He argued that the object of granting the land-gift to men is to induce them to make home on the prairie – home in the centre of their agricultural pursuit. He held the first requirement of the genuine home-maker to be a wife: he marries, he has a family, etc. etc. Women, he assumes, are already averse to marriage, and he considered that to admit them to the opportunities of the land-grant would be to make them more independent of marriage than ever. The reason was at least flattering to the Woman-Farmer if it was unpromising for the race; but the birthrate of Canada is not nearly as high as it should be, so perhaps Maeterlinck's 'Blue-Bird' has warned the myriad of 'winged thoughts' eagerly awaiting their human moment against the trap of the 'homesteader's requirement.'

Since there was not the smallest hope of official encouragement, the only way of going on seemed to lie in refusing to give up, so I did what I could alone and very imperfectly. I had neither sufficient capital nor experience to carry out my 'women and wheat' experiment in any other way than by teaching my would-be women-farmers what to avoid, and to give them the opportunity of learning by actually working with the horses and implements on the land. The double responsibility naturally needed even more knowledge and training and patience and endurance than the chronicled end of my experiment, but over and over again I recognized the splendid qualities I had always believed to be in women, and I don't think a woman ever worked on my wheat-land without discovering a finer energy and a stronger and more independent Self than she dreamed she possessed.

But what is really wanted is such an experiment in complete form: the average farm-plot, the average farm-buildings of the prosperous farmer with sufficient capital to prove the result of suggestion, worked out on the best possible method of increase; the proof that, given sufficient capital, £500 net profit can be made by any qualified woman-farmer on three hundred and twenty acres of land through demonstrating inch by inch and dollar by dollar how it is made on one particular half-section. It is easy to work out propositions on paper, although if more were sketched out carefully in this manner finer results would be obtained from the land and the man and the woman. For instance, it is easy, but it is also inspiring, to demonstrate on paper that, against the average power of increase of £100 to £200 in the space of twenty years, the power of increase of £100 invested in cattle on the present scale of commercial value will reach £5645 in twenty years, after allowing for natural death and then striking off 25 per cent. from the full sum of result to allow for unnatural death or disaster; but it would also be possible and convincing to demonstrate the experiment in action at any period of its development – so many cows, so many calves, yearlings, heifers and steers, and so many butcher's receipts standing for that original £100. In the same way, through adequate capital and careful experiment one should be able to foretell approximately what £100 invested in poultry, pigs, cattle, sheep, horses, may be expected to yield to the owner of so many acres of land in five, ten, or twenty years. What is needed is an experimental farm which is a commercial success, where women may learn by doing and know by seeing that through agriculture the farmer may arrive at independence and wealth. In such a proposition there should be no room for philanthropy except in the foundation, and even that should always be reclaimable. Any business proposition that is not a commercial success is practically a failure. The experimental training farm must produce a net profit: of this a portion should be set aside for depreciation and development, a portion should go towards a fund to assist women-farmers of true vocation but insufficient capital to make a fair start, and a portion should be placed to the fund for the repayment of initial capital in whatever form of advance it was obtained. Nothing can cancel the grace of giving, none can repay an act of generosity, but the law 'Unto Caesar the things that are Caesar's' is only second to its better half. Besides, the philanthropic fund of the world is wanted in so many different corners of the world, and it should be kept moving.

At present the nearest approach to such a proposition in action is Mr. Kingsley Fairbridge's experiment in Western Australia, which, of course, for many years must mainly depend on philanthropic contributions. Mr. Fairbridge has been aptly named a practical idealist. On a reclaimed fruit-farm he makes home for a certain number of destitute and forsaken children and instructs them in mental culture and manual labour until they reach the age of sixteen. The experiment is only in the second year of its development. The increase from the produce of the land has risen from less than £20 to nearly £80 in its first year, and a fund is to be established in connexion with the work to provide boys and girls with a *dot* towards their first start on leaving home. Mr. Fairbridge is a Rhodes scholar hailing from South Africa. He conceived the idea during his sojourn at Exeter College, Oxford, and it is significant that he has planted it, not in the wonderful country of his birth, not in the nearer and matchless country of Canada, but far off in Western Australia, where women are honoured in deed as well as in word, where a voice is given them in the selection of their law-makers, and the opportunity of the land-grant is open to them.

If there had been no pause in the amazing development of Canada I cannot think there would have been any hope for the extension of the land-grant to women, although I believe that had the Province of Saskatchewan been given that administration of her own natural resources, for which Mr. Haultain fought without ceasing, in Saskatchewan the land-grant would have been extended to women, and that both the Liberal and Conservative Governments would have been of one mind in wiping out the shame of this injustice from their home province, which is destined to become the richest and the most powerful in the Dominion. But to-day the fact that Canada is in vital need of the producer may inspire the Dominion Government to seek a virtue in necessity.

Industrial development has selected the great cities of the North-West. A great population is gathering in those centres; the land and the farmer should have been ready to supply their great demand for food, but in the rapid development of the last few years the producer – starved at seed-time and squeezed at harvest, through lack of foresight in the financial administration of the country – has failed to keep up. For a moment *under-production* has thrown a veil over the face of Canadian prosperity, and has already proved to the investor that production alone can support the development which production compelled.

Canada's food-bill is enormous. The most fertile pasture and food-producing country in the world is buying everything she should be selling but wheat. Demand for food even to feed the present population is years ahead of supply. For Christmas season of 1912 Pat Burns, the big supply merchant of Calgary, imported thirty-eight carloads of eggs, 13,500 dozen to a car, from the United States, for which he had to pay duty at the rate of three cents per dozen. Vancouver is at the gate of the richest dairy country in the world. During the late financial depression she found it difficult to meet the weekly wages bill in connexion with local development, yet between September 1912 and May 1913 she contracted for seventy million pounds of butter from New Zealand, the value being three million dollars. Calgary also feeds from New Zealand, and sent to Minneapolis eight thousand dollars for eggs in one month. Potatoes of the value of £1,000,000 sterling were sent last year from Britain to Canada and the United States. Meantime the housekeepers of Canada are very justly in revolt against the high price of food. As they have been trained to limit their consideration to the point of view of their own kitchen table, they can hardly be expected to remember that a fall in the tariff means a fall in the revenue of their country; so the consumer is loud in demand for the outward healing of the complaint which can only be truly healed from within, by the increase of production, through State aid and encouragement to the producer – man or woman.

The first consideration of the woman-farmer contemplating the business of farming in order to contribute to the supply of the demand for farm produce should be the relation of her place of produce to her market. She should study the map and digest statistics, especially as to population and industrial development. It is well to remember that there is no more desirable customer than the workman and his family, and that in countries of great natural resources the place which labour selects to-day is the industrial centre of to-morrow, and in such places land-values are sound and certain to increase. The Prairie Provinces, Vancouver Island, and the twin cities of Fort William and Port Arthur mark the chief industrial districts in Canada. Stock, meat, fish, poultry, eggs, vegetables, flowers and fruit of the berry order may all be produced with a little trouble within a reasonable feeding distance of many of the chief centres in these districts of Canada, and sold at a highly remunerative price. It is true that the winter is severe in the Prairie Provinces, but the commercial farmer should bear in mind that, although in a very few years her commercial farm should yield her a pleasure farm, it must be long waiting before the pleasure-farm could yield her the value of the commercial undertaking.

Never has the opening for the woman on the land in Canada been so easy or so full of promise as just now in the hour that Canada, in spite of all her gifts, is shining through the film of a breath of suspicion, which no more emanates from her pure and splendid self than the burst of noisy enthusiasm that preceded it. Neither one nor the other can affect the value of her matchless natural resources. Whichever way one tests her values Canada is rock-bottom. If she can hit hard, she strikes to urge and wounds to heal. True daughter of a new day, she has the energy and will-power of health and strength and self-knowledge. Less tender yet passionately loving is this virgin side of the Great

Mother. Living much, giving much, she asks much. 'This new land with vibrations in the air that stir up every particle in those who breathe it' demands of its nation – character. Out of the heart of her virgin soil, new life; but from the children who would claim her mother, courage and kindness, swiftness and patience, strength and sympathy, unflinching purpose, unfailing energy, untiring philosophy.

She yields the milk, but all her mind
Is vowed to thresh for stouter stock.
Earth's passion for old giant kind
That scaled the mount, upheaved the rock
Devolves on them who read aright
   Her meaning and devoutly serve.